The Pilgrim's Progress
&
Grace Abounding *to the*
Chief *of* Sinners

The Pilgrim's Progress

From This World *to* That Which Is *to* Come

&

Grace Abounding *to the*

Chief *of* Sinners

John Bunyan

EDITED BY

John F. Thornton and *Susan B. Varenne*

PREFACE BY

W. Clark Gilpin

VINTAGE SPIRITUAL CLASSICS

VINTAGE BOOKS

A DIVISION OF RANDOM HOUSE, INC.

NEW YORK

A VINTAGE SPIRITUAL CLASSICS ORIGINAL, APRIL 2004
FIRST EDITION

Library of Congress Cataloging-in-Publication Data
Bunyan, John, 1628–1688.
The pilgrim's progress ; &, Grace abounding to the chief of sinners / John Bunyan ;
edited by John F. Thornton and Susan B. Varenne ; preface by W. Clark Gilpin.
p. cm. — (Vintage spiritual classics)
Includes bibliographical references (p.).
ISBN 0-375-72568-7 (trade paper)
1. Christian pilgrims and pilgrimages—Fiction.   2. Authors, English—Early modern,
1500–1700—Biography.   3. Puritans—England—Biography.   4. Christian
biography—England.   5. Bunyan, John, 1628–1688.   I. Title: Pilgrim's progress ; &,
Grace abounding to the chief of sinners.   II. Thornton, John F., 1942–   III. Varenne,
Susan B.   IV. Bunyan, John, 1628–1688. Grace abounding to the chief of
sinners.   V. Title: Grace abounding to the chief of sinners.   VI. Title.   VII. Series.
PR3330.A2T48 2004
823'.4—dc22   2003062169

Book design by Fritz Metsch

www.vintagebooks.com

Manufactured in the United States of America
10 9 8 7 6 5 4 3 2 1

CONTENTS

by John F. Thornton and Susan B. Varenne, General Editors

A turn or shift of sorts is becoming evident in the reflections of men and women today on their life experiences. Not quite as adamantly secular and, perhaps, a little less insistent on material satisfactions, the reading public has recently developed a certain attraction to testimonies that human life is leavened by a Presence that blesses and sanctifies. Recovery, whether from addictions or personal traumas, illness, or even painful misalignments in human affairs, is evolving from the standard therapeutic goal of enhanced self-esteem. Many now seek a deeper healing that embraces the whole person, including the soul. Contemporary books provide accounts of the invisible assistance of angels. The laying on of hands in prayer has made an appearance at the hospital bedside. Guides for the spiritually perplexed have risen to the tops of best-seller lists. The darkest shadows of skepticism and unbelief, which have eclipsed the presence of the Divine in our materialistic age, are beginning to lighten and part.

If the power and presence of God are real and effective, what do they mean for human experience? What does He offer to men and women, and what does He ask in return? How do we recognize Him? Know Him? Respond to Him? God has a reputation for being both benevolent and wrathful. Which will He be for me and when? Can these aspects of the Divine somehow be reconciled? Where is God when I suffer? Can I lose Him? Is God truthful, and are His promises to be trusted?

Are we really as precious to God as we are to ourselves and our loved ones? Do His providence and amazing grace guide our faltering steps toward Him, even in spite of ourselves? Will God abandon us if the sin is serious enough, or if we have episodes of resistance and forgetfulness? These are fundamental questions any person might address to God during a lifetime. They are pressing and difficult, often becoming wounds in the soul of the person who yearns for the power and courage of hope, especially in stressful times.

The Vintage Spiritual Classics present the testimony of writers across the centuries who have considered all these difficulties and who have pondered the mysterious ways, unfathomable mercies, and deep consolations afforded by God to those who call upon Him from out of the depths of their lives. These writers, then, are our companions, even our champions, in a common effort to discern the meaning of God in personal experience. For God is personal to us. To whom does He speak if not to us, provided we have the desire to hear Him deep within our hearts?

Each volume opens with a specially commissioned essay by a well-known contemporary writer that offers the reader an appreciation of its intrinsic value. A chronology of the general historical context of each author and his work is provided, as are suggestions for further reading.

We offer a final word about the act of reading these spiritual classics. From the very earliest accounts of monastic practice—dating back to the fourth century—it is evident that a form of reading called *lectio divina* ("divine" or "spiritual reading") was essential to any deliberate spiritual life. This kind of reading is quite different from that of scanning a text for useful facts and bits of information, or advancing along an exciting plotline to a climax in the action. It is, rather, a meditative approach by which the reader seeks to savor and taste the beauty and truth of every phrase and passage. This process of contemplative reading has the effect of enkindling in the reader compunction for past behavior that has been less than beautiful and true. At the same time, it increases the desire to seek a realm where all that is lovely and unspoiled may be found. There are four steps in *lectio divina:* first, to read, next to meditate, then to rest in the sense of God's nearness, and, ultimately, to resolve to govern one's actions in the light of new understanding. This kind of reading is itself an act of prayer. And, indeed, it is in prayer that God manifests His Presence to us.

PREFACE TO THE
VINTAGE SPIRITUAL CLASSICS
EDITION

by W. Clark Gilpin

The core spiritual disciplines of the Puritans were retrospective. Their ministers preached sermons and published devotional manuals that urged the faithful to search their lives for evidence of God's presence, in both mercy and judgment. Individuals acted on the ministers' advice, assiduously composing journals, diaries, and autobiographies that recorded life's passage in order to look back on the course traveled, trace its major contours, and therein discern the providential hand of God. By means of this retrospective spirituality, the Puritans sought to discover and then cultivate the principle that would unify a person's life by orienting it toward a single end. In their search for this unifying plot to the story of life, they turned to the Christian Bible for both model narratives and evaluative norms. Hence, the Puritans' principal contribution to modern religious thought lay in conceiving of theology as a practical wisdom about the coherence of one's life over time. John Bunyan's spiritual autobiography, *Grace Abounding to the Chief of Sinners* (1666), and his great allegory of the Christian life, *The Pilgrim's Progress* (1678), were culminating masterworks of this Puritan spirituality of retrospection.

It may seem surprising that John Bunyan (1628–88), a tradesman and preacher of modest family and limited education, should produce *The Pilgrim's Progress,* one of the great narrative works of the English language. And, indeed, critics have not infrequently represented him as a singular genius, whose powerful imagination transcended the limitations of his time, place, and culture. But a more fruitful approach to reading Bunyan's two most famous books interprets him as an author who was both a product of the Puritan tradition and evidence of Puritanism's educative and literary power.

The Puritan Background

Bunyan composed *Grace Abounding* and *The Pilgrim's Progress* while he was in prison. He had been arrested in November 1660, as he was preparing to preach to an illegally gathered congregation. Although the magistrate offered to release him if he would promise to cease preaching, Bunyan refused and was imprisoned in the county jail, where he would remain, with some brief periods of parole, until 1672. By the time of Bunyan's imprisonment, the great epoch of Puritan protest and experimentation with parliamentary government had passed. Oliver Cromwell had died in 1658, and on May 25, 1660, the Stuart king, Charles II, landed at Dover to reclaim his throne. Puritan clergy who refused to conform to the reestablished Church of England were ousted from their parishes or jailed, if they persisted in illegal preaching.

Despite the subsequent eclipse of Puritanism as a political and social movement, its dissenting habits of mind continued. Since its beginnings in Elizabethan England during the 1560s, the Puritan movement had protested that the Church of England needed a thorough reformation: erroneous human opinions had accumulated over time to corrupt the church's worship, doctrines, and moral standards. With increasingly militant zeal during the early seventeenth century, the Puritans preached, debated, and organized in order to purify these errors according to standards they found revealed in scripture. They considered themselves the faithful church within an errant church and aimed to leaven the whole loaf. By the time Bunyan was a young man, the points of controversy between the Puritans and the establishment had expanded beyond early Elizabethan disputes over, for example, proper ministerial apparel and encompassed much broader issues, such as the government of the church by bishops, the laws governing poverty and debt, and the scope of parliamentary authority. Puritan dissent thus contributed to the great political clashes of the mid-seventeenth century: the opposition government of the Long Parliament, the English Civil Wars, the execution of Charles I, and the rise of Oliver Cromwell. The young Bunyan served in the Parliamentary army during the Civil Wars and assumed his calling as a preacher in the 1650s, when Cromwell was at the height of his power.

The Puritans were convinced that the motivating energy for reformation in church and society arose from personal spiritual transformation—conversion. Hence, even worse than the corrupt practices of the established church, the Puritans declared, was the church's complacent acceptance of merely nominal conformity on the part of its members, when what God actually required was a change of heart. Their zeal for transformations of society and the self were unified by the sense that divine power was effecting its purposes in history, for society and individual alike. The proper conduct of life required careful attention to the evidences of history, especially the internal history of the soul. The power of God was welling up and expressing itself through human devotion to the divine cause, the Puritans declared, and this required a scrupulous examination of personal religious motives.

The high value that Bunyan placed on the self-critical evaluation of past conduct is immediately apparent in the preface to *Grace Abounding,* in which he explained his reasons for writing. Not only was the book "a relation of the work of God upon my own soul, even from the very first, till now," but Bunyan enjoined his readers to probe their own memories, where they, too, would find "treasure hid" of the "experience of the grace of God toward you." In this brief preface to his readers, Bunyan underscored his advice by employing the words *remember* and *remembrance* nearly twenty times. Just as Moses had commanded the Israelites to remember their deliverance from Egypt and their forty years of travel in the wilderness, said Bunyan, so his own readers should look back on their spiritual histories. "Have you forgot the close, the milk-house, the stable, the barn, and the like, where God did visit your soul?"

The memory of past dealings with God provided consolation in present troubles and hope for the future. Most importantly, it was the great source of spiritual education. On first encounter, temptation advanced like a roaring lion, but once overcome, it yielded self-knowledge to those who remembered. The experienced Christian was like Samson, who returned to a lion he had slain and found honey in its carcass (Judg. 14:5–9). Bunyan, recounting his own spiritual history in light of this biblical story, explained that he was presenting his readers with "a drop of that honey, that I have taken out of the carcass of a lion."

As the Samson analogy suggests, Bunyan and the Puritans used biblical narrative to make an armature on which to build an individual life. The self, as fashioned in the Puritan tradition of retrospective spirituality, arrived at responsible self-knowledge by discerning the way in which a particular life distinctively expressed a general human pattern, revealed in scripture. This classic narrative assumed that the sinful self simultaneously grasped the world in pride, clung to it in desperation, but could not preserve itself from ultimate destruction without a conversion, effected by the infusion of a supernatural and saving grace. The truth or authenticity of any individual Puritan's conversion rested on the recognizable enactment of this archetypal narrative of redemption in a form that, at the same time, displayed those singular features that served to make it one's personal narrative. For this reason, seemingly "conventional" features of Bunyan's autobiography should not be thought of as existing in an uneasy tension with its original and individual qualities. Instead, Bunyan's creativity expressed itself precisely in the way he incorporated distinctive, individual experience into a grand narrative of the history of salvation. This assumption that personal narrative disclosed its meaning through participation in universal narrative decisively shaped the spiritual geography of *The Pilgrim's Progress*. When, for example, characters pass through the same terrain—the Slough of Despond or the Valley of Humiliation—they encounter differing dangers and experiences.

"The Dangers of His Solitary Way"—The Journey Narrative

The classic Puritan model of the self assumed that the life of holiness was a long, spiritual warfare—a battle against the world, the flesh, and the devil—in which the new, active principle of interior grace struggled toward consistent expression in exterior conduct. This drive toward consistency between the inner and the outer, culminating in unified devotion to the will and glory of God, was the lifelong vocation of the Puritan saint. Pretense and hypocrisy were vices of the first order. Both *Grace Abounding* and *The Pilgrim's Progress* made this spiritual battle for consistency of life a central theme. In *Grace Abounding,* Bunyan recalled that he had once been "a brisk talker" about religion until the day on a street in his town of Bedford when he overheard a conversation among pious women. They spoke about the work of God in their hearts, but in a manner that was so far beyond his own experience that he simply could not understand them. This same contrast between mere speech about religion and the interior disposition of religion reappeared in allegorical form in a classic scene from *The Pilgrim's Progress*. The pilgrim Christian and his companion, Faithful, were recounting their religious experiences in a lively discussion as they walked together toward the heavenly city. In the midst of their walk, they encountered a man named Talkative, who, it so happened, spoke very eloquently of religious matters but had little experience of religion's inward power and whose behavior in household and business did not match his fine speech: "a saint abroad and a devil at home." Bunyan's deft portrait of Talkative's fatal inconsistency of life simultaneously criticized the general superficiality of English religion, issued a self-critical warning about the temptations of pious conversation, and recalled and reinterpreted Bunyan's own religious journey.

Bunyan and the Puritans were concerned not only that one's life consistently cohere but also that it be coherent. They devoutly reflected on the day, the month, the year just passed in order to discern the continuities that bound life into a meaningful whole and placed it in some larger scheme of significance. They meditated on past trials and deliverances in order to cultivate the vivid sense that God's work was worthy of their best efforts and to sustain energetic commitment through difficult times and over the long term. Identifying himself with the biblical David, Bunyan declared that he could remember his "sad months with comfort; they are as the head of Goliath in my hand."

Retrospection played a regulative role for the Puritans, functioning to adjudicate among responsibilities in terms of an overarching claim on life. It harmonized competing responsibilities so that they pointed forward toward goals worthy of accomplishment. The backward look over the course of life also performed the nourishing function of reminding about the reason for and the worth of daily labor. It worked to explore and achieve richer understanding of the overarching goals by which the Puritan measured longer-term achievement and the social purposes to which the Puritan believed his or her work contributed. What I have called "the spirituality of retrospection" addressed these purposes by exploring the nature of a life as a cumulative process in which coherence and meaning cannot be known in advance but only appraised by looking backward.

At the same time, Bunyan recognized that even religious commitment itself might be, as he expressed it in *Grace Abounding,* nothing more than "a mere think so," i.e., wishful thinking that would prove unable to withstand the tests of either time or eternity. He understood that socially constructed meanings—"worldly," in the Puritan's preferred terminology—were ephemeral "human inventions," likely to wither under the divine gaze. Doubt, and in Bunyan's case even stark despair, could overwhelm human assertions of worth and meaning. Christian's imprisonment in Doubting Castle by the Giant Despair, who advised Christian that suicide would be his only release, was a telling representation not only of Bunyan's personal bouts of depression but also of the wider Puritan confrontation with the transience of life.

Bunyan knew that hard-won experience could never be mistaken for a sure knowledge of the future, and his narratives therefore invoked utter reliance on the providence of God as a way of coming to terms with the imponderable uncertainty of life as it actually unfolds. The order achieved by human purposes might sometimes dimly reflect divine purpose, but, more often, one found human schemes dramatically reordered by the hidden purpose or secret counsel of God. For this reason, the actual meaning of events, in contrast to what human actors intended, was seldom visible at the time but revealed itself only in retrospect. *The Pilgrim's Progress* portrayed this tension between human and divine purposes in those numerous scenes in which Christian must retrace his steps to some earlier point on his journey. At one point, he retrieves a scroll that had fallen from his pack while he slept; at another, he returns to a gate through which he had mistakenly passed in search of an easier route; at still another, he remembers that he has the key that will release him from the dungeon of Doubting Castle.

Bunyan understood life to be inescapably cumulative. Past circumstances and the decisions made within those circumstances did not slip away into insignificance but instead left persistent traces in, even constraints on, the current conduct of life. His narratives thus proceeded on the assumption that the shape of a life emerges gradually from the mixture of accumulating choices, chance encounters, and unforeseen circumstances. The most carefully planned decisions inevitably have unanticipated consequences, and actions that seemed minor at the time may loom much larger in retrospect. Even when things work out pretty much as expected, it remains the case that the choices made have foreclosed other possibilities. There is always a "road not taken."

Given these considerations, Bunyan and the Puritans engaged in what might be called "imaginative retrospection" in order to evaluate each action or decision for its contribution to the cumulative pattern of action. How, they asked, might this decision measure up when I look back at it from "the future world" where I no longer have the capacity to change or ameliorate its consequences? As I look back on a day's work from the perspective of eternity, how consistently does it express what I take to be my governing purpose?

"The City Shone Like the Sun"— Imagination and Moral Judgment

Bunyan amplified the Puritan mandate to review, chart, and appraise one's past, by imaginatively extending the metaphor that life is a journey. The journey motif had wide currency, of course, not only in Christianity but in many religious traditions, and Puritan ministers had employed it in sermons and devotional manuals for a full century by the time Bunyan wrote *Grace Abounding*. Its influence was clearly evident, for example, in the title of a frequently reprinted book by the English clergyman Arthur Dent, *The Plaine Mans Path-Way to Heaven* (1601), a book that was part of the dowry of Bunyan's first wife. However, the title of Dent's book obscured a pivotal feature of the journey metaphor that Bunyan would fully exploit both in his autobiography and in *The Pilgrim's Progress:* life's journey moves toward a goal not simply beyond present reach but, in some important sense, even beyond present comprehension. The progress of the pilgrim, as the full title of Bunyan's allegory explained, was "from this world to that which is to come." But "the world to come" was unknown to those who hoped they were traveling toward it, and, even with resources from the Bible and personal experience, the traveler could not fully understand the ultimate destination. Thus, toward the end of *The*

Pilgrim's Progress, when the pilgrim was afforded an opportunity to gaze on the Celestial City through a "perspective glass," his hand shook with fear of the journey, preventing a clear view of the city gate and the glory of the place.

The spirituality of retrospection as practiced by John Bunyan was, in short, an act of imagination. The "look backward" by which Bunyan advised his Puritan reader to discern a plot and coherence to life was not a look backward merely from the present situation. It was a look backward over the whole journey of life from an imagined end point, a view that sought to create distance from the immediacies of success and disappointment, frustration and confidence. Bunyan made vividly concrete the spiritual advice of Puritan sermons and devotional manuals. These had typically proposed a kind of mortuary meditation, in which the pious person would lie in bed at night as if it were the grave and, from that imagined end point, evaluate his or her conduct during the day just concluded. They even imagined the ultimate future, the millennium, and the Last Judgment as absolute vantage points from which to gaze back in divine hindsight on the course of life and discern its direction of movement. Bunyan had practiced these disciplines himself, and, as he pondered in prison, his religious memories began to multiply "like sparks that from the coals of fire do fly," igniting the allegories of *The Pilgrim's Progress.* Thus the spirituality of retrospection cultivated imaginative vision as one of its constitutive features. Bunyan's literary artistry and imaginative interpretation were not departures from the biblical and moral sensibilities of the Puritans but were extensions of those sensibilities.

Seventeenth-Century England

In 1620, just a few years before the birth of John Bunyan in 1628, the first pilgrims to the New World disembarked from the *Mayflower* at what would become Plymouth Rock in Massachusetts. They had sailed there determined to live free of English rule, and to create their own religious and political society. These austere and single-minded Puritans had been the principal victims of the repressive measures of England's Court of High Commission, which had consolidated the power of the Anglican Church and its episcopacy in line with the monarchy. The Calvinists thus found themselves subject to intolerance and persecution. The stage was set for civil war.

Charles I (1600–1649) came to power during the Thirty Years' War (1618–48) and ruled England from 1625 to 1649. By reaffirming the divine right of kings and the lines connecting the power of government to the power of the High Church, he had provoked the dissenting Puritans. The first Civil War ensued from 1642 to 1645, in which the king's troops opposed the army of the Parliament. Parliament had come under Puritan power when William Laud, archbishop of Canterbury and counselor of the king, was imprisoned and then executed in January 1645. Four years later, after a second Civil War, Charles I was tried and executed on January 30, 1649.

A time of social ferment ensued in England in which the landed gentry continued to accrue ever more capital and wealth while the landless poor, especially the agricultural peasantry, found themselves to be victims of increasing scarcity. Those without capital simply could not gain access to any and were unable to improve their lot either by labor or by education. Their condition was insufferable, hence the revolt against their perceived oppressors, the Anglican episcopacy and the gentry. English laws of enclosure, removing the freedom to use former common land, and forced labor caused riots as desperation fueled the fires of dissent. The Puritan ethic, justification by faith, and predestination offered hope of deliverance to the desperate, who looked to their own clergy for advice and guidance. Ministers upbraided the landed rich for living off the rents and labor of the poor, branding them as thieves.

The period of the Commonwealth and of the Protectorate of Oliver Cromwell (1653–58) revealed the divisions that perdured at the heart of the national church. Since the reign of Elizabeth I (1558–1603), separatists from the High Church had successively formed various sects: Robert Brown founded the Congregationists, ca. 1580; John Smyth the Baptists, ca. 1612; and George Fox the Quakers, ca. 1647. During the period of Puritan power, the division of the church went in several directions: the majority of Anglicans (anti-Rome and Puritan at heart) adhered to the Presbyterian model; others rallied to the new order that would dispense with the Book of Common Prayer and the Anglican form of sacraments. The Laudians, High Church Anglicans loyal to the ideals of Archbishop Laud and faithful to the monarchy, were forced to live in obscurity for the time being.

Two years after the death of Cromwell his Protectorate collapsed, and the monarchy was restored in 1660 in the person of Charles II. The Long Parliament was dissolved, and the House of Lords restored. The trial and execution of regicides followed. Anglicanism was officially reestablished along with government of the High Church by the episcopacy. All ministers who refused to conform to the restored Episcopal Church were expelled. These numbered more than 1,700.

John Bunyan (1628–88) wrote of his background: "My descent was of a low and inconsiderable generation, my father's house being of that rank that is meanest and most despised of all the families of the land." He was poorly educated, though he did learn to read and write. His schooling was often interrupted by the need to work for his father, a mender of pots and pans. At the age of sixteen he fought in the Parliamentary army during the first segment of the Civil War. Next, marriage to a good woman, who brought into their poor home two religious books, wakened in him a sense of

God. Inspired by the sincerity of a conversation he overheard one day among some women discussing the things of God, he began to undergo a great inner spiritual conflict, which he recounted in *Grace Abounding to the Chief of Sinners,* his spiritual autobiography. A few years later, in 1653, Bunyan joined the Baptist Church in Bedford and was baptized in the River Ouse. Two years later he became a deacon and began preaching. In 1658 he was arrested for preaching without the requisite license but kept on until, not long after the Restoration in 1660, he was imprisoned for the same offense. He then spent the better part of the next twelve years in prison writing his masterpieces.

In 1672 Charles II, with a secret agenda to reestablish the Roman Catholic Church in England, issued the second Declaration of Indulgence by which penal statutes against Nonconformists to the Church of England were suspended. Bunyan was thus pardoned on September 13, 1672. He received a license to preach and was called to pastor the Bedford church. He began to travel throughout his county and beyond, preaching to large gatherings as far away as London. He even became the spiritual advisor to Sir John Shorter, the Lord Mayor of London.

John Bunyan died of a fever on August 31, 1688, after being drenched and chilled in the rain while traveling to visit a friend.

Chronology

1628   John Bunyan is born in Elstow, Bedfordshire, England, to Thomas Bunyan and his second wife, Margaret Bentley. Thomas is a tinker, a mender of pots and pans. Though the family is extremely poor, John is sent to school to learn the rudiments of reading and writing.

Charles I (1600–1649) is king, ruling without benefit of Parliament. By reaffirming the divine right of kings and establishing the power of the episcopacy of the High Church, he provokes the dissenting Puritans, who are struggling as well with grave social inequities brought about by the enclosure laws that favor the landed gentry. The poor are being driven ever closer to desperation.

1642   Civil war breaks out in England. The royal troops of the king are opposed to the Parliamentary army, largely made up of Dissenters. The war will last three years.

1644   Bunyan's mother dies. His father remarries two months later. Bunyan leaves home to enlist as a soldier in the Parliamentary army.

John Milton (1608–74) writes *Areopagitica,* his defense of freedom of the press, which had been restricted by Parliament.

1645   The Parliamentary army wins a victory at the Battle of Naseby in June. The war comes to an end. However, Bunyan is not demobilized for two more years.

William Laud (1573–1645), archbishop of Canterbury and counselor to the king, is executed for treason in January.

1646   The feudal tenures and the Court of Wards are abolished as is the episcopacy of the High Church.

1647   Bunyan is demobilized and returns home to Elstow in July. During his time in the army, John has listened to many radical discussions about people's rights, political democracy, and economic equality.

In August the Parliamentary army occupies London.

1648   The second Civil War begins.

1649   Around this time, Bunyan marries. Although he does not mention her name, his wife is a good woman and enriches their destitution with two pious books and a deep sense of God. These influences incline Bunyan to give up swearing, at which he had learned to excel in the army, and to attend church services regularly.

In January Charles I is tried and executed. In the spring, the House of Lords is abolished and a republic is established.

1650   Compulsory attendance at the local parish church is abolished.

1651   The Battle of Worcester takes place in September. The invasion of Charles II (1630–85) is defeated.

Thomas Hobbes (1588–1679) publishes *Leviathan,* which describes the life of man without government as "nasty, brutish, and short." His preferred form of government was a sovereign whose powers derived from the governed.

1653   Oliver Cromwell (1599–1658), leader of the Puritan Dissenters, dissolves the Rump of the Long Parliament. Cromwell's Protectorate begins and will last until 1658.

1654   The First Parliament of the Protectorate commences.

1655   Bunyan now has two children: Mary, born blind, and Elizabeth. His strong physical constitution enables him to fight off an attack of consumption, so often deadly for those thus affected.

   Bunyan is received into the Bedford congregation, a Baptist church, and is baptized in the River Ouse. Previous to this he had spent several years in a state of spiritual torment, which is to be recounted in his spiritual autobiography, *Grace Abounding to the Chief of Sinners* (1666). He had questioned the existence of God and the truth of revealed religion, doubted the Bible, was skeptical of the afterlife, and was sometimes overwhelmed by fears and scruples. However, ultimately he determines to hold on to the Bible and the historical Christ.

1656   Bunyan writes pamphlets against the contemporary religious sect of Quakers in order to point out what he thinks is their lack of a proper sense of sin. He considers consciousness of sin essential to any true conversion to God. He believes that Satan tempts men to love their sins for the pleasure they receive from committing them and encourages them to disregard any anxiety about sin as simply "a melancholy fit." He is certain that Satan uses consciousness of sin to induce sinners to despair, as well as to delude people about their own state of righteousness. He believes in the mercy of Christ for the sinner.

   The kingship of England is offered to Oliver Cromwell. He ultimately rejects it.

1657   A Second Protectorate is established.

1658   Bunyan's *A Few Sighs from Hell* is published. It is an expansion of his sermon on the parable of the rich man and Lazarus told in the gospel of Luke (16:19–31). In it he condemns pride, greed, loose living, and covetousness, saying it is "better to hear the Gospel under a hedge than to sit roaring in a tavern." Bunyan's attacks on the well-to-do gentry hit their mark, and they begin to look for an opportunity to silence him.

By this date Bunyan's family has grown to four children.

Oliver Cromwell dies in September. He is succeeded by his son, Richard.

1659 Richard Cromwell abdicates in May. The Long Parliament and the republic are restored.

Bunyan's first wife dies (date and name unknown), and he marries a second time, to Elizabeth.

During the period of the English Civil Wars, the idea that the end of the world is coming soon is widespread. Millenarian ideas give rise to the belief that the lower classes are the enemy of the Antichrist, who finds support among the nobles and gentlemen who rebel against God. Bunyan subscribes to these millenarian theories and sees the monarchy as anti-Christian. He preaches the judgment of the Royalists at the hand of God.

1660 In March the Long Parliament is dissolved. In May Charles II is accepted as king of England. In October the regicides are tried and executed. By December the Episcopal Church is restored, as is the House of Lords.

Punishments for Nonconformists are revived. It is now illegal to conduct a church service not in accord with the rituals of the High Church or for anyone not episcopally ordained to preach. Nearly two thousand ministers who refuse to conform to the Episcopal Church are ejected.

Bunyan continues to preach and is consequently arrested on November 12. He would not promise the court to forbear preaching and so is sentenced to jail.

1661 Bunyan's wife, Elizabeth, travels to London to petition the House of Lords for a legal trial for her husband. Bunyan had been convicted without a proper trial and the necessary two witnesses. She tries and fails three times to plead his cause. He remains in jail for the better part of the next twelve years. He embraces steadfast endurance as his stabilizing virtue. He busies himself making hundreds of shoelaces to be sold for the support of his family. He preaches to fellow prisoners, gives religious instruction to visitors, reads the Bible and Foxe's *Book of Martyrs*. He begins to write and produces books, tracts, verse, meditations, and expanded sermons. He will achieve literary immortality for himself with *Grace Abounding to the Chief of Sinners* and *The Pilgrim's Progress.*

1662   Post-Restoration legislation aims at putting down the insurrection of those in English society "of no degree and quality." Servile dependence of the poor on their landlords increases, and laws to restrict mobility confine men and women to their villages to earn there whatever living they can, or to starve if they cannot. Dissent against the gentry is suppressed as is the freedom of religion that had allowed for discussion and preaching. The restoration of a single state church is effective in silencing those who are opposed to it. Parliament now controls the church.

Bunyan's prison library of books expands, and he enters into argument with other prominent religious perspectives of his time. He strongly contests the liberal, rational tendencies of Fowler, the Quakers, and the Latitudinarians, all of whom taught an optimistic view of the human potential for good and downplayed the necessity of absolute dependence on the divine grace won for us by Christ's righteousness.*

The Royal Society receives its charter from Charles II. The Act of Settlement, which forbids people to circulate outside the confines of their farms and villages, is passed. This clampdown on mobility is particularly aimed at itinerant preachers. In December, Charles II's first Declaration of Indulgence is proclaimed.

1667   John Milton publishes *Paradise Lost.* In this great work, he justifies the ways of God to men and extols the workings of God's eternal Providence.

1671   Milton publishes *Paradise Regained,* a brief epic account of the temptations of Christ, and *Samson Agonistes,* "an Hebraic tragedy."

---

*Christopher Hill, in *A Tinker and a Poor Man: John Bunyan and His Church, 1628–1688* (New York, 1988), p. 142, notes that Bunyan mentions in his writings works by "Origen, Machiavelli, Luther, Tyndale, Cranmer, Ainsworth, Samuel Clarke's *A Mirrour and Looking-glass for both Saints and Sinners* (1646), Owen, Baxter, Jessey, and the Koran." Martin Luther's writings, especially his *Commentary on the Epistle to the Galatians,* are of great importance to Bunyan.

1672 During his twelve years of incarceration, John Bunyan writes his masterpieces: *Grace Abounding to the Chief of Sinners,* his spiritual autobiography, and *The Pilgrim's Progress,* his allegory on the Christian life as a pilgrimage through temptation to salvation. In addition, he produces numerous sermons, poems, and theological treatises.

In January of this year Bunyan is called to pastor the Bedford congregation when, through Charles II's second Declaration of Indulgence, he receives a pardon. He is released from prison in March. The Bedford congregation applies for a license as a "Congregational" church. Bunyan continues his prolific work as a writer on spiritual themes at the same time as he preaches throughout the county and beyond to ever-larger congregations.

1673 Parliament withdraws the Declaration of Indulgence. Nonconformists to the High Church of England are again in peril. Bunyan continues to travel and preach, putting himself at risk of being arrested again.

1676 Bunyan is again imprisoned, though briefly, from December to June 1677.

1678 A national crisis occurs that will cause unrest for the next four years. A "Popish Plot," by means of which the king was to be murdered and Roman Catholicism established once again in England, is uncovered. James II (1633–1700), who will rule from 1685 to 1688, wants to revive the power of the papacy in England. Charles II tries to substitute his illegitimate son, the Duke of Monmouth, as successor to the throne.

1679 Three years in succession see the constitution of three parliaments.

1681 Bills are passed to exclude James, Duke of York, from succession. Protestant Dissenters are very uneasy about possible religious persecution if Catholics gain power in England.

1685 Charles II dies, and James II succeeds him to the throne. Laws against Nonconformists are put into vigorous operation once again. The Duke of Monmouth leads a rebellion but is defeated. Bunyan, fearful of being arrested again, has all his property put in the name of his wife.

1687 The first Declaration of Indulgence is issued by James II. He pursues a policy of toleration by involving Catholics, Cromwellians, and Dissenters in his government. The landed gentry feel betrayed by his actions. James dismantles the charters of town corporations set up by Charles II in order to secure a favorable Parliament. The social climate begins to deteriorate under the stress of opposition to James's policies favoring papal influence.

1688 In April a second Declaration of Indulgence proclaims full liberty of worship for Catholics and dissidents, and suspends all the penal laws against religious practice. Seven Anglican bishops refuse to read the Declaration from their pulpits. They are charged with, but acquitted of, seditious libel. Parliament fights back against the king and succeeds in gaining control of the judiciary and the corporations. The struggle against Catholic influence and the absolute power of the king is won by Anglicanism.

In November the Protestant William of Orange arrives in England from France at the invitation of some Whigs, Tories, and Anglican bishops to supplant his father-in-law, James II, on the throne. In December James II is forced to flee to France, and William and Mary, daughter of James II and a Protestant, mount the throne. Anglicanism is fully victorious over Catholicism. No Catholic will be allowed to rule England.

John Bunyan dies on August 31. He had undertaken a long journey on horseback to London from Reading to help a father achieve reconciliation with his estranged son. Caught in a heavy downpour, Bunyan sickens and dies from fever at the house of his friend, John Strudwick. He is buried in the Strudwick vault in Bunhill Fields, Finsbury. His devoted wife, Elizabeth, dies a year and a half later, in 1691. Five of his six children survive him. (His much-beloved, blind oldest daughter, Mary, born in 1650, had died before him.)

Between 1689 and 1692, Bunyan's posthumous works are published. In 1736 the first complete collection of his works appears in print. He is the adopted champion of lower-class working people, and his contempt for the rich resounds throughout his work. A Dissenter and a Nonconformist, a man who accepted prison rather than betray his convictions, John Bunyan's fiery voice speaks in word and print in defense of the burdened poor as God's chosen and beloved people.

A NOTE ON THE TEXTS

So as not to encumber the modern reader with unnecessary difficulty in reading these works of seventeenth-century colloquial English prose, the editors of the present volume have modernized spelling, punctuation, capitalization, and any other elements that might distract from reasonable, direct access to the words and ideas on Bunyan's pages. Scholarly text editions as well as editions essentially rewritten in simplified contemporary paraphrase are available elsewhere for readers seeking those respective approaches. Our effort was to minimize the use of the traditional sidebars, antiquarian flourishes, and notes full of pious ejaculations that have accrued to these oft-reprinted works. Instead we respect both the reader's general background and intelligence as well as his or her willingness to make an occasional trip to the dictionary or encyclopedia to pursue any odd usage or allusion that puzzles. Information about the standard edition of Bunyan's works may be found in "Suggestions for Further Reading" on page 370.

As to handling direct quotes from the Bible, typically a source note is provided. However, like many an earlier writer on religious topics, Bunyan pored so thoroughly over Holy Writ that many phrases, half-phrases, allusions, and other references creep into every other sentence he wrote. To offer a source for each example—and sometimes several sources of the same phrase or idea—would, once again, be to embark on a scholarly edition, which the editors have no intention of providing, beyond offering directions to the same for the interested reader.

Finally, some of Bunyan's original marginal notes have been retained and are indicated with initial **[B]** at the end of each.

The Pilgrim's Progress
Part I

THE

PILGRIM'S PROGRESS

FROM THIS WORLD TO THAT WHICH

IS TO COME

———

DELIVERED

UNDER THE SIMILITUDE OF A DREAM

WHEREIN IS DISCOVERED

THE MANNER OF HIS SETTING OUT,

HIS DANGEROUS JOURNEY,

AND SAFE ARRIVAL AT

THE DESIRED COUNTRY

———

BY JOHN BUNYAN

"I have used similitudes." —Hos. 12:10

The Author's Apology for His Book

When at the first I took my pen in hand
Thus for to write, I did not understand
That I at all should make a little book
In such a mode; nay, I had undertook
To make another; which, when almost done,
Before I was aware, I this begun.

    And thus it was: I, writing of the way
And race of saints, in this our gospel day,
Fell suddenly into an allegory
About their journey, and the way to glory,
In more than twenty things which I set down.
This done, I twenty more had in my crown;
And they again began to multiply,
Like sparks that from the coals of fire do fly.
Nay, then, thought I, if that you breed so fast,
I'll put you by yourselves, lest you at last
Should prove *ad infinitum,* and eat out
The book that I already am about.

    Well, so I did; but yet I did not think
To show to all the world my pen and ink
In such a mode; I only thought to make
I knew not what; nor did I undertake
Thereby to please my neighbour: no, not I;
I did it my own self to gratify.

    Neither did I but vacant seasons spend
In this my scribble; nor did I intend
But to divert myself in doing this
From worser thoughts which make me do amiss.

    Thus I set pen to paper with delight,
And quickly had my thoughts in black and white.
For, having now my method by the end,
Still as I pulled, it came; and so I penned
It down: until it came at last to be,
For length and breadth, the bigness which you see.

    Well, when I had thus put mine ends together,
I showed them others, that I might see whether

They would condemn them, or them justify:
And some said, Let them live; some, Let them die;
Some said, John, print it; others said, Not so;
Some said it might do good; others said, No.

Now was I in a strait, and did not see
Which was the best thing to be done by me:
At last I thought, Since you are thus divided,
I print it will, and so the case decided.

For, thought I, some, I see, would have it done,
Though others in that channel do not run:
To prove, then, who advised for the best,
Thus I thought fit to put it to the test.

I further thought, if now I did deny
Those that would have it, thus to gratify;
I did not know but hinder them I might
Of that which would to them be great delight.

For those which were not for its coming forth,
I said to them, Offend you I am loath,
Yet, since your brethren pleasèd with it be,
Forbear to judge till you do further see.

If that thou wilt not read, let it alone;
Some love the meat, some love to pick the bone.
Yea, that I might them better palliate,
I did too with them thus expostulate:

May I not write in such a style as this?
In such a method, too, and yet not miss
My end, thy good? Why may it not be done?
Dark clouds bring waters, when the bright bring none.
Yea, dark or bright, if they their silver drops
Cause to descend, the earth, by yielding crops,
Gives praise to both, and carpeth not at either,
But treasures up the fruit they yield together;
Yea, so commixes both, that in her fruit
None can distinguish this from that: they suit
Her well when hungry; but, if she be full,
She spews out both, and makes their blessings null.

You see the ways the fisherman doth take
To catch the fish; what engines doth he make!
Behold! how he engageth all his wits;
Also his snares, lines, angles, hooks, and nets;

Yet fish there be, that neither hook, nor line,
Nor snare, nor net, nor engine can make thine:
They must be groped for, and be tickled too,
Or they will not be catch'd, whate'er you do.
    How doth the fowler seek to catch his game
By diverse means! all which one cannot name:
His guns, his nets, his lime-twigs, light, and bell;
He creeps, he goes, he stands; yea, who can tell
Of all his postures? Yet there's none of these
Will make him master of what fowls he please.
Yea, he must pipe and whistle to catch *this;*
Yet, if he does so, *that* bird he will miss.
    If that a pearl may in a toad's head dwell,[1]
And may be found too in an oyster-shell;
If things that promise nothing do contain
What better is than gold; who will disdain,
That have an inkling of it, there to look
That they may find it? Now, my little book
(Though void of all these paintings that may make
It with this or the other man to take)
Is not without those things that do excel
What do in brave but empty notions dwell.
    "Well, yet I am not fully satisfied,
That this your book will stand, when soundly tried."
    Why, what's the matter? "It is dark." What though?
"But it is feignèd." What of that? I trow
Some men, by feignèd words, as dark as mine,
Make truth to spangle and its rays to shine.
"But they want solidness." Speak, man, thy mind.
"They drown the weak; metaphors make us blind."
    Solidity, indeed, becomes the pen
Of him that writeth things divine to men;
But must I needs want solidness, because
By metaphors I speak? Were not God's laws,
His gospel laws, in olden times held forth
By types, shadows, and metaphors? Yet loath
Will any sober man be to find fault

---

1. Refers to a contemporary belief that toads formed healing gemstones in their heads.

With them, lest he be found for to assault
The highest wisdom. No, he rather stoops,
And seeks to find out what by pins and loops,
By calves and sheep, by heifers and by rams,
By birds and herbs, and by the blood of lambs,
God speaketh to him; and happy is he
That finds the light and grace that in them be.
   Be not too forward, therefore, to conclude
That I want solidness, that I am rude;
All things solid in show not solid be;
All things in parables despise not we,
Lest things most hurtful lightly we receive,
And things that good are, of our souls bereave.
My dark and cloudy words, they do but hold
The truth, as cabinets enclose the gold.
   The prophets usèd much by metaphors
To set forth truth; yea, who so considers
Christ, his apostles too, shall plainly see,
That truths to this day in such mantles be.
   Am I afraid to say that holy writ,
Which for its style and phrase puts down all wit
Is everywhere so full of all these things
(Dark figures, allegories), yet there springs
From that same book that lustre, and those rays
Of light, that turns our darkest nights to days?
   Come, let my carper to his life now look,
And find there darker lines than in my book
He findeth any; yea, and let him know,
That in his best things there are worse lines too.
   May we but stand before impartial men,
To his poor one I dare adventure ten,
That they will take my meaning in these lines
Far better than his lies in silver shrines.
Come, truth, although in swaddling clouts, I find,
Informs the judgement, rectifies the mind;
Pleases the understanding, makes the will
Submit; the memory too it doth fill
With what doth our imaginations please;
Likewise it tends our troubles to appease.

Sound words, I know, Timothy is to use,
And old wives' fables he is to refuse;
But yet grave Paul him nowhere did forbid
The use of parables; in which lay hid
That gold, those pearls, and precious stones that were
Worth digging for, and that with greatest care.
    Let me add one word more. O man of God,
Art thou offended? Dost thou wish I had
Put forth my matter in another dress?
Or that I had in things been more express?
Three things let me propound; then I submit
To those that are my betters, as is fit.
    1. I find not that I am denied the use
Of this method, so I no abuse
Put on the words, things, readers; or be rude
In handling figure or similitude,
In appreciation; but, all that I may,
Seek the advance of truth this or that way:
Denied, did I say? Nay, I have leave
(Example too, and that from them that have
God better pleased, by their words or ways,
Than any man that breatheth now-a-days)
Thus to express my mind, thus to declare
Things unto thee that excellentest are.
    2. I find that men (as high as trees) will write
Dialogue-wise; yet no man doth them slight
For writing so: indeed, if they abuse
Truth, cursèd be they, and the craft they use
To that intent; but yet let truth be free
To make her sallies upon thee and me,
Which way it pleases God; for who knows how,
Better than he that taught us first to plough,
To guide our mind and pens for his design?
And he makes base things usher in divine.
    3. I find that holy writ in many places
Hath semblance with this method, where the cases
Do call for one thing, to set forth another;
Use it I may, then, and yet nothing smother
Truth's golden beams: nay, by this method may

Make it cast forth its rays as light as day.
    And now before I do put up my pen,
I'll show the profit of my book, and then
Commit both thee and it unto that hand
That pulls the strong down, and makes weak ones stand.
    This book it chalketh out before thine eyes
The man that seeks the everlasting prize;
It shows you whence he comes, whither he goes;
What he leaves undone, also what he does;
It also shows you how he runs and runs,
Till he unto the gate of glory comes.
    It shows, too, who set out for life amain,
As if the lasting crown they would obtain;
Here also you may see the reason why
They lose their labour, and like fools do die.
    This book will make a traveller of thee,
If by its counsel thou wilt rulèd be;
It will direct thee to the Holy Land,
If thou wilt its directions understand:
Yea, it will make the slothful active be;
The blind also delightful things to see.
    Art thou for something rare and profitable?
Wouldst thou see a truth within a fable?
Art thou forgetful? Wouldst thou remember
From New Year's day to the last of December?
Then read my fancies; they will stick like burrs,
And may be, to the helpless, comforters.
    This book is writ in such a dialect
As may the minds of listless men affect:
It seems a novelty, and yet contains
Nothing but sound and honest gospel strains.
    Wouldst thou divert thyself from melancholy?
Wouldst thou be pleasant, yet be far from folly?
Wouldst thou read riddles, and their explanation?
Or else be drownèd in thy contemplation?
Dost thou love picking meat? Or wouldst thou see
A man i' the clouds, and hear him speak to thee?
Wouldst thou be in a dream, and yet not sleep?
Or wouldst thou in a moment laugh and weep?
Wouldst thou lose thyself and catch no harm,

And find thyself again without a charm?
Wouldst read thyself, and read thou knowst not what,
And yet know whether thou art blest or not,
By reading the same lines? Or, then come hither,
And lay my book, thy head, and heart together.

JOHN BUNYAN

In the Similitude of a Dream

As I walked through the wilderness of this world, I lighted on a certain place where was a Den,[2] and I laid me down in that place to sleep; and as I slept I dreamed a dream. I dreamed, and behold I saw a man clothed with rags,[3] standing in a certain place, with his face from his own house, a book in his hand, and a great burden[4] upon his back. I looked, and saw him open the book and read therein; and as he read, he wept and trembled; and not being able longer to contain, he brake out with a lamentable cry, saying, "What shall I do?"[5]

In this plight, therefore, he went home and refrained himself as long as he could, that his wife and children should not perceive his distress; but he could not be silent long, because that his trouble increased. Wherefore at length he brake his mind to his wife and children, and thus he began to talk to them. O my dear wife, said he, and you the children of my bowels, I, your dear friend, am in myself undone by reason of a burden that lieth hard upon me; moreover, I am for certain informed that this our city will be burned with fire from heaven, in which fearful overthrow both myself, with thee my wife, and you my sweet babes, shall miserably come to ruin, except (the which yet I see not) some way of escape can be found, whereby we may be delivered. At this his relations were sore amazed; not for that they believed that what he had said to them was true, but because they thought that some frenzy distemper had got into his head; therefore, it drawing towards night, and they hoping that sleep might settle his brains, with all haste they got him to bed. But the night was as troublesome to him as the day; wherefore, instead of sleeping, he spent it in sighs and tears. So, when the morning was come, they would know how he did. He told them, Worse and worse. He also set to talking to them again,

---

2. The Jail. [B]
3. Isa. 64:6.
4. Ps. 38:4.
5. Acts 2:37; 16:30, 31.

but they began to be hardened. They also thought to drive away his distemper by harsh and surly carriages[6] to him; sometimes they would deride, sometimes they would chide, and sometimes they would quite neglect him. Wherefore he began to retire himself to his chamber, to pray for and pity them, and also to condole his own misery; he would also walk solitarily in the fields, sometimes reading, and sometimes praying, and thus for some days he spent his time.

Now I saw, upon a time when he was walking in the fields, that he was (as he was wont) reading in his book, and greatly distressed in his mind; and as he read, he burst out, as he had done before, crying, "What shall I do to be saved?"

I saw also that he looked this way and that way, as if he would run; yet he stood still, because (as I perceived) he could not tell which way to go. I looked then, and saw a man named Evangelist coming to him, who asked, Wherefore dost thou cry?

He answered, Sir, I perceive by the book in my hand that I am condemned to die, and after that to come to judgement, and I find that I am not willing to do the first, nor able to do the second.

Then said Evangelist, Why not willing to die, since this life is attended with so many evils? The man answered, Because I fear that this burden that is upon my back will sink me lower than the grave, and I shall fall into Tophet. And, sir, if I be not fit to go to prison, I am not fit to go to judgement, and from thence to execution; and the thoughts of these things make me cry.

Then said Evangelist, If this be thy condition, why standest thou still? He answered, Because I know not whither to go. Then he gave him a parchment roll, and there was written within, "Fly from the wrath to come."[7]

The man therefore read it, and looking upon Evangelist very carefully, said, Whither must I fly? Then said Evangelist, pointing with his finger over a very wide field, Do you see yonder wicket-gate?[8] The man said, No. Then said the other, Do you see yonder shining light?[9] He said, I think I do. Then said Evangelist, Keep that light in your eye, and go up directly thereto: so shalt thou see the gate,[10] at which when thou knockest it shall be told thee what

6. Acts of behaviour.
7. Matt. 3:7.
8. Matt. 7:13, 14.
9. Ps. 119:105; 2 Pet. 1:19.
10. Christ, and the way to him, cannot be found without the Word. [B]

thou shalt do. So I saw in my dream that the man began to run. Now, he had not run far from his own door, but his wife and children perceiving it, began to cry after him to return; but the man put his fingers in his ears, and ran on, crying, Life! life! eternal life! So he looked not behind him, but fled towards the middle of the plain.

The neighbour also came out to see him run, and as he ran, some mocked, others threatened, and some cried after him to return; and, among those that did so, there were two that resolved to fetch him back by force. The name of the one was Obstinate, and the name of the other Pliable. Now by this time the man was got a good distance from them; but, however, they were resolved to pursue him, which they did, and in a little time they overtook him. Then said the man, Neighbours, wherefore are ye come? They said, To persuade you to go back with us. But he said, That can by no means be; you dwell, said he, in the City of Destruction,[11] the place also where I was born: I see it to be so, and dying there, sooner or later, you will sink lower than the grave, into a place that burns with fire and brimstone. Be content, good neighbours, and go along with me.

OBST. What! said Obstinate, and leave our friends and our comforts behind us?

CHR. Yes, said Christian (for that was his name), because that all which you shall forsake is not worthy to be compared with a little of that which I am seeking to enjoy; and if you will go along with me, and hold it, you shall fare as I myself, for there where I go is enough and to spare. Come away, and prove my words.

OBST. What are the things you seek, since you leave all the world to find them?

CHR. I seek "an inheritance incorruptible, undefiled, and that fadeth not away,"[12] and it is laid up in heaven, and safe there, to be bestowed, at the time appointed, on them that diligently seek it. Read it so, if you will, in my book.

OBST. Tush! said Obstinate, away with your book. Will you go back with us or no?

CHR. No, not I, said the other, because I have laid my hand to the plough.[13]

OBST. Come then, neighbour Pliable, let us turn again and go

---

11. Isa. 19:18.
12. 1 Pet. 1:4.
13. Luke 9:62.

home without him; there is a company of these crazed-headed cox-combs, that, when they take a fancy by the end, are wiser in their own eyes "than seven men that can render a reason."[14]

PLI. Then said Pliable, Don't revile; if what the good Christian says is true, the things he looks after are better than ours: my heart inclines to go with my neighbour.

OBST. What! more fools still! Be ruled by me, and go back; who knows whither such a brain-sick fellow will lead you? Go back, go back, and be wise.

CHR. Nay, but do thou come with thy neighbour, Pliable; there are such things to be had which I spoke of, and many more glories besides. If you believe not me, read here in this book, and for the truth of what is expressed therein, behold all is confirmed by the blood of Him that made it.

PLI. Well, neighbour Obstinate, said Pliable, I begin to come to a point; I intend to go along with this good man, and to cast in my lot with him, but, my good companion, do you know the way to this desired place?

CHR. I am directed by a man whose name is Evangelist, to speed me to a little gate that is before us, where we shall receive instructions about the way.

PLI. Come then, good neighbour, let us be going. Then they went both together.

OBST. And I will go back to my place, said Obstinate; I will be no companion of such misled, fantastical fellows.

Now I saw in my dream that, when Obstinate was gone back, Christian and Pliable went talking over the plain, and thus they began their discourse.

CHR. Come, neighbour Pliable, how do you do? I am glad you are persuaded to go along with me. Had even Obstinate himself but felt what I have felt of the powers and terrors of what is yet unseen, he would not thus lightly have given us the back.

PLI. Come, neighbour Christian, since there are none but us two here, tell me now further what the things are, and how to be enjoyed, whither we are going.

CHR. I can better conceive of them with my mind, than speak of them with my tongue, but yet, since you are desirous to know, I will read of them in my book.

---

14. Prov. 26:16.

PLI. And do you think that the words of your book are certainly true?

CHR. Yes, verily, for it was made by Him that cannot lie.[15]

PLI. Well said; what things are they?

CHR. There is an endless kingdom to be inhabited, and everlasting life to be given us, that we may inhabit that kingdom for ever.

PLI. Well said; and what else?

CHR. There are crowns of glory to be given us, and garments that will make us shine like the sun in the firmament of heaven!

PLI. This is very pleasant; and what else?

CHR. There shall be no more crying nor sorrow, for He that is owner of the place will wipe all tears from our eyes.[16]

PLI. And what company shall we have there?

CHR. There we shall be with seraphims and cherubims, creatures that will dazzle your eyes to look on them. There also you shall meet with thousands and ten thousands that have gone before us to that place; none of them are hurtful, but loving and holy; every one walking in the sight of God, and standing in his presence with acceptance for ever. In a word, there we shall see the elders with their golden crowns; there we shall see the holy virgins with their golden harps;[17] there we shall see men that by the world were cut in pieces, burnt in flames, eaten of beasts, drowned in the seas, for the love that they bare to the Lord of the place, all well, and clothed with immortality as with a garment.

PLI. The hearing of this is enough to ravish one's heart. But are these things to be enjoyed? How shall we get to be sharers thereof?

CHR. The Lord, the Governor of the country, hath recorded that in this book; the substance of which is: If we be truly willing to have it, he will bestow it upon us freely.

PLI. Well, my good companion, glad am I to hear of these things; come on, let us mend our pace.

CHR. I cannot go so fast as I would, by reason of this burden that is on my back.

Now I saw in my dream that just as they had ended this talk they drew near to a very miry slough that was in the midst of the plain, and they, being heedless, did both fall suddenly into the bog. The

15. Titus 1:2.
16. Rev. 21:4.
17. Rev. 5:11; 4:4; 14:2–4.

name of the slough was Despond. Here, therefore, they wallowed for a time, being grievously bedaubed with the dirt, and Christian, because of the burden that was on his back, began to sink in the mire.

PLI. Then said Pliable, Ah, neighbour Christian, where are you now?

CHR. Truly, said Christian, I do not know.

PLI. At that Pliable began to be offended, and angrily said to his fellow, Is this the happiness you have told me all this while of? If we have such ill speed at our first setting out, what may we expect 'twixt this and our journey's end? May I get out again with my life, you shall possess the brave[18] country alone for me. And with that he gave a desperate struggle or two, and got out of the mire on that side of the slough which was next[19] to his own house. So away he went, and Christian saw him no more.

Wherefore Christian was left to tumble in the Slough of Despond alone. But still he endeavoured to struggle to that side of the slough that was still further from his own house, and next to the wicket-gate; the which he did, but could not get out, because of the burden that was upon his back. But I beheld in my dream that a man came to him, whose name was Help, and asked him, What he did there?

CHR. Sir, said Christian, I was bid go this way by a man called Evangelist, who directed me also to yonder gate, that I might escape the wrath to come, and as I was going thither I fell in here.

HELP. But why did you not look for the steps?

CHR. Fear followed me so hard that I fled the next way and fell in.

HELP. Then said he, Give me thy hand. So he gave him his hand, and he drew him out, and set him upon sound ground, and bid him go on his way.[20]

Then I stepped to him that plucked him out, and said, Sir, wherefore, since over this place is the way from the City of Destruction to yonder gate, is it that this plat is not mended, that poor travellers might go thither with more security? And he said unto me, This miry slough is such a place as cannot be mended; it is the descent whither the scrum and filth that attends conviction for sin doth continually run, and therefore it is called the Slough of Despond. For still,[21] as the sinner is awakened about his lost condition, there

---

18. Excellent, "fine."   20. Ps. 40:2.
19. Nearest.   21. Always, continually.

ariseth in his soul many fears, and doubts, and discouraging apprehensions, which all of them get together, and settle in this place.
And this is the reason of the badness of this ground.

It is not the pleasure of the King that this place should remain so
bad. His labourers also have, by the direction of His Majesty's sur-
veyors, been for above these sixteen hundred years employed about
this patch of ground, if perhaps it might have been mended. Yea,
and to my knowledge, said he, here have been swallowed up at
least twenty thousand cartloads, yea, millions of wholesome instructions, that have at all seasons been brought from all places of the
King's dominions, and they that can tell, say they are the best mate-
rials to make good ground of the place; if so be, it might have been
mended, but it is the Slough of Despond still, and so will be when
they have done what they can.

True, there are, by the direction of the Lawgiver, certain good
and substantial steps,[22] placed even through the very midst of the
slough, but at such time as this place doth much spew out its filth,
as it doth against change of weather, these steps are hardly seen. Or
if they be, men, through the dizziness of their heads, step besides,
and then they are bemired to purpose, notwithstanding the steps be
there; but the ground is good when they are once got in at the gate.

Now I saw in my dream that by this time Pliable was got home
to his house again, so that his neighbours came to visit him, and some
of them called him wise man for coming back, and some called him
fool for hazarding himself with Christian. Others, again, did mock
at his cowardliness, saying, Surely, since you began to venture, I
would not have been so base to have given out for a few difficulties.
So Pliable sat sneaking among them. But at last he got more confidence, and then they all turned their tales, and began to deride poor
Christian behind his back. And thus much concerning Pliable.

Now as Christian was walking solitarily by himself, he espied
one afar off come crossing over the field to meet him, and their hap
was to meet just as they were crossing the way of each other. The
gentleman's name that met him was Mr. Worldly Wiseman. He
dwelt in the town of Carnal Policy, a very great town, and also hard
by from whence Christian came. This man, then, meeting with
Christian, and having some inkling of him, for Christian's setting

---

22. The promises of forgiveness and acceptance to life by faith in Christ. [B]

forth from the City of Destruction was much noised abroad, not only in the town where he dwelt, but also it began to be the town-talk in some other places—Master Worldly Wiseman, therefore, having some guess of him, by beholding his laborious going, by observing his sighs and groans, and the like, began thus to enter into some talk with Christian.

WORLD. How now, good fellow, whither away after this bur-dened manner?

CHR. A burdened manner indeed, as ever, I think, poor creature had. And whereas you ask me, Whither away, I tell you, Sir, I am going to yonder wicket-gate before me, for there, as I am informed, I shall be put into a way to be rid of my heavy burden.

WORLD. Hast thou a wife and children?

CHR. Yes, but I am so laden with this burden that I cannot take that pleasure in them as formerly; methinks I am as if I had none.[23]

WORLD. Wilt thou harken unto me if I give thee counsel?

CHR. If it be good, I will, for I stand in need of good counsel.

WORLD. I would advise thee, then, that thou with all speed get thyself rid of thy burden, for thou wilt never be settled in thy mind till then; nor canst thou enjoy the benefits of the blessing which God hath bestowed upon thee till then.

CHR. That is that which I seek for, even to be rid of this heavy burden, but get it off myself, I cannot; nor is there any man in our country that can take it off my shoulders; therefore am I going this way, as I told you, that I may be rid of my burden.

WORLD. Who bid thee go this way to be rid of thy burden?

CHR. A man that appeared to me to be a very great and hon-ourable person; his name, as I remember, is Evangelist.

WORLD. I beshrew him for his counsel; there is not a more dan-gerous and troublesome way in the world than is that unto which he hath directed thee, and that thou shalt find, if thou will be ruled by his counsel. Thou hast met with something (as I perceive) already, for I see the dirt of the Slough of Despond is upon thee; but that slough is the beginning of the sorrows that do attend those that go on in that way. Hear me, I am older than thou; thou art like to meet with, in the way which thou goest, wearisomeness, painfulness, hunger, perils, nakedness, sword, lions, dragons, dark-ness, and, in a word, death, and what not? These things are cer-

---

23. 1 Cor. 7:29.

tainly true, having been confirmed by many testimonies. And why should a man so carelessly cast away himself, by giving heed to a stranger?

CHR. Why, Sir, this burden upon my back is more terrible to me than are all these things which you have mentioned; nay, methinks I care not what I meet with in the way, if so be I can also meet with deliverance from my burden.

WORLD. How camest thou by the burden at first?

CHR. By reading this book in my hand.

WORLD. I thought so, and it is happened unto thee as to other weak men, who meddling with things too high for them, do suddenly fall into thy distractions; which distractions do not only unman men, as thine, I perceive, has done thee, but they run them upon desperate ventures to obtain they know not what.

CHR. I know what I would obtain; it is ease for my heavy burden.

WORLD. But why wilt thou seek for ease this way, seeing so many dangers attend it? Especially since (hadst thou but patience to hear me) I could direct thee to the obtaining of what thou desirest, without the dangers that thou in this way wilt run thyself into; yea, and the remedy is at hand. Besides, I will add that instead of those dangers thou shalt meet with much safety, friendship, and content.

CHR. Pray, Sir, open this secret to me.

WORLD. Why, in yonder village (the village is named Morality) there dwells a gentleman whose name is Legality, a very judicious man, and a man of a very good name, that has skill to help men off with such burdens as thine are from their shoulders. Yea, to my knowledge, he hath done a great deal of good this way; ay, and besides, he hath skill to cure those that are somewhat crazed in their wits with their burdens. To him, as I said, thou mayest go, and be helped presently.[24] His house is not quite a mile from this place, and if he should not be at home himself, he hath a pretty young man to his son, whose name is Civility,[25] that can do it (to speak on) as well as the old gentleman himself. There, I say, thou mayest be eased of thy burden, and if thou art not minded to go back to thy former habitation, as indeed I would not wish thee, thou mayest send for thy wife and children to thee to this village, where there are

---

24. Quickly.
25. A theological term: the quality of being morally good, as a citizen, but not sanctified by Faith.

houses now standing empty, one of which thou mayest have at reasonable rates; provision is there also cheap and good, and that which will make thy life the more happy is, to be sure, there thou shalt live by honest neighbours, in credit and good fashion.

Now was Christian somewhat at a stand, but presently he concluded, If this be true which this gentleman hath said, my wisest course is to take his advice; and with that he thus further spoke.

CHR. Sir, which is my way to this honest man's house?

WORLD. Do you see yonder high hill?[26]

CHR. Yes, very well.

WORLD. By that hill you must go, and the first house you come at is his.

So Christian turned out of his way to go to Mr. Legality's house for help. But behold, when he was got now hard by the hill, it seemed so high, and also that side of it that was next the wayside did hang so much over, that Christian was afraid to venture further, lest the hill should fall on his head; wherefore there he stood still, and wotted not what to do. Also his burden now seemed heavier to him than while he was in his way. There came also flashes of fire out of the hill, that made Christian afraid that he should be burned.[27] Here, therefore, he sweat and did quake for fear. And now he began to be sorry that he had taken Mr. Worldy Wiseman's counsel. And with that he saw Evangelist coming to meet him; at the sight also of whom he began to blush for shame. So Evangelist drew nearer and nearer, and coming up to him, he looked upon him with a severe and dreadful countenance, and thus began to reason with Christian.

EVAN. What dost thou here, Christian? said he. At which words Christian knew not what to answer; wherefore at present he stood speechless before him. Then said Evangelist further, Art not thou the man that I found crying without the walls of the City of Destruction?

CHR. Yes, dear Sir, I am the man.

EVAN. Did not I direct thee the way to the little wicket-gate?

CHR. Yes, dear Sir, said Christian.

EVAN. How is it, then, that thou art so quickly turned aside? For thou art now out of the way.

---

26. Mount Sinai. [B]
27. Exod. 19:16, 18.

CHR. I met with a gentleman so soon as I had got over the Slough of Despond, who persuaded me that I might, in the village before me, find a man that could take off my burden.

EVAN. What was he?

CHR. He looked like a gentleman, and talked much to me, and got me at last to yield, so I came hither. But when I beheld this hill, and how it hangs over the way, I suddenly made a stand, lest it should fall on my head.

EVAN. What said that gentleman to you?

CHR. Why, he asked me whither I was going, and I told him.

EVAN. And what said he then?

CHR. He asked me if I had a family, and I told him. But, said I, I am so loaden with the burden that is on my back, that I cannot take pleasure in them as formerly.

EVAN. And what said he then?

CHR. He bid me with speed get rid of my burden, and I told him 'twas ease that I sought. And, said I, I am therefore going to yonder gate, to receive further direction how I may get to the place of deliverance. So he said that he would show me a better way, and short, not so attended with difficulties as the way, Sir, that you set me in; which way, said he, will direct you to a gentleman's house that hath skill to take off these burdens. So I believed him, and turned out of that way into this, if haply I might be soon eased of my burden. But when I came to this place, and beheld things as they are, I stopped for fear (as I said) of danger; but I now know not what to do.

EVAN. Then, said Evangelist, stand still a little, that I may show thee the words of God. So he stood trembling. Then said Evangelist, "See that ye refuse not him that speaketh. For if they escaped not who refused him that spake on earth, much more shall not we escape, if we turn away from him that speaketh from heaven." He said, moreover, "Now the just shall live by faith: but if any man draw back, my soul shall have no pleasure in him."[28] He also did thus apply them: Thou art the man that art running into this misery; thou hast begun to reject the counsel of the Most High, and to draw back thy foot from the way of peace, even almost to the hazarding of thy perdition.

Then, Christian fell down at his feet as dead, crying, "Woe is

---

28. Heb. 12:25; 10:38.

me, for I am undone!"[29] At the sight of which, Evangelist caught him by the right hand, saying, "All manner of sin and blasphemies shall be forgiven unto men." "Be not faithless, but believing."[30] Then did Christian again a little revive, and stood up trembling, as at first, before Evangelist.

Then Evangelist proceeded, saying, Give more earnest heed to the things that I shall tell thee of. I will now show thee who it was that deluded thee, and who it was also to whom he sent thee. The man that met thee is one Worldly Wiseman, and rightly is he so called; partly because he favoureth only the doctrine of this world (therefore he always goes to the town of Morality to church), and partly because he loveth that doctrine best, for it saveth him best from the cross. And because he is of this carnal temper, therefore he seeketh to prevent my ways, though right. Now there are three things in this man's counsel that thou must utterly abhor.

1. His turning thee out of the way. 2. His labouring to render the cross odious to thee. 3. His setting thy feet in that way that leadeth unto the administration of death.

First, thou must abhor his turning thee out of the way; yea, and thine own consenting thereto, because this is to reject the counsel of God for the sake of the counsel of a Worldly Wiseman. The Lord says, "Strive to enter in at the strait gate," the gate to which I send thee; for "strait is the gate that leadeth unto life, and few there be that find it."[31] From this little wicket-gate, and from the way thereto, hath this wicked man turned thee, to the bringing of thee almost to destruction; hate, therefore, his turning thee out of the way, and abhor thyself for hearkening to him.

Secondly, thou must abhor his labouring to render the cross odious unto thee, for thou art to prefer it before "the treasures in Egypt." Besides, the King of Glory hath told thee that he that "will save his life shall lose it"; and he that comes after him, "and hates not his father, and mother, and wife, and children, and brethren, and sisters, yea, and his own life also, he cannot be my disciple."[32] I say, therefore, for man to labour to persuade thee that that shall be thy death, without which, the truth hath said, thou canst not have eternal life; this doctrine thou must abhor.

---

29. Isa. 6:5.   31. Luke 13:24; Matt. 7:14.
30. Matt. 12:31; John 20:27.   32. Heb. 11:26; Mark 8:35; Luke 14:26.

Thirdly, thou must hate his setting of thy feet in the way that leadeth to the ministration of death. And for this thou must consider to whom he sent thee, and also how unable that person was to deliver thee from thy burden.

He to whom thou wast sent for ease, being by name Legality, is the son of the bondwoman which now is in bondage with her children,[33] and is, in a mystery,[34] this Mount Sinai, which thou hast feared will fall on thy head. Now if she, with her children, are in bondage, how canst thou expect by them to be made free? This Legality, therefore, is not able to set thee free from thy burden. No man was as yet ever rid of his burden by him; no, nor ever is like to be. Ye cannot be justified by the works of the law,[35] for by the deeds of the law no man living can be rid of his burden. Therefore, Mr. Worldly Wiseman is an alien, and Mr. Legality is a cheat; and for his son Civility, notwithstanding his simpering looks, he is but a hypocrite and cannot help thee. Believe me, there is nothing in all this noise that thou hast heard of these sottish men, but a design to beguile thee of thy salvation, by turning thee from the way in which I had set thee. After this, Evangelist called aloud to the heavens for confirmation of what he had said, and with that there came words and fire out of the mountain under which poor Christian stood, that made the hair of his flesh stand up. The words were thus pronounced: "As many as are of the works of the law are under the curse; for it is written, Cursed is every one that continueth not in all things which are written in the book of the law to do them."[36]

Now Christian looked for nothing but death, and began to cry out lamentably, even cursing the time in which he met with Mr. Worldly Wiseman, still calling himself a thousand fools for hearkening to his counsel. He also was greatly ashamed to think that this gentleman's arguments, flowing only from the flesh, should have the prevalency with him as to cause him to forsake the right way. This done, he applied himself again to Evangelist in words and sense as follows:

CHR. Sir, what think you? Is there hope? May I now go back and go up to the wicket-gate? Shall I not be abandoned for this, and

---

33. Gal. 4:21–31.   35. Gal. 2:16.
34. Symbolically, in a spiritual sense.   36. Gal. 3:10.

sent back from thence ashamed? I am sorry I have hearkened to this man's counsel. But may my sin be forgiven?

EVAN. Then said Evangelist to him, Thy sin is very great, for by it thou hast committed two evils: thou hast forsaken the way that is good, to tread in forbidden paths, yet will the man at the gate receive thee, for he has goodwill for men; only, said he, take heed that thou turn not aside again, "lest thou perish from the way, when his wrath is kindled but a little."[37] Then did Christian address himself to go back, and Evangelist, after he had kissed him, gave him one smile, and bid him God-speed. So he went on with haste, neither spake he to any man by the way, nor, if any asked him, would he vouchsafe them an answer. He went like one that was all the while treading on forbidden ground, and could by no means think himself safe, till again he was got into the way which he left to follow Mr. Worldly Wiseman's counsel. So in process of time Christian got up to the gate. Now, over the gate there was written, "Knock, and it shall be opened unto you."[38] He knocked, therefore, more than once or twice, saying,

> May I now enter here? Will he within
> Open to sorry me, though I have been
> An undeserving rebel? Then shall I
> Not fail to sing his lasting praise on high.

At last there came a grave person to the gate, named Good-will, who asked who was there? and whence he came? and what he would have?

CHR. Here is a poor burdened sinner. I come from the City of Destruction, but am going to Mount Zion, that I may be delivered from the wrath to come. I would, therefore, Sir, since I am informed that by this gate is the way thither, know if you are willing to let me in?

GOOD-WILL. I am willing with all my heart, said he; and with that he opened the gate.[39]

So when Christian was stepping in, the other gave him a pull. Then said Christian, What means that? The other told him, A little distance from this gate, there is erected a strong castle, of which

---

37. Ps. 2:12.
38. Matt. 7:8.
39. The gate will be opened to broken-hearted sinners. [B]

Beelzebub is the captain; from thence, both he and them that are with him shoot arrows at those that come up to this gate, if haply they may die before they can enter in. Then said Christian, I rejoice and tremble. So when he was got in, the man of the gate asked him who directed him thither?

CHR. Evangelist bid me come hither and knock (as I did), and he said that you, Sir, would tell me what I must do.

GOOD-WILL. An open door is set before thee, "and no man can shut it."[40]

CHR. Now I begin to reap the benefits of my hazards.

GOOD-WILL. But how is it that you came alone?

CHR. Because none of my neighbours saw their danger, as I saw mine.

GOOD-WILL. Did any of them know of your coming?

CHR. Yes, my wife and children saw me at the first, and called after me to turn again; also some of my neighbours stood crying and calling after me to return, but I put my fingers in my ears, and so came on my way.

GOOD-WILL. But did none of them follow you to persuade you to go back?

CHR. Yes, both Obstinate and Pliable, but when they saw that they could not prevail, Obstinate went railing back, but Pliable came with me a little way.

GOOD-WILL. But why did he not come through?

CHR. We indeed came both together, until we came at the Slough of Despond, into the which we also suddenly fell. And then was my neighbour Pliable discouraged, and would not adventure further. Wherefore, getting out again on that side next to his own house, he told me I should possess the brave country alone for him, so he went his way, and I came mine; he after Obstinate, and I to this gate.[41]

GOOD-WILL. Then said Good-will, Alas, poor man, is the celestial glory of so small esteem with him, that he counteth it not worth running the hazards of a few difficulties to obtain it?

CHR. Truly, said Christian, I have said the truth of Pliable, and if I should also say all the truth of myself, it will appear there is no betterment 'twixt him and myself. 'Tis true, he went back to his

---

40. Rev. 3:8
41. A man may have company when he sets out for heaven, and yet go thither alone. [B]

own house, but I also turned aside to go in the way of death, being persuaded thereto by the carnal arguments of one Mr. Worldly Wiseman.

Good-will. Oh, did he light upon you? What, he would have had you a sought for ease at the hands of Mr. Legality. They are, both of them, a very cheat. But did you take his counsel?

Chr. Yes, as far as I durst; I went to find Mr. Legality, until I thought that the mountain that stands by his house would have fallen upon my head; wherefore, there I was forced to stop.

Good-will. That mountain has been the death of many, and will be the death of many more; 'tis well you escaped being by it dashed in pieces.

Chr. Why, truly, I do not know what had become of me there, had not Evangelist happily met me again, as I was musing in the midst of my dumps; but 'twas God's mercy that he came to me again, for else I had never come hither. But now I am come, such a one as I am, more fit indeed for death by that mountain, than thus to stand talking with my Lord; but, oh, what a favour is this to me, that yet I am admitted entrance here.

Good-will. We make no objections against any, notwithstanding all that they have done before they came hither: they "in no wise are cast out."[42] And therefore, good Christian, come a little way with me, and I will teach thee about the way thou must go. Look before thee; dost thou see this narrow way? That is the way thou must go. It was cast up by the patriarchs, prophets, Christ, and his apostles, and it is as straight as a rule can make it. This is the way thou must go.

Chr. But, said Christian, are there no turnings or windings, by which a stranger may lose his way?

Good-will. Yes, there are many ways butt down upon this, and they are crooked and wide. But thus thou may'st distinguish the right from the wrong, the right only being straight and narrow.[43]

Then I saw in my dream that Christian asked him further if he could not help him off with his burden that was upon his back; for as yet he had not got rid thereof, nor could he by any means get it off without help.

---

42. John 6:37.
43. Matt. 7:13, 14. [Bunyan is here taking liberties with the word "strait," which in the biblical passage means simply "narrow."]

He told him, As to thy burden, be content to bear it until thou comest to the place of deliverance, for there it will fall from thy back of itself.[44]

Then Christian began to gird up his loins, and to address himself to his journey. So the other told him, that by that he was gone some distance from the gate, he would come at the house of the Interpreter, at whose door he should knock, and he would show him excellent things. Then Christian took his leave of his friend, and he again bid him God-speed.

Then he went on till he came to the house of the Interpreter, where he knocked over and over; at last one came to the door and asked who was there.

CHR. Sir, here is a traveller, who was bid by an acquaintance of the goodman of this house to call here for my profit; I would therefore speak with the master of the house. So he called for the master of the house, who after a little time came to Christian and asked him what he would have.

CHR. Sir, said Christian, I am a man that am come from the City of Destruction, and am going to the Mount Zion, and I was told by the man that stands at the gate, at the head of this way, that if I called here, you would show me excellent things, such as would be an help to me in my journey.

INTER. Then said the Interpreter, Come in; I will show thee that which will be profitable to thee. So he commanded his man to light the candle,[45] and bid Christian follow him. So he had him into a private room, and bid his man open a door, the which when he had done, Christian saw the picture of a very grave person hang up against the wall; and this was the fashion of it. It had eyes lifted up to heaven, the best of books in his hand, the law of truth was written upon his lips, the world was behind his back. It stood as if it pleaded with men, and a crown of gold did hang over its head.

CHR. Then said Christian, What meaneth this?

INTER. The man whose picture this is, is one of a thousand; he can beget children, travail in birth with children,[46] and nurse them himself when they are born. And whereas thou seest him with his

---

44. There is no deliverance from the guilt and burden of sin, but by the death and blood of Christ. [B]
45. Illumination (that is, Divine inspiration). [B]
46. 1 Cor. 4:15; Gal. 4:19.

eyes lift up to heaven, the best of books in his hand, and the law of
truth writ on his lips, it is to show thee that his work is to know and
unfold dark things to sinners, even as also thou seest him stand as
if he pleaded with men; and whereas thou seest the world as cast
behind him, and that a crown hangs over his head, that is to show
thee that slighting and despising the things that are present, for the
love that he hath to his Master's service, he is sure in the world that
comes next to have glory for his reward. Now, said the Interpreter,
I have showed thee this picture first because the man whose picture
this is, is the only man whom the Lord of the place whither thou art
going hath authorized to be thy guide in all difficult places thou
mayest meet with in the way; wherefore, take good heed to what I
have showed thee, and bear well in thy mind what thou hast seen,
lest in thy journey thou meet with some that pretend to lead thee
right, but their way goes down to death.

Then he took him by the hand and led him into a very large parlour that was full of dust, because never swept; the which, after he
had reviewed a little while, the Interpreter called for a man to
sweep. Now when he began to sweep, the dust began so abun-
dantly to fly about that Christian had almost therewith been
choked. Then said the Interpreter to a damsel that stood by, Bring
hither the water and sprinkle the room; the which, when she had
done, it was swept and cleansed with pleasure.

CHR. Then said Christian, What means this?

INTER. The Interpreter answered, This parlour is the heart of a
man that was never sanctified by the sweet grace of the Gospel; the
dust is his original sin and inward corruptions that have defiled the
whole man. He that began to sweep at first is the Law, but she that
brought water and did sprinkle it is the Gospel. Now whereas thou
sawest that so soon as the first began to sweep, the dust did so fly
about that the room by him could not be cleansed, but that thou
wast almost choked therewith, this is to show thee that the law,
instead of cleansing the heart (by its working) from sin, doth revive,
put strength into, and increase it in the soul, even as it doth discover
and forbid it, for it doth not give power to subdue.

Again, as thou sawest the damsel sprinkle the room with water,
upon which it was cleansed with pleasure, this is to show thee that
when the Gospel comes in the sweet and precious influences
thereof to the heart, then, I say, even as thou sawest the damsel lay
the dust by sprinkling the floor with water, so is sin vanquished

and subdued, and the soul made clean through the faith of it, and consequently fit for the King of glory to inhabit.

I saw, moreover, in my dream, that the Interpreter took him by the hand and had him into a little room, where sat two little children, each one in his chair. The name of the eldest was Passion, and the name of the other Patience. Passion seemed to be much discontented, but Patience was very quiet. Then Christian asked, What is the reason of the discontent of Passion? The Interpreter answered, The Governor of them would have him stay for his best things till the beginning of the next year, but he will have all now; but Patience is willing to wait.

Then I saw that one came to Passion, and brought him a bag of treasure, and poured it down at his feet; the which he took up and rejoiced therein, and withal laughed Patience to scorn. But I beheld but a while, and he had lavished all away, and had nothing left him but rags.

CHR. Then said Christian to the Interpreter, Expound this matter more fully to me.

INTER. So he said, These two lads are figures: Passion, of the men of this world; and Patience, of the men of that which is to come. For, as here thou seest, Passion will have all now this year, that is to say, in this world; so are the men of this world: they must have all their good things now, they cannot stay till next year, that is, until the next world, for their portion of good. That proverb, "A bird in the hand is worth two in the bush," is of more authority with them than are all the Divine testimonies of the good of the world to come. But as thou sawest that he had quickly lavished all away, and had presently left him nothing but rags; so will it be with all such men at the end of this world.

CHR. Then said Christian, Now I see that Patience has the best wisdom, and that upon many accounts. 1. Because he stays for the best things. 2. And also because he will have the glory of his, when the other has nothing but rags.

INTER. Nay, you may add another, to wit, the glory of the next world will never wear out, but these are suddenly gone. Therefore Passion had not so much reason to laugh at Patience, because he had his good things first, as Patience will have to laugh at Passion, because he had his best things last; for first must give place to last, because last must have his time to come, but last gives place to nothing, for there is not another to succeed. He, therefore, that hath his portion first, must needs have a time to spend it, but he that hath his portion last, must have it lastingly; therefore it is said of Dives, "In thy life thou receivedst thy good things, and likewise Lazarus evil things: but now he is comforted, and thou art tormented."[47]

CHR. Then I perceive 'tis not best to covet things that are now, but to wait for things to come.

INTER. You say truth, "For the things that are seen are temporal; but the things that are not seen are eternal."[48] But though this be so, yet since things present and our fleshly appetite are such near neighbours one to another, and again, because things to come and carnal sense are such strangers one to another, therefore it is that the first of these so suddenly fall into amity, and that distance is so continued between the second.

Then I saw in my dream that the Interpreter took Christian by the hand and led him into a place where was a fire burning against a wall, and one standing by it, always casting much water upon it to quench it; yet did the fire burn higher and hotter.

Then said Christian, What means this?

The Interpreter answered, This fire is the work of grace that is wrought in the heart; he that casts water upon it, to extinguish and put it out, is the Devil; but in that thou seest the fire notwithstanding burn higher and hotter, thou shalt also see the reason of that. So he had him about to the backside of the wall, where he saw a man with a vessel of oil in his hand, of the which he did also continually cast (but secretly) into the fire.

Then said Christian, What means this?

The Interpreter answered, This is Christ, who continually, with the oil of his grace, maintains the work already begun in the heart, by the means of which, notwithstanding what the Devil can do, the souls of his people prove gracious still. And in that thou sawest that the man stood behind the wall to maintain the fire, that is to teach thee that it is hard for the tempted to see how this work of grace is maintained in the soul.

I saw also that the Interpreter took him again by the hand and led him into a pleasant place, where was builded a stately palace, beautiful to behold; at the sight of which Christian was greatly

---

47. Luke 16:25.
48. 2 Cor. 4:18.

delighted. He saw also, upon the top thereof, certain persons walk-ing, who were clothed all in gold.

Then said Christian, May we go in thither?

Then the Interpreter took him and led him up toward the door of the palace, and behold, at the door stood a great company of men, as desirous to go in, but durst not. There also sat a man at a little distance from the door, at a tableside, with a book and his ink-horn before him, to take the name of him that should enter therein; he saw also that in the doorway stood many men in armour to keep it, being resolved to do the men that would enter what hurt and mischief they could. Now was Christian somewhat in a maze. At last, when every man started back for fear of the armed men, Christian saw a man of very stout countenance come up to the man that sat there to write, saying, "Set down my name, Sir"; the which when he had done, he saw the man draw his sword, and put an hel-met upon his head, and rush toward the door upon the armed men, who laid upon him with deadly force. But the man, not at all dis-couraged, fell to cutting and hacking most fiercely. So after he had received and given many wounds to those that attempted to keep him out, he cut his way through them all, and pressed forward into the palace, at which there was a pleasant voice heard from those that were within, even of those that walked upon the top of the palace, saying,

> Come in, come in;
> Eternal glory thou shalt win.

So he went in, and was clothed with such garments as they. Then Christian smiled and said, I think verily I know the meaning of this.

Now, said Christian, let me go hence. Nay, stay, said the Inter-preter, till I have showed thee a little more, and after that thou shalt go on thy way. So he took him by the hand again and led him into a very dark room, where there sat a man in an iron cage.

Now the man, to look on, seemed very sad; he sat with his eyes looking down to the ground, his hands folded together, and he sighed as if he would break his heart. Then said Christian, What means this? At which the Interpreter bid him talk with the man.

Then said Christian to the man, What art thou? The man an-swered, I am what I was not once.

CHR. What wast thou once?

MAN. The man said, I was once a fair and flourishing professor,[49] both in mine own eyes and also in the eyes of others; I once was, as I thought, fair for the Celestial City, and had then even joy at the thoughts that I should get thither.

CHR. Well, but what art thou now?

MAN. I am now a man of despair, and am shut up in it, as in this iron cage. I cannot get out. Oh, now I cannot!

CHR. But how camest thou in this condition?

MAN. I left off to watch and be sober; I laid the reins upon the neck of my lusts; I sinned against the light of the Word and the goodness of God; I have grieved the Spirit, and he is gone; I tempted the Devil, and he is come to me; I have provoked God to anger, and he has left me; I have so hardened my heart that I cannot repent.

Then said Christian to the Interpreter, But is there no hope for such a man as this? Ask him, said the Interpreter. Nay, said Christian, pray Sir, do you.

INTER. Then said the Interpreter, Is there no hope, but you must be kept in the iron cage of despair?

MAN. No, none at all.

INTER. Why, the Son of the Blessed is very pitiful.

MAN. I have crucified him to myself afresh, I have despised his person, I have despised his righteousness, I have counted his blood an unholy thing, I have "done despite to the Spirit of Grace."[50] Therefore I have shut myself out of all the promises, and there now remains to me nothing but threatenings, dreadful threatenings, fearful threatenings of certain judgement and fiery indignation, which shall devour me as an adversary.

INTER. For what did you bring yourself into this condition?

MAN. For the lusts, pleasures, and profits of this world; in the enjoyment of which I did then promise myself much delight. But now every one of those things also bite me and gnaw me like a burning worm.

INTER. But canst thou not now repent and turn?

MAN. God hath denied me repentance. His Word gives me no encouragement to believe; yea, himself hath shut me up in this iron cage, nor can all the men in the world let me out. O eternity! eter-

---

49. One who makes an open declaration (profession) of his religious faith.
50. Heb. 6:6; 10:28, 29.

nity! how shall I grapple with the misery that I must meet with in eternity!

INTER. Then said the Interpreter to Christian, Let this man's misery be remembered by thee and be an everlasting caution to thee.

CHR. Well, said Christian, this is fearful; God help me to watch and be sober, and to pray that I may shun the cause of this man's misery. Sir, is it not time for me to go on my way now?

INTER. Tarry till I shall show thee one thing more, and then thou shalt go on thy way.

So he took Christian by the hand again and led him into a chamber, where there was one rising out of bed; and as he put on his raiment, he shook and trembled. Then said Christian, Why doth this man thus tremble? The Interpreter then bid him to tell to Christian the reason of his so doing. So he began and said, This night, as I was in my sleep, I dreamed, and behold the heavens grew exceeding black; also it thundered and lightened in most fearful wise, that it put me into an agony. So I looked up in my dream, and saw the clouds rack at an unusual rate, upon which I heard a great sound of a trumpet, and saw also a man sit upon a cloud, attended with the thousands of heaven; they were all in flaming fire. Also the heavens were in a burning flame. I heard then a voice saying, "Arise, ye dead, and come to judgement"; and with that the rocks rent, the graves opened, and the dead that were therein came forth. Some of them were exceeding glad, and looked upward; and some sought to hide themselves under the mountains. Then I saw the man that sat upon the cloud open the book, and bid the world draw near. Yet there was, by reason of a fierce flame which issued out and came from before him, a convenient[51] distance betwixt him and them, as betwixt the judge and the prisoners at the bar. I heard it also proclaimed to them that attended on the man that sat on the cloud, "Gather together the tares, the chaff, and stubble, and cast them into the burning lake." And with that the bottomless pit opened, just whereabout I stood; out of the mouth of which there came, in an abundant manner, smoke and coals of fire, with hideous noises. It was also said to the same persons, "Gather my wheat into the garner." And with that I saw many catched up and carried away into the clouds, but I was left behind. I also sought to hide myself, but I could not, for the man that sat upon the cloud still kept his eye

---

51. Suitable to the conditions; appropriate; proper.

upon me. My sins also came into my mind, and my conscience did accuse me on every side. Upon this I awaked from my sleep.[52]

CHR. But what was it that made you so afraid of this sight?

MAN. Why, I thought that the day of judgement was come, and that I was not ready for it. But this frighted me most, that the angels gathered up several, and left me behind; also the pit of hell opened her mouth just where I stood. My conscience, too, afflicted me, and (as I thought) the Judge had always his eye upon me, showing indignation in his countenance.

Then said the Interpreter to Christian, Hast thou considered all these things?

CHR. Yes, and they put me in hope and fear.

INTER. Well, keep all things so in thy mind that they may be as a goad in thy sides, to prick thee forward in the way thou must go. Then Christian began to gird up his loins, and to address himself to his journey. Then said the Interpreter, The Comforter be always with thee, good Christian, to guide thee in the way that leads to the City. So Christian went on his way, saying,

> Here I have seen things rare and profitable;
> Things pleasant, dreadful, things to make me stable
> In what I have begun to take in hand;
> Then let me think on them, and understand
> Wherefore they showed me was, and let me be
> Thankful, O good Interpreter, to thee.

Now I saw in my dream that the highway up which Christian was to go was fenced on either side with a wall, and that wall was called Salvation.[53] Up this way, therefore, did burdened Christian run, but not without great difficulty, because of the load on his back.

He ran thus till he came at a place somewhat ascending, and upon that place stood a Cross, and a little below, in the bottom, a Sepulchre. So I saw in my dream that just as Christian came up with the Cross, his burden loosed from off his shoulders, and fell from off his back, and began to tumble, and so continued to do, till it came to the mouth of the Sepulchre, where it fell in, and I saw it no more.

---

52. For this vision, recalling dozens of biblical passages, see especially 1 Cor. 15:52; Rev. 14:14; 20:11–15; Matt. 3:12; 13:30.
53. Isa. 26:1.

Then was Christian glad and lightsome,[54] and said with a merry heart, "He hath given me rest by his sorrow, and life by his death." Then he stood still awhile to look and wonder, for it was very surprising to him that the sight of the Cross should thus ease him of his burden. He looked, therefore, and looked again, even till the springs that were in his head sent the waters down his cheeks. Now, as he stood looking and weeping, behold, three Shining Ones came to him and saluted him with "Peace be to thee." So the first said to him, "Thy sins be forgiven"; the second stripped him of his rags, and clothed him "with change of raiment"; the third also set a mark on his forehead, and gave him a roll with a seal upon it, which he bade him look on as he ran, and that he should give it in at the Celestial Gate.[55] So they went their way. Then Christian gave three leaps for joy, and went on, singing,

> Thus far did I come loaden with my sin;
> Nor could aught ease the grief that I was in
> Till I came hither: What a place is this!
> Must here be the beginning of my bliss?
> Must here the burden fall from off my back?
> Must here the strings that bound it to me crack?
> Blest Cross! blest Sepulchre! blest rather be
> The Man that there was put to shame for me![56]

I saw then in my dream that he went on thus, even until he came at a bottom, where he saw, a little out of the way, three men fast asleep, with fetters upon their heels. The name of the one was Simple, another Sloth, and the third Presumption.

Christian then seeing them lie in this case, went to them, if peradventure he might awake them, and cried, You are like them that sleep on the top of a mast, for the Dead Sea is under you, a gulf that hath no bottom.[57] Awake therefore, and come away; be willing also, and I will help you off with your irons. He also told them, If he that goeth about like "a roaring lion" comes by, you will cer-

---

54. When God releases us of our guilt and burden we are as those that leap for joy. [B]

55. Mark 2:5; Zech. 3:3–5; Eph. 1:13.

56. A Christian can sing though alone, when God doth give him the joy of his heart. [B]

57. Prov. 23:34.

tainly become a prey to his teeth.[58] With that they looked upon him, and began to reply in this sort: Simple said, "I see no danger"; Sloth said, "Yet a little more sleep"; and Presumption said, "Every fat[59] must stand upon his own bottom." And so they lay down to sleep again, and Christian went on his way.[60]

Yet was he troubled to think that men in that danger should so little esteem the kindness of him that so freely offered to help them, both by awakening of them, counseling of them, and proffering to help them off with their irons. And as he was troubled thereabout, he espied two men come tumbling over the wall, on the left hand of the narrow way, and they made up apace to him. The name of the one was Formalist, and the name of the other Hypocrisy. So, as I said, they drew up unto him, who thus entered with them into discourse.

CHR. Gentlemen, whence came you, and whither do you go?

FORM. and HYP. We were born in the land of Vainglory, and are going for praise to Mount Sion.

CHR. Why came you not in at the gate which standeth at the beginning of the way? Know you not that it is written, that "he that cometh not in by the door, but climbeth up some other way, the same is a thief and a robber"?[61]

FORM. and HYP. They said, That to go to the gate for entrance was by all their countrymen counted too far about, and that therefore their usual way was to make a short cut of it, and to climb over the wall, as they had done.

CHR. But will it not be counted a trespass against the Lord of the city whither we are bound, thus to violate his revealed will?

FORM. and HYP. They told him, that, as for that, he needed not to trouble his head thereabout, for what they did they had custom for, and could produce (if need were) testimony that would witness it for more than a thousand years.

CHR. But, said Christian, will your practice stand a trial at law?

FORM. and HYP. They told him, That custom, it being of so long a standing as above a thousand years, would doubtless now be admitted as a thing legal by any impartial judge; and beside, said

---

58. 1 Pet. 5:8.
59. A large vessel for liquids; a tub, cask, vat.
60. There is no persuasion will do, if God openeth not the eyes. [B]
61. John 10:1.

they, if we get into the way, what's matter which way we get in? If we are in, we are in; thou art but in the way, who, as we perceive, came in at the gate, and we are also in the way that came tumbling over the wall. Wherein now is thy condition better than ours?

CHR. I walk by the rule of my Master; you walk by the rude working of your fancies. You are counted thieves already by the Lord of the way; therefore I doubt[62] you will not be found true men at the end of the way. You come in by yourselves without his direction, and shall go out by yourselves without his mercy.

To this they made him but little answer; only they bid him look to himself. Then I saw that they went on every man in his way, without much conference one with another, save that these two men told Christian, that as to laws and ordinances, they doubted not but they should as conscientiously do them as he; therefore, said they, we see not wherein thou differest from us but by the coat that is on thy back, which was, as we trow, given thee by some of thy neighbours, to hide the shame of thy nakedness.

CHR. By laws and ordinances you will not be saved, since you came not in by the door. And as for this coat that is on my back, it was given me by the Lord of the place whither I go, and that, as you say, to cover my nakedness with. And I take it as a token of his kindness to me, for I had nothing but rags before. And besides, thus I comfort myself as I go: Surely, think I, when I come to the gate of the city, the Lord thereof will know me for good, since I have his coat on my back, a coat that he gave me freely in the day that he stripped me of my rags. I have, moreover, a mark in my forehead, of which perhaps you have taken no notice, which one of my Lord's most intimate associates fixed there in the day that my burden fell off my shoulders. I will tell you, moreover, that I had then given me a roll, sealed, to comfort me by reading as I go on the way; I was also bid to give it in at the Celestial Gate, in token of my certain going in after it, all which things I doubt you want,[63] and want them because you came not in at the gate.

To these things they gave him no answer; only they looked upon each other and laughed. Then I saw that they went on all, save that Christian kept before, who had no more talk but with himself, and that sometimes sighingly and sometimes comfortably; also he

---

62. Fear, or suspect.
63. Fear that you lack.

would be often reading in the roll that one of the Shining Ones gave him, by which he was refreshed.

I beheld then that they all went on till they came to the foot of the Hill Difficulty, at the bottom of which was a spring. There were also in the same place two other ways besides that which came straight from the gate; one turned to the left hand, and the other to the right, at the bottom of the hill, but the narrow way lay right up the hill (and the name of the going up the side of the hill is called Difficulty). Christian now went to the spring,[64] and drank thereof to refresh himself, and then began to go up the hill, saying,

> The hill, though high, I covet to ascend,
> The difficulty will not me offend;
> For I perceive the way to life lies here.
> Come, pluck up heart, let's neither faint nor fear;
> Better, though difficult, the right way to go,
> Than wrong, though easy, where the end is woe.

The other two also came to the foot of the hill, but when they saw that the hill was steep and high, and that there were two other ways to go, and supposing also that these two ways might meet again with that up which Christian went, on the other side of the hill, therefore they were resolved to go in those ways. Now the name of one of those ways was Danger, and the name of the other Destruction. So the one took the way which is called Danger, which led him into a great wood, and the other took directly up the way to Destruction, which led him into a wide field, full of dark mountains, where he stumbled and fell, and rose no more.

I looked then after Christian, to see him go up the hill, where I perceived he fell from running to going,[65] and from going to clambering upon his hands and his knees, because of the steepness of the place. Now about the midway to the top of the hill was a pleasant arbour, made by the Lord of the hill for the refreshing of weary travellers; thither, therefore, Christian got, where also he sat down to rest him. Then he pulled his roll out of his bosom, and read therein to his comfort; he also now began afresh to take a review of the coat or garment that was given him as he stood by the Cross.

---

64. Isa. 49:10.
65. Walking.

Thus pleasing himself awhile, he at last fell into a slumber, and thence into a fast sleep, which detained him in that place until it was almost night, and in his sleep his roll fell out of his hand. Now as he was sleeping, there came one to him and awaked him, saying, "Go to the ant, thou sluggard; consider her ways, and be wise."[66] And with that Christian suddenly started up, and sped him on his way, and went apace till he came to the top of the hill.

Now when he was got up to the top of the hill, there came two men running against him amain; the name of the one was Timorous, and of the other, Mistrust, to whom Christian said, Sirs, what's the matter you run the wrong way? Timorous answered, that they were going to the City of Zion, and had got up that difficult place, but, said he, the further we go, the more danger we meet with; wherefore we turned, and are going back again.

Yes, said Mistrust, for just before us lie a couple of lions in the way, whether sleeping or waking we know not, and we could not think, if we came within reach, but they would presently pull us in pieces.

CHR. Then said Christian, You make me afraid, but whither shall I fly to be safe? If I go back to mine own country, *that* is prepared for fire and brimstone, and I shall certainly perish there. If I can get to the Celestial City, I am sure to be in safety there. I must venture. To go back is nothing but death; to go forward is fear of death, and life everlasting beyond it. I will yet go forward. So Mistrust and Timorous ran down the hill, and Christian went on his way. But, thinking again of what he had heard from the men, he felt in his bosom for his roll, that he might read therein and be comforted; but he felt, and found it not. Then was Christian in great distress, and knew not what to do, for he wanted that which used to relieve him, and that which should have been his pass into the Celestial City. Here, therefore, he began to be much perplexed, and knew not what to do. At last he bethought himself that he had slept in the arbour that is on the side of the hill, and, falling down upon his knees, he asked God's forgiveness for that his foolish act, and then went back to look for his roll. But all the way he went back, who can sufficiently set forth the sorrow of Christian's heart? Sometimes he sighed, sometimes he wept, and oftentimes he chid himself for being so foolish to fall asleep in that place which was erected only for a little refreshment for his weariness. Thus, there-

---

66. Prov. 6:6.

fore, he went back, carefully looking on this side and on that, all the way as he went, if happily[67] he might find his roll, that had been his comfort so many times in his journey. He went thus till he came again within sight of the arbour where he sat and slept, but that sight renewed his sorrow the more by bringing again, even afresh, his evil of sleeping into his mind. Thus, therefore, he now went on bewailing his sinful sleep, saying, "O wretched man that I am!"[68] that I should sleep in the daytime! that I should sleep in the midst of difficulty! that I should so indulge the flesh, as to use that rest for ease to my flesh, which the Lord of the hill hath erected only for the relief of the spirits of pilgrims! How many steps have I took in vain! (Thus it happened to Israel, for their sin; they were sent back again by the way of the Red Sea.) And I am made to tread those steps with sorrow, which I might have trod with delight, had it not been for this sinful sleep. How far might I have been on my way by this time! I am made to tread those steps thrice over, which I needed not to have trod but once; yea, now also I am like to be benighted, for the day is almost spent. Oh, that I had not slept!

Now by this time he was come to the arbour again, where for a while he sat down and wept; but at last, as Christian would have it, looking sorrowfully down under the settle, there he espied his roll, the which he with trembling and haste catched up, and put it into his bosom. But who can tell how joyful this man was when he had gotten his roll again! For this roll was the assurance of his life, and acceptance at the desired haven. Therefore he laid it up in his bosom, gave thanks to God for directing his eye to the place where it lay, and with joy and tears betook himself again to his journey. But oh, how nimbly now did he go up the rest of the hill! Yet before he got up, the sun went down upon Christian, and this made him again recall the vanity of his sleeping to his remembrance; and thus he again began to condole with himself. O thou sinful sleep: how for thy sake am I like to be benighted in my journey! I must walk without the sun; darkness must cover the path of my feet; and I must hear the noise of the doleful creatures, because of my sinful sleep. Now also he remembered the story that Mistrust and Timorous told him of, how they were frighted with the sight of the lions. Then said Christian to himself again, These beasts range in the

---

67. Luckily, fortunately (see "haply").
68. Rom. 7:24.

night for their prey, and if they should meet with me in the dark, how should I shift[69] them? How should I escape being by them torn in pieces? Thus he went on his way. But while he was thus bewailing his unhappy miscarriage, he lift up his eyes, and behold there was a very stately palace before him, the name of which was Beautiful, and it stood just by the highway side.

So I saw in my dream that he made haste and went forward, that if possible he might get lodging there. Now before he had gone far he entered into a very narrow passage, which was about a furlong off of the porter's lodge, and looking very narrowly before him as he went, he espied two lions in the way. Now, thought he, I see the dangers that Mistrust and Timorous were driven back by. (The lions were chained, but he saw not the chains.) Then he was afraid, and thought also himself to go back after them, for he thought nothing but death was before him. But the porter at the lodge, whose name is Watchful,[70] perceiving that Christian made a halt as if he would go back, cried unto him, saying, Is thy strength so small? Fear not the lions, for they are chained, and are placed there for trial of faith where it is, and for discovery of those that had none. Keep in the midst of the path, and no hurt shall come unto thee.

Then I saw that he went on, trembling for fear of the lions, but taking good heed to the directions of the porter; he heard them roar, but they did him no harm. Then he clapped his hands, and went on till he came and stood before the gate where the porter was. Then said Christian to the porter, Sir, what house is this? And may I lodge here tonight? The porter answered, This house was built by the Lord of the hill, and he built it for the relief and security of pilgrims. The porter also asked whence he was, and whither he was going.

CHR. I am come from the City of Destruction, and am going to Mount Zion, but because the sun is now set, I desire, if I may, to lodge here tonight.

POR. What is your name?

CHR. My name is now Christian, but my name at the first was Graceless; I came of the race of Japheth, whom God will persuade to dwell in the tents of Shem.[71]

POR. But how doth it happen that you come so late? The sun is set.

---

69. Escape.
70. Mark 13:34–37.
71. Gen. 9:27.

Chr. I had been here sooner, but that, "wretched man that I am!" I slept in the arbour that stands on the hillside; nay, I had, notwithstanding that, been here much sooner, but that in my sleep I lost my evidence, and came without it to the brow of the hill; and then feeling for it and finding it not, I was forced with sorrow of heart to go back to the place where I slept my sleep, where I found it, and now I am come.

Por. Well, I will call out one of the virgins of this place, who will, if she likes your talk, bring you into the rest of the family, according to the rules of the house. So Watchful, the porter, rang a bell, at the sound of which came out at the door of the house a grave and beautiful damsel, named Discretion, and asked why she was called.

The porter answered, This man is in a journey from the City of Destruction to Mount Zion, but being weary and benighted, he asked me if he might lodge here tonight; so I told him I would call for thee, who, after discourse had with him, mayest do as seemeth thee good, even according to the law of the house.

Then she asked him whence he was and whither he was going, and he told her. She asked him also how he got into the way, and he told her. Then she asked him what he had seen and met with in the way, and he told her. And last she asked his name, so he said, It is Christian, and I have so much the more a desire to lodge here tonight, because, by what I perceive, this place was built by the Lord of the hill, for the relief and security of pilgrims. So she smiled, but the water stood in her eyes, and after a little pause she said, I will call forth two or three more of the family. So she ran to the door and called out Prudence, Piety, and Charity, who after a little more discourse with him had him into the family, and many of them, meeting him at the threshold of the house, said, "Come in, thou blessed of the Lord";[72] this house was built by the Lord of the hill, on purpose to entertain such pilgrims in. Then he bowed his head and followed them into the house. So when he was come in and sat down, they gave him something to drink, and consented[73] together that until supper was ready some of them should have some particular discourse with Christian, for the best improvement of time, and they appointed Piety, and Prudence, and Charity to discourse with him; and thus they began:

---

72. Gen. 24:31.
73. Agreed.

PIETY. Come, good Christian, since we have been so loving to you, to receive you in our house this night, let us, if perhaps we may better ourselves thereby, talk with you of all things that have happened to you in your pilgrimage.

CHR. With a very good will, and I am glad that you are so well disposed.

PIETY. What moved you at first to betake yourself to a pilgrim's life?

CHR. I was driven out of my native country by a dreadful sound that was in mine ears: to wit, that unavoidable destruction did attend me, if I abode in that place where I was.

PIETY. But how did it happen that you came out of your country this way?

CHR. It was as God would have it, for when I was under the fears of destruction, I did not know whither to go, but by chance there came a man, even to me, as I was trembling and weeping, whose name is Evangelist, and he directed me to the wicket-gate, which else I should never have found, and so set me into the way that hath led me directly to this house.

PIETY. But did you not come by the house of the Interpreter?

CHR. Yes, and did see such things there, the remembrance of which will stick by me as long as I live; especially three things: to wit, how Christ, in despite of Satan, maintains his work of grace in the heart; how the man had sinned himself quite out of hopes of God's mercy; and also the dream of him that thought in his sleep the day of judgement was come.

PIETY. Why, did you hear him tell his dream?

CHR. Yes, and a dreadful one it was. I thought it made my heart ache as he was telling of it, but yet I am glad I heard it.

PIETY. Was that all that you saw at the house of the Interpreter?

CHR. No; he took me and had me where he showed me a stately palace, and how the people were clad in gold that were in it, and how there came a venturous man and cut his way through the armed men that stood in the door to keep him out, and how he was bid to come in, and win eternal glory. Methought those things did ravish my heart! I would have stayed at that good man's house a twelvemonth, but that I knew I had further to go.

PIETY. And what saw you else in the way?

CHR. Saw! why, I went but a little further, and I saw one, as I thought in my mind, hang bleeding upon the tree, and the very sight of him made my burden fall off my back (for I groaned under a very heavy burden), but then it fell down from off me. It was a strange thing to me, for I never saw such a thing before; yea, and while I stood looking up, for then I could not forbear looking, three Shining Ones came to me. One of them testified that my sins were forgiven me; another stripped me of my rags and gave me this broidered coat which you see; and the third set the mark which you see in my forehead, and gave me this sealed roll. (And with that he plucked it out of his bosom.)

PIETY. But you saw more than this, did you not?

CHR. The things that I have told you were the best, yet some other matters I saw, as, namely: I saw three men, Simple, Sloth, and Presumption, lie asleep a little out of the way, as I came, with irons upon their heels, but do you think I could awake them? I also saw Formality and Hypocrisy come tumbling over the wall, to go (as they pretended) to Zion, but they were quickly lost, even as I myself did tell them, but they would not believe. But above all, I found it hard work to get up this hill, and as hard to come by the lions' mouths, and truly if it had not been for the good man, the porter that stands at the gate, I do not know but that after all I might have gone back again; but now I thank God I am here, and I thank you for receiving of me.

Then Prudence thought good to ask him a few questions, and desired his answer to them.

PRUD. Do you think sometimes of the country from whence you came?

CHR. Yes, but with much shame and detestation: "Truly, if I had been mindful of that country from whence I came out, I might have had opportunity to have returned; but now I desire a better country, that is, an heavenly."[74]

PRUD. Do you not yet bear away with you some of the things that then you were conversant withal?

CHR. Yes, but greatly against my will, especially my inward and carnal cogitations, with which all my countrymen, as well as myself, were delighted. But now all those things are my grief, and might I but choose mine own things, I would choose never to think of those things more; but when I would be doing of that which is best, that which is worst is with me.

---

74. Heb. 11:15, 16.

Prud. Do you not find sometimes, as if those things were vanquished, which at other times are your perplexity?

Chr. Yes, but that is seldom; but they are to me golden hours in which such things happen to me.

Prud. Can you remember by what means you find your annoyances, at times, as if they were vanquished?

Chr. Yes, when I think what I saw at the Cross, that will do it; and when I look upon my broidered coat, that will do it; also when I look into the roll that I carry in my bosom, that will do it; and when my thoughts wax warm about whither I am going, that will do it.

Prud. And what is it that makes you so desirous to go to Mount Zion?

Chr. Why, there I hope to see him alive that did hang dead on the Cross; and there I hope to be rid of all those things that to this day are in me an annoyance to me; there, they say, there is no death; and there I shall dwell with such company as I like best. For to tell you truth, I love him, because I was by him eased of my burden, and I am weary of my inward sickness. I would fain be where I shall die no more, and with the company that shall continually cry, "Holy, Holy, Holy!"[75]

Then said Charity to Christian, Have you a family? Are you a married man?

Chr. I have a wife and four small children.

Char. And why did you not bring them along with you?

Chr. Then Christian wept and said, Oh how willingly would I have done it, but they were all of them utterly averse to my going on pilgrimage.

Char. But you should have talked to them, and have endeavoured to have shown them the danger of being behind.

Chr. So I did, and told them also what God had showed to me of the destruction of our city, but I seemed to them "as one that mocked,"[76] and they believed me not.

Char. And did you pray to God that he would bless your counsel to them?

Chr. Yes, and that with much affection: for you must think that my wife and poor children were very dear unto me.

---

75. Rev. 4:8.
76. Gen. 19:14.

CHAR. But did you tell them of your own sorrow and fear of destruction? For I suppose that destruction was visible enough to you.

CHR. Yes, over, and over, and over. They might also see my fears in my countenance, in my tears, and also in my trembling under the apprehension of the judgement that did hang over our heads; but all was not sufficient to prevail with them to come with me.

CHAR. But what could they say for themselves, why they came not?

CHR. Why, my wife was afraid of losing this world, and my children were given to the foolish delights of youth; so what by one thing, and what by another, they left me to wander in this manner alone.

CHAR. But did you not with your vain life damp all that you by words used by way of persuasion to bring them away with you?

CHR. Indeed, I cannot commend my life, for I am conscious to myself of many failings therein. I know also that a man by his conversation[77] may soon overthrow what by argument or persuasion he doth labour to fasten upon others for their good. Yet this I can say, I was very wary of giving them occasion, by any unseemly action, to make them averse to going on pilgrimage. Yea, for this very thing they would tell me I was too precise, and that I denied myself of things (for their sakes) in which they saw no evil. Nay, I think I may say that if what they saw in me did hinder them, it was my great tenderness in sinning against God, or of doing any wrong to my neighbour.

CHAR. Indeed Cain hated his brother, "because his own works were evil, and his brother's righteous,"[78] and if thy wife and children have been offended with thee for this, they thereby show themselves to be implacable to good, and "thou hast delivered thy soul" from their blood.[79]

Now I saw in my dream that thus they sat talking together until supper was ready. So when they had made ready, they sat down to meat. Now the table was furnished with fat things and with wine that was well refined,[80] and all their talk at the table was about the Lord of the hill; as, namely, about what he had done, and where-

---

77. Way of life, conduct.
78. 1 John 3:12.
79. Ezek. 3:19.
80. Isa. 25:6.

fore he did what he did, and why he had built that house. And by what they said I perceived that he had been a great warrior, and had fought with and slain "him that had the power of death,"[81] but not without great danger to himself, which made me love him the more.

For, as they said, and as I believe (said Christian), he did it with the loss of much blood; but that which put glory of grace into all he did was, that he did it out of pure love to his country. And besides, there were some of them of the household that said they had been and spoke with him since he did die on the Cross, and they have attested that they had it from his own lips, that he is such a lover of poor pilgrims, that the like is not to be found from the east to the west.

They, moreover, gave an instance of what they affirmed, and that was, he had stripped himself of his glory, that he might do this for the poor; and that they heard him say and affirm that he would not dwell in the mountain of Zion alone. They said, moreover, that he had made many pilgrims princes, though by nature they were beggars born, and their original had been the dunghill.[82]

Thus they discoursed together till late at night, and after they had committed themselves to their Lord for protection, they betook themselves to rest. The Pilgrim they laid in a large upper chamber, whose window opened towards the sun rising. The name of the chamber was Peace, where he slept till break of day, and then he awoke and sang:

> Where am I now? Is this the love and care
> Of Jesus for the men that pilgrims are
> Thus to provide? That I should be forgiven!
> And dwell already the next door to heaven!

So in the morning they all got up, and after some more discourse they told him that he should not depart till they had shown him the rarities of that place. And first they had him into the study, where they showed him records of the greatest antiquity, in which, as I remember in my dreams, they showed him first the pedigree of the Lord of the hill, that he was the son of the Ancient of Days, and came by that eternal generation. Here also was more fully recorded the acts that he had done, and the names of many hundreds that he had taken

---

81. Heb. 2:14.
82. 1 Sam. 2:8.

into his service, and how he had placed them in such habitations that could neither by length of days nor decays of nature be dissolved.

Then they read to him some of the worthy acts that some of his servants had done: as, how they had "subdued kingdoms, wrought righteousness, obtained promises, stopped the mouths of lions, quenched the violence of fire, escaped the edge of the sword, out of weakness were made strong, waxed valiant in fight, and turned to flight the armies of the aliens."[83]

They then read again, in another part of the records of the house, where it was showed how willing their Lord was to receive into his favour any, even any, though they in time past had offered great affronts to his person and proceedings. Here also were several other histories of many other famous things, of all which Christian had a view; as of things both ancient and modern, together with prophecies and predictions of things that have their certain accomplishment, both to the dread and amazement of enemies, and the comfort and solace of pilgrims.

The next day they took him and had him into the armoury, where they showed him all manner of furniture,[84] which their Lord had provided for pilgrims, as sword, shield, helmet, breastplate, *all prayer,* and shoes that would not wear out.[85] And there was here enough of this to harness out[86] as many men for the service of their Lord as there be stars in heaven for multitude.

They also showed him some of the engines with which some of his servants had done wonderful things. They showed him Moses' rod; the hammer and nail with which Jael slew Sisera; the pitchers, trumpets, and lamps too, with which Gideon put to flight the armies of Midian. Then they showed him the ox's goad wherewith Shamgar slew six hundred men. They showed him also the jawbone with which Samson did such mighty feats. They showed him, moreover, the sling and stone with which David slew Goliath of Gath, and the sword also with which their Lord will kill the Man of Sin, in the day that he shall rise up to the prey. They showed him besides many excellent things, with which Christian was much delighted. This done, they went to their rest again.

---

83. Heb. 11:33, 34.
84. Equipment; armor and weapons.
85. Eph. 6:13–18.
86. Equip, arm.

Then I saw in my dream that on the morrow he got up to go forward, but they desired him to stay till the next day also. And then, said they, we will, if the day be clear, show you the Delectable Mountains, which, they said, would yet further add to his comfort, because they were nearer the desired haven than the place where at present he was; so he consented and stayed. When the morning was up, they had him to the top of the house, and bade him look south, so he did. And behold at a great distance he saw a most pleasant mountainous country, beautified with woods, vineyards, fruits of all sorts, flowers also, with springs and fountains, very delectable to behold. Then he asked the name of the country. They said it was Immanuel's Land, and it is as common,[87] said they, as this hill is, to and for all the pilgrims. And when thou comest there from hence, said they, thou mayest see to the gate of the Celestial City, as the shepherds that live there will make appear.

Now he bethought himself of setting forward, and they were willing he should. But first, said they, let us go again into the armoury. So they did, and when they came there, they harnessed him from head to foot with what was of proof,[88] lest perhaps he should meet with assaults in the way. He being therefore thus accoutred, walketh out with his friends to the gate, and there he asked the porter if he saw any pilgrims pass by. Then the porter answered, Yes.

CHR. Pray, did you know him? said he.

POR. I asked him his name, and he told me it was Faithful.

CHR. Oh, said Christian, I know him; he is my townsman, my near neighbour. He comes from the place where I was born. How far do you think he may be before?

POR. He is got by this time below the hill.

CHR. Well, said Christian, good Porter, the Lord be with thee, and add to all thy blessings much increase, for the kindness that thou hast showed to me.

Then he began to go forward, but Discretion, Piety, Charity, and Prudence would accompany him down to the foot of the hill. So they went on together, reiterating their former discourses, till they came to go down the hill. Then said Christian, As it was difficult coming up, so (so far as I can see) it is dangerous going down. Yes,

---

87. Public, open to anyone's use.
88. Of tested strength, invulnerable.

said Prudence, so it is, for it is a hard matter for a man to go down into the Valley of Humiliation, as thou art now, and to catch no slip by the way; therefore, said they, are we come out to accompany thee down the hill. So he began to go down, but very warily, yet he caught a slip or two.

Then I saw in my dream that these good companions, when Christian was gone to the bottom of the hill, gave him a loaf of bread, a bottle of wine, and a cluster of raisins, and then he went on his way.

But now in this Valley of Humiliation poor Christian was hard put to it, for he had gone but a little way before he espied a foul fiend coming over the field to meet him; his name is Apollyon.[89] Then did Christian begin to be afraid, and to cast in his mind whether to go back or to stand his ground. But he considered again that he had no armour for his back, and therefore thought that to turn the back to him might give him the greater advantage with ease to pierce him with his darts. Therefore he resolved to venture and stand his ground; for, thought he, had I no more in mine eye than the saving of my life, it would be the best way to stand.

So he went on, and Apollyon met him. Now the monster was hideous to behold; he was clothed with scales like a fish (and they are his pride), he had wings like a dragon, feet like a bear, and out of his belly came fire and smoke, and his mouth was as the mouth of a lion.[90] When he was come up to Christian, he beheld him with a disdainful countenance, and thus began to question with him.

APOL. Whence come you, and whither are you bound?

CHR. I am come from the City of Destruction, which is the place of all evil, and am going to the City of Zion.

APOL. By this I perceive thou art one of my subjects, for all that country is mine, and I am the prince and god of it. How is it then that thou hast run away from thy king? Were it not that I hope thou mayest do me more service, I would strike thee now at one blow to the ground.

CHR. I was born indeed in your dominions, but your service was hard, and your wages such as a man could not live on, "for the wages of sin is death";[91] therefore when I was come to years, I did as other considerate persons do, look out if perhaps I might mend myself.

---

89. Rev. 9:11.
90. See especially Job 41:15; Rev. 13:2.
91. Rom. 6:23.

APOL. There is no prince that will thus lightly lose his subjects, neither will I as yet lose thee, but since thou complainest of thy service and wages, be content to go back; what our country will afford, I do here promise to give thee.

CHR. But I have let myself to another, even to the King of princes, and how can I with fairness go back with thee?

APOL. Thou hast done in this, according to the proverb, "changed a bad for a worse"; but it is ordinary for those that have professed themselves his servants, after a while to give him the slip, and return again to me. Do thou so too, and all shall be well.

CHR. I have given him my faith, and sworn my allegiance to him; how then can I go back from this, and not be hanged as a traitor?

APOL. Thou didst the same to me, and yet I am willing to pass by all, if now thou wilt yet turn again and go back.

CHR. What I promised thee was in my nonage, and besides, I count that the Prince under whose banner now I stand is able to absolve me, yea, and to pardon also what I did as to my compliance with thee; and besides (O thou destroying Apollyon), to speak truth, I like his service, his wages, his servants, his government, his company and country, better than thine, and therefore leave off to persuade me further. I am his servant, and I will follow him.

APOL. Consider again when thou art in cool blood, what thou art like to meet with in the way that thou goest. Thou knowest that, for the most part, his servants come to an ill end, because they are transgressors against me and my ways. How many of them have been put to shameful deaths; and besides, thou countest his service better than mine, whereas he never came yet from the place where he is to deliver any that served him out of their hands. But as for me, how many times, as all the world very well knows, have I delivered, either by power or fraud, those that have faithfully served me from him and his, though taken by them; and so I will deliver thee.

CHR. His forbearing at present to deliver them is on purpose to try their love, whether they will cleave to him to the end; and as for the ill end thou sayest they come to, that is most glorious in their account, for, for present deliverance, they do not much expect it, for they stay for their glory, and then they shall have it, when their Prince comes in his and the glory of the angels.

APOL. Thou hast already been unfaithful in thy service to him; and how dost thou think to receive wages of him?

CHR. Wherein, O Apollyon, have I been unfaithful to him?

APOL. Thou didst faint at first setting out, when thou wast almost choked in the Gulf of Despond; thou didst attempt wrong ways to be rid of thy burden, whereas thou shouldest have stayed till thy Prince had taken it off; thou didst sinfully sleep and lose thy choice thing; thou wast also almost persuaded to go back at the sight of the lions; and when thou talkest of thy journey, and of what thou hast heard and seen, thou art inwardly desirous of vainglory in all that thou sayest or doest.

CHR. All this is true, and much more which thou hast left out, but the Prince whom I serve and honour is merciful and ready to forgive. But besides, these infirmities possessed me in thy country, for there I sucked them in, and I have groaned under them, been sorry for them, and have obtained pardon of my Prince.

APOL. Then Apollyon broke out into a grievous rage, saying, I am an enemy to this Prince; I hate his person, his laws, and people; I am come out on purpose to withstand thee.

CHR. Apollyon, beware what you do, for I am in the king's highway, the way of holiness; therefore take heed to yourself.

APOL. Then Apollyon straddled quite over the whole breadth of the way, and said, I am void of fear in this matter: prepare thyself to die, for I swear by my infernal den that thou shalt go no further; here will I spill thy soul.

And with that he threw a flaming dart at his breast, but Christian had a shield in his hand, with which he caught it, and so prevented the danger of that. Then did Christian draw, for he saw 'twas time to bestir him, and Apollyon as fast made at him, throwing darts as thick as hail; by the which, notwithstanding all that Christian could do to avoid it, Apollyon wounded him in his head, his hand, and foot.[92] This made Christian give a little back; Apollyon therefore followed his work amain, and Christian again took courage and resisted as manfully as he could. This sore combat lasted for above half a day, even till Christian was almost quite spent; for you must know that Christian, by reason of his wounds, must needs grow weaker and weaker.

Then Apollyon, espying his opportunity, began to gather up close to Christian, and wrestling with him, gave him a dreadful fall; and with that Christian's sword flew out of his hand. Then said Apollyon, I am sure of thee now. And with that he had almost

---

92. Christian wounded in his understanding, faith, and conversation. [B]

pressed him to death, so that Christian began to despair of life. But as God would have it, while Apollyon was fetching of his last blow, thereby to make a full end of this good man, Christian nimbly reached out his hand for his sword and caught it, saying, "Rejoice not against me, O mine enemy: when I fall I shall arise";[93] and with that gave him a deadly thrust, which made him give back, as one that had received his mortal wound. Christian perceiving that, made at him again, saying, "Nay, in all these things we are more than conquerors through him that loved us."[94] And with that Apollyon spread forth his dragon's wings and sped him away, that Christian for a season saw him no more.

In this combat no man can imagine, unless he had seen and heard as I did, what yelling and hideous roaring Apollyon made all the time of the fight—he spake like a dragon;[95] and on the other side, what sighs and groans burst from Christian's heart. I never saw him all the while give so much as one pleasant look, till he perceived he had wounded Apollyon with his two-edged sword; then indeed he did smile and look upward, but 'twas the dreadfulest sight that ever I saw.

So when the battle was over, Christian said, I will here give thanks to him that hath delivered me "out of the mouth of the lion,"[96] to him that did help me against Apollyon. And so he did, saying,

> Great Beelzebub, the captain of this fiend,
> Designed my ruin; therefore to this end
> He sent him harnessed out: and he with rage
> That hellish was did fiercely me engage.
> But blessed Michael helped me, and I
> By dint of sword did quickly make him fly.
> Therefore to him let me give lasting praise,
> And thank and bless his holy name always.

Then there came to him an hand with some of the leaves of the Tree of Life, the which Christian took and applied to the wounds that he had received in the battle, and was healed immediately. He also sat down in that place to eat bread, and to drink of the bottle that was given him a little before; so being refreshed, he

93. Mic. 7:8.   95. Rev. 13:11.
94. Rom. 8:37.   96. 2 Tim. 4:17.

addressed himself to his journey, with his sword drawn in his hand, for he said, I know not but some other enemy may be at hand. But he met with no other affront from Apollyon quite through this valley.

Now at the end of this valley was another, called the Valley of the Shadow of Death, and Christian must needs go through it, because the way to the Celestial City lay through the midst of it. Now this valley is a very solitary place. The prophet Jeremiah thus describes it: "A wilderness, a land of deserts and of pits, a land of drought, and of the shadow of death, a land that no man" (but a Christian) "passeth through, and where no man dwelt."[97]

Now here Christian was worse put to it than in his fight with Apollyon, as by the sequel you shall see.

I saw then in my dream that when Christian was got to the borders of the Shadow of Death, there met him two men, children of them that brought up an evil report of the good land,[98] making haste to go back; to whom Christian spake as follows:

CHR. Whither are you going?

MEN. They said, Back, back; and we would have you to do so too, if either life or peace is prized by you.

CHR. Why, what's the matter? said Christian.

MEN. Matter! said they; we were going that way as you are going, and went as far as we durst, and indeed we were almost past coming back, for had we gone a little further, we had not been here to bring the news to thee.

CHR. But what have you met with? said Christian.

MEN. Why, we were almost in the Valley of the Shadow of Death, but that by good hap we looked before us, and saw the danger before we came to it.

CHR. But what have you seen? said Christian.

MEN. Seen! Why, the Valley itself, which is as dark as pitch; we also saw there the hobgoblins, satyrs, and dragons of the pit; we heard also in that Valley a continual howling and yelling, as of a people under unutterable misery, who there sat bound in affliction and irons; and over that Valley hang the discouraging clouds of confusion. Death also doth always spread his wings over it. In a word, it is every whit dreadful, being utterly without order.

---

97. Jer. 2:6.
98. Num. 13:31, 32.

CHR. Then said Christian, I perceive not yet, by what you have said, but that this is my way to the desired haven.

MEN. Be it thy way; we will not choose it for ours. So they parted, and Christian went on his way, but still with his sword drawn in his hand, for fear lest he should be assaulted.

I saw then in my dream, so far as this valley reached, there was on the right hand a very deep ditch; that ditch is it into which the blind have led the blind in all ages, and have both there miserably perished.[99] Again, behold on the left hand, there was a very dangerous quag, into which, if even a good man falls, he can find no bottom for his foot to stand on. Into that quag King David once did fall,[100] and had no doubt therein been smothered, had not he that is able plucked him out.

The pathway was here also exceeding narrow, and therefore good Christian was the more put to it, for when he sought in the dark to shun the ditch on the one hand, he was ready to tip over into the mire on the other; also when he sought to escape the mire, without great carefulness he would be ready to fall into the ditch. Thus he went on, and I heard him here sigh bitterly, for, besides the dangers mentioned above, the pathway was here so dark that ofttimes, when he lift up his foot to set forward, he knew not where or upon which he should set it next.

About the midst of this valley I perceived the mouth of hell to be, and it stood also hard by the wayside. Now thought Christian, what shall I do? And ever and anon the flame and smoke would come out in such abundance, with sparks and hideous noises (things that cared not for Christian's sword, as did Apollyon before), that he was forced to put up his sword, and betake himself to another weapon, called *all prayer*. So he cried in my hearing, "O Lord, I beseech thee, deliver my soul!"[101] Thus he went on a great while, yet still the flames would be reaching towards him. Also he heard doleful voices, and rushings to and fro, so that sometimes he thought he should be torn in pieces, or trodden down like mire in the streets. This frightful sight was seen and these dreadful noises were heard by him for several miles together, and coming to a place where he thought he heard a company of fiends coming forward to

---

99. Matt. 15:14.
100. Ps. 69:2, 14.
101. Ps. 116:4.

meet him, he stopped, and began to muse what he had best to do. Sometimes he had half a thought to go back; then again he thought he might be halfway through the valley; he remembered also how he had already vanquished many a danger, and that the danger of going back might be much more than for to go forward; so he resolved to go on. Yet the fiends seemed to come nearer and nearer, but when they were come even almost at him, he cried out with a most vehement voice, "I will walk in the strength of the Lord God!"[102] so they gave back, and came no further.

One thing I would not let slip; I took notice that now poor Christian was so confounded that he did not know his own voice, and thus I perceived it. Just when he was come over against the mouth of the burning pit, one of the wicked ones got behind him, and stepped up softly to him and whisperingly suggested many grievous blasphemies to him, which he verily thought had proceeded from his own mind. This put Christian more to it than anything that he met with before, even to think that he should now blaspheme him that he loved so much before, yet if he could have helped it, he would not have done it; but he had not the discretion either to stop his ears, or to know from whence these blasphemies came.

When Christian had travelled in this disconsolate condition some considerable time, he thought he heard the voice of a man, as going before him, saying, "Though I walk through the valley of the shadow of death, I will fear no evil, for thou art with me."[103]

Then he was glad, and that for these reasons:

First, Because he gathered from thence that some who feared God were in this valley as well as himself.

Secondly, For that he perceived God was with them, though in that dark and dismal state; and why not, thought he, with me? though, by reason of the impediment that attends this place, I cannot perceive it.

Thirdly, For that he hoped (could he overtake them) to have company by and by. So he went on and called to him that was before, but he knew not what to answer, for that he also thought himself to be alone, and by and by the day broke; then said Christian, He hath turned "the shadow of death into the morning."[104]

---

102. Ps. 71:16.
103. Ps. 23:4.
104. Amos 5:8.

Now morning being come, he looked back, not out of desire to return, but to see by the light of the day what hazards he had gone through in the dark. So he saw more perfectly the ditch that was on the one hand and the quag that was on the other; also how narrow the way was which led betwixt them both; also now he saw the hobgoblins, and satyrs, and dragons of the pit, but all afar off (for after break of day they came not nigh); yet they were discovered to him, according to that which is written, "He discovereth deep things out of darkness, and bringeth out to light the shadow of death."[105]

Now was Christian much affected with his deliverance from all the danger of his solitary way, which dangers, though he feared them more before, yet he saw them more clearly now, because the light of the day made them conspicuous to him. And about this time, the sun was rising, and this was another mercy to Christian, for you must note that though the first part of the Valley of the Shadow of Death was dangerous, yet this second part which he was yet to go was, if possible, far more dangerous. For from the place where he now stood, even to the end of the valley, the way was all along set so full of snares, traps, gins, and nets here, and so full of pits, pitfalls, deep holes, and shelvings down there, that, had it now been dark, as it was when he came the first part of the way, had he had a thousand souls, they had in reason been cast away; but, as I said just now, the sun was rising. Then said he, "His candle shineth on my head and by his light I go through darkness."[106]

In this light, therefore, he came to the end of the valley. Now I saw in my dream that at the end of this valley lay blood, bones, ashes, and mangled bodies of men, even of pilgrims that had gone this way formerly, and while I was musing what should be the reason, I espied a little before me a cave, where two giants, Pope and Pagan, dwelt in old time, by whose power and tyranny the men whose bones, blood, ashes, &c., lay there, were cruelly put to death. But by this place Christian went without much danger, whereat I somewhat wondered; but I have learnt since that Pagan has been dead many a day, and as for the other, though he be yet alive, he is by reason of age and also of the many shrewd[107] brushes that he met with in his younger days, grown so crazy and stiff in his

---

105. Job 12:22.
106. Job 29:3.
107. Severe, hard.

joints, that he can now do little more than sit in his cave's mouth, grinning at pilgrims as they go by, and biting his nails because he cannot come at them.

So I saw that Christian went on his way, yet at the sight of the Old Man that sat in the mouth of the cave, he could not tell what to think, especially because he spake to him, though he could not go after him, saying, "You will never mend till more of you be burned." But he held his peace and set a good face on't, and so went by and catched no hurt. Then sang Christian,

> O world of wonders! (I can say no less)
> That I should be preserved in that distress
> That I have met with here! O blessed be
> That hand that from it hath delivered me!
> Dangers in darkness, devils, hell, and sin,
> Did compass me, while I this vale was in:
> Yea, snares and pits, and traps, and nets, did lie
> My path about, that worthless, silly I
> Might have been catched, entangled, and cast down;
> But since I live, let Jesus wear the crown.

Now as Christian went on his way, he came to a little ascent, which was cast up on purpose that pilgrims might see before them. Up there, therefore, Christian went, and looking forward, he saw Faithful before him upon his journey. Then said Christian aloud, Ho, ho, Soho: stay, and I will be your companion. At that Faithful looked behind him; to whom Christian cried again, Stay, stay, till I come up to you. But Faithful answered, No, I am upon my life, and the avenger of blood is behind me. At this Christian was somewhat moved, and putting to all his strength, he quickly got up with Faithful and did also overrun him; so the last was first. Then did Christian vaingloriously smile, because he had gotten the start of his brother; but not taking good heed to his feet, he suddenly stumbled and fell, and could not rise again until Faithful came up to help him.

Then I saw in my dream they went very lovingly on together, and had sweet discourse of all things that had happened to them in their pilgrimage, and thus Christian began:

CHR. My honoured and well-beloved brother Faithful, I am glad that I have overtaken you, and that God has so tempered our spirits that we can walk as companions in this so pleasant a path.

FAITH. I had thought, dear friend, to have had your company quite from our town, but you did get the start of me, wherefore I was forced to come thus much of the way alone.

CHR. How long did you stay in the City of Destruction before you set out after me on your pilgrimage?

FAITH. Till I could stay no longer, for there was great talk presently after you were gone out, that our city would in short time with fire from heaven be burned down to the ground.

CHR. What? Did your neighbours talk so?

FAITH. Yes, it was for a while in everybody's mouth.

CHR. What? And did no more of them but you come out to escape the danger?

FAITH. Though there was, as I said, a great talk thereabout, yet I do not think they did firmly believe it. For in the heat of the discourse I heard some of them deridingly speak of you and of your desperate journey (for so they called this your pilgrimage), but I did believe, and do still, that the end of our city will be with fire and brimstone from above, and therefore I have made my escape.

CHR. Did you hear no talk of neighbour Pliable?

FAITH. Yes, Christian, I heard that he followed you till he came at the Slough of Despond, where, as some said, he fell in, but he would not be known to have so done; but I am sure he was soundly bedabbled with that kind of dirt.

CHR. And what said the neighbours to him?

FAITH. He hath since his going back been had greatly in derision, and that among all sorts of people; some do mock and despise him, and scarce will any set him on work. He is now seven times worse than if he had never gone out of the city.

CHR. But why should they be so set against him, since they also despise the way that he forsook?

FAITH. Oh, they say, hang him, he is a turncoat, he was not true to his profession. I think God has stirred up even his enemies to hiss at him and make him a proverb, because he hath forsaken the way.

CHR. Had you no talk with him before you came out?

FAITH. I met him once in the streets, but he leered[108] away on the other side, as one ashamed of what he had done; so I spake not to him.

CHR. Well, at my first setting out I had hopes of that man, but

108. Walked stealthily; slunk.

now I fear he will perish in the overthrow of the city, for "it is happened to him according to the true proverb, The dog is turned to his vomit again, and the sow that was washed to her wallowing in the mire."[109]

FAITH. These are my fears of him too, but who can hinder that which will be?

CHR. Well, neighbour Faithful, said Christian, let us leave him and talk of things that more immediately concern ourselves. Tell me now what you have met with in the way as you came, for I know you have met with some things, or else it may be writ for a wonder.

FAITH. I escaped the Slough that I perceived you fell into, and got up to the gate without that danger; only I met with one whose name was Wanton, who had like to have done me a mischief.

CHR. It was well you escaped her net; Joseph was hard put to it by her, and he escaped her as you did, but it had like to have cost him his life.[110] But what did she do to you?

FAITH. You cannot think (but that you know something) what a flattering tongue she had; she lay at me hard to turn aside with her, promising me all manner of content.

CHR. Nay, she did not promise you the content of a good conscience.

FAITH. You know what I mean; all carnal and fleshly content.

CHR. Thank God you have escaped her: the "abhorred of the Lord" shall fall into her ditch.[111]

FAITH. Nay, I know not whether I did wholly escape her or no.

CHR. Why, I trow you did not consent to her desires?

FAITH. No, not to defile myself, for I remembered an old writing that I had seen, which said, "Her steps take hold of hell."[112] So I shut mine eyes, because I would not be bewitched with her looks. Then she railed on me, and I went my way.

CHR. Did you meet with no other assault as you came?

FAITH. When I came to the foot of the hill called Difficulty, I met with a very aged man, who asked me what I was and whither bound. I told him that I was a pilgrim going to the Celestial City. Then said

---

109. 2 Pet. 2:22.
110. Gen. 39.
111. Prov. 22:14.
112. Prov. 5:5.

the old man, Thou lookest like an honest fellow; wilt thou be content to dwell with me for the wages that I shall give thee? Then I asked him his name and where he dwelt. He said his name was Adam the First, and that he dwelt in the town of Deceit.[113] I asked him then what was his work and what the wages that he would give. He told me that his work was many delights, and his wages that I should be his heir at last. I further asked him what house he kept and what other servants he had. So he told me that his house was maintained with all the dainties in the world, and that his servants were those of his own begetting. Then I asked how many children he had. He said that he had but three daughters: "the lust of the flesh, the lust of the eyes, and the pride of life,"[114] and that I should marry them all if I would. Then I asked how long time he would have me live with him. And he told me, As long as he lived himself.

CHR. Well, and what conclusion came the old man and you to at last?

FAITH. Why, at first, I found myself somewhat inclinable to go with the man, for I thought he spake very fair, but looking in his forehead, as I talked with him, I saw there written, "Put off the old man with his deeds."[115]

CHR. And how then?

FAITH. Then it came burning hot into my mind, whatever he said and however he flattered, when he got me home to his house, he would sell me for a slave. So I bid him forbear to talk, for I would not come near the door of his house. Then he reviled me and told me that he would send such a one after me that should make my way bitter to my soul. So I turned to go away from him, but just as I turned myself to go thence, I felt him take hold of my flesh and give me such a deadly twitch back that I thought he had pulled part of me after himself. This made me cry, "Oh, wretched man!" So I went on my way up the hill.

Now when I had got about halfway up, I looked behind and saw one coming after me swift as the wind; so he overtook me just about the place where the settle stands.

CHR. Just there, said Christian, did I sit down to rest me, but being overcome with sleep, I there lost this roll out of my bosom.

---

113. Eph. 4:22.
114. John 2:16.
115. Col. 3:9.

FAITH. But, good brother, hear me out. So soon as the man overtook me, he was but a word and a blow, for down he knocked me and laid me for dead. But when I was a little come to myself again, I asked him wherefore he served me so. He said, because of my secret inclining to Adam the First: and with that he strook me another deadly blow on the breast and beat me down backward, so I lay at his foot as dead as before. So when I came to myself again, I cried him mercy, but he said, I know not how to show mercy, and with that knocked me down again. He had doubtless made an end of me, but that one came by and bid him forbear.

CHR. Who was that that bid him forbear?

FAITH. I did not know him at first, but as he went by I perceived the holes in his hands and his side; then I concluded that he was our Lord. So I went up the hill.

CHR. That man that overtook you was Moses. He spareth none, neither knoweth he how to show mercy to those that transgress his law.

FAITH. I know it very well; it was not the first time that he has met with me. It was he that came to me when I dwelt securely at home, and that told me he would burn my house over my head if I stayed there.

CHR. But did you not see the house that stood there on the top of the hill on the side of which Moses met you?

FAITH. Yes, and the lions too, before I came at it; but for the lions, I think they were asleep, for it was about noon, and because I had so much of the day before me, I passed by the porter and came down the hill.

CHR. He told me, indeed, that he saw you go by, but I wish you had called at the house, for they would have showed you so many rarities that you would scarce have forgot them to the day of your death. But pray tell me, did you meet nobody in the Valley of Humility?

FAITH. Yes, I met with one Discontent, who would willingly have persuaded me to go back again with him; his reason was, for that the valley was altogether without honour. He told me, moreover, that there to go was the way to disobey all my friends, as Pride, Arrogancy, Self-conceit, Worldly Glory, with others, who he knew, as he said, would be very much offended if I made such a fool of myself as to wade through this valley.

CHR. Well, and how did you answer him?

FAITH. I told him that although all these that he named might claim kindred of me, and that rightly (for indeed they were my relations according to the flesh), yet since I became a pilgrim they have disowned me, as I also have rejected them; and therefore they were to me now no more than if they had never been of my lineage. I told him, moreover, that as to this valley, he had quite misrepresented the thing, for "before honour is humility, and a haughty spirit before a fall."[116] Therefore, said I, I had rather go through this valley to the honour that was so accounted by the wisest, than choose that which he esteemed most worthy our affections.

CHR. Met you with nothing else in that valley?

FAITH. Yes, I met with Shame; but of all the men that I met with in my pilgrimage, he, I think, bears the wrong name. The other would be said nay after a little argumentation (and somewhat else), but this bold-faced Shame would never have done.

CHR. Why, what did he say to you?

FAITH. What! why, he objected against religion itself; he said it was a pitiful, low, sneaking business for a man to mind religion; he said that a tender conscience was an unmanly thing; and that for a man to watch over his words and ways, so as to tie up himself from that hectoring liberty that the brave spirits of the times accustom themselves unto, would make him the ridicule of the times. He objected also that but few of the mighty, rich, or wise, were ever of my opinion; nor any of them neither before they were persuaded to be fools and to be of a voluntary fondness,[117] to venture the loss of all for nobody knows what. He, moreover, objected the base and low estate and condition of those that were chiefly the pilgrims of the times in which they lived; also their ignorance and want of understanding in all natural science. Yea, he did hold me to it at that rate also about a great many more things than here I relate; as that it was a *shame* to sit whining and mourning under a sermon, and a *shame* to come sighing and groaning home; that it was a *shame* to ask my neighbour forgiveness for petty faults, or to make restitution where I have taken from any. He said also that religion made a man grow strange to the great because of a few vices (which he called by finer names), and made him own and respect the base because of the same religious fraternity. And is not this, said he, a *shame*?

CHR. And what did you say to him?

---

116. Prov. 18:12; 16:18.
117. Foolishness.

FAITH. Say! I could not tell what to say at first. Yea, he put me so to it that my blood came up in my face; even this Shame fetched it up and had almost beat me quite off. But at last I began to consider that "that which is highly esteemed among men is had in abomination with God."[118] And I thought again, this Shame tells me what men are, but it tells me nothing what God or the Word of God is. And I thought, moreover, that at the day of doom we shall not be doomed to death or life according to the hectoring spirits of the world, but according to the wisdom and law of the Highest. Therefore, thought I, what God says is best, is best, though all the men in the world are against it. Seeing then that God prefers his religion; seeing God prefers a tender conscience; seeing they that make themselves fools for the kingdom of heaven are wisest; and that the poor man that loveth Christ is richer than the greatest man in the world that hates him; Shame, depart, thou art an enemy to my salvation! Shall I entertain thee against my sovereign Lord? How then shall I look him in the face at his coming? Should I now be ashamed of his ways and servants, how can I expect the blessing? But indeed this Shame was a bold villain; I could scarce shake him out of my company. Yea, he would be haunting of me and continually whispering me in the ear, with some one or other of the infirmities that attend religion, but at last I told him it was but in vain to attempt further in this business, for those things that he disdained, in those did I see most glory; and so at last I got past this importunate one. And when I had shaken him off, then I began to sing:

> The trials that those men do meet withal
> That are obedient to the heavenly call,
> Are manifold and suited to the flesh,
> And come, and come, and come again afresh;
> That now, or sometime else, we by them may
> Be taken, overcome, and cast away.
> O, let the pilgrims, let the pilgrims then
> Be vigilant, and quit themselves like men.

CHR. I am glad, my brother, that thou didst withstand this villain so bravely, for of all, as thou sayest, I think he has the wrong name, for he is so bold as to follow us in the streets and to attempt

118. Luke 16:15.

to put us to shame before all men; that is, to make us ashamed of that which is good. But if he was not himself audacious, he would never attempt to do as he does. But let us still resist him; for notwithstanding all his bravadoes he promoteth the fool and none else. "The wise shall inherit glory," said Solomon, "but shame shall be the promotion of fools."[119]

FAITH. I think we must cry to him, for help against Shame, that would have us be valiant for truth upon the earth.

CHR. You say true; but did you meet nobody else in that valley?

FAITH. No, not I; for I had sunshine all the rest of the way through that, and also through the Valley of the Shadow of Death.

CHR. 'Twas well for you. I am sure it fared far otherwise with me. I had for a long season, as soon almost as I entered into that valley, a dreadful combat with that foul fiend Apollyon; yea, I thought verily he would have killed me, especially when he got me down and crushed me under him, as if he would have crushed me to pieces. For as he threw me, my sword flew out of my hand; nay, he told me he was sure of me, but I cried to God, and he heard me, and delivered me out of all my troubles. Then I entered into the Valley of the Shadow of Death, and had no light for almost half the way through it. I thought I should have been killed there, over and over, but at last day broke and the sun rose, and I went through that which was behind with far more ease and quiet.

Moreover, I saw in my dream that as they went on, Faithful, as he chanced to look on one side, saw a man whose name is Talkative, walking at a distance besides them (for in this place there was room enough for them all to walk). He was a tall man and something more comely at a distance than at hand. To this man Faithful addressed himself in this manner:

FAITH. Friend, whither away? Are you going to the heavenly country?

TALK. I am going to the same place.

FAITH. That is well; then I hope we may have your good company.

TALK. With a very good will, will I be your companion.

FAITH. Come on then, and let us go together, and let us spend our time in discoursing of things that are profitable.

TALK. To talk of things that are good, to me is very acceptable, with you or with any other, and I am glad that I have met with

---

119. Prov. 3:35.

those that incline to so good a work; for to speak the truth, there are but few that care thus to spend their time (as they are in their travels), but choose much rather to be speaking of things to no profit, and this hath been a trouble to me.

FAITH. That is indeed a thing to be lamented; for what things so worthy of the use of the tongue and mouth of men on earth, as are the things of the God of heaven?

TALK. I like you wonderful well, for your sayings are full of conviction; and I will add, what thing is so pleasant, and what so profitable, as to talk of the things of God? What things so pleasant (that is, if a man hath any delight in things that are wonderful)? For instance, if a man doth delight to talk of the history or the mystery of things, or if a man doth love to talk of miracles, wonders, or signs, where shall he find things recorded so delightful and so sweetly penned as in the Holy Scripture?

FAITH. That is true; but to be profited by such things in our talk should be that which we design.

TALK. That is it that I said, for to talk of such things is most profitable. For by so doing a man may get knowledge of many things, as of the vanity of earthly things, and the benefit of things above; (thus in general) but more particularly, by this a man may learn the necessity of the new birth, the insufficiency of our works, the need of Christ's righteousness, &c. Besides, by this a man may learn what it is to repent, to believe, to pray, to suffer, or the like; by this also a man may learn what are the great promises and consolations of the gospel, to his own comfort. Further, by this a man may learn to refute false opinions, to vindicate the truth, and also to instruct the ignorant.

FAITH. All this is true, and glad am I to hear these things from you.

TALK. Alas, the want of this is the cause why so few understand the need of faith and the necessity of a work of grace in their soul, in order to eternal life, but ignorantly live in the works of the law, by which a man can by no means obtain the kingdom of heaven.

FAITH. But by your leave, heavenly knowledge of these is the gift of God; no man attaineth to them by human industry, or only by the talk of them.

TALK. All this I know very well. For a man can receive nothing except it be given him from heaven; all is of grace, not of works. I could give you a hundred Scriptures for the confirmation of this.

FAITH. Well then, said Faithful, what is that one thing that we shall at this time found our discourse upon?

TALK. What you will. I will talk of things heavenly, or things earthly; things moral, or things evangelical; things sacred, or things profane; things past, or things to come; things foreign, or things at home; things more essential, or things circumstantial; provided that all be done to our profit.

FAITH. Now did Faithful begin to wonder, and stepping to Christian (for he walked all this while by himself), he said to him (but softly), What a brave companion have we got! Surely this man will make a very excellent pilgrim.

CHR. At this Christian modestly smiled and said, This man with whom you are so taken will beguile with this tongue of his twenty of them that know him not.

FAITH. Do you know him then?

CHR. Know him! Yes, better than he knows himself.

FAITH. Pray what is he?

CHR. His name is Talkative; he dwelleth in our town. I wonder that you should be a stranger to him, only I consider that our town is large.

FAITH. Whose son is he? And whereabout doth he dwell?

CHR. He is the son of one Say-well; he dwelt in Prating Row; and he is known of all that are acquainted with him by the name of Talkative in Prating Row; and notwithstanding his fine tongue he is but a sorry fellow.

FAITH. Well, he seems to be a very pretty man.

CHR. That is, to them who have not thorough acquaintance with him, for he is best abroad; near home he is ugly enough. Your saying that he is a pretty man brings to my mind what I have observed in the work of the painter, whose pictures show best at a distance, but very near, more unpleasing.

FAITH. But I am ready to think you do but jest, because you smiled.

CHR. God forbid that I should jest (although I smiled) in this matter, or that I should accuse any falsely. I will give you a further discovery of him. This man is for any company and for any talk; as he talketh now with you, so will he talk when he is on the ale-bench, and the more drink he hath in his crown, the more of these things he hath in his mouth. Religion hath no place in his heart, or house, or conversation; all he hath lieth in his tongue, and his religion is to make a noise therewith.

FAITH. Say you so? Then am I in this man greatly deceived.

CHR. Deceived! you may be sure of it; remember the proverb,

"They say and do not," but "the kingdom of God is not in word, but in power."[120] He talketh of prayer, of repentance, of faith, and of the new birth; but he knows but only to talk of them. I have been in his family and have observed him both at home and abroad, and I know what I say of him is the truth. His house is as empty of religion as the white of an egg is of savour. There is there neither prayer, nor sign of repentance for sin; yea, the brute in his kind serves God far better than he. He is the very stain, reproach, and shame of religion to all that know him; it can hardly have a good word in all that end of the town where he dwells, through him. Thus say the common people that know him. A saint abroad and a devil at home. His poor family finds it so; he is such a churl, such a railer at and so unreasonable with his servants, that they neither know how to do for, or speak to him. Men that have any dealings with him say it is better to deal with a Turk than with him, for fairer dealing they shall have at their hands. This Talkative (if it be possible) will go beyond them, defraud, beguile, and overreach them. Besides, he brings up his sons to follow his steps, and if he findeth in any of them a foolish timorousness (for so he calls the first appearance of a tender conscience), he calls them fools and blockheads, and by no means will employ them in much, or speak to their commendations before others. For my part, I am of opinion that he has by his wicked life caused many to stumble and fall, and will be, if God prevent not, the ruin of many more.

FAITH. Well, my brother, I am bound to believe you; not only because you say you know him, but also because like a Christian you make your reports of men. For I cannot think that you speak these things of ill-will, but because it is even so as you say.

CHR. Had I known him no more than you, I might perhaps have thought of him as at the first you did; yea, had he received this report at their hands only that are enemies to religion, I should have thought it had been a slander (a lot that often falls from bad men's mouths upon good men's names and professions). But all these things, yea, and a great many more as bad, of my own knowledge I can prove him guilty of. Besides, good men are ashamed of him; they can neither call him brother nor friend. The very naming of him among them makes them blush, if they know him.

FAITH. Well, I see that saying and doing are two things, and hereafter I shall better observe this distinction.

---

120. Matt. 23:3; 1 Cor. 4:20.

CHR. They are two things indeed, and are as diverse as are the
soul and the body; for as the body without the soul is but a dead
carcass, so saying, if it be alone, is but a dead carcass also. The soul
of religion is the practic part: "Pure religion and undefiled before
God and the Father is this, to visit the fatherless and widows in
their affliction, and to keep himself unspotted from the world."[121]
This Talkative is not aware of; he thinks that hearing and saying
will make a good Christian, and thus he deceiveth his own soul.
Hearing is but as the sowing of the seed; talking is not sufficient to
prove that fruit is indeed in the heart and life, and let us assure
ourselves that at the day of doom men shall be judged according
to their fruits. It will not be said then, Did you believe? but, Were
you doers or talkers only? and accordingly shall they be judged.
The end of the world is compared to our harvest, and you know
men at harvest regard nothing but fruit.[122] Not that anything can
be accepted that is not of faith, but I speak this to show you how
insignificant the profession of Talkative will be at that day.

FAITH. This brings to my mind that of Moses, by which he
describeth the beast that is clean.[123] He is such a one that parteth
the hoof and cheweth the cud; not that parteth the hoof only, or
that cheweth the cud only. The hare cheweth the cud, but yet is
unclean, because he parteth not the hoof. And this truly resembleth
Talkative; he cheweth the cud, he seeketh knowledge, he cheweth
upon the Word, but he divideth not the hoof, he parteth not with
the way of sinners, but as the hare, he retaineth the foot of a dog or
bear, and therefore he is unclean.

CHR. You have spoken, for aught I know, the true gospel sense of
those texts. And I will add another thing. Paul calleth some men,
yea, and those great talkers too, "sounding brass and tinkling cymbals"; that is, as he expounds them in another place, "things without life, giving sound."[124] Things without life, that is, without the
true faith and grace of the gospel; and consequently, things that
shall never be placed in the kingdom of heaven among those that
are the children of life, though their sound, by their talk, be as if it
were the tongue or voice of an angel.

---

121. James 1:27.
122. Matt. 13.
123. Lev. 11:3–8.
124. 1 Cor. 13:1; 14:7.

FAITH. Well, I was not so fond of his company at first, but I am as sick of it now. What shall we do to be rid of him?

CHR. Take my advice and do as I bid you, and you shall find that he will soon be sick of your company too, except God shall touch his heart and turn it.

FAITH. What would you have me to do?

CHR. Why, go to him and enter into some serious discourse about the power of religion, and ask him plainly (when he has approved of it, for that he will) whether this thing be set up in his heart, house, or conversation.

FAITH. Then Faithful stepped forward again and said to Talkative, Come, what cheer? How is it now?

TALK. Thank you, well. I thought we should have had a great deal of talk by this time.

FAITH. Well, if you will, we will fall to it now, and since you left it with me to state the question, let it be this: How doth the saving grace of God discover itself, when it is in the heart of man?

TALK. I perceive then that our talk must be about the power of things. Well, it is a very good question, and I shall be willing to answer you. And take my answer in brief, thus: First, Where the grace of God is in the heart, it causeth there a great outcry against sin. Secondly——

FAITH. Nay hold, let us consider of one at once. I think you should rather say, It shows itself by inclining the soul to abhor its sin.

TALK. Why, what difference is there between crying out against, and abhorring of sin?

FAITH. Oh, a great deal. A man may cry out against sin, of policy,[125] but he cannot abhor it but by virtue of a godly antipathy against it. I have heard many cry out against sin in the pulpit, who yet can abide it well enough in the heart, house, and conversation. Joseph's mistress cried out with a loud voice, as if she had been very holy, but she would willingly, notwithstanding that, have committed uncleanness with him.[126] Some cry out against sin even as the mother cries out against her child in her lap, when she calleth it slut and naughty girl, and then falls to hugging and kissing it.

---

125. By cunning or prudence, for personal advantage.
126. Gen. 39:14–15.
127. Lie in wait for an opportunity to make objections.

TALK. You lie at the catch,[127] I perceive.

FAITH. No, not I; I am only for setting things right. But what is the second thing whereby you would prove a discovery of a work of grace in the heart?

TALK. Great knowledge of gospel mysteries.

FAITH. This sign should have been first; but first or last, it is also false, for knowledge, great knowledge, may be obtained in the mysteries of the gospel, and yet no work of grace in the soul. Yea, if a man have all knowledge, he may yet be nothing, and so consequently be no child of God.[128] When Christ said, "Do you know all these things?" and the disciples had answered, "Yes," he addeth, "Blessed are ye if ye do them."[129] He doth not lay the blessing in the knowing of them, but in the doing of them. For there is a knowledge that is not attended with doing. "He that knoweth his Master's will and doth it not."[130] A man may know like an angel, and yet be no Christian; therefore your sign of it is not true. Indeed, *to know* is a thing that pleaseth talkers and boasters; but *to do* is that which pleaseth God. Not that the heart can be good without knowledge; for without that the heart is naught. There is, therefore, knowledge and knowledge. Knowledge that resteth in the bare speculation of things, and knowledge that is accompanied with the grace of faith and love, which puts a man upon doing even the will of God from the heart. The first of these will serve the talker, but without the other the true Christian is not content. "Give me understanding, and I shall keep thy law; yea, I shall observe it with my whole heart."[131]

TALK. You lie at the catch again; this is not for edification.

FAITH. Well, if you please, propound another sign how this work of grace discovereth itself where it is.

TALK. Not I, for I see we shall not agree.

FAITH. Well, if you will not, will you give me leave to do it?

TALK. You may use your liberty.

FAITH. A work of grace in the soul discovereth itself either to him that hath it, or to standers by.

To him that hath it, thus: It gives him conviction of sin, especially of the defilement of his nature and the sin of unbelief (for the sake of which he is sure to be damned, if he findeth not mercy at God's hand

128. 1 Cor. 13:2.   130. James 4:15–17.
129. Matt. 13:51, 52; John 13:17.   131. Ps. 119:34.

by faith in Jesus Christ). This sight and sense of things worketh in him sorrow and shame for sin; he findeth, moreover, revealed in him the Saviour of the world, and the absolute necessity of closing with him for life, at the which he findeth hungerings and thirstings after him, to which hungerings, &c., the promise is made.[132] Now, according to the strength or weakness of his faith in his Saviour, so is his joy and peace, so is his love to holiness, so are his desires to know him more, and also to serve him in this world. But though I say it discovereth itself thus unto him, yet it is but seldom that he is able to conclude that this is a work of grace, because his corruptions now and his abused reason makes his mind to misjudge in this matter; therefore in him that hath this work, there is required a very sound judgement before he can with steadiness conclude that this is a work of grace.

To others, it is thus discovered:

1. By an experimental confession[133] of his faith in Christ. 2. By a life answerable to that confession; to wit, a life of holiness, heart-holiness, family-holiness (if he hath a family), and by conversation-holiness in the world, which in the general teacheth him inwardly to abhor his sin, and himself for that in secret, to suppress it in his family, and to promote holiness in the world, not by talk only, as a hypocrite or talkative person may do, but by a practical subjection, in faith and love, to the power of the Word. And now, Sir, as to this brief description of the work of grace, and also the discovery of it, if you have aught to object, object; if not, then give me leave to propound to you a second question.

TALK. Nay, my part is not now to object, but to hear; let me therefore have your second question.

FAITH. It is this: Do you experience this first part of this description of it? and doth your life and conversation testify the same? or standeth your religion in word or in tongue, and not in deed and truth? Pray, if you incline to answer me in this, say no more than you know the God above will say Amen to, and also nothing but what your conscience can justify you in, "for not he that commendeth himself is approved, but whom the Lord commendeth."[134] Besides, to say I am thus and thus, when my conversation and all my neighbours tell me I lie, is great wickedness.

---

132. Matt. 5:6.
133. A confession based on personal experience.
134. 2 Cor. 10:18.

TALK. Then Talkative at first began to blush, but recovering himself, thus he replied: You come now to experience, to conscience, and God, and to appeal to him for justification of what is spoken. This kind of discourse I did not expect; nor am I disposed to give an answer to such questions, because I count not myself bound thereto, unless you take upon you to be a catechiser, and, though you should so do, yet I may refuse to make you my judge. But I pray, will you tell me why you ask me such questions?

FAITH. Because I saw you forward to talk, and because I knew not that you had aught else but notion. Besides, to tell you all the truth, I have heard of you, that you are a man whose religion lies in talk, and that your conversation gives this your mouth-profession the lie. They say, you are a spot among Christians, and that religion fareth the worse for your ungodly conversation; that some have already stumbled at your wicked ways, and that more are in danger of being destroyed thereby. Your religion, and an ale-house, and covetousness, and uncleanness, and swearing, and lying, and vain company-keeping, &c., will stand together. The proverb is true of you which is said of a whore, to wit, that she is a shame to all women; so are you a shame to all professors.

TALK. Since you are ready to take up reports and to judge so rashly as you do, I cannot but conclude you are some peevish or melancholy man, not fit to be discoursed with; and so adieu.

CHR. Then came up Christian and said to his brother, I told you how it would happen: your words and his lusts could not agree; he had rather leave your company than reform his life. But he is gone, as I said; let him go, the loss is no man's but his own. He has saved us the trouble of going from him, for he continuing (as I suppose he will do) as he is, he would have been but a blot in our company; besides, the apostle says, "From such withdraw thyself."[135]

FAITH. But I am glad we had this little discourse with him; it may happen that he will think of it again. However, I have dealt plainly with him, and so am clear of his blood, if he perisheth.

CHR. You did well to talk so plainly to him as you did; there is but little of this faithful dealing with men nowadays, and that makes religion to stink so in the nostrils of many, as it doth, for they are these talkative fools whose religion is only in word, and are debauched and vain in their conversation, that (being so much

135. 1 Tim. 6:5.

admitted into the fellowship of the godly) do puzzle the world, blemish Christianity, and grieve the sincere. I wish that all men would deal with such as you have done; then should they either be made more comfortable to religion, or the company of saints would be too hot for them. Then did Faithful say,

> How Talkative at first lifts up his plumes!
> How bravely doth he speak! How he presumes
> To drive down all before him! But so soon
> As Faithful talks of heart-work, like the moon
> That's past the full, into the wane he goes.
> And so will all, but he that heart-work knows.

Thus they went on talking of what they had seen by the way, and so made that way easy which would otherwise, no doubt, have been tedious to them; for now they went through a wilderness.

Now when they were got almost quite out of this wilderness, Faithful chanced to cast his eye back, and espied one coming after them, and he knew him. Oh! said Faithful to his brother, Who comes yonder? Then Christian looked and said, It is my good friend Evangelist. Aye, and my good friend too, said Faithful, for 'twas he that set me the way to the gate. Now was Evangelist come up to them, and thus saluted them:

EVAN. Peace be with you, dearly beloved; and peace be to your helpers.

CHR. Welcome, welcome, my good Evangelist. The sight of thy countenance brings to my remembrance thy ancient kindness and unwearied labouring for my eternal good.

FAITH. And a thousand times welcome, said good Faithful. Thy company, O sweet Evangelist, how desirable it is to us poor pilgrims!

EVAN. Then said Evangelist, How hath it fared with you, my friends, since the time of our last parting? What have you met with, and how have you behaved yourselves?

Then Christian and Faithful told him of all things that had happened to them in the way; and how, and with what difficulty, they had arrived to that place.

EVAN. Right glad am I, said Evangelist, not that you have met with trials, but that you have been victors, and for that you have (notwithstanding many weaknesses) continued in the way to this very day.

I say, right glad am I of this thing, and that for mine own sake and yours. I have sowed, and you have reaped, and the day is coming when both he that sowed and they that reaped shall rejoice together; that is, if you hold out, for in due time ye shall reap, if you faint not. The crown is before you, and it is an incorruptible one; so run that you may obtain it. Some there be that set out for this crown, and after they have gone far for it, another comes in and takes it from them. Hold fast therefore that you have; let no man take your crown.[136] You are not yet out of the gunshot of the devil; you have not resisted unto blood, striving against sin. Let the kingdom be always before you, and believe steadfastly concerning things that are invisible. Let nothing that is on this side the other world get within you, and above all, look well to your own hearts and to the lusts thereof, for they are deceitful above all things and desperately wicked. Set your faces like a flint; you have all power in heaven and earth on your side.

CHR. Then Christian thanked him for his exhortation, but told him withal that they would have him speak further to them for their help the rest of the way, and the rather, for that they well knew that he was a prophet, and could tell them of things that might happen unto them, and also how they might resist and overcome them. To which request Faithful also consented. So Evangelist began as followeth:

EVAN. My sons, you have heard, in the words of the truth of the gospel, that you must through many tribulations enter into the kingdom of heaven. And, again, that in every city bonds and afflictions abide in you, and therefore you cannot expect that you should go long on your pilgrimage without them in some sort or other. You have found something of the truth of these testimonies upon you already, and more will immediately follow. For now, as you see, you are almost out of this wilderness, and therefore you will soon come into a town that you will by and by see before you. And in that town you will be hardly beset with enemies who will strain hard but they will kill you, and be you sure that one or both of you must seal the testimony which you hold with blood; but be you faithful unto death, and the King will give you a crown of life. He that shall die there, although his death will be unnatural, and his pain perhaps great, he will yet have the better of his fellow; not only

---

136. John 4:36; Gal. 6:9; 1 Cor. 9:24, 25; Rev. 3:11.

because he will be arrived at the Celestial City soonest, but because he will escape many miseries that the other will meet with in the rest of his journey. But when you are come to the town, and shall find fulfilled what I have here related, then remember your friend, and quit yourselves like men, and commit the keeping of your souls to your God in well-doing, as unto a faithful Creator.

Then I saw in my dream that when they were got out of the wilderness, they presently saw a town before them, and the name of that town is Vanity, and at the town there is a fair kept, called Vanity Fair. It is kept all the year long; it beareth the name of Vanity Fair, because the town where it is kept is lighter than vanity, and also because all that is there sold, or that cometh thither, is vanity. As is the saying of the wise, "all that cometh is vanity."[137]

This fair is no new-erected business, but a thing of ancient standing; I will show you the original of it.

Almost five thousand years agone there were pilgrims walking to the Celestial City, as these two honest persons are, and Beelzebub, Apollyon, and Legion,[138] with their companions, perceiving by the path that the pilgrims made that their way to the city lay through this town of Vanity, they contrived here to set up a fair; a fair wherein should be sold all sorts of vanity, and that it should last all the year long. Therefore at this fair are all such merchandise sold, as houses, lands, trades, places, honours, preferments, titles, countries, kingdoms, lusts, pleasures, and delights of all sorts, as whores, bawds, wives, husbands, children, masters, servants, lives, blood, bodies, souls, silver, gold, pearls, precious stones, and what not.

And, moreover, at this fair there is at all times to be seen jugglings, cheats, games, plays, fools, apes, knaves, and rogues, and that of every kind.

Here are to be seen too, and that for nothing, thefts, murders, adulteries, false swearers, and that of a blood-red colour.

And as in other fairs of less moment there are the several rows and streets under their proper names, where such and such wares are vended; so here likewise you have the proper places, rows, streets (viz. countries and kingdoms), where the wares of this fair are soonest to be found. Here is the Britain Row, the French Row, the Italian Row, the Spanish Row, the German Row, where several

137. See Eccles. especially chaps. 1 and 2.
138. Mark 5:1–9.

sorts of vanities are to be sold. But as in other fairs some one com-
modity is as the chief of all the fair, so the ware of Rome and her
merchandise is greatly promoted in this fair; only our English
nation, with some others, have taken a dislike thereat.

Now, as I said, the way to the Celestial City lies just through this
town where this lusty fair is kept, and he that will go to the City,
and yet not go through this town, must needs "go out of the
world."[139] The Prince of princes himself, when here, went through
this town to his own country, and that upon a fair day too; yea, and
as I think, it was Beelzebub, the chief lord of this fair, that invited
him to buy of his vanities, yea, would have made him lord of the
fair, would he but have done him reverence as he went through the
town.[140] Yea, because he was such a person of honour, Beelzebub
had him from street to street, and showed him all the kingdoms of
the world in a little time, that he might, if possible, allure the Blessed
One to cheapen[141] and buy some of his vanities; but he had no mind
to the merchandise, and therefore left the town without laying out
so much as one farthing upon these vanities. This fair therefore is
an ancient thing, of long standing, and a very great fair. Now these
pilgrims, as I said, must needs go through this fair. Well, so they
did. But behold, even as they entered into the fair, all the people in
the fair were moved, and the town itself as it were in a hubbub
about them, and that for several reasons: for,

First, The Pilgrims were clothed with such kind of raiment as
was diverse from the raiment of any that traded in that fair. The
people therefore of the fair made a great gazing upon them: some
said they were fools, some they were bedlams, and some they are
outlandish[142] men.

Secondly, And as they wondered at their apparel, so they did
likewise at their speech, for few could understand what they said;
they naturally spoke the language of Canaan, but they that kept the
fair were the men of this world, so that from one end of the fair to
the other they seemed barbarians[143] each to the other.

Thirdly, But that which did not a little amuse[144] the merchandisers was that these pilgrims set very light by all their wares; they
cared not so much as to look upon them, and if they called upon

---

139. 1 Cor. 5:10.
140. Matt. 4:8, 9; Luke 4:5–7.
141. To bargain for, offer a price for.

142. Foreign.
143. Foreigners.
144. Cause to stare in astonishment.

them to buy, they would put their fingers in their ears and cry, "Turn away mine eyes from beholding vanity,"[145] and look upwards, signifying that their trade and traffic was in heaven.

One chanced mockingly, beholding the carriage of the men, to say unto them, What will ye buy? But they, looking gravely upon him, answered, "We buy the truth."[146] At that there was an occasion taken to despise the men the more; some mocking, some taunting, some speaking reproachfully, and some calling upon others to smite them. At last things came to a hubbub and great stir in the fair, insomuch that all order was confounded. Now was word presently brought to the great one of the fair, who quickly came down and deputed some of his most trusty friends to take these men into examination, about whom the fair was almost overturned. So the men were brought to examination; and they that sat upon them asked them whence they came, whither they went, and what they did there in such an unusual garb? The men told them that they were pilgrims and strangers in the world, and that they were going to their own country, which was the heavenly Jerusalem,[147] and that they had given no occasion to the men of the town, nor yet to the merchandisers, thus to abuse them and to let[148] them in their journey, except it was for that, when one asked them what they would buy, they said they would buy the truth. But they that were appointed to examine them did not believe them to be any other than bedlams and mad, or else such as came to put all things into a confusion in the fair. Therefore they took them and beat them, and besmeared them with dirt, and then put them into the cage, that they might be made a spectacle to all the men of the fair.

There, therefore, they lay for some time and were made the objects of any man's sport, or malice, or revenge, the great one of the fair laughing still at all that befell them. But the men being patient and not rendering railing for railing, but contrariwise blessing, and giving good words for bad and kindness for injuries done, some men in the fair that were more observing and less prejudiced than the rest, began to check[149] and blame the baser sort for their continual abuses done by them to the men; they therefore in angry manner let fly at them again, counting them as bad as the men in the

---

145. Ps. 119:37.
146. Prov. 23:23.
147. Heb. 11:13–16.

148. Hinder, obstruct.
149. Rebuke.

cage, and telling them that they seemed confederates and should be made partakers of their misfortunes. The other replied that for aught they could see, the men were quiet, and sober, and intended nobody any harm, and that there were many that traded in their fair that were more worthy to be put into the cage, yea, and pillory too, than were the men they had abused. Thus after diverse words had passed on both sides (the men behaving themselves all the while very wisely and soberly before them) they fell to some blows among themselves and did harm one to another. Then were these two poor men brought before their examiners again, and there charged as being guilty of the late hubbub that had been in the fair. So they beat them pitifully, and hanged irons upon them, and led them in chains up and down the fair, for an example and a terror to others, lest any should speak in their behalf or join themselves unto them. But Christian and Faithful behaved themselves yet more wisely, and received the ignominy and shame that was cast upon them with so much meekness and patience that it won to their side (though but few in comparison of the rest) several of the men in the fair. This put the other party yet into greater rage, insomuch that they concluded the death of these two men. Wherefore they threatened that neither cage nor irons should serve their turn, but that they should die for the abuse they had done and for deluding the men of the fair.

Then were they remanded to the cage again, until further order should be taken with them. So they put them in and made their feet fast in the stocks.

Here also they called again to mind what they had heard from their faithful friend Evangelist, and were the more confirmed in their way and sufferings by what he told them would happen to them. They also now comforted each other that whose lot it was to suffer, even he should have the best of it; therefore each man secretly wished that he might have that preferment, but committing themselves to the all-wise dispose of him that ruleth all things, with much content they abode in the condition in which they were, until they should be otherwise disposed of.

Then a convenient time being appointed, they brought them forth to their trial in order to their condemnation. When the time was come, they were brought before their enemies and arraigned. The Judge's name was Lord Hate-good. Their indictment was one and the same in substance, though somewhat varying in form; the contents whereof was this:

"That they were enemies to and disturbers of their trade; that they had made commotions and divisions in the town, and had won a party to their own most dangerous opinions, in contempt of the law of their prince."

Then Faithful began to answer, That he had only set himself against that which hath set itself against him that is higher than the highest. And, said he, as for disturbance, I make none, being myself a man of peace; the parties that were won to us were won by beholding our truth and innocence, and they are only turned from the worse to the better. And as to the king you talk of, since he is Beelzebub, the enemy of our Lord, I defy him and all his angels.

Then proclamation was made that they that had aught to say for their lord the king against the prisoner at the bar should forthwith appear and give in their evidence. So there came in three witnesses, to wit, Envy, Superstition, and Pickthank. They were then asked if they knew the prisoner at the bar, and what they had to say for their lord the king against him.

Then stood forth Envy and said to this effect: My Lord, I have known this man a long time, and will attest upon my oath before this honourable bench that he is——

JUDGE. Hold, give him his oath. (So they sware him.) Then he said, My Lord, this man, notwithstanding his plausible name, is one of the vilest men in our country. He neither regardeth prince nor people, law nor custom, but doth all that he can to possess all men with certain of his disloyal notions, which he in the general calls principles of faith and holiness. And, in particular, I heard him once myself affirm that Christianity and the customs of our town of Vanity were diametrically opposite and could not be reconciled. By which saying, my Lord, he doth at once not only condemn all our laudable doings, but us in the doing of them.

JUDGE. Then did the judge say to him, Hast thou any more to say?

ENVY. My Lord, I could say much more, only I would not be tedious to the court. Yet, if need be, when the other gentlemen have given in their evidence, rather than anything shall be wanting that will dispatch him, I will enlarge my testimony against him. So he was bid stand by. Then they called Superstition and bid him look upon the prisoner. They also asked what he could say for their lord the king against him. Then they sware him; so he began.

SUPER. My Lord, I have no great acquaintance with this man, nor do I desire to have further knowledge of him; however, this I know, that he is a very pestilent fellow, from some discourse that the other day I had with him in this town, for then talking with him, I heard him say that our religion was naught, and such by which a man could by no means please God. Which sayings of his, my Lord, your Lordship very well knows what necessarily thence will follow, to wit, that we do still worship in vain, are yet in our sins, and finally shall be damned, and this is that which I have to say.

Then was Pickthank sworn and bid say what he knew in behalf of their lord the king against the prisoner at the bar.

PICK. My Lord, and you gentlemen all, this fellow I have known of a long time, and have heard him speak things that ought not to be spoke. For he hath railed on our noble prince Beelzebub, and hath spoken contemptibly of his honourable friends, whose names are the Lord Old Man, the Lord Carnal Delight, the Lord Luxurious, the Lord Desire of Vain Glory, my old Lord Lechery, Sir Having Greedy, with all the rest of our nobility,[150] and he hath said, moreover, that if all men were of his mind, if possible, there is not one of these noblemen should have any longer a being in this town. Besides, he hath not been afraid to rail on you, my Lord, who are now appointed to be his judge, calling you an ungodly villain, with many other such like vilifying terms, with which he hath bespattered most of the gentry of our town. When this Pickthank had told his tale, the Judge directed his speech to the prisoner at the bar, saying, Thou runagate, heretic, and traitor, hast thou heard what these honest gentlemen have witnessed against thee?

FAITH. May I speak a few words in my own defence?

JUDGE. Sirrah, Sirrah, thou deservest to live no longer, but to be slain immediately upon the place, yet that all men may see our gentleness towards thee, let us hear what thou, vile runagate, hast to say.

FAITH. 1. I say then in answer to what Mr. Envy hath spoken, I never said aught but this, That what rule, or laws, or custom, or people, were flat against the Word of God, are diametrically opposite to Christianity. If I have said amiss in this, convince me of my error, and I am ready here before you to make my recantation.

2. As to the second, to wit, Mr. Superstition, and his charge against me, I said only this, That in the worship of God there is required a Divine faith; but there can be no Divine faith without a Divine revelation of the will of God. Therefore whatever is thrust into the

150. Sins are all Lords and great ones. [B]

worship of God that is not agreeable to Divine revelation cannot be done but by a human faith, which faith will not be profitable to eternal life.

3. As to what Mr. Pickthank hath said, I say (avoiding terms, as that I am said to rail and the like) that the prince of this town, with all the rabblement[151] his attendants by this gentleman named, are more fit for a being in hell, than in this town and country; and so the Lord have mercy upon me!

Then the Judge called to the jury (who all this while stood by to hear and observe): Gentlemen of the jury, you see this man about whom so great an uproar hath been made in this town. You have also heard what these worthy gentlemen have witnessed against him. Also you have heard his reply and confession. It lieth now in your breasts to hang him or save his life; but yet I think meet to instruct you into our law.

There was an Act made in the days of Pharaoh the Great, servant to our prince, that lest those of a contrary religion should multiply and grow too strong for him, their males should be thrown into the river. There was also an Act made in the days of Nebuchadnezzar the Great, another of his servants, that whosoever would not fall down and worship his golden image should be thrown into a fiery furnace. There was also an Act made in the days of Darius, that whoso for some time called upon any god but him should be cast into the lion's den.[152] Now the substance of these laws this rebel has broken, not only in thought (which is not to be borne), but also in word and deed; which must therefore needs be intolerable.

For that of Pharaoh, his law was made upon a supposition, to prevent mischief, no crime being yet apparent, but here is a crime apparent. For the second and third, you see he disputeth against our religion, and for the treason he hath confessed, he deserveth to die the death.

Then went the jury out, whose names were, Mr. Blind-man, Mr. No-good, Mr. Malice, Mr. Love-lust, Mr. Live-loose, Mr. Heady, Mr. High-mind, Mr. Enmity, Mr. Liar, Mr. Cruelty, Mr. Hate-light, and Mr. Implacable; who every one gave in his private verdict against him among themselves, and afterwards unanimously con-

---

151. Rabble; disorderly crowd.
152. Exod. 1:22; Dan. 3:6; 6:7.

cluded to bring him in guilty before the Judge. And first, among themselves, Mr. Blind-man, the foreman, said, I see clearly that this man is an heretic. Then said Mr. No-good, Away with such a fellow from the earth. Ay, said Mr. Malice, for I hate the very looks of him. Then said Mr. Love-lust, I could never endure him. Nor I, said Mr. Live-loose, for he would always be condemning my way. Hang him, hang him, said Mr. Heady. A sorry scrub, said Mr. High-mind. My heart riseth against him, said Mr. Enmity. He is a rogue, said Mr. Liar. Hanging is too good for him, said Mr. Cruelty. Let's dispatch him out of the way, said Mr. Hate-light. Then said Mr. Implacable, Might I have all the world given me, I could not be reconciled to him; therefore let us forthwith bring him in guilty of death. And so they did; therefore he was presently condemned to be had from the place where he was, to the place from whence he came, and there to be put to the most cruel death that could be invented.

They therefore brought him out, to do with him according to their law; and first they scourged him, then they buffeted him, then they lanced his flesh with knives; after that they stoned him with stones, then pricked him with their swords; and last of all they burned him to ashes at the stake. Thus came Faithful to his end. Now I saw that there stood behind the multitude a chariot and a couple of horses, waiting for Faithful, who (so soon as his adversaries had dispatched him) was taken up into it, and straightway was carried up through the clouds, with sound of trumpet, the nearest way to the celestial gate.

But for Christian, he had some respite, and was remanded back to prison. So he there remained for a space; but he that overrules all things, having the power of their rage in his own hand, so wrought it about that Christian for that time escaped them and went his way, and as he went he sang, saying,

> Well, Faithful, thou hast faithfully professed
> Unto thy Lord; with whom thou shalt be blest,
> When faithless ones, with all their vain delights,
> Are crying out under their hellish plights:
> Sing, Faithful, sing, and let thy name survive;
> For though they killed thee, thou art yet alive.

Now I saw in my dream that Christian went not forth alone, for there was one whose name was Hopeful (being made so by the beholding of Christian and Faithful in their words and behaviour in their sufferings at the Fair), who joined himself unto him, and entering into a brotherly covenant, told him that he would be his companion. Thus one died to bear testimony to the truth, and another rises out of his ashes to be a companion with Christian in his pilgrimage. This Hopeful also told Christian that there were many more of the men in the Fair that would take their time and follow after.

So I saw that quickly after they were got out of the Fair, they overtook one that was going before them, whose name was By-ends;[153] so they said to him, What countryman, Sir? and how far go you this way? He told him that he came from the town of Fair-speech, and he was going to the Celestial City, but told them not his name.

From Fair-speech, said Christian; is there any good that lives there?

By-ends. Yes, said By-ends, I hope.

Chr. Pray Sir, what may I call you? said Christian.

By-ends. I am a stranger to you, and you to me. If you be going this way, I shall be glad of your company; if not, I must be content.

Chr. This town of Fair-speech, said Christian, I have heard of it; and as I remember, they say it's a wealthy place.

By-ends. Yes, I will assure you that it is; and I have very many rich kindred there.

Chr. Pray, who are your kindred there? if a man may be so bold.

By-ends. Almost the whole town, and in particular, my Lord Turn-about, my Lord Time-server, my Lord Fair-speech (from whose ancestors that town first took its name), also Mr. Smooth-man, Mr. Facing-both-ways, Mr. Any-thing, and the parson of our parish, Mr. Two-tongues, was my mother's own brother by father's side; and to tell you the truth, I am become a gentleman of good quality, yet my great-grandfather was but a waterman, looking one way and rowing another, and I got most of my estate by the same occupation.

Chr. Are you a married man?

By-ends. Yes, and my wife is a very virtuous woman, the daughter of a virtuous woman; she was my Lady Feigning's daughter, therefore she came of a very honourable family, and is arrived to such a pitch of breeding that she knows how to carry it to all, even to prince and peasant. 'Tis true, we somewhat differ in religion

---

153. Subordinate purposes, concealed aims at personal gain, aside from one's professedly "chief" purpose.

from those of the stricter sort, yet but in two small points: first, we never strive against wind and tide; secondly, we are always most zealous when Religion goes in his silver slippers; we love much to walk with him in the street, if the sun shines and the people applaud him.

Then Christian stepped a little aside to his fellow Hopeful, saying, It runs in my mind that this is one By-ends of Fair-speech; and if it be he, we have as very a knave in our company as dwelleth in all these parts. Then said Hopeful, Ask him, methinks he should not be ashamed of his name. So Christian came up with him again and said, Sir, you talk as if you knew something more than all the world doth; and if I take not my mark amiss, I deem I have half a guess of you: Is not your name Mr. By-ends of Fair-speech?

By-ends. This is not my name, but indeed it is a nickname that is given me by some that cannot abide me, and I must be content to bear it as a reproach, as other good men have borne theirs before me.

Chr. But did you never give an occasion to men to call you by this name?

By-ends. Never, never! The worst that ever I did to give them an occasion to give me this name was that I had always the luck to jump in my judgement with the present way of the times, whatever it was, and my chance was to get thereby, but if things are thus cast upon me, let me count them a blessing; but let not the malicious load me therefore with reproach.

Chr. I thought indeed that you were the man that I heard of; and to tell you what I think, I fear this name belongs to you more properly than you are willing we should think it doth.

By-ends. Well, if you will thus imagine, I cannot help it; you shall find me a fair company-keeper, if you will still admit me your associate.

Chr. If you will go with us, you must go against the wind and tide; the which, I perceive, is against your opinion. You must also own Religion in his rags, as well as when in his silver slippers, and stand by him too when bound in irons, as well as when he walketh the streets with applause.

By-ends. You must not impose, nor lord it over my faith; leave me to my liberty, and let me go with you.

Chr. Not a step further, unless you will do in what I propound as we.

Then said By-ends, I shall never desert my old principles, since they are harmless and profitable. If I may not go with you, I must do as I did before you overtook me, even go by myself, until some overtake me that will be glad of my company.

Now I saw in my dream that Christian and Hopeful forsook him, and kept their distance before him; but one of them looking back saw three men following Mr. By-ends, and behold, as they came up with him, he made them a very low *congé,* and they also gave him a compliment. The men's names were Mr. Hold-the-world, Mr. Money-love, and Mr. Save-all; men that Mr. By-ends had formerly been acquainted with. For in their minority, they were schoolfellows, and were taught by one Mr. Gripe-man, a schoolmaster in Love-gain, which is a market town in the county of Coveting in the north. This schoolmaster taught them the art of getting, either by violence, cozenage, flattery, lying, or by putting on a guise of religion; and these four gentlemen had attained much of the art of their master, so that they could each of them have kept such a school themselves.

Well, when they had, as I said, thus saluted each other, Mr. Money-love said to Mr. By-ends, Who are they upon the road before us? (for Christian and Hopeful were yet within view).

By-ENDS. They are a couple of far countrymen, that, after their mode, are going on pilgrimage.

MONEY-LOVE. Alas, why did they not stay, that we might have had their good company? for they, and we, and you, Sir, I hope, are all going on pilgrimage.

By-ENDS. We are so indeed; but the men before us are so rigid, and love so much their own notions, and do also so lightly esteem the opinions of others, that let a man be never so godly, yet if he jumps not with them in all things, they thrust him quite out of their company.

SAVE-ALL. That is bad, but we read of some that are righteous overmuch; and such men's rigidness prevails with them to judge and condemn all but themselves. But I pray, what and how many were the things wherein you differed?

By-ENDS. Why, they, after their headstrong manner, conclude that it is duty to rush on their journey all weathers, and I am for waiting for wind and tide. They are for hazarding all for God at a clap, and I am for taking all advantages to secure my life and estate. They are for holding their notions, though all other men are against them, but I am for religion in what and so far as the times and my safety will bear it. They are for Religion when in rags and contempt, but I am for him when he walks in his golden slippers in the sunshine and with applause.

HOLD-THE-WORLD. Aye, and hold you there still, good Mr. By-ends; for, for my part, I can count him but a fool that, having the liberty to keep what he has, shall be so unwise as to lose it. Let us be wise as serpents; it is best to make hay when the sun shines. You see how the bee lieth still all winter, and bestirs her only when she can have profit with pleasure. God sends sometimes rain and sometimes sunshine; if they be such fools to go through the first, yet let us be content to take fair weather along with us. For my part, I like that religion best that will stand with the security of God's good blessings unto us; for who can imagine, that is ruled by his reason, since God has bestowed upon us the good things of this life, but that he would have us keep them for his sake? Abraham and Solomon grew rich in religion. And Job says that a good man "shall lay up gold as dust." But he must not be such as the men before us, if they be as you have described them.

SAVE-ALL. I think that we are all agreed in this matter, and therefore there needs no more words about it.

MONEY-LOVE. No, there needs no more words about this matter indeed; for he that believes neither Scripture nor reason (and you see we have both on our side) neither knows his own liberty, nor seeks his own safety.

BY-ENDS. My brethren, we are, as you see, going all on pilgrimages, and for our better diversion from things that are bad, give me leave to propound unto you this question:

Suppose a man, a minister, or a tradesman, &c., should have an advantage lie before him to get the good blessings of this life, yet so as that he can by no means come by them except, in appearance at least, he becomes extraordinary zealous in some points of religion that he meddled not with before; may he not use this means to attain his end, and yet be a right honest man?

MONEY-LOVE. I see the bottom of your question; and, with these gentlemen's good leave, I will endeavour to shape you an answer. And first, to speak to your question as it concerns a minister himself: Suppose a minister, a worthy man, possessed but of a very small benefice, and has in his eye a greater, more fat and plump by far; he has also now an opportunity of getting of it, yet so as by being more studious, by preaching more frequently and zealously, and, because the temper of the people requires it, by altering of some of his principles. For my part, I see no reason but a man may do this (provided he has a call), aye, and more a great deal besides, and yet be an honest man. For why,

1. His desire of a greater benefice is lawful (this cannot be contradicted), since 'tis set before him by Providence; so then, he may get it, if he can, making no question for conscience sake.

2. Besides, his desire after that benefice makes him more studious, a more zealous preacher, &c., and so makes him a better man; yea, makes him better improve his parts,[154] which is according to the mind of God.

3. Now as for his complying with the temper of his people by dissenting, to serve them, some of his principles, this argueth, (1) That he is of a self-denying temper; (2) Of a sweet and winning deportment; (3) and so more fit for the ministerial function.

4. I conclude, then, that a minister that changes a small for a great should not, for so doing, be judged as covetous, but rather, since he has improved in his parts and industry thereby, be counted as one that pursues his call and the opportunity put into his hand to do good.

And now to the second part of the question, which concerns the tradesman you mentioned. Suppose such an one to have but a poor employ in the world, but by becoming religious, he may mend his market, perhaps get a rich wife, or more and far better customers to his shop; for my part, I see no reason but that this may be lawfully done. For why,

1. To become religious is a virtue, by what means soever a man becomes so.

2. Nor is it unlawful to get a rich wife, or more custom to my shop.

3. Besides, the man that gets these by becoming religious, gets that which is good of them that are good, by becoming good himself. So then here is a good wife, and good customers, and good gain, and all these by becoming religious, which is good; therefore to become religious to get all these is a good and profitable design.

This answer, thus made by this Mr. Money-love to Mr. By-ends' question, was highly applauded by them all; wherefore they concluded, upon the whole, that it was most wholesome and advanta-

---

154. Abilities.

geous. And because, as they thought, no man was able to contradict it, and because Christian and Hopeful were yet within call, they joyfully agreed to assault them with the question as soon as they overtook them; and the rather because they had opposed Mr. By-ends before. So they called after them, and they stopped and stood still till they came up to them; but they concluded, as they went, that not Mr. By-ends, but old Mr. Hold-the-world, should propound the question to them, because, as they supposed, their answer to him would be without the remainder of that heat that was kindled betwixt Mr. By-ends and them, at their parting a little before.

So they came up to each other, and after a short salutation, Mr. Hold-the-world propounded the question to Christian and his fellow, and bid them to answer it if they could.

Chr. Then said Christian, Even a babe in religion may answer ten thousand such questions. For if it be unlawful to follow Christ for loaves, as it is,[155] how much more abominable is it to make of him and religion a stalking-horse to get and enjoy the world. Nor do we find any other than heathens, hyprocrites, devils, and witches, that are of this opinion.

1. Heathens; for when Hamor and Shechem had a mind to the daughter and cattle of Jacob, and saw that there was no ways for them to come at them, but by becoming circumcised, they say to their companions, If every male of us be circumcised as they are circumcised, shall not their cattle, and their substance, and every beast of theirs, be ours? Their daughter and their cattle were that which they sought to obtain, and their religion the stalking-horse they made use of to come at them. Read the whole story.[156]

2. The hypocritical Pharisees were also of this religion; long prayers were their pretence, but to get widows' houses was their intent, and greater damnation was from God their judgement.[157]

3. Judas the devil was also of this religion; he was religious for the bag, that he might be possessed of what was therein, but he was lost, cast away, and the very son of perdition.

4. Simon the witch was of this religion too; for he would have had the Holy Ghost, that he might have got money therewith, and his sentence from Peter's mouth was according.[158]

---

155. John 6, especially verses 26, 27.
156. Gen. 3:20–23.

157. Luke 20:46, 47.
158. Acts 8:18–24.

5. Neither will it out of my mind, but that that man that takes up religion for the world will throw away religion for the world; for so surely as Judas designed the world in becoming religious, so surely did he also sell religion and his Master for the same. To answer the question therefore affirmatively, as I perceive you have done, and to accept of as authentic such answer, is both heathenish, hypocritical, and devilish; and your reward will be according to your works. Then they stood staring one upon another, but had not wherewith to answer Christian. Hopeful also approved of the soundness of Christian's answer; so there was a great silence among them. Mr. By-ends and his company also staggered and kept behind, that Christian and Hopeful might outgo them. Then said Christian to his fellow, If these men cannot stand before the sentence of men, what will they do with the sentence of God? And if they are mute when dealt with by vessels of clay, what will they do when they shall be rebuked by the flames of a devouring fire?

Then Christian and Hopeful outwent them again, and went till they came at a delicate plain called Ease, where they went with much content; but that plain was but narrow, so they were quickly got over it.[159] Now at the further side of that plain was a little hill called Lucre, and in that hill a silver mine, which some of them that had formerly gone that way, because of the rarity of it, had turned aside to see, but going too near the brink of the pit, the ground being deceitful under them broke, and they were slain; some also had been maimed there, and could not to their dying day be their own men again.

Then I saw in my dream that a little off the road, over against the silver mine, stood Demas[160] (gentleman-like) to call to passengers to come and see; who said to Christian and his fellow, Ho! turn aside hither, and I will show you a thing.

CHR. What thing so deserving as to turn us out of the way?

DEMAS. Here is a silver mine, and some digging in it for treasure. If you will come, with a little pains you may richly provide for yourselves.

HOPE. Then said Hopeful, Let us go see.

CHR. Not I, said Christian. I have heard of this place before now, and how many have there been slain; and besides that, treasure is a

---

159. The ease that pilgrims have is but little in this life. [B]
160. 2 Tim. 4:10.

snare to those that seek it, for it hindereth them in their pilgrimage. Then Christian called to Demas, saying, Is not the place dangerous? Hath it not hindered many in their pilgrimage?

DEMAS. Not very dangerous, except to those that are careless (but withal, he blushed as he spake).

CHR. Then said Christian to Hopeful, Let us not stir a step, but still keep on our way.

HOPE. I will warrant you, when By-ends comes up, if he hath the same invitation as we, he will turn in thither to see.

CHR. No doubt thereof, for his principles lead him that way, and a hundred to one but he dies there.

DEMAS. Then Demas called again, saying, But will you not come over and see?

CHR. Then Christian roundly answered, saying, Demas, thou art an enemy to the right ways of the Lord of this way, and hast been already condemned for thine own turning aside by one of his Majesty's judges; and why seekest thou to bring us into the like condemnation? Besides, if we at all turn aside, our Lord the King will certainly hear thereof, and will there put us to shame, where we would stand with boldness before him.

Demas cried again that he also was one of their fraternity, and that if they would tarry a little, he also himself would walk with them.

CHR. Then said Christian, What is thy name? Is it not the same by the which I have called thee?

DEMAS. Yes, my name is Demas; I am the son of Abraham.

CHR. I know you; Gehazi[161] was your great-grandfather and Judas your father, and you have trod their steps. It is but a devilish prank that thou usest; thy father was hanged for a traitor, and thou deservest no better reward. Assure thyself that when we come to the King, we will do him word of this thy behaviour. Thus they went their way.

By this time By-ends and his companions were come again within sight, and they at the first beck went over to Demas. Now whether they fell into the pit by looking over the brink thereof, or whether they went down to dig, or whether they were smothered in the bottom by the damps that commonly arise, of these things I am not certain; but this I observed, that they never were seen again in the way. Then sang Christian,

---

161. 2 Kings 5:20–27.

> By-ends and silver Demas both agree;
> One calls, the other runs, that he may be
> A sharer in his lucre; so these do
> Take up in this world, and no further go.

Now I saw that just on the other side of this plain the pilgrims came to a place where stood an old monument, hard by the highway side, at the sight of which they were both concerned, because of the strangeness of the form thereof, for it seemed to them as if it had been a woman transformed into the shape of a pillar; here therefore they stood looking and looking upon it, but could not for a time tell what they should make thereof. At last Hopeful espied written above upon the head thereof, a writing in an unusual hand, but he being no scholar, called to Christian (for he was learned) to see if he could pick out the meaning; so he came, and after a little laying of letters together, he found the same to be this, "Remember Lot's wife." So he read it to his fellow; after which they both concluded that that was the pillar of salt into which Lot's wife was turned, for her looking back with a covetous heart, when she was going from Sodom for safety,[162] which sudden and amazing sight gave them occasion of this discourse.

CHR. Ah my brother, this is a seasonable sight; it came opportunely to us after the invitation which Demas gave us to come over to view the Hill Lucre, and had we gone over as he desired us, and as thou wast inclining to do, my brother, we had, for aught I know, been made ourselves like this woman, a spectacle for those that shall come after to behold.

HOPE. I am sorry that I was so foolish, and am made to wonder that I am not now as Lot's wife; for wherein was the difference 'twixt her sin and mine? She only looked back; and I had a desire to go see. Let grace be adored, and let me be ashamed that ever such a thing should be in mine heart.

CHR. Let us take notice of what we see here for our help for time to come. This woman escaped one judgement, for she fell not by the destruction of Sodom, yet she was destroyed by another; as we see, she is turned into a pillar of salt.

HOPE. True, and she may be to us both caution and example; caution, that we should shun her sin; or a sign of what judgement

---

162. Gen. 19:26.

will overtake such as shall not be prevented by this caution. So Korah, Dathan, and Abiram, with the two hundred and fifty men that perished in their sin, did also become a sign or example to others to beware.[163] But above all, I muse at one thing, to wit, how Demas and his fellows can stand so confidently yonder to look for that treasure, which this woman, but for looking behind her after (for we read not that she stepped one foot out of the way), was turned into a pillar of salt; specially since the judgement which overtook her did make her an example within sight of where they are, for they cannot choose but see her, did they but lift up their eyes.

CHR. It is a thing to be wondered at, and it argueth that their heart is grown desperate in the case; and I cannot tell who to compare them to so fitly, as to them that pick pockets in the presence of the judge, or that will cut purses under the gallows. It is said of the men of Sodom "that they were sinners exceedingly," because they were sinners "before the Lord," that is, in his eyesight, and notwithstanding the kindnesses that he had showed them; for the land of Sodom was now like the garden of Eden heretofore.[164] This therefore provoked him the more to jealousy, and made their plague as hot as the fire of the Lord out of heaven could make it. And it is most rationally to be concluded that such, even such as these are, that shall sin in the sight, yea, and that too in despite of such examples that are set continually before them, to caution them to the contrary, must be partakers of severest judgements.

HOPE. Doubtless thou hast said the truth; but what a mercy is it that neither thou, but especially I, am not made myself this example. This ministereth occasion to us to thank God, to fear before him, and always to remember Lot's wife.

I saw then that they went on their way to a pleasant river, which David the king called "the river of God," but John, "the river of the water of life."[165] Now their way lay just upon the bank of the river; here therefore Christian and his companion walked with great delight. They drank also of the water of the river, which was pleasant and enlivening to their weary spirits. Besides, on the banks of this river, on either side, were green trees that bore all manner of fruit; and the leaves of the trees were good for medicine; with the fruit of

---

163. Num. 26:9, 10.
164. Gen. 13:13, 10.
165. Ps. 65:9; Rev. 22:1, 2.

these trees they were also much delighted; and the leaves they ate to prevent surfeits and other diseases that are incident to those that heat their blood by travels.[166] On either side of the river was also a meadow, curiously beautified with lilies, and it was green all the year long. In this meadow they lay down and slept; for here they might lie down safely.[167] When they awoke, they gathered again of the fruit of the trees, and drank again of the water of the river, and then lay down again to sleep. Thus they did several days and nights. Then they sang,

> Behold ye how these crystal streams do glide
> (To comfort pilgrims) by the highway side;
> The meadows green, besides their fragrant smell,
> Yield dainties for them: and he that can tell
> What pleasant fruit, yea, leaves, these trees do yield,
> Will soon sell all, that he may buy this field.

So when they were disposed to go on (for they were not, as yet, at their journey's end), they ate and drank, and departed.

Now I beheld in my dream that they had not journeyed far, but the river and the way (for a time) parted; at which they were not a little sorry, yet they durst not go out of the way. Now the way from the river was rough, and their feet tender by reason of their travels; "so the souls of the pilgrims were much discouraged because of the way."[168] Wherefore still as they went on, they wished for better way. Now a little before them, there was on the left hand of the road a meadow, and a stile to go over into it; and that meadow is called By-path Meadow. Then said Christian to his fellow, If this meadow lieth along by our wayside, let's go over into it.[169] Then he went to the stile to see, and behold, a path lay along by the way on the other side of the fence. 'Tis according to my wish, said Christian. Here is the easiest going; come, good Hopeful, and let us go over.

HOPE. But how if this path should lead us out of the way?

CHR. That's not like, said the other. Look, doth it not go along by the wayside? So Hopeful, being persuaded by his fellow, went after him over the stile.[170] When they were gone over and were got into

---

166. Ezek. 47:7, 12.
167. Ps. 23:2.
168. Num. 21:4.
169. One temptation does make way for another. [B]
170. Strong Christians may lead weak ones out of the way. [B]

the path, they found it very easy for their feet, and withal, they looking before them, espied a man walking as they did (and his name was Vain-confidence); so they called after him and asked him whither that way led. He said, To the Celestial Gate.[171] Look, said Christian, did not I tell you so? By this you may see we are right. So they followed, and he went before them. But behold, the night came on and it grew very dark, so that they that were behind lost the sight of him that went before.

He therefore that went before (Vain-confidence by name), not seeing the way before him, fell into a deep pit which was on purpose there made by the Prince of those grounds, to catch vainglorious fools withal, and was dashed in pieces with his fall.

Now Christian and his fellow heard him fall. So they called to know the matter, but there was none to answer, only they heard a groaning. Then said Hopeful, Where are we now? Then was his fellow silent, as mistrusting that he had led him out of the way; and now it began to rain and thunder, and lighten in a very dreadful manner, and the water rose amain.

Then Hopeful groaned in himself, saying, Oh, that I had kept on my way!

CHR. Who could have thought that this path should have led us out of the way?

HOPE. I was afraid on't at very first, and therefore gave you that gentle caution. I would have spoke plainer, but that you are older than I.

CHR. Good brother, be not offended; I am sorry I have brought thee out of the way, and that I have put thee into such eminent[172] danger. Pray, my brother, forgive me; I did not do it of an evil intent.

HOPE. Be comforted, my brother, for I forgive thee; and believe too that this shall be for our good.

CHR. I am glad I have with me a merciful brother, but we must not stand thus; let's try to go back again.

HOPE. But good brother, let me go before.

CHR. No, if you please, let me go first, that if there be any danger, I may be first therein, because by my means we are both gone out of the way.

---

171. See what it is too suddenly to fall in with strangers. [B]
172. Imminent.

HOPE. No, said Hopeful, you shall not go first; for your mind being troubled may lead you out of the way again. Then for their encouragement they heard the voice of one saying, "Let thine heart be towards the highway, even the way that thou wentest; turn again."[173] But by this time the waters were greatly risen, by reason of which the way of going back was very dangerous. (Then I thought that it is easier going out of the way when we are in, than going in when we are out.) Yet they adventured to go back, but it was so dark, and the flood was so high, that in their going back they had like to have been drowned nine or ten times.

Neither could they, with all the skill they had, get again to the stile that night. Wherefore, at last, lighting under a little shelter, they sat down there till the day brake; but being weary, they fell asleep. Now there was, not far from the place where they lay, a castle called Doubting Castle, the owner whereof was Giant Despair, and it was in his grounds they now were sleeping. Wherefore he, getting up in the morning early, and walking up and down in his fields, caught Christian and Hopeful asleep in his grounds. Then with a grim and surly voice he bid them awake, and asked them whence they were and what they did in his grounds. They told him they were pilgrims and that they had lost their way. Then said the Giant, You have this night trespassed on me by trampling in and lying on my grounds, and therefore you must go along with me. So they were forced to go, because he was stronger than they. They also had but little to say, for they knew themselves in a fault. The Giant therefore drove them before him and put them into his castle, into a very dark dungeon, nasty and stinking to the spirits of these two men. Here then they lay from Wednesday morning till Saturday night, without one bit of bread, or drop of drink, or light, or any to ask how they did; they were therefore here in evil case, and were far from friends and acquaintance. Now in this place Christian had double sorrow, because 'twas through his unadvised haste that they were brought into this distress.

Now Giant Despair had a wife, and her name was Diffidence. So when he was gone to bed, he told his wife what he had done; to wit, that he had taken a couple of prisoners and cast them into his dungeon for trespassing on his grounds. Then he asked her also what he had best to do further to them. So she asked him what they

<hr>

173. Jer. 31:21.

were, whence they came, and whither they were bound; and he told her. Then she counselled him that when he arose in the morning he should beat them without any mercy. So when he arose, he getteth him a grievous crab-tree cudgel, and goes down into the dungeon to them, and there first falls to rating of them as if they were dogs, although they never gave him a word of distaste. Then he falls upon them and beats them fearfully, in such sort that they were not able to help themselves, or to turn them upon the floor. This done, he withdraws and leaves them there to condole their misery and to mourn under their distress. So all that day they spent the time in nothing but sighs and bitter lamentations. The next night she talking with her husband about them further, and understanding they were yet alive, did advise him to counsel them to make away themselves. So when morning was come, he goes to them in a surly manner as before, and perceiving them to be very sore with the stripes that he had given them the day before, he told them that since they were never like to come out of that place, their only way would be forthwith to make an end of themselves, either with knife, halter, or poison. For why, said he, should you choose life, seeing it is attended with so much bitterness? But they desired him to let them go. With that he looked ugly upon them, and rushing to them, had doubtless made an end of them himself, but that he fell into one of his fits (for he sometimes in sunshine weather fell into fits), and lost for a time the use of his hand; wherefore he withdrew, and left them as before to consider what to do. Then did the prisoners consult between themselves, whether 'twas best to take his counsel or no; and thus they began to discourse:

CHR. Brother, said Christian, what shall we do? The life that we now live is miserable. For my part I know not whether it is best to live thus, or to die out of hand. "My soul chooseth strangling rather than life," and the grave is more easy for me than this dungeon.[174] Shall we be ruled by the Giant?

HOPE. Indeed our present condition is dreadful, and death would be far more welcome to me than thus for ever to abide, but yet let us consider, the Lord of the country to which we are going hath said, Thou shalt do no murder: no, not to another man's person; much more then are we forbidden to take his counsel to kill ourselves. Besides, he that kills another can but commit murder

---

174. Job 7:15.

upon his body; but for one to kill himself is to kill body and soul at once. And moreover, my brother, thou talkest of ease in the grave, but hast thou forgotten the hell whither for certain the murderers go? For "no murderer hath eternal life," &c.[175] And let us consider again that all the law is not in the hand of Giant Despair. Others, so far as I can understand, have been taken by him, as well as we, and yet have escaped out of his hand. Who knows but that God that made the world may cause that Giant Despair may die? or that at some time or other he may forget to lock us in? or but he may in short time have another of his fits before us, and may lose the use of his limbs? And if ever that should come to pass again, for my part, I am resolved to pluck up the heart of a man, and to try my utmost to get from under his hand. I was a fool that I did not try to do it before; but however, my brother, let's be patient, and endure a while. The time may come that may give us a happy release; but let us not be our own murderers. With these words Hopeful at present did moderate the mind of his brother; so they continued together (in the dark) that day, in their sad and doleful condition.

Well, towards evening the Giant goes down into the dungeon again, to see if his prisoners had taken his counsel, but when he came there he found them alive; and truly, alive was all, for now, what for want of bread and water, and by reason of the wounds they received when he beat them, they could do little but breathe. But, I say, he found them alive; at which he fell into a grievous rage, and told them that, seeing they had disobeyed his counsel, it should be worse with them than if they had never been born.

At this they trembled greatly, and I think that Christian fell into a swoon, but coming a little to himself again, they renewed their discourse about the Giant's counsel, and whether yet they had best to take it or no. Now Christian again seemed to be for doing it, but Hopeful made his second reply as followeth:

HOPE. My brother, said he, rememberest thou not how valiant thou hast been heretofore? Apollyon could not crush thee, nor could all that thou didst hear, or see, or feel, in the Valley of the Shadow of Death. What hardship, terror, and amazement hast thou already gone through, and art thou now nothing but fear? Thou seest that I am in the dungeon with thee, a far weaker man by nature than thou art; also this Giant has wounded me as well as thee, and

---

175. John 3:15.

hath also cut off the bread and water from my mouth, and with thee I mourn without the light. But let us exercise a little more patience; remember how thou playedst the man at Vanity Fair, and wast neither afraid of the chain, nor cage, nor yet of bloody death. Wherefore let us (at least to avoid the shame that becomes not a Christian to be found in) bear up with patience as well as we can.

Now night being come again, and the Giant and his wife being in bed, she asked him concerning the prisoners, and if they had taken his counsel. To which he replied, They are sturdy rogues, they choose rather to bear all hardship, than to make away themselves. Then said she, Take them into the castle-yard tomorrow, and show them the bones and skulls of those that thou hast already dispatched, and make them believe, ere a week comes to an end, thou also wilt tear them into pieces, as thou hast done their fellows before them.

So when the morning was come, the Giant goes to them again, and takes them into the castle-yard, and shows them, as his wife had bidden him. These, said he, were pilgrims as you are once, and they trespassed in my grounds, as you have done, and when I thought fit, I tore them in pieces, and so within ten days I will do you. Go, get you down to your den again; and with that he beat them all the way thither. They lay therefore all day on Saturday in a lamentable case, as before. Now when night was come, and when Mrs. Diffidence and her husband the Giant were got to bed, they began to renew their discourse of their prisoners; and withal the old Giant wondered that he could neither by his blows nor his counsel bring them to an end. And with that his wife replied, I fear, said she, that they live in hope that some will come to relieve them, or that they have pick-locks about them, by the means of which they hope to escape. And sayest thou so, my dear? said the Giant; I will therefore search them in the morning.

Well, on Saturday about midnight they began to pray, and continued in prayer till almost break of day.

Now a little before it was day, good Christian, as one half amazed, brake out in this passionate speech: What a fool (quoth he) am I, thus to lie in a stinking dungeon, when I may as well walk at liberty! I have a key in my bosom called Promise, that will (I am persuaded) open any lock in Doubting Castle. Then said Hopeful, That is good news, good brother; pluck it out of thy bosom and try. Then Christian pulled it out of his bosom, and began to try at the dungeon door, whose bolt (as he turned the key) gave back, and the door flew open with ease, and Christian and Hopeful both came out. Then he went to the outward door that leads into the castle-yard, and with his key opened that door also. After, he went to the iron gate, for that must be opened too; but that lock went damnable hard, yet the key did open it. Then they thrust open the gate to make their escape with speed, but that gate, as it opened, made such a creaking that it waked Giant Despair, who, hastily rising to pursue his prisoners, felt his limbs to fail, for his fits took him again, so that he could by no means go after them. Then they went on and came to the King's highway, and so were safe because they were out of his jurisdiction.

Now when they were gone over the stile, they began to contrive with themselves what they should do at that stile to prevent those that should come after from falling into the hands of Giant Despair. So they consented to erect there a pillar, and to engrave upon the side thereof this sentence: "Over this stile is the way to Doubting Castle, which is kept by Giant Despair, who despiseth the King of the Celestial Country, and seeks to destroy his holy pilgrims." Many therefore that followed after, read what was written and escaped the danger. This done, they sang as follows:

> Out of the way we went, and then we found
> What 'twas to tread upon forbidden ground;
> And let them that come after have a care,
> Lest heedlessness makes them, as we, to fare.
> Lest they for trespassing his prisoners are,
> Whose castle's Doubting and whose name's Despair.

They went then till they came to the Delectable Mountains, which mountains belong to the Lord of that hill of which we have spoken before; so they went up to the mountains, to behold the gardens and orchards, the vineyards and fountains of water, where also they drank and washed themselves, and did freely eat of the vineyards. Now there were on the tops of these mountains shepherds feeding their flocks, and they stood by the highway side. The pilgrims therefore went to them, and leaning upon their staves (as is common with weary pilgrims, when they stand to talk with any by the way), they asked, Whose delectable mountains are these? And whose be the sheep that feed upon them?

SHEP. These mountains are Immanuel's Land, and they are

within sight of his city; and the sheep also are his, and he laid down his life for them.

CHR. Is this the way to the Celestial City?

SHEP. You are just in your way.

CHR. How far is it thither?

SHEP. Too far for any but those that shall get thither indeed.

CHR. Is the way safe or dangerous?

SHEP. Safe for those for whom it is to be safe; "but transgressors shall fall therein."[176]

CHR. Is there in this place any relief for pilgrims that are weary and faint in the way?

SHEP. The Lord of these mountains hath given us a charge, "not to be forgetful to entertain strangers";[177] therefore the good of the place is before you.

I saw also in my dream that when the Shepherds perceived that they were wayfaring men, they also put questions to them (to which they made answer as in other places), as, Whence came you? and, How got you into the way? and, By what means have you so persevered therein? For but few of them that begin to come hither do show their face on these mountains. But when the Shepherds heard their answers, being pleased therewith, they looked very lovingly upon them and said, Welcome to the Delectable Mountains.

The Shepherds, I say, whose names were Knowledge, Experience, Watchful, and Sincere, took them by the hand, and had them to their tents, and made them partake of that which was ready at present. They said, moreover, We would that ye should stay here awhile, to be acquainted with us, and yet more to solace yourselves with the good of these Delectable Mountains. They then told them that they were content to stay; so they went to their rest that night, because it was very late.

Then I saw in my dream that in the morning the Shepherds called up Christian and Hopeful to walk with them upon the mountains; so they went forth with them and walked a while, having a pleasant prospect on every side. Then said the Shepherds one to another, Shall we show these pilgrims some wonders? So when they had concluded to do it, they had them first to the top of a hill called Error, which was very steep on the furthest side, and

---

176. Hos. 14:9.
177. Heb. 13:2.

bid them look down to the bottom. So Christian and Hopeful looked down, and saw at the bottom several men dashed all to pieces by a fall that they had from the top. Then said Christian, What meaneth this? The Shepherds answered, Have you not heard of them that were made to err, by hearkening to Hymeneus and Philetus, as concerning the faith of the resurrection of the body?[178] They answered, Yes. Then said the Shepherds, Those that you see lie dashed in pieces at the bottom of this mountain are they; and they have continued to this day unburied, as you see, for an example to others to take heed how they clamber too high, or how they come too near the brink of this mountain.

Then I saw that they had them to the top of another mountain, and the name of that is Caution, and bid them look afar off; which when they did, they perceived, as they thought, several men walking up and down among the tombs that were there, and they perceived that the men were blind, because they stumbled sometimes upon the tombs, and because they could not get out from among them. Then said Christian, What means this?

The Shepherds then answered, Did you not see a little below these mountains a stile, that led into a meadow, on the left hand of this way? They answered, Yes. Then said the Shepherds, From that stile there goes a path that leads directly to Doubting Castle, which is kept by Giant Despair, and these men (pointing to them among the tombs) came once on pilgrimage, as you do now, even till they came to that same stile; and because the right way was rough in that place, they chose to go out of it into that meadow, and there were taken by Giant Despair, and cast into Doubting Castle, where, after they had been a while kept in the dungeon, he at last did put out their eyes, and led them among those tombs, where he has left them to wander to this very day, that the saying of the wise man might be fulfilled, "He that wandereth out of the way of understanding shall remain in the congregation of the dead."[179] Then Christian and Hopeful looked upon one another with tears gushing out, but yet said nothing to the Shepherds.

Then I saw in my dream that the Shepherds had them to another place, in a bottom, where was a door in the side of a hill, and they

---

178. 2 Tim. 2:17, 18.
179. Prov. 21:16.

opened the door and bid them look in. They looked in therefore and saw that within, it was very dark and smoky; they also thought that they heard there a rumbling noise as of fire, and a cry of some tormented, and that they smelt the scent of brimstone. Then said Christian, What means this? The Shepherds told them, This is a by-way to hell, a way that hypocrites go in at; namely, such as sell their birthright, with Esau; such as sell their master, with Judas; such as blaspheme the gospel, with Alexander; and that lie and dissemble, with Ananias and Sapphira his wife. Then said Hopeful to the Shepherds, I perceive that these had on them, even every one, a show of pilgrimage, as we have now; had they not?

SHEP. Yes, and held it a long time too.

HOPE. How far might they go on pilgrimage in their day, since they notwithstanding were thus miserably cast away?

SHEP. Some further, and some not so far as these mountains.

Then said the pilgrims one to another, We had need cry to the strong for strength.

SHEP. Ay, and you will have need to use it when you have it too.

By this time the pilgrims had a desire to go forward, and the Shepherds a desire they should; so they walked together towards the end of the mountains. Then said the Shepherds one to another, Let us here show to the pilgrims the gates of the Celestial City, if they have skill to look through our perspective glass. The pilgrims then lovingly accepted the motion; so they had them to the top of a high hill called Clear, and gave them their glass to look.

Then they essayed to look, but the remembrance of that last thing that the Shepherds had shown them made their hands shake; by means of which impediment they could not look steadily through the glass, yet they thought they saw something like the gate, and also some of the glory of the place. Then they went away and sang this song:

> Thus by the Shepherds secrets are revealed,
> Which from all other men are kept concealed.
> Come to the Shepherds then, if you would see
> Things deep, things hid, and that mysterious be.

When they were about to depart, one of the Shepherds gave them a note of the way. Another of them bid them beware of the

Flatterer. The third bid them take heed that they sleep not upon the Enchanted Ground. And the fourth bid them God-speed. So I awoke from my dream.

And I slept, and dreamed again, and saw the same two pilgrims going down the mountains along the highway towards the city. Now a little below these mountains, on the left hand, lieth the country of Conceit, from which country there comes into the way in which the pilgrims walked, a little crooked lane. Here therefore they met with a very brisk lad that came out of that country, and his name was Ignorance. So Christian asked him from what parts he came and whither he was going.

IGNOR. Sir, I was born in the country that lieth off there a little on the left hand, and I am going to the Celestial City.

CHR. But how do you think to get in at the gate? for you may find some difficulty there.

IGNOR. As other good people do, said he.

CHR. But what have you to show at the gate, that may cause that the gate should be opened to you?

IGNOR. I know my Lord's will, and I have been a good liver; I pay every man his own; I pray, fast, pay tithes, and give alms, and have left my country for whither I am going.

CHR. But thou camest not in at the wicket-gate that is at the head of this way; thou camest in hither through that same crooked lane, and therefore I fear, however thou mayest think of thyself, when the reckoning day shall come, thou wilt have laid to thy charge that thou art a thief and a robber, instead of getting admittance into the city.

IGNOR. Gentlemen, ye be utter strangers to me, I know you not; be content to follow the religion of your country, and I will follow the religion of mine. I hope all will be well. And as for the gate that you talk of, all the world knows that that is a great way off of our country. I cannot think that any man in all our parts doth so much as know the way to it, nor need they matter whether they do or no, since we have, as you see, a fine pleasant green lane that comes down from our country, the next way into the way.

When Christian saw that the man was "wise in his own conceit,"[180] he said to Hopeful whisperingly, "There is more hopes of a fool than of him." And said, moreover, "When he that is a fool

---

180. Private opinion or judgement.

walketh by the way, his wisdom faileth him, and he saith to every one that he is a fool."[181] What, shall we talk further with him, or out-go him at present, and so leave him to think of what he hath heard already, and then stop again for him afterwards, and see if by degrees we can do any good to him? Then said Hopeful,

> Let Ignorance a little while now muse
> On what is said, and let him not refuse
> Good counsel to embrace, lest he remain
> Still ignorant of what's the chiefest gain.
> God saith, those that no understanding have
> (Although he made them), them he will not save.

HOPE. He further added, It is not good, I think, to say all to him at once; let us pass him by, if you will, and talk to him anon, even as he is able to bear it.

So they both went on, and Ignorance he came after. Now when they had passed him a little way, they entered into a very dark lane, where they met a man whom seven devils had bound with seven strong cords, and were carrying of him back to the door that they saw on the side of the hill.[182] Now good Christian began to tremble, and so did Hopeful his companion, yet as the devils led away the man, Christian looked to see if he knew him; and he thought it might be one Turn-away, that dwelt in the town of Apostasy. But he did not perfectly see his face, for he did hang his head like a thief that is found. But being once past, Hopeful looked after him, and espied on his back a paper with this inscription, "Wanton professor and damnable apostate." Then said Christian to his fellow, Now I call to remembrance that which was told me of a thing that happened to a good man hereabout. The name of the man was Little-faith, but a good man, and he dwelt in the town of Sincere. The thing was this: At the entering in at this passage, there comes down from Broad-way Gate a lane called Dead Man's Lane, so called because of the murders that are commonly done there; and this Little-faith going on pilgrimage, as we do now, chanced to sit down there, and slept. Now there happened at that time to come down the lane from Broad-way Gate, three sturdy rogues, and

---

181. Prov. 26:12; Eccles. 10:3.
182. Matt. 12:45; Prov. 5:22.

their names were Faint-heart, Mistrust, and Guilt (three brothers), and they espying Little-faith where he was, came galloping up with speed. Now the good man was just awake from his sleep, and was getting up to go on his journey. So they came up all to him, and with threatening language bid him stand. At this Little-faith looked as white as a clout, and had neither power to fight nor fly. Then said Faint-heart, Deliver thy purse. But he making no haste to do it (for he was loth to lose his money), Mistrust ran up to him, and thrusting his hand into his pocket, pulled out thence a bag of silver. Then he cried out, Thieves! Thieves! With that, Guilt with a great club that was in his hand struck Little-faith on the head, and with that blow felled him flat to the ground, where he lay bleeding as one that would bleed to death. All this while the thieves stood by. But at last, they hearing that some were upon the road, and fearing lest it should be one Great-grace that dwells in the city of Good-confidence, they betook themselves to their heels, and left this good man to shift for himself. Now after a while, Little-faith came to himself, and getting up, made shift to scrabble on his way. This was the story.

HOPE. But did they take from him all that ever he had?

CHR. No; the place where his jewels were they never ransacked, so those he kept still. But as I was told, the good man was much afflicted for his loss, for the thieves got most of his spending-money. That which they got not (as I said) were jewels, also he had a little odd money left, but scarce enough to bring him to his journey's end; nay (if I was not misinformed) he was forced to beg as he went, to keep himself alive (for his jewels he might not sell). But beg and do what he could, he went (as we say) with many a hungry belly the most part of the rest of the way.

HOPE. But is it not a wonder they got not from him his certificate, by which he was to receive his admittance at the Celestial Gate?

CHR. 'Tis a wonder, but they got not that, though they missed it not through any good cunning of his; for he, being dismayed with their coming upon him, had neither power nor skill to hide anything, so 'twas more by good Providence than by his endeavour that they missed of "that good thing."[183]

HOPE. But it must needs be a comfort to him that they got not his jewels from him.

---

183. 2 Tim. 1:14.

CHR. It might have been great comfort to him, had he used it as he should, but they that told me the story said that he made but little use of it all the rest of the way, and that because of the dismay that he had in their taking away his money; indeed he forgot it a great part of the rest of his journey. And besides, when at any time it came into his mind, and he began to be comforted therewith, then would fresh thoughts of his loss come again upon him, and those thoughts would swallow up all.

HOPE. Alas, poor man! This could not but be a great grief to him.

CHR. Grief! ay, a grief indeed! Would it not have been so to any of us, had we been used as he, to be robbed, and wounded too, and that in a strange place, as he was? It is a wonder he did not die with grief, poor heart! I was told that he scattered almost all the rest of the way with nothing but doleful and bitter complaints, telling also to all that overtook him, or that he overtook in the way as he went, where he was robbed, and how; who they were that did it, and what he lost; how he was wounded, and that he hardly escaped with his life.

HOPE. But 'tis a wonder that his necessity did not put him upon selling or pawning some of his jewels, that he might have wherewith to relieve himself in his journey.

CHR. Thou talkest like one upon whose head is the shell to this very day; for what should he pawn them, or to whom should he sell them?[184] In all that country where he was robbed his jewels were not accounted of; nor did he want that relief which could from thence be administered to him. Besides, had his jewels been missing at the gate of the Celestial City, he had (and that he knew well enough) been excluded from an inheritance there; and that would have been worse to him than the appearance and villainy of ten thousand thieves.

HOPE. Why art thou so tart, my brother? Esau sold his birthright, and that for a mess of pottage,[185] and that birthright was his greatest jewel; and if he, why might not Little-faith do so too?

CHR. Esau did sell his birthright indeed, and so do many besides, and by so doing exclude themselves from the chief blessing, as also that caitiff did; but you must put a difference betwixt Esau and Little-faith, and also betwixt their estates. Esau's birthright was typ-

184. Christian snibbeth his fellow for unadvised speaking. [B]
185. Gen. 25:29–34; Heb. 12:16.

ical,[186] but Little-faith's jewels were not so. Esau's belly was his god, but Little-faith's belly was not so. Esau's want lay in his fleshly appetite, Little-faith's did not so. Besides, Esau could see no further than to the fulfilling of his lusts; "for I am at the point to die (said he), and what good will this birthright do me?" But Little-faith, though it was his lot to have but a little faith, was by his little faith kept from such extravagancies, and made to see and prize his jewels more than to sell them, as Esau did his birthright. You read not anywhere that Esau had faith, no, not so much as a little; therefore no marvel if, where the flesh only bears sway (as it will in that man where no faith is to resist), if he sells his birthright, and his soul and all, and that to the Devil of hell, for it is with such, as it is with the ass, "who in her occasions[187] cannot be turned away."[188] When their minds are set upon their lusts, they will have them whatever they cost. But Little-faith was of another temper, his mind was on things divine; his livelihood was upon things that were spiritual and from above;[189] therefore to what end should he that is of such a temper sell his jewels (had there been any that would have bought them) to fill his mind with empty things? Will a man give a penny to fill his belly with hay; or can you persuade the turtle-dove to live upon the carrion like the crow? Though faithless ones can, for carnal lusts, pawn, or mortgage, or sell what they have, and themselves outright to boot, yet they that have faith, saving faith, though but a little of it, cannot do so. Here therefore, my brother, is thy mistake.

HOPE. I acknowledge it; but yet your severe reflection had almost made me angry.

CHR. Why, I did but compare thee to some of the birds that are of the brisker sort, who will run to and fro in untrodden paths with the shell upon their heads; but pass by that, and consider the matter under debate, and all shall be well betwixt thee and me.

HOPE. But Christian, these three fellows, I am persuaded in my heart, are but a company of cowards; would they have run else, think you, as they did, at the noise of one that was coming on the road? Why did not Little-faith pluck up a greater heart? He

---

186. Symbolical; in theological usage, something in Old Testament history that prefigures something revealed in the New Testament.
187. Needs, requirements.
188. Jer. 2:24.
189. Little-faith could not live upon Esau's pottage. [B]

might, methinks, have stood one brush with them, and have yielded when there had been no remedy.[190]

CHR. That they are cowards, many have said, but few have found it so in the time of trial. As for a great heart, Little-faith had none; and I perceive by thee, my brother, hadst thou been the man concerned, thou art but for a brush, and then to yield. And verily, since this is the height of thy stomach,[191] now they are at a distance from us, should they appear to thee as they did to him, they might put thee to second thoughts.[192]

But consider again, they are but journeymen thieves; they serve under the king of the bottomless pit, who, if need be, will come in to their aid himself, and his voice is as the roaring of a lion. I myself have been engaged as this Little-faith was, and I found it a terrible thing. These three villains set upon me, and I beginning like a Christian to resist, they gave but a call, and in came their master. I would, as the saying is, have given my life for a penny; but that, as God would have it, I was clothed with armour of proof. Ay, and yet, though I was so harnessed, I found it hard work to quit myself like a man. No man can tell what in that combat attends us, but he that hath been in the battle himself.

HOPE. Well, but they ran, you see, when they did but suppose that one Great-grace was in the way.

CHR. True, they have often fled, both they and their master, when Great-grace hath but appeared; and no marvel, for he is the King's champion. But I trow, you will put some difference between Little-faith and the King's champion. All the King's subjects are not his champions, nor can they, when tried, do such feats of war as he. Is it meet to think that a little child should handle Goliath as David did? Or that there should be the strength of an ox in a wren? Some are strong, some are weak; some have great faith, some have little. This man was one of the weak, and therefore he went to the walls.

HOPE. I would it had been Great-grace for their sakes.

CHR. If it had been he, he might have had his hands full; for I must tell you that though Great-grace is excellent good at his weapons, and has, and can, so long as he keeps them at sword's point, do well

---

190. Hopeful swaggers. [B]
191. Courage.
192. No great heart for God where there is but little faith. We have more courage when out, than when we are in. [B]

enough with them, yet if they get within him, even Faint-heart, Mistrust, or the other, it shall go hard but they will throw up his heels. And when a man is down, you know, what can he do?

Whoso looks well upon Great-grace's face shall see those scars and cuts there that shall easily give demonstration of what I say. Yea, once I heard that he should say (and that when he was in the combat), "We despaired even of life."[193] How did these sturdy rogues and their fellows make David groan, mourn, and roar? Yea, Heman and Hezekiah too, though champions in their day, were forced to bestir them, when by these assaulted; and yet, notwith-standing, they had their coats soundly brushed by them. Peter upon a time would go try what he could do; but though some do say of him that he is the prince of the apostles, they handled him so that they made him at last afraid of a sorry girl.[194]

Besides, their king is at their whistle. He is never out of hearing, and if at any time they be put to the worst, he, if possible, comes in to help them; and of him it is said, "The sword of him that layeth at him cannot hold; the spear, the dart, nor the habergeon; he esteemeth iron as straw, and brass as rotten wood. The arrow can-not make him fly, sling-stones are turned with him into stubble, darts are counted as stubble; he laugheth at the shaking of a spear."[195] What can a man do in this case? 'Tis true, if a man could at every turn have Job's horse, and had skill and courage to ride him, he might do notable things. "For his neck is clothed with thunder, he will not be afraid as the grasshopper, the glory of his nostrils is terrible, he paweth in the valley, rejoiceth in his strength, and goeth out to meet the armed men. He mocketh at fear, and is not affrighted, neither turneth back from the sword. The quiver rattleth against him, the glittering spear, and the shield. He swal-loweth the ground with fierceness and rage, neither believeth he that it is the sound of the trumpet. He saith among the trumpets, Ha, ha! and he smelleth the battle afar off, the thundering of the captains, and the shoutings."[196]

But for such footmen as thee and I are, let us never desire to meet with an enemy, nor vaunt as if we could do better, when we

---

193. 2 Cor. 1:8.
194. Matt. 26:69–72; Luke 22:56, 57.
195. Job 41:26–29.
196. Job 39:19–25.

hear of others that they have been foiled, nor be tickled at the thoughts of our own manhood; for such commonly come by the worst when tried. Witness Peter, of whom I made mention before. He would swagger, ay, he would; he would, as his vain mind prompted him to say, do better, and stand more for his Master than all men, but who so foiled and run down by these villains as he?

When therefore we hear that such robberies are done on the King's highway, two things become us to do: first, to go out harnessed, and to be sure to take a shield with us; for it was for want of that, that he that laid so lustily at Leviathan could not make him yield: for indeed, if that be wanting, he fears us not at all. Therefore he that had skill hath said, "Above all take the shield of faith, wherewith ye shall be able to quench all the fiery darts of the wicked."[197]

'Tis good also that we desire of the King a convoy, yea, that he will go with us himself. This made David rejoice when in the Valley of the Shadow of Death; and Moses was rather for dying where he stood, than to go one step without his God. O my brother, if he will but go along with us, what need we be afraid of ten thousands that shall set themselves against us? But without him, "the proud helpers fall under the slain."[198]

I for my part have been in the fray before now, and though (through the goodness of him that is best) I am, as you see, alive, yet I cannot boast of my manhood. Glad shall I be, if I meet with no more such brunts; though I fear we are not got beyond all danger. However, since the lion and the bear have not as yet devoured me, I hope God will also deliver us from the next uncircumcised Philistine. Then sang Christian,

> Poor Little-faith! Hast been among the thieves?
> Wast robbed? Remember this, whoso believes:
> And get more faith; then shall you victors be
> Over ten thousand, else scarce over three.

So they went on, and Ignorance followed. They went then till they came at a place where they saw a way put itself into their way, and seemed withal to lie as straight as the way which they should go: and here they knew not which of the two to take, for both seemed

---

197. Eph. 6:16.
198. Ps. 3:6; Job 9:13; Isa. 10:4.

straight before them; therefore hence they stood still to consider. And as they were thinking about the way, behold, a man black of flesh, but covered with a very light robe, came to them, and asked them why they stood there. They answered, They were going to the Celestial City, but knew not which of these ways to take. Follow me, said the man, it is thither that I am going. So they followed him in the way that but now came into the road, which by degrees turned, and turned them so from the city that they desired to go to, that in little time their faces were turned away from it, yet they followed him. But by and by, before they were aware, he led them both within the compass of a net, in which they were both so entangled that they knew not what to do; and with that the white robe fell off the black man's back. Then they saw where they were. Wherefore there they lay crying some time, for they could not get themselves out.

CHR. Then said Christian to his fellow, Now do I see myself in error. Did not the Shepherds bid us beware of the flatterers? As is the saying of the wise man, so we have found it this day, "A man that flattereth his neighbour spreadeth a net for his feet."[199]

HOPE. They also gave us a note of directions about the way, for our more sure finding thereof; but therein we have also forgotten to read, and have not kept ourselves from the paths of the destroyer. Here David was wiser than we; for saith he, "Concerning the works of men, by the word of thy lips I have kept me from the paths of the destroyer."[200] Thus they lay bewailing themselves in the net. At last they espied a Shining One coming towards them with a whip of small cord in his hand. When he was come to the place where they were, he asked them whence they came, and what they did there. They told him that they were poor pilgrims going to Zion, but were led out of their way by a black man, clothed in white, who bid us, said they, follow him, for he was going thither too. Then said he with the whip, It is Flatterer, a false apostle, that hath transformed himself into an angel of light.[201] So he rent the net, and let the men out. Then said he to them, Follow me, that I may set you in your way again. So he led them back to the way which they had left to follow the Flatterer. Then he asked them, saying, Where did you lie the last night? They said, With the Shepherds,

---

199. Prov. 29:5.
200. Ps. 17:4.
201. 2 Cor. 11:13, 14.

upon the Delectable Mountains. He asked them then, if they had not of those Shepherds a note of direction for the way. They answered, Yes. But did you, said he, when you were at a stand, pluck out and read your note? They answered, No. He asked them, Why? They said, they forgot. He asked, moreover, if the Shepherds did not bid them beware of the Flatterer. They answered, Yes, but we did not imagine, said they, that this fine-spoken man had been he.

Then I saw in my dream that he commanded them to lie down, which when they did, he chastised them sore, to teach them the good way wherein they should walk; and as he chastised them he said, "As many as I love, I rebuke and chasten; be zealous, therefore, and repent."[202] This done, he bid them go on their way, and take good heed to the other directions of the Shepherds. So they thanked him for all his kindness, and went softly along the right way, singing,

> Come hither, you that walk along the way;
> See how the pilgrims fare that go astray!
> They catchèd are in an entangling net,
> 'Cause they good counsel lightly did forget:
> 'Tis true they rescued were, but yet you see,
> They're scourged to boot. Let this your caution be.

Now after a while they perceived, afar off, one coming softly and alone all along the highway to meet them. Then said Christian to his fellow, Yonder is a man with his back towards Zion, and he is coming to meet us.

Hope. I see him; let us take heed to ourselves now, lest he should prove a flatterer also. So he drew nearer and nearer, and at last came up unto them. His name was Atheist, and he asked them whither they were going.

Chr. We are going to Mount Zion.

Then Atheist fell into a very great laughter.

Chr. What is the meaning of your laughter?

Atheist. I laugh to see what ignorant persons you are, to take upon you so tedious a journey; and yet are like to have nothing but your travel for your pains.

---

202. Rev. 3:19.

CHR. Why, man, do you think we shall not be received?

ATHEIST. Received! There is no such place as you dream of in all this world.

CHR. But there is in the world to come.

ATHEIST. When I was at home in mine own country, I heard as you now affirm, and from that hearing went out to see, and have been seeking this city this twenty years; but find no more of it than I did the first day I set out.

CHR. We have both heard and believe that there is such a place to be found.

ATHEIST. Had not I, when at home, believed, I had not come thus far to seek; but finding none (and yet I should, had there been such a place to be found, for I have gone to seek it further than you), I am going back again, and will seek to refresh myself with the things that I then cast away for hopes of that which I now see is not.

CHR. Then said Christian to Hopeful his fellow, Is it true which this man hath said?

HOPE. Take heed, he is one of the flatterers; remember what it hath cost us once already for our hearkening to such kind of fellows. What! no Mount Zion? Did we not see from the Delectable Mountains the gate of the city? Also, are we not now to walk by faith? Let us go on, said Hopeful, lest the man with the whip overtakes us again.[203]

You should have taught me that lesson, which I will round you in the ears[204] withal: "Cease, my son, to hear the instruction that causeth to err from the words of knowledge." I say, my brother, cease to hear him, and let us "believe to the saving of the soul."[205]

CHR. My brother, I did not put the question to thee for that I doubted of the truth of our belief myself, but to prove thee, and to fetch from thee a fruit of the honesty of thy heart. As for this man, I know that he is blinded by the god of this world. Let thee and I go on, knowing that we have belief of the truth, and "no lie is of the truth."[206]

HOPE. Now do I rejoice in hope of the glory of God. So they turned away from the man; and he, laughing at them, went his way.

---

203. A remembrance of former chastisements is an help against present temptations. [B].

204. Whisper, or murmur in your ears; take to task privately.

205. Prov. 19:27; Heb. 10:39.

206. John 2:21.

I saw then in my dream that they went till they came into a certain country whose air naturally tended to make one drowsy, if he came a stranger into it. And here Hopeful began to be very dull and heavy of sleep. Wherefore he said unto Christian, I do now begin to grow so drowsy that I can scarcely hold up mine eyes; let us lie down here and take one nap.

CHR. By no means, said the other; lest sleeping, we never awake more.

HOPE. Why, my brother? Sleep is sweet to the labouring man; we may be refreshed if we take a nap.

CHR. Do you not remember that one of the Shepherds bid us beware of the Enchanted Ground? He meant by that, that we should beware of sleeping; wherefore "let us not sleep as do others, but let us watch and be sober."[207]

HOPE. I acknowledge myself in a fault; and had I been here alone, I had by sleeping run the danger of death. I see it is true that the wise man saith, "Two are better than one." Hitherto hath thy company been my mercy, "and thou shalt have a good reward for thy labour."[208]

CHR. Now then, said Christian, to prevent drowsiness in this place, let us fall into good discourse.

HOPE. With all my heart, said the other.

CHR. Where shall we begin?

HOPE. Where God began with us. But do you begin, if you please.[209]

CHR. Then Christian began and said, I will ask you a question. How came you to think at first of so doing as you do now?

HOPE. Do you mean, how came I at first to look after the good of my soul?

CHR. Yes, that is my meaning.

---

207. 1 Thess. 5:6.
208. Eccles. 4:9.
209. When saints do sleepy grow, let them come hither,
And hear how these two pilgrims talk together:
Yea, let them learn of them in any wise
Thus to keep ope their drowsy slumbering eyes.
Saints' fellowship, if it be managed well,
Keeps them awake, and that in spite of hell.
[In the first three editions these verses occur in the body of the text without linkage to the prose; later editions add the clumsy connection: "Chr. I will sing you first this song."]

118]   THE PILGRIM'S PROGRESS

HOPE. I continued a great while in the delight of those things which were seen and sold at our fair; things which, I believe now, would have (had I continued in them still) drowned me in perdition and destruction.

CHR. What things are they?

HOPE. All the treasures and riches of the world. Also I delighted much in rioting, revelling, drinking, swearing, lying, uncleanness, Sabbath-breaking, and what not, that tended to destroy the soul. But I found at last, by hearing and considering of things that are divine, which indeed I heard of you, as also of beloved Faithful, that was put to death for his faith and good living in Vanity Fair, that "the end of these things is death." And that for these things' sake "the wrath of God cometh upon the children of disobedience."[210]

CHR. And did you presently fall under the power of this conviction?

HOPE. No, I was not willing presently to know the evil of sin, nor the damnation that follows upon the commission of it; but endeavoured, when my mind at first began to be shaken with the Word, to shut mine eyes against the light thereof.

CHR. But what was the cause of your carrying of it thus to the first workings of God's blessed Spirit upon you?

HOPE. The causes were, 1. I was ignorant that this was the work of God upon me. I never thought that by awakenings for sin God at first begins the conversion of a sinner. 2. Sin was yet very sweet to my flesh, and I was loath to leave it. 3. I could not tell how to part with mine old companions, their presence and actions were so desirable unto me. 4. The hours in which convictions were upon me were such troublesome and such heart-affrighting hours, that I could not bear, no not so much as the remembrance of them upon my heart.

CHR. Then, as it seems, sometimes you got rid of your trouble.

HOPE. Yes, verily, but it would come into my mind again, and then I should be as bad, nay, worse, than I was before.

CHR. Why, what was it that brought your sins to mind again?

HOPE. Many things, as,

1. If I did but meet a good man in the streets; or,
2. If I have heard any read in the Bible; or,

---

210. Rom. 6:21; Eph. 5:6.

3. If mine head did begin to ache; or,

4. If I were told that some of my neighbours were sick; or,

5. If I heard the bell toll for some that were dead; or,

6. If I thought of dying myself; or,

7. If I heard that sudden death happened to others;

8. But especially, when I thought of myself, that I must quickly come to judgement.

CHR. And could you at any time with ease get off the guilt of sin, when by any of these ways it came upon you?

HOPE. No, not I, for then they got faster hold of my conscience; and then, if I did but think of going back to sin (though my mind was turned against it), it would be double torment to me.

CHR. And how did you do then?

HOPE. I thought I must endeavour to mend my life; for else, thought I, I am sure to be damned.

CHR. And did you endeavour to mend?

HOPE. Yes; and fled from not only my sins, but sinful company too, and betook me to religious duties, as prayer, reading, weeping for sin, speaking truth to my neighbours, &c. These things did I, with many others, too much here to relate.

CHR. And did you think yourself well then?

HOPE. Yes, for a while; but at the last my trouble came tumbling upon me again, and that over the neck of all my reformations.

CHR. How came that about, since you were now reformed?

HOPE. There were several things brought it upon me, especially such sayings as these: "All our righteousnesses are as filthy rags." "By the works of the Law no man shall be justified." "When you have done all things, say, We are unprofitable";[211] with many more such like. From whence I began to reason with myself thus: If *all* my righteousnesses are filthy rags; if by the deeds of the Law *no* man can be justified; and if, when we have done *all,* we are yet unprofitable, then 'tis but a folly to think of heaven by the Law. I further thought thus: If a man runs an hundred pound into the shopkeeper's debt, and after that shall pay for all that he shall fetch, yet his old debt stands still in the book uncrossed; for the which the shopkeeper may sue him, and cast him into prison till he shall pay the debt.

CHR. Well, and how did you apply this to yourself?

---

211. Isa. 64:6; Gal. 2:16; Luke 17:10.

HOPE. Why, I thought thus with myself: I have by my sins run a great way into God's book, and that my now reforming will not pay off that score; therefore I should think still under all my present amendments, But how shall I be freed from that damnation that I have brought myself in danger of by my former transgressions?

CHR. A very good application: but pray, go on.

HOPE. Another thing that hath troubled me, even since my late amendments, is, that if I look narrowly into the best of what I do now, I still see sin, new sin, mixing itself with the best of that I do; so that now I am forced to conclude that notwithstanding my former fond conceits[212] of myself and duties, I have committed sin enough in one duty to send me to hell, though my former life had been faultless.

CHR. And what did you do then?

HOPE. Do! I could not tell what to do, till I brake my mind to Faithful; for he and I were well acquainted. And he told me that unless I could obtain the righteousness of a man that never had sinned, neither mine own, nor all the righteousness of the world could save me.

CHR. And did you think he spake true?

HOPE. Had he told me so when I was pleased and satisfied with mine own amendment, I had called him fool for his pains; but now, since I see mine own infirmity, and the sin that cleaves to my best performance, I have been forced to be of his opinion.

CHR. But did you think, when at first he suggested it to you, that there was such a man to be found, of whom it might justly be said, that he never committed sin?

HOPE. I must confess the words at first sounded strangely, but after a little more talk and company with him, I had full conviction about it.

CHR. And did you ask him what man this was, and how you must be justified by him?

HOPE. Yes, and he told me it was the Lord Jesus, that dwelleth on the right hand of the Most High. And thus, said he, you must be justified by him, even by trusting to what he hath done by himself in the days of his flesh, and suffered when he did hang on the tree. I asked him further, how that man's righteousness could be of that

212. Foolish favorable opinions.

efficacy to justify another before God? And he told me he was the mighty God, and did what he did, and died the death also, not for himself, but for me; to whom his doings and the worthiness of them should be imputed, if I believed on him.

CHR. And what did you do then?

HOPE. I made my objections against my believing, for that I thought he was not willing to save me.

CHR. And what said Faithful to you then?

HOPE. He bid me go to him and see. Then I said it was presumption; but he said, No, for I was invited to come. Then he gave me a book of Jesus his inditing, to encourage me the more freely to come; and he said concerning that book, that every jot and tittle thereof stood firmer than heaven and earth. Then I asked him what I must do when I came; and he told me, I must entreat upon my knees with all my heart and soul, the Father to reveal him to me. Then I asked him further, how I must make my supplication to him. And he said, Go, and thou shalt find him upon a mercy-seat, where he sits all the year long, to give pardon and forgiveness to them that come. I told him that I knew not what to say when I came. And he bid me say to this effect: God be merciful to me a sinner, and make me to know and believe in Jesus Christ; for I see that if his righteousness had not been, or I have not faith in that righteousness, I am utterly cast away. Lord, I have heard that thou art a merciful God, and hast ordained that thy Son Jesus Christ should be the Saviour of the world, and moreover, that thou art willing to bestow him upon such a poor sinner as I am (and I am a sinner indeed); Lord, take therefore this opportunity, and magnify thy grace in the salvation of my soul, through thy Son Jesus Christ. Amen.

CHR. And did you do as you were bidden?

HOPE. Yes, over, and over, and over.

CHR. And did the Father reveal his Son to you?

HOPE. Not at the first, nor second, nor third, nor fourth, nor fifth; no, nor at the sixth time neither.

CHR. What did you do then?

HOPE. What! why I could not tell what to do.

CHR. Had you not thoughts of leaving off praying?

HOPE. Yes; an hundred times twice told.

CHR. And what was the reason you did not?

HOPE. I believed that that was true which had been told me, to wit, that without the righteousness of this Christ, all the world could not save me; and therefore, thought I with myself, if I leave off I die, and I can but die at the throne of grace. And withal, this came into my mind, "If it tarry, wait for it, because it will surely come, and will not tarry."[213] So I continued praying until the Father showed me his Son.

CHR. And how was he revealed unto you?

HOPE. I did not see him with my bodily eyes, but with the eyes of my understanding; and thus it was. One day I was very sad, I think sadder than at any one time in my life, and this sadness was through a fresh sight of the greatness and vileness of my sins. And as I was then looking for nothing but hell, and the everlasting damnation of my soul, suddenly, as I thought, I saw the Lord Jesus Christ look down from heaven upon me, and saying, "Believe on the Lord Jesus Christ, and thou shalt be saved."[214]

But I replied, Lord, I am a great, a very great sinner. And he answered, "My grace is sufficient for thee."[215] Then I said, But Lord, what is believing? And then I saw from that saying, "He that cometh to me shall never hunger, and he that believeth on me shall never thirst,"[216] that believing and coming was all one; and that he that came, that is, ran out in his heart and affections after salvation by Christ, he indeed believed in Christ. Then the water stood in mine eyes, and I asked further, But Lord, may such a great sinner as I am be indeed accepted of thee, and be saved by thee? And I heard him say, "And him that cometh to me, I will in no wise cast out."[217] Then I said, But how, Lord, must I consider of thee in my coming to thee, that my faith may be placed aright upon thee? Then he said, "Christ Jesus came into the world to save sinners." "He is the end of the law for righteousness to every one that believes." "He died for our sins, and rose again for our justification." "He loved us, and washed us from our sins in his own blood." "He is mediator between God and us." "He ever liveth to make intercession for us."[218] From all which I gathered that I must look for righteousness in his person, and for satisfaction for my sins by his blood; that what he did in obedience to his Father's law, and in sub-

---

213. Hab. 2:3.
214. Acts 16:31.
215. 2 Cor. 12:9.
216. John 6:35.
217. John 6:37.
218. 1 Tim. 1:15; Rom. 10:4; 4:25; Rev. 1:5; 1 Tim. 2:5; Heb. 7:25.

mitting to the penalty thereof, was not for himself, but for him that will accept it for his salvation, and be thankful. And now was my heart full of joy, mine eyes full of tears, and mine affections running over with love to the name, people, and ways of Jesus Christ.

CHR. This was a revelation of Christ to your soul indeed; but tell me particularly what effect this had upon your spirit.

HOPE. It made me see that all the world, notwithstanding all the righteousness thereof, is in a state of condemnation. It made me see that God the Father, though he be just, can justly justify the coming sinner. It made me greatly ashamed of the vileness of my former life, and confounded me with the sense of mine own ignorance; for there never came thought into my heart before now that showed me so the beauty of Jesus Christ. It made me love a holy life, and long to do something for the honour and glory of the name of the Lord Jesus; yea, I thought that had I now a thousand gallons of blood in my body, I could spill it all for the sake of the Lord Jesus.

I saw then in my dream that Hopeful looked back and saw Ignorance, whom they had left behind, coming after. Look, said he to Christian, how far yonder youngster loitereth behind.

CHR. Ay, ay, I see him; he careth not for our company.

HOPE. But I trow, it would not have hurt him, had he kept pace with us hitherto.

CHR. That's true, but I warrant you he thinketh otherwise.

HOPE. That, I think, he doth; but however, let us tarry for him. So they did.

Then Christian said to him, Come away, man, why do you stay so behind?

IGNOR. I take my pleasure in walking alone, even more a great deal than in company, unless I like it the better.

Then said Christian to Hopeful (but softly), Did I not tell you he cared not for our company? But however, said he, come up, and let us talk away the time in this solitary place. Then directing his speech to Ignorance, he said, Come, how do you? How stands it between God and your soul now?

IGNOR. I hope well; for I am always full of good motions, that come into my mind to comfort me as I walk.

CHR. What good motions? pray, tell us.

IGNOR. Why, I think of God and heaven.

CHR. So do the devils and damned souls.

IGNOR. But I think of them and desire them.

CHR. So do many that are never like to come there. "The soul of the sluggard desires, and hath nothing."[219]

IGNOR. But I think of them, and leave all for them.

CHR. That I doubt, for leaving all is a hard matter; yea, a harder matter than many are aware of. But why, or by what, art thou persuaded that thou hast left all for God and heaven?

IGNOR. My heart tells me so.

CHR. The wise man says, "He that trusts his own heart is a fool."[220]

IGNOR. This is spoken of an evil heart, but mine is a good one.

CHR. But how dost thou prove that?

IGNOR. It comforts me in hopes of heaven.

CHR. That may be through its deceitfulness; for a man's heart may minister comfort to him in the hopes of that thing for which he yet has no ground to hope.

IGNOR. But my heart and life agree together, and therefore my hope is well grounded.

CHR. Who told thee that thy heart and life agree together?

IGNOR. My heart tells me so.

CHR. Ask my fellow if I be a thief! Thy heart tells thee so! Except the Word of God beareth witness in this matter, other testimony is of no value.

IGNOR. But is it not a good heart that hath good thoughts? and is not that a good life that is according to God's commandments?

CHR. Yes, that is a good heart that hath good thoughts, and that is a good life that is according to God's commandments; but it is one thing indeed to have these, and another thing only to think so.

IGNOR. Pray, what count you good thoughts, and a life according to God's commandments?

CHR. There are good thoughts of diverse kinds; some respecting ourselves, some God, some Christ, and some other things.

IGNOR. What be good thoughts respecting ourselves?

CHR. Such as agree with the Word of God.

IGNOR. When do our thoughts of ourselves agree with the Word of God?

CHR. When we pass the same judgement upon ourselves which the Word passes. To explain myself: the Word of God saith of persons in a natural condition, "There is none righteous, there is none

---

219. Prov. 13:4.
220. Prov. 28:26.

that doth good." It saith also, that "every imagination of the heart of man is only evil, and that continually." And again, "The imagination of man's heart is evil from his youth."[221] Now then, when we think thus of ourselves, having sense[222] thereof, then are our thoughts good ones, because according to the Word of God.

IGNOR. I will never believe that my heart is thus bad.

CHR. Therefore thou never hadst one good thought concerning thyself in thy life. But let me go on. As the Word passeth a judgement upon our heart, so it passeth a judgement upon our ways; and when our thoughts of our hearts and ways agree with the judgement which the Word giveth of both, then are both good, because agreeing thereto.

IGNOR. Make out your meaning.

CHR. Why, the Word of God saith that man's ways are crooked ways, not good, but perverse. It saith they are naturally out of the good way, that they have not known it. Now when a man thus thinketh of his ways, I say when he doth sensibly[223] and with heart-humiliation thus think, then hath he good thoughts of his own ways, because his thoughts now agree with the judgement of the Word of God.

IGNOR. What are good thoughts concerning God?

CHR. Even (as I have said concerning ourselves) when our thoughts of God do agree with what the Word saith of him. And that is, when we think of his being and attributes as the Word hath taught; of which I cannot now discourse at large. But to speak of him with reference to us: Then we have right thoughts of God, when we think that he knows us better than we know ourselves, and can see sin in us when and where we can see none in ourselves; when we think he knows our inmost thoughts, and that our heart, with all its depths, is always open unto his eyes; also when we think that all our righteousness stinks in his nostrils, and that therefore he cannot abide to see us stand before him in any confidence, even of all our best performances.

IGNOR. Do you think that I am such a fool as to think God can see no further than I? or that I would come to God in the best of my performances?

---

221. Rom. 3:10, 12; Gen. 6:5; 8:21.
222. Emotional awareness.
223. With strong feeling.

CHR. Why, how dost thou think in this matter?

IGNOR. Why, to be short, I think I must believe in Christ for justification.

CHR. How! think thou must believe in Christ, when thou seest not thy need of him! Thou neither seest thy original nor actual[224] infirmities, but hast such an opinion of thyself, and of what thou dost, as plainly renders thee to be one that did never see a necessity of Christ's personal righteousness to justify thee before God. How then dost thou say, I believe in Christ?

IGNOR. I believe well enough for all that.

CHR. How dost thou believe?

IGNOR. I believe that Christ died for sinners, and that I shall be justified before God from the curse, through his gracious acceptance of my obedience to his Law. Or thus, Christ makes my duties that are religious acceptable to his Father by virtue of his merits; and so shall I be justified.

CHR. Let me give an answer to this confession of thy faith.

1. Thou believest with a fantastical faith, for this faith is nowhere described in the Word.

2. Thou believest with a false faith, because it taketh justification from the personal righteousness of Christ, and applies it to thy own.

3. This faith maketh not Christ a justifier of thy person, but of thy actions; and of thy person for thy actions' sake, which is false.

4. Therefore this faith is deceitful, even such as will leave thee under wrath in the day of God Almighty. For true justifying faith puts the soul (as sensible of its lost condition by the Law) upon flying for refuge unto Christ's righteousness; which righteousness of his is, not an act of grace by which he maketh for justification thy obedience accepted with God, but his personal obedience to the Law in doing and suffering for us what that required at our hands. This righteousness, I say, true faith accepteth; under the skirt of which the soul being shrouded, and by it presented as spotless before God, it is accepted, and acquit from condemnation.

IGNOR. What! would you have us trust to what Christ in his own person has done without us? This conceit would loosen the reins of our lust, and tolerate us to live as we list. For what matter how we live, if we may be justified by Christ's personal righteousness from all, when we believe it?

---

224. Pertaining to acts; shown in acts.

CHR. Ignorance is thy name, and as thy name is, so art thou; even this thy answer demonstrateth what I say. Ignorant thou art of what justifying righteousness is, and as ignorant how to secure thy soul through the faith of it from the heavy wrath of God. Yea, thou also art ignorant of the true effects of saving faith, in this righteousness of Christ, which is to bow and win over the heart of God in Christ, to love his name, his word, ways, and people, and not as thou ignorantly imaginest.

HOPE. Ask him if ever he had Christ revealed to him from heaven.

IGNOR. What! you are a man for revelations! I believe that what both you and all the rest of you say about that matter is but the fruit of distracted brains.[225]

HOPE. Why, man! Christ is so hid in God from the natural apprehensions of the flesh, that he cannot by any man be savingly known, unless God the Father reveals him to them.

IGNOR. That is your faith, but not mine; yet mine, I doubt not, is as good as yours, though I have not in my head so many whimsies as you.[226]

CHR. Give me leave to put in a word. You ought not so slightly to speak of this matter; for this I will boldly affirm (even as my good companion hath done), that no man can know Jesus Christ but by the revelation of the Father. Yea, and faith too, by which the soul layeth hold upon Christ (if it be right), must be wrought by the exceeding greatness of his mighty power; the working of which faith, I perceive, poor Ignorance, thou art ignorant of. Be awakened then, see thine own wretchedness, and fly to the Lord Jesus; and by his righteousness, which is the righteousness of God (for he himself is God), thou shalt be delivered from condemnation.

IGNOR. You go so fast, I cannot keep pace with you. Do you go on before; I must stay a while behind.

Then they said,

> Well, Ignorance, wilt thou yet foolish be,
> To slight good counsel, ten times given thee?
> And if thou yet refuse it, thou shalt know
> Ere long the evil of thy doing so.

---

225. Ignorance jangles with them. [B]
226. He speaks reproachfully of what he knows not. [B]

Remember, man, in time; stoop, do not fear,
Good counsel taken well, saves: therefore hear.
But if thou yet shalt slight it, thou wilt be
The loser (Ignorance), I'll warrant thee.

Then Christian addressed thus himself to his fellow:

CHR. Well, come, my good Hopeful, I perceive that thou and I must walk by ourselves again.

So I saw in my dream that they went on apace before, and Ignorance he came hobbling after. Then said Christian to his companion, It pities me much for this poor man, it will certainly go ill with him at last.

HOPE. Alas, there are abundance in our town in his condition; whole families, yea, whole streets (and that of pilgrims too), and if there be so many in our parts, how many, think you, must there be in the place where he was born?

CHR. Indeed the Word saith, "He hath blinded their eyes, lest they should see," &c.[227] But now we are by ourselves, what do you think of such men? Have they at no time, think you, convictions of sin, and so consequently fears that their state is dangerous?

HOPE. Nay, do you answer that question yourself, for you are the elder man.

CHR. Then I say, sometimes (as I think) they may; but they being naturally ignorant, understand not that such convictions tend to their good, and therefore they do desperately seek to stifle them, and presumptuously continue to flatter themselves in the way of their own hearts.

HOPE. I do believe, as you say, that fear tends much to men's good, and to make them right, at their beginning to go on pilgrimage.

CHR. Without all doubt it doth, if it be right; for so says the Word, "The fear of the Lord is the beginning of wisdom."[228]

HOPE. How will you describe right fear?

CHR. True or right fear is discovered by three things:

1. By its rise; it is caused by saving convictions for sin.
2. It driveth the soul to lay fast hold of Christ for salvation.
3. It begetteth and continueth in the soul a great reverence of God, his Word, and ways, keeping it tender, and making it afraid

227. John 12:40.
228. Prov. 9:10.

to turn from them, to the right hand or to the left, to anything that may dishonour God, break its peace, grieve the Spirit, or cause the enemy to speak reproachfully.

HOPE. Well said; I believe you have said the truth. Are we now almost got past the Enchanted Ground?

CHR. Why, art thou weary of this discourse?

HOPE. No, verily, but that I would know where we are.

CHR. We have not now above two miles further to go thereon. But let us return to our matter. Now the ignorant know not that such convictions as tend to put them in fear are for their good, and therefore they seek to stifle them.

HOPE. How do they seek to stifle them?

CHR. 1. They think that those fears are wrought by the Devil (though indeed they are wrought of God); and thinking so, they resist them as things that directly tend to their overthrow. 2. They also think that these fears tend to the spoiling of their faith (when, alas for them, poor men that they are! they have none at all), and therefore they harden their hearts against them. 3. They presume they ought not to fear, and therefore, in despite of them, wax presumptuously confident. 4. They see that those fears tend to take away from them their pitiful old self-holiness, and therefore they resist them with all their might.

HOPE. I know something of this myself; for before I knew myself it was so with me.

CHR. Well, we will leave at this time our neighbour Ignorance by himself, and fall upon another profitable question.

HOPE. With all my heart, but you shall still begin.

CHR. Well then, did you not know, about ten years ago, one Temporary in your parts, who was a forward man in religion then?

HOPE. Know him! yes, he dwelt in Graceless, a town about two miles off of Honesty, and he dwelt next door to one Turnback.

CHR. Right, he dwelt under the same roof with him. Well, that man was much awakened once; I believe that then he had some sight of his sins, and of the wages that was due thereto.

HOPE. I am of your mind, for, my house not being above three miles from him, he would ofttimes come to me, and that with many tears. Truly I pitied the man, and was not altogether without hope of him; but one may see, it is not every one that cries, Lord, Lord.

CHR. He told me once that he was resolved to go on pilgrimage, as we do now; but all of a sudden he grew acquainted with one Save-self, and then he became a stranger to me.

HOPE. Now since we are talking about him, let us a little inquire into the reason of the sudden backsliding of him and such others.

CHR. It may be very profitable, but do you begin.

HOPE. Well then, there are in my judgement four reasons for it:

1. Though the consciences of such men are awakened, yet their minds are not changed; therefore when the power of guilt weareth away, that which provoked them to be religious ceaseth. Wherefore they naturally turn to their own course again, even as we see the dog that is sick of what he has eaten, so long as his sickness prevails, he vomits and casts up all; not that he doth this of a free mind (if we may say a dog has a mind), but because it troubleth his stomach. But now when his sickness is over, and so his stomach eased, his desires being not at all alienate from his vomit, he turns him about and licks up all. And so it is true which is written, "The dog is turned to his own vomit again."[229] Thus I say, being hot for heaven, by virtue only of the sense and fear of the torments of hell, as their sense of hell and the fears of damnation chills and cools, so their desires for heaven and salvation cool also. So then it comes to pass that when their guilt and fear is gone, their desires for heaven and happiness die, and they return to their course again.

2. Another reason is, they have slavish fears that do overmaster them. I speak now of the fears that they have of men, for "the fear of men bringeth a snare."[230] So then, though they seem to be hot for heaven, so long as the flames of hell are about their ears, yet when that terror is a little over, they betake themselves to second thoughts; namely, that 'tis good to be wise, and not to run (for they know not what) the hazard of losing all, or at least, of bringing themselves into unavoidable and unnecessary troubles, and so they fall in with the world again.

3. The shame that attends religion lies also as a block in their way; they are proud and haughty, and religion in their eye is low and contemptible. Therefore, when they have lost their sense of hell and wrath to come, they return again to their former course.

4. Guilt, and to meditate terror, are grievous to them. They like not to see their misery before they come into it; though perhaps the

---

229. 2 Pet. 2:22.
230. Prov. 29:25.

sight of it first, if they loved that sight, might make them fly whither the righteous fly and are safe. But because they do, as I hinted before, even shun the thoughts of guilt and terror, therefore when once they are rid of their awakenings about the terrors and wrath of God, they harden their hearts gladly, and choose such ways as will harden them more and more.

CHR. You are pretty near the business, for the bottom of all is, for want of a change in their mind and will. And therefore they are but like the felon that standeth before the judge; he quakes and trembles, and seems to repent most heartily, but the bottom of all is the fear of the halter, not that he hath any detestation of the offence, as is evident because, let but this man have his liberty, and he will be a thief, and so a rogue still, whereas if his mind was changed, he would be otherwise.

HOPE. Now I have showed you the reasons of their going back, do you show me the manner thereof.

CHR. So I will willingly.

1. They draw off their thoughts, all that they may, from the remembrance of God, death, and judgement to come.

2. Then they cast off by degrees private duties, as closet-prayer,[231] curbing their lusts, watching, sorrow for sin, and the like.

3. Then they shun the company of lively and warm Christians.

4. After that they grow cold to public duty, as hearing, reading, godly conference, and the like.

5. Then they begin to pick holes, as we say, in the coats of some of the godly; and that devilishly, that they may have a seeming colour to throw religion (for the sake of some infirmity they have spied in them) behind their backs.

6. Then they begin to adhere to and associate themselves with carnal, loose, and wanton men.

7. Then they give way to carnal and wanton discourses in secret; and glad are they if they can see such things in any that are counted honest, that they may the more boldly do it through their example.

8. After this they begin to play with little sins openly.

9. And then, being hardened, they show themselves as they are. Thus, being launched again into the gulf of misery, unless a miracle of grace prevent it, they everlastingly perish in their own deceivings.

---

231. Prayer in one's private room.

Now I saw in my dream that by this time the pilgrims were got over the Enchanted Ground, and entering into the country of Beulah, whose air was very sweet and pleasant; the way lying directly through it, they solaced themselves there for a season. Yea, here they heard continually the singing of birds, and saw every day the flowers appear in the earth, and heard the voice of the turtle in the land.[232] In this country the sun shineth night and day; wherefore this was beyond the Valley of the Shadow of Death, and also out of the reach of Giant Despair, neither could they from this place so much as see Doubting Castle. Here they were within sight of the city they were going to; also here met them some of the inhabitants thereof. For in this land the Shining Ones commonly walked, because it was upon the borders of heaven. In this land also the contract between the bride and the bridegroom was renewed; yea, here, "As the bridegroom rejoiceth over the bride, so did their God rejoice over them." Here they had no want of corn and wine; for in this place they met with abundance of what they had sought for in all their pilgrimage. Here they heard voices from out of the city, loud voices, saying, "Say ye to the daughter of Zion, Behold, thy salvation cometh; behold, his reward is with him." Here all the inhabitants of the country called them "the holy people, the redeemed of the Lord, sought out," &c.[233]

Now, as they walked in this land, they had more rejoicing than in parts more remote from the kingdom to which they were bound; and drawing near to the city, they had yet a more perfect view thereof. It was builded of pearls and precious stones, also the street thereof was paved with gold, so that by reason of the natural glory of the city, and the reflection of the sunbeams upon it, Christian with desire fell sick; Hopeful also had a fit or two of the same disease. Wherefore here they lay by it a while, crying out because of their pangs, "If you see my beloved, tell him that I am sick of love."[234]

But being a little strengthened, and better able to bear their sickness, they walked on their way, and came yet nearer and nearer, where were orchards, vineyards, and gardens, and their gates opened into the highway. Now, as they came up to these places, behold the gardener stood in the way, to whom the pilgrims said, Whose goodly vineyards and gardens are these? He answered,

---

232. Isa. 62:4; Song of Sol. 2:12 (turtle: turtle-dove).
233. Isa. 62:5–12.
234. Song of Sol. 5:8.

They are the King's, and are planted here for his own delight, and also for the solace of pilgrims. So the gardener had them into the vineyards, and bid them refresh themselves with the dainties. He also showed them there the King's walks, and the arbours where he delighted to be; and here they tarried and slept.

Now I beheld in my dream that they talked more in their sleep at this time than ever they did in all their journey; and being in a muse thereabout, the gardener said even to me, Wherefore musest thou at the matter? It is the nature of the fruit of the grapes of these vineyards to go down so sweetly as to cause "the lips of them that are asleep to speak."[235]

So I saw that when they awoke, they addressed themselves to go up to the city. But, as I said, the reflections of the sun upon the city (for "the city was pure gold")[236] was so extremely glorious, that they could not as yet with open face behold it, but through an instrument made for that purpose.[237] So I saw that as they went on, there met them two men in raiment that shone like gold; also their faces shone as the light.

These men asked the pilgrims whence they came; and they told them. They also asked them where they had lodged, what difficulties and dangers, what comforts and pleasures they had met in the way; and they told them. Then said the men that met them, You have but two difficulties more to meet with, and then you are in the city.

Christian then and his companion asked the men to go along with them; so they told them they would. But, said they, you must obtain it by your own faith. So I saw in my dream that they went on together till they came in sight of the gate.

Now I further saw that betwixt them and the gate was a river,[238] but there was no bridge to go over; the river was very deep. At the sight therefore of this river, the pilgrims were much stunned; but the men that went with them said, You must go through, or you cannot come at the gate.

The pilgrims then began to inquire if there was no other way to the gate;[239] to which they answered, Yes, but there hath not any,

---

235. Song of Sol. 7:9.
236. Rev. 21:18.
237. 2 Cor. 3:18; 1 Cor. 13:12.
238. Death. [B]
239. Death is not welcome to nature, though by it we pass out of this world into glory. [B]

save two, to wit, Enoch and Elijah, been permitted to tread that path, since the foundation of the world, nor shall, until the last trumpet shall sound. The pilgrims then, especially Christian, began to despond in their minds, and looked this way and that, but no way could be found by them, by which they might escape the river. Then they asked the men if the waters were all of a depth. They said, No; yet they could not help them in that case, for, said they, you shall find it deeper or shallower, as you believe in the King of the place.[240]

They then addressed themselves to the water, and entering, Christian began to sink, and crying out to his good friend Hopeful, he said, I sink in deep waters; the billows go over my head, all his waves go over me![241] Selah.

Then said the other, Be of good cheer, my brother, I feel the bottom, and it is good. Then said Christian, Ah! my friend, the sorrows of death have compassed me about; I shall not see the land that flows with milk and honey, and with that a great darkness and horror fell upon Christian, so that he could not see before him. Also here he in great measure lost his senses, so that he could neither remember, nor orderly talk of any of those sweet refreshments that he had met with in the way of his pilgrimage. But all the words that he spake still tended to discover that he had horror of mind and heart-fears that he should die in that river, and never obtain entrance in at the gate. Here also, as they that stood perceived, he was much in the troublesome thoughts of the sins that he had committed, both since and before he began to be a pilgrim. It was also observed that he was troubled with apparitions of hobgoblins and evil spirits, for ever and anon he would intimate so much by words. Hopeful therefore here had much ado to keep his brother's head above water; yea, sometimes he would be quite gone down, and then ere a while he would rise up again half dead. Hopeful also would endeavour to comfort him, saying, Brother, I see the gate, and men standing by to receive us, but Christian would answer, 'Tis you, 'tis you they wait for; you have been hopeful ever since I knew you. And so have you, said he to Christian. Ah, brother, said he, surely if I was right he would now arise to help me; but for my sins he hath brought me into the snare and hath left me. Then said Hopeful, My brother,

---

240. Angels help us not comfortably through death. [B]
241. Jon. 2:3–6.

you have quite forgot the text where it is said of the wicked, "There is no band[242] in their death, but their strength is firm. They are not troubled as other men, neither are they plagued like other men."[243] These troubles and distresses that you go through in these waters are no sign that God hath forsaken you, but are sent to try you, whether you will call to mind that which heretofore you have received of his goodness, and live upon him in your distresses.

Then I saw in my dream that Christian was as in a muse a while. To whom also Hopeful added this word, Be of good cheer; Jesus Christ maketh thee whole. And with that Christian brake out with a loud voice, Oh! I see him again, and he tells me, "When thou passest through the waters, I will be with thee; and through the rivers, they shall not overflow thee."[244] Then they both took courage, and the enemy was after that as still as a stone, until they were gone over. Christian therefore presently found ground to stand upon, and so it followed that the rest of the river was but shallow. Thus they got over. Now upon the bank of the river on the other side, they saw two shining men again, who there waited for them; wherefore, being come out of the river, they saluted them saying, "We are ministering spirits, sent forth to minister for those that shall be heirs of salvation."[245] Thus they went along towards the gate. Now you must note that the city stood upon a mighty hill, but the pilgrims went up that hill with ease, because they had these two men to lead them up by the arms; also they had left their mortal garments behind them in the river, for though they went in with them, they came out without them. They therefore went up here with much agility and speed, though the foundation upon which the city was framed was higher than the clouds. They therefore went up through the regions of the air, sweetly talking as they went, being comforted, because they safely got over the river, and had such glorious companions to attend them.

The talk they had with the Shining Ones was about the glory of the place, who told them that the beauty and glory of it was inexpressible. There, said they, is the Mount Zion, the heavenly Jerusalem, the innumerable company of angels, and the spirits of just

242. Shackle, bond, restraint (implying, apparently, torment).
243. Ps. 73:4, 5.
244. Isa. 43:2.
245. Heb. 1:14.

men made perfect. You are going now, said they, to the paradise of God, wherein you shall see the tree of life, and eat of the never-fading fruits thereof; and when you come there, you shall have white robes given you, and your walk and talk shall be every day with the King, even all the days of eternity.[246] There you shall not see again such things as you saw when you were in the lower region upon the earth, to wit, sorrow, sickness, affliction, and death, "for the former things are passed away."[247] You are now going to Abraham, to Isaac, and Jacob, and to the prophets; men that God hath taken away from the evil to come, and that are now resting upon their beds, each one walking in his righteousness. The men then asked, What must we do in the holy place? To whom it was answered, You must there receive the comforts of all your toil, and have joy for all your sorrow; you must reap what you have sown, even the fruit of all your prayers, and tears, and sufferings for the King by the way. In that place you must wear crowns of gold, and enjoy the perpetual sight and vision of the Holy One, "for there you shall see him as he is."[248] There also you shall serve him continually with praise, with shouting, and thanksgiving, whom you desired to serve in the world, though with much difficulty, because of the infirmity of your flesh. There your eyes shall be delighted with seeing, and your ears with hearing the pleasant voice of the Mighty One. There you shall enjoy your friends again that are gone thither before you; and there you shall with joy receive even every one that follows into the holy place after you. There also shall you be clothed with glory and majesty, and put into an equipage fit to ride out with the King of glory. When he shall come with sound of trumpet in the clouds, as upon the wings of the wind, you shall come with him; and when he shall sit upon the throne of judgement, you shall sit by him; yea, and when he shall pass sentence upon all the workers of iniquity, let them be angels or men, you also shall have a voice in that judgement, because they were his and your enemies. Also when he shall again return to the city, you shall go too, with sound of trumpet, and be ever with him.

Now while they were thus drawing towards the gate, behold a company of the heavenly host came out to meet them; to whom it was said, by the other two Shining Ones, These are the men that

---

246. Heb. 12:22–24; Rev. 2:7; 3:4, 5.
247. Rev. 21:4.
248. 1 John 3:2.

have loved our Lord when they were in the world, and that have left all for his holy name; and he hath sent us to fetch them, and we have brought them thus far on their desired journey, that they may go in and look their Redeemer in the face with joy. Then the heavenly host gave a great shout, saying, "Blessed are they that are called to the marriage supper of the Lamb."[249] There came out also at this time to meet them several of the King's trumpeters, clothed in white and shining raiment, who with melodious noises and loud, made even the heavens to echo with their sound. These trumpeters saluted Christian and his fellow with ten thousand welcomes from the world; and this they did with shouting and sound of trumpet.

This done, they compassed them round on every side; some went before, some behind, and some on the right hand, some on the left (as 'twere to guard them through the upper regions), continually sounding as they went, with melodious noise, in notes on high, so that the very sight was, to them that could behold it, as if heaven itself was come down to meet them. Thus therefore they walked on together; and as they walked, ever and anon these trumpeters, even with joyful sound, would, by mixing their music with looks and gestures, still signify to Christian and his brother how welcome they were into their company, and with what gladness they came to meet them. And now were these two men, as 'twere, in heaven before they came at it, being swallowed up with the sight of angels, and with hearing of their melodious notes. Here also they had the city itself in view, and they thought they heard all the bells therein to ring, to welcome them thereto. But above all, the warm and joyful thoughts that they had about their own dwelling there, with such company, and that for ever and ever. Oh, by what tongue or pen can their glorious joy be expressed! And thus they came up to the gate.

Now when they were come up to the gate, there was written over it in letters of gold, "Blessed are they that do his commandments, that they may have right to the tree of life, and may enter in through the gates into the city."[250]

Then I saw in my dream that the Shining Men bid them call at the gate, the which when they did, some looked from above over the gate, to wit, Enoch, Moses, and Elijah, &c., to whom it was said, These pilgrims are come from the City of Destruction for the love

---

249. Rev. 19:9.
250. Rev. 22:14.

that they bear to the King of this place. And then the pilgrims gave in unto them each man his certificate, which they had received in the beginning; those therefore were carried in to the King, who, when he had read them, said, Where are the men? To whom it was answered, They are standing without the gate. The King then commanded to open the gate, "That the righteous nation," said he, "that keepeth truth, may enter in."[251]

Now I saw in my dream that these two men went in at the gate: and lo, as they entered, they were transfigured, and they had raiment put on that shone like gold. There was also that met them with harps and crowns, and gave them to them; the harps to praise withal, and the crowns in token of honour. Then I heard in my dream that all the bells in the city rang again for joy, and that it was said unto them, "Enter ye into the joy of our Lord." I also heard the men themselves, that they sang with a loud voice, saying, "Blessing, honour, glory, and power, be to him that sitteth upon the throne, and to the Lamb, for ever and ever."[252]

Now just as the gates were opened to let in the men, I looked in after them, and behold, the city shone like the sun; the streets also were paved with gold, and in them walked many men, with crowns on their heads, palms in their hands, and golden harps to sing praises withal.

There were also of them that had wings, and they answered one another without intermission, saying, "Holy, holy, holy is the Lord."[253] And after that, they shut up the gates; which when I had seen, I wished myself among them.

Now while I was gazing upon all these things, I turned my head to look back, and saw Ignorance come up to the riverside; but he soon got over, and that without half that difficulty which the other two men met with. For it happened that there was then in that place one Vain-hope, a ferryman, that with his boat helped him over, so he, as the other I saw, did ascend the hill to come up to the gate, only he came alone; neither did any man meet him with the least encouragement. When he was come up to the gate, he looked up to the writing that was above, and then began to knock, supposing that entrance should have been quickly administered to him; but he was

251. Isa. 26:2.
252. Matt. 25:21; Rev. 5:13.
253. Rev. 4:8.

asked by the men that looked over the top of the gate, Whence came you? and what would you have? He answered, I have eat and drank in the presence of the King, and he has taught in our streets. Then they asked him for his certificate, that they might go in and show it to the King; so he fumbled in his bosom for one, and found none. Then said they, Have you none? But the man answered never a word. So they told the King, but he would not come down to see him, but commanded the two Shining Ones that conducted Christian and Hopeful to the City, to go out and take Ignorance, and bind him hand and foot, and have him away. Then they took him up, and carried him through the air to the door that I saw in the side of the hill, and put him in there. Then I saw that there was a way to hell, even from the gates of heaven, as well as from the City of Destruction. So I awoke, and behold it was a dream.

THE CONCLUSION

Now, Reader, I have told my dream to thee;
See if thou canst interpret it to me,
Or to thyself, or neighbour; but take heed
Of misinterpreting; for that, instead
Of doing good, will but thyself abuse:
By misinterpreting evil ensues.

Take heed also that thou be not extreme,
In playing with the outside of my dream:
Nor let my figure or similitude
Put thee into a laughter or a feud.
Leave this for boys and fools; but as for thee,
Do thou the substance of my matter see.

Put by the curtains, look within my veil,
Turn up my metaphors, and do not fail,
There, if thou seekest them, such things to find,
As will be helpful to an honest mind.

What of my dross thou findest there, be bold
To throw away, but yet preserve the gold;
What if my gold be wrapped up in ore?
None throws away the apple for the core.
But if thou shalt cast all away as vain,
I know not but 'twill make me dream again.

END OF THE FIRST PART

The Pilgrim's Progress
Part II

THE

PILGRIM'S PROGRESS

FROM THIS WORLD TO THAT WHICH

IS TO COME

THE SECOND PART

———

DELIVERED

UNDER THE SIMILITUDE OF A DREAM

WHEREIN IS SET FORTH

THE MANNER OF THE SETTING OUT OF

CHRISTIAN'S WIFE AND CHILDREN,

THEIR DANGEROUS JOURNEY,

AND SAFE ARRIVAL AT THE

DESIRED COUNTRY

———

BY JOHN BUNYAN

"I have used similitudes." —HOS. 12:10

The Author's Way
of Sending Forth His
Second Part of the Pilgrim

Go now, my little book, to every place
Where my first Pilgrim has but shown his face,
Call at their door. If any say, Who's there?
Then answer thou, Christiana is here.
If they bid thee come in, then enter thou,
With all thy boys; and then, as thou know'st how,
Tell who they are, also from whence they came;
Perhaps they know them by their looks or name.
But if they should not, ask them yet again
If formerly they did not entertain
One Christian, a Pilgrim? If they say
They did; and was delighted in his way:
Then let them know that those related were
Unto him; yea, his wife and children are.
   Tell them that they have left their house and home,
Are turnèd Pilgrims, seek a world to come;
That they have met with hardships in the way,
That they do meet with troubles night and day,
That they have trod on serpents, fought with devils,
Have also overcome a many evils.
Yea, tell them also of the next, who have
Of love to pilgrimage been stout and brave
Defenders of that way, and how they still
Refuse this world, to do their Father's will.
   Go, tell them also of those dainty things
That pilgrimage unto the Pilgrim brings.
Let them acquainted be, too, how they are
Beloved of their King, under his care:
What goodly mansions for them he provides,
Though they meet with rough winds and swelling tides.
How brave a calm they will enjoy at last,
Who to their Lord and by his ways hold fast.
   Perhaps with heart and hand they will embrace
Thee, as they did my firstling, and will grace

Thee and thy fellows with such cheer and fare,
As show will, they of Pilgrims lovers are.

OBJECTION I

But how if they will not believe of me
That I am truly thine; 'cause some there be
That counterfeit the Pilgrim and his name,
Seek by disguise to seem the very same;
And by that means have wrought themselves into
The hands and houses of I know not who?

ANSWER

'Tis true, some have of late, to counterfeit
My Pilgrim, to their own my title set;
Yea others, half my name and title too
Have stitched to their book, to make them do;
But yet they by their features do declare
Themselves not mine to be, whose e'er they are.
If such thou meet'st with, then thine only way
Before them all, is, to say out thy say,
In thine own native language, which no man
Now useth, nor with ease dissemble can.
If, after all, they still of you shall doubt,
Thinking that you like gipsies go about,
In naughty wise the country to defile,
Or that you seek good people to beguile
With things unwarrantable; send for me,
And I will testify you Pilgrims be.
Yea, I will testify that only you
My Pilgrims are; and that alone will do.

OBJECTION II

But yet, perhaps, I may inquire for him
Of those that wish him damned, life and limb.
What shall I do, when I at such a door
For Pilgrims ask, and they shall rage the more?

ANSWER

Fright not thyself, my book, for such bugbears
Are nothing else but ground for groundless fears.
My Pilgrim's book has travelled sea and land,
Yet could I never come to understand
That it was slighted, or turned out of door
By any kingdom, were they rich or poor.
    In France and Flanders, where men kill each other,
My Pilgrim is esteemed a friend, a brother.
    In Holland too, 'tis said, as I am told,
My Pilgrim is with some worth more than gold.
    Highlanders and wild Irish can agree
My Pilgrim should familiar with them be.
    'Tis in New England under such advance,
Receives there so much loving countenance,
As to be trimmed, new clothed, and decked with gems
That it may show its features and its limbs,
Yet more; so comely doth my Pilgrim walk,
That of him thousands daily sing and talk.
    If you draw nearer home, it will appear,
My Pilgrim knows no ground of shame or fear;
City and country will him entertain
With, Welcome, Pilgrim; yea, they can't refrain
From smiling, if my Pilgrim be but by,
Or shows his head in any company.
    Brave gallants do my Pilgrim hug and love,
Esteem it much, yea, value it above
Things of a greater bulk: yea, with delight,
Say my lark's leg is better than a kite.
    Young ladies, and young gentlewomen too,
Do no small kindness to my Pilgrim show.
Their cabinets, their bosoms, and their hearts,
My Pilgrim has, 'cause he to them imparts
His pretty riddles in such wholesome strains,
As yields them profit double to their pains
Of reading; yea, I think I may be bold
To say some prize him far above their gold.
    The very children that do walk the street,
If they do but my holy Pilgrim meet,

Salute him will, will wish him well, and say,
He is the only stripling of the day.
    They that have never seen him, yet admire
What they have heard of him, and much desire
To have his company, and hear him tell
Those Pilgrim stories which he knows so well.
    Yea, some who did not love him at the first,
But called him fool and noddy, say they must,
Now they have seen and heard him, him commend,
And to those whom they love they do him send.
    Wherefore, my Second Part, thou need'st not be
Afraid to show thy head; none can hurt thee,
That wish but well to him that went before,
'Cause thou com'st after with a second store
Of things as good, as rich, as profitable,
For young, for old, for stagg'ring, and for stable.

OBJECTION III

    But some there be that say he laughs too loud;
And some do say his head is in a cloud.
Some say his words and stories are so dark,
They know not how, by them, so find his mark.

ANSWER

    One may, I think, say, Both his laughs and cries
May well be guessed at by his watery eyes.
Some things are of that nature as to make
One's fancy chuckle while his heart doth ache.
When Jacob saw his Rachel with the sheep,
He did at the same time both kiss and weep.
    Whereas some say, A cloud is in his head,
That doth but show how wisdom's covered
With its own mantles, and to stir the mind
To a search after what it fain would find.
Things that seem to be hid in words obscure,
Do but the godly mind the more allure
To study what those sayings should contain,
That speak to us in such a cloudy strain.

I also know a dark similitude
Will on the fancy more itself intrude,
And will stick faster in the heart and head,
Than things from similes not borrowed.
    Wherefore, my book, let no discouragement
Hinder thy travels. Behold, thou art sent
To friends, not foes; to friends that will give place
To thee, thy pilgrims, and thy words embrace.
    Besides, what my first Pilgrim left concealed,
Thou, my brave second Pilgrim, hast revealed;
What Christian left locked up, and went his way,
Sweet Christiana opens with her key.

OBJECTION IV

But some love not the method of your first;
Romance they count it, throw 't away as dust;
If I should meet with such, what should I say?
Must I slight them as they slight me, or nay?

ANSWER

My Christiana, if with such thou meet,
By all means, in all loving-wise, them greet;
Render them not reviling for revile;
But if they frown, I prithee on them smile;
Perhaps 'tis nature, or some ill report,
Has made them thus despise, or thus retort.
    Some love no cheese, some love no fish, and some
Love not their friends, nor their own house or home;
Some start at pig, slight chicken, love not fowl,
More than they love a cuckoo, or an owl;
Leave such, my Christiana, to their choice,
And seek those who to find thee will rejoice;
By no means strive, but in humble wise
Present thee to them in thy Pilgrim's guise.
    Go then, my little book, and show to all
That entertain, and bid thee welcome shall,
What thou shalt keep close, shut up from the rest,
And wish what thou shalt show them may be blest

To them for good, may make them choose to be
Pilgrims better by far than thee or me.
　　Go then, I say, tell all men who thou art;
Say, I am Christiana, and my part
Is now, with my four sons, to tell you what
It is for men to take a Pilgrim's lot.
　　Go also, tell them who and what they be,
That now do go on pilgrimage with thee;
Say, Here's my neighbour, Mercy, she is one
That has long time with me a Pilgrim gone.
Come, see her in her virgin face, and learn
'Twixt idle ones and Pilgrims to discern.
Yea, let young damsels learn of her to prize
The world which is to come, in any wise.
When little tripping maidens follow God,
And leave old doting sinners to his rod;
'Tis like those days wherein the young ones cried
Hosanna! to whom old ones did deride.
　　Next tell them of old Honest, whom you found
With his white hairs, treading the Pilgrim's ground.
Yea, tell them how plain-hearted this man was,
How after his good Lord he bare his cross;
Perhaps with some grey head this may prevail
With Christ to fall in love, and sin bewail.
　　Tell them also how Master Fearing went
On pilgrimage, and how the time he spent
In solitariness, with fears and cries;
And how, at last, he won the joyful prize.
He was a good man, though much down in spirit,
He is a good man, and doth life inherit.
　　Tell them of Master Feeble-mind also,
Who, not before, but still behind would go.
Show them also how he had like been slain,
And how one Great-heart did his life regain.
This man was true of heart, though weak in grace,
One might true godliness read in his face.
　　Then tell them of Master Ready-to-halt,
A man with crutches, but much without fault;
Tell them how Master Feeble-mind and he
Did love, and in opinions much agree.

And let all know, though weakness was their chance,
Yet sometimes one could sing, the other dance.
    Forget not Master Valiant-for-the-truth,
That man of courage, though a very youth.
Tell every one his spirit was so stout,
No man could ever make him face about;
And how Great-heart and he could not forbear,
But put down Doubting Castle, slay Despair.
    Overlook not Master Despondency,
Nor Much-afraid, his daughter, though they lie
Under such mantles, as may make them look
(With some) as if their God had them forsook.
They softly went, but sure, and at the end
Found that the Lord of Pilgrims was their friend.
    When thou hast told the world of all these things,
Then turn about, my book, and touch these strings,
Which, if but touchèd, will such music make,
They'll make a cripple dance, a giant quake.
Those riddles that lie couched within thy breast,
Freely propound, expound; and for the rest
Of thy mysterious lines, let them remain
For those whose nimble fancies shall them gain.
    Now may this little book a blessing be
To those who love this little book and me,
And may its buyer have no cause to say,
His money is but lost or thrown away;
Yea, may this Second Pilgrim yield that fruit,
As may with each good Pilgrim's fancy suit;
And may it persuade some that go astray,
To turn their feet and heart to the right way,

Is the hearty prayer

of the Author,

JOHN BUNYAN

In the Similitude of a Dream
The Second Part

Courteous companions, sometime since, to tell you my dream that I had of Christian the pilgrim, and of his dangerous journey toward the Celestial Country, was pleasant to me and profitable to you. I told you then also what I saw concerning his wife and children, and how unwilling they were to go with him on pilgrimage; insomuch that he was forced to go on his progress without them, for he durst not run the danger of that destruction which he feared would come by staying with them in the City of Destruction. Wherefore, as I then showed you, he left them and departed.

Now it hath so happened, through the multiplicity of business, that I have been much hindered and kept back from my wonted travels into those parts whence he went, and so could not till now obtain an opportunity to make further inquiry after whom he left behind, that I might give you an account of them. But having had some concerns that way of late, I went down again thitherward. Now, having taken up my lodgings in a wood about a mile off the place, as I slept I dreamed again.

And as I was in my dream, behold, an aged gentleman came by where I lay; and because he was to go some part of the way that I was travelling, methought I got up and went with him. So as we walked, and as travellers usually do, I was as if we fell into discourse, and our talk happened to be about Christian and his travels; for thus I began with the old man:

Sir, said I, what town is that there below, that lieth on the left hand of our way?

Then said Mr. Sagacity (for that was his name), It is the City of Destruction, a populous place, but possessed with a very ill-conditioned[1] and idle[2] sort of people.

---

1. Having bad qualities; disposed to evil.
2. Worthless.

I thought that was that city, quoth I; I went once myself through that town, and therefore know that this report you give of it is true.

SAG. Too true; I wish I could speak truth in speaking better of them that dwell therein.

Well, Sir, quoth I, then I perceive you to be a well-meaning man; and so one that takes pleasure to hear and tell of that which is good. Pray, did you never hear what happened to a man some time ago in this town, whose name was Christian, that went on pilgrimage up towards the higher regions?

SAG. Hear of him! Ay, and I also heard of the molestations, troubles, wars, captivities, cries, groans, frights, and fears that he met with and had in his journey; besides, I must tell you, all our country rings of him. There are but few houses that have heard of him and his doings but have sought after and got the records of his pilgrimage; yea, I think I may say that his hazardous journey has got a many well-wishers to his ways, for though, when he was here, he was fool in every man's mouth, yet now he is gone, he is highly commended of all. For, it is said, he lives bravely where he is; yea, many of them that are resolved never to run his hazards, yet have their mouths water at his gains.

They may, quoth I, well think, if they think anything that is true, that he liveth well where he is; for he now lives at and in the Fountain of Life, and has what he has without labour and sorrow, for there is no grief mixed therewith. But pray, what talk have the people about him?

SAG. Talk! the people talk strangely about him; some say that he now walks in white; that he has a chain of gold about his neck; that he has a crown of gold, beset with pearls, upon his head. Others say that the Shining Ones, that sometimes showed themselves to him in his journey, are become his companions, and that he is as familiar with them in the place where he is, as here one neighbour is with another. Besides, it is confidently affirmed concerning him, that the King of the place where he is has bestowed upon him already a rich and pleasant dwelling at court; and that he every day eateth, and drinketh, and walketh, and talketh with him, and receiveth of the smiles and favours of him that is Judge of all there. Moreover, it is expected of some that his Prince, the Lord of that country, will shortly come into these parts, and will know the reason, if they can give any, why his neighbours set so little by him, and had him so much in derision, when they perceived that he would be a pilgrim.

For they say that now he is so in the affections of his Prince, and that his Sovereign is so much concerned with the indignities that were cast upon Christian when he became a pilgrim, that he will look upon all as if done unto himself; and no marvel, for it was for the love that he had to his Prince that he ventured as he did.

I dare say, quoth I, I am glad on't, I am glad for the poor man's sake, for that he now has rest from his labour; and for that he now reapeth the benefit of his tears with joy; and for that he has got beyond the gunshot of his enemies, and is out of the reach of them that hate him. I also am glad for that a rumour of these things is noised abroad in this country; who can tell but that it may work some good effect on some that are left behind? But, pray Sir, while it is fresh in my mind, do you hear anything of his wife and children? Poor hearts, I wonder in my mind what they do.

Sag. Who! Christiana and her sons? They are like to do as well as did Christian himself, for though they all played the fool at the first, and would by no means be persuaded by either the tears or entreaties of Christian, yet second thoughts have wrought wonderfully with them; so they have packed up and are also gone after him.

Better and better, quoth I. But what! wife and children and all?

Sag. It is true; I can give you an account of the matter, for I was upon the spot at the instant, and was thoroughly acquainted with the whole affair.

Then, said I, a man, it seems, may report it for a truth?

Sag. You need not fear to affirm it; I mean that they are all gone on pilgrimage, both the good woman and her four boys. And being we are, as I perceive, going some considerable way together, I will give you an account of the whole matter.

This Christiana (for that was her name from the day that she with her children betook themselves to a pilgrim's life) after her husband was gone over the river, and she could hear of him no more, her thoughts began to work in her mind. First, for that she had lost her husband, and for that the loving bond of that relation was utterly broken betwixt them. For you know, said he to me, nature can do no less but entertain the living with many a heavy cogitation in the remembrance of the loss of loving relations. This therefore of her husband did cost her many a tear. But this was not all; for Christiana did also begin to consider with herself, whether her unbecoming behaviour towards her husband was not one cause that she saw him no more, and that in such sort he was taken away from her.[3] And upon this, came into her mind, by swarms, all her kind, unnatural, and ungodly carriages to her dear friend; which also clogged her conscience, and did load her with guilt. She was, moreover, much broken with calling to remembrance the restless groans, brinish tears, and self-bemoanings of her husband, and how she did harden her heart against all his entreaties and loving persuasions (of her and her sons) to go with him; yea, there was not anything that Christian either said to her or did before her all the while that his burden did hang on his back, but it returned upon her like a flash of lightning, and rent the caul of her heart in sunder. Specially that bitter outcry of his, "What shall I do to be saved?" did ring in her ears most dolefully.

Then said she to her children, Sons, we are all undone. I have sinned away your father, and he is gone; he would have had us with him, but I would not go myself. I also have hindered you of life. With that the boys fell all into tears, and cried out to go after their father. Oh! said Christiana, that it had been but our lot to go with him, then had it fared well with us beyond what 'tis like to do now. For though I formerly foolishly imagined, concerning the troubles of your father, that they proceeded of a foolish fancy that he had, or for that he was overrun with melancholy humours, yet now 'twill not out of my mind, but that they sprang from another cause, to wit, for that the Light of Light was given him, by the help of which, as I perceive, he has escaped the snares of death. Then they all wept again, and cried out, "O woe worth the day!"

The next night Christiana had a dream; and behold, she saw as if a broad parchment was opened before her, in which were recorded the sum of her ways, and the times, as she thought, looked very black upon her. Then she cried out aloud in her sleep, "Lord, have mercy upon me a sinner!" and the little children heard her.

After this she thought she saw two very ill-favoured[4] ones standing by her bedside and saying, What shall we do with this woman? For she cries out for mercy waking and sleeping; if she be suffered to go on as she begins, we shall lose her as we have lost her husband. Wherefore we must, by one way or other, seek to take her off from

---

3. Mark this, you that are churls to your godly relations. [B]
4. Of ugly appearance.

the thoughts of what shall be hereafter, else all the world cannot help it but she will become a pilgrim.[5]

Now she awoke in a great sweat, also a trembling was upon her; but after a while she fell to sleeping again. And then she thought she saw Christian her husband in a place of bliss among many immortals, with a harp in his hand, standing and playing upon it before one that sat on a throne with a rainbow about his head. She saw also as if he bowed his head with his face to the paved work that was under the Prince's feet, saying, I heartily thank my Lord and King, for bringing of me into this place. Then shouted a company of them that stood round about, and harped with their harps; but no man living could tell what they said, but Christian and his companions.

Next morning, when she was up, had prayed to God, and talked with her children a while, one knocked hard at the door, to whom she spake out, saying, If thou comest in God's name, come in. So he said, Amen, and opened the door, and saluted her with "Peace be to this house." The which when he had done, he said, Christiana, knowest thou wherefore I am come? Then she blushed and trembled, also her heart began to wax warm with desires to know whence he came, and what was his errand to her. So he said unto her, My name is Secret; I dwell with those that are high. It is talked of, where I dwell, as if thou hadst a desire to go thither; also there is a report that thou art aware of the evil thou hast formerly done to thy husband in hardening of thy heart against his way, and in keeping of these thy babes in their ignorance. Christiana, the Merciful One has sent me to tell thee that he is a God ready to forgive, and that he taketh delight to multiply to pardon offences. He also would have thee know that he inviteth thee to come into his presence, to his table, and that he will feed thee with the fat of his house, and with the heritage of Jacob thy father.

There is Christian thy husband (that was), with legions more his companions, ever beholding that face that doth minister life to beholders; and they will all be glad when they shall hear the sound of thy feet over thy Father's threshold.

Christiana at this was greatly abashed in herself, and bowing her head to the ground, this visitor proceeded and said, Christiana, here is also a letter for thee, which I have brought from thy hus-

---

5. Mark this, this is the quintessence of hell. [B]

band's King. So she took it, and opened it, but it smelt after the manner of the best perfume, also it was written in letters of gold. The contents of the letter was, That the King would have her do as did Christian her husband; for that was the way to come to his city, and to dwell in his presence with joy for ever. At this the good woman was quite overcome; so she cried out to her visitor, Sir, will you carry me and my children with you, that we also may go and worship this King?

Then said the visitor, Christiana, the bitter is before the sweet. Thou must through troubles, as did he that went before thee, enter this Celestial City. Wherefore I advise thee to do as did Christian thy husband. Go to the wicket-gate yonder, over the plain, for that stands in the head of the way up which thou must go, and I wish thee all good speed. Also I advise that thou put this letter in thy bosom; that thou read therein to thyself and to thy children, until you have got it by root-of-heart,[6] for it is one of the songs that thou must sing while thou art in this house of thy pilgrimage. Also this thou must deliver in at the further gate.

Now I saw in my dream that this old gentleman, as he told me this story, did himself seem to be greatly affected therewith. He, moreover, proceeded and said, So Christiana called her sons together, and began thus to address herself unto them: My sons, I have, as you may perceive, been of late under much exercise in my soul about the death of your father; not for that I doubt at all of his happiness, for I am satisfied now that he is well. I have also been much affected with the thoughts of mine own state and yours, which I verily believe is by nature miserable. My carriages also to your father in his distress is a great load to my conscience; for I hardened both my own heart and yours against him, and refused to go with him on pilgrimage.

The thoughts of these things would now kill me outright, but that for a dream which I had last night, and but that for the encouragement that this stranger has given me this morning. Come, my children, let us pack up and be gone to the gate that leads to the Celestial Country, that we may see your father, and be with him and his companions in peace, according to the laws of that land.

Then did her children burst out into tears for joy, that the heart

---

6. Perhaps a variant form of "rote," combined with suggestions of "the bottom of the heart."

of their mother was so inclined. So their visitor bade them farewell; and they began to prepare to set out for their journey.

But while they were thus about to be gone, two of the women that were Christiana's neighbours came up to her house and knocked at her door. To whom she said as before, If you come in God's name, come in. At this the women were stunned; for this kind of language they used not to hear, or to perceive to drop from the lips of Christiana. Yet they came in; but behold, they found the good woman a-preparing to be gone from her house.

So they began and said, Neighbour, pray what is your meaning by this?

Christiana answered and said to the eldest of them, whose name was Mrs. Timorous, I am preparing for a journey. (This Timorous was daughter to him that met Christian upon the Hill Difficulty, and would have had him go back for fear of the lions.)

TIM. For what journey, I pray you?

CHRIS. Even to go after my good husband. And with that she fell a-weeping.

TIM. I hope not so, good neighbour; pray, for your poor children's sakes, do not so unwomanly cast away yourself.

CHRIS. Nay, my children shall go with me, not one of them is willing to stay behind.

TIM. I wonder, in my very heart, what or who has brought you into this mind.

CHRIS. Oh, neighbour, knew you but as much as I do, I doubt not but that you would go with me.

TIM. Prithee, what new knowledge hast thou got, that so worketh off thy mind from thy friends, and that tempteth thee to go nobody knows where?

CHRIS. Then Christiana replied, I have been sorely afflicted since my husband's departure from me; but specially since he went over the river. But that which troubleth me most is my churlish carriages to him when he was under his distress. Besides, I am now as he was then; nothing will serve me but going on pilgrimage. I was a-dreaming last night that I saw him. Oh that my soul was with him! He dwelleth in the presence of the King of the country; he sits and eats with him at his table; he is become a companion of immortals, and has a house now given him to dwell in, to which the best palaces on earth, if compared, seems to me to be but as a dunghill. The Prince of the place has also sent for me, with promise of entertainment if I shall come to him; his messenger was here even now, and has brought me a letter which invites me to come. And with that she plucked out her letter, and read it, and said to them, What now will ye say to this?

Tim. Oh the madness that has possessed thee and thy husband, to run yourselves upon such difficulties! You have heard, I am sure, what your husband did meet with, even in a manner at the first step that he took on his way, as our neighbour Obstinate can yet testify, for he went along with him; yea, and Pliable too, until they, like wise men, were afraid to go any further. We also heard, over and above, how he met with the lions, Apollyon, the Shadow of Death, and many other things. Nor is the danger that he met with at Vanity Fair to be forgotten by thee; for if he, though a man, was hard put to it, what canst thou, being but a poor woman, do? Consider also that these four sweet babes are thy children, thy flesh and thy bones. Wherefore, though thou shouldest be so rash as to cast away thyself, yet for the sake of the fruit of thy body, keep thou at home.[7]

But Christiana said unto her, Tempt me not, my neighbour. I have now a price put into my hand to get gain, and I should be a fool of the greatest size, if I should have no heart to strike in with the opportunity. And for that you tell me of all these troubles that I am like to meet with in the way, they are so far off from being to me a discouragement, that they show I am in the right. "The bitter must come before the sweet," and that also will make the sweet the sweeter. Wherefore, since you came not to my house in God's name, as I said, I pray you to be gone, and not disquiet me further.

Then Timorous also reviled her, and said to her fellow, Come, neighbour Mercy, let us leave her in her own hands, since she scorns our counsel and company. But Mercy was at a stand, and could not so readily comply with her neighbour, and that for a twofold reason. First, her bowels[8] yearned over Christiana. So she said within herself, If my neighbour will needs be gone, I will go a little way with her and help her. Secondly, her bowels yearned over her own soul, for what Christiana had said had taken some hold upon her mind. Wherefore she said within herself again, I will yet have more talk with this Christiana, and if I find truth and life in what

---

7. The reasonings of the flesh. [B]
8. Biblical: the interior of the body, considered as the source of sympathetic emotions; hence in general, pity, compassion.

she shall say, myself with my heart shall also go with her. Wherefore Mercy began thus to reply to her neighbour Timorous.

MERCY. Neighbour, I did indeed come with you to see Christiana
this morning; and since she is, as you see, a-taking of her last
farewell of her country, I think to walk, this sunshine morning, a
little way with her, to help her on the way. But she told her not of
the second reason, but kept that to herself.

TIM. Well, I see you have a mind to go a-fooling too, but take
heed in time and be wise. While we are out of danger we are out;
but when we are in, we are in. So Mrs. Timorous returned to her
house, and Christiana betook herself to her journey. But when
Timorous was got home to her house, she sends for some of her
neighbours, to wit, Mrs. Bat's-eyes, Mrs. Inconsiderate,[9] Mrs. Light-
mind, and Mrs. Know-nothing. So when they were come to her
house, she falls to telling of the story of Christiana, and of her
intended journey. And thus she began her tale.

TIM. Neighbours, having had little to do this morning, I went to
give Christiana a visit; and when I came at the door, I knocked, as
you know 'tis our custom. And she answered, If you come in God's
name, come in. So in I went, thinking all was well. But when I
came in, I found her preparing herself to depart the town, she and
also her children. So I asked her what was her meaning by that.
And she told me, in short, that she was now of a mind to go on pilgrimage, as did her husband. She told me also a dream that she
had, and how the King of the country where her husband was had
sent her an inviting letter to come thither.

Then said Mrs. Know-nothing, And what! do you think she
will go?

TIM. Ay, go she will, whatever come on't, and methinks I know
it by this: for that which was my great argument to persuade her to
stay at home (to wit, the troubles she was like to meet with in the way)
is one great argument with her to put her forward on her journey.
For she told me in so many words, "The bitter goes before the sweet."
Yea, and forasmuch as it so doth, it makes the sweet the sweeter.

MRS. BAT'S-EYES. Oh, this blind and foolish woman! said she;
will she not take warning by her husband's afflictions? For my
part, I see, if he was here again, he would rest him content in a
whole skin, and never run so many hazards for nothing.

9. Thoughtless, imprudent, rash.

Mrs. Inconsiderate also replied, saying, Away with such fantastical fools from the town! A good riddance, for my part I say, of her. Should she stay where she dwells, and retain this her mind, who could live quietly by her? for she will either be dumpish or unneighbourly, or talk of such matters as no wise body can abide; wherefore, for my part, I shall never be sorry for her departure. Let her go, and let better come in her room. It was never a good world since these whimsical fools dwelt in it.

Then Mrs. Light-mind added as followeth: Come, put this kind of talk away. I was yesterday at Madame Wanton's,[10] where we were as merry as the maids. For who do you think should be there, but I, and Mrs. Love-the-Flesh, and three or four more, with Mr. Lechery, Mrs. Filth, and some others. So there we had music and dancing, and what else was meet to fill up the pleasure. And I dare say my lady herself is an admirably well-bred gentlewoman, and Mr. Lechery is as pretty a fellow.

By this time Christiana was got on her way, and Mercy went along with her. So as they went, her children being there also, Christiana began to discourse. And, Mercy, said Christiana, I take this as an unexpected favour, that thou shouldest set foot out of doors with me to accompany me a little in my way.

MERCY. Then said young Mercy (for she was but young), If I thought it would be to purpose to go with you, I would never go near the town any more.

CHRIS. Well, Mercy, said Christiana, cast in thy lot with me; I well know what will be the end of our pilgrimage. My husband is here he would not but be for all the gold in the Spanish mines. Nor shalt thou be rejected, though thou goest but upon my invitation. The King who hath sent for me and my children is one that delighteth in mercy. Besides, if thou wilt, I will hire thee, and thou shalt go along with me as my servant. Yet we will have all things in common betwixt thee and me; only go along with me.

MERCY. But how shall I be ascertained that I also shall be entertained? Had I this hope but from one that can tell, I would make no stick at all, but would go, being helped by him that can help, though the way was never so tedious.

---

10. Madame Wanton, she that had like to a been too hard for Faithful in time past. [B]

CHRIS. Well, loving Mercy, I will tell thee what thou shalt do. Go with me to the wicket-gate,[11] and there I will further inquire for thee; and if there thou shalt not meet with encouragement, I will be content that thou shalt return to thy place. I also will pay thee for thy kindness which thou showest to me and my children, in thy accompanying us in our way as thou dost.

MERCY. Then will I go thither, and will take what shall follow; and the Lord grant that my lot may there fall even as the King of Heaven shall have his heart upon me.

Christiana then was glad at her heart, not only that she had a companion, but also for that she had prevailed with this poor maid to fall in love with her own salvation. So they went on together, and Mercy began to weep. Then said Christiana, Wherefore weepeth my sister so?

MERCY. Alas! said she, who can but lament that shall but rightly consider what a state and condition my poor relations are in that yet remain in our sinful town? and that which makes my grief the more heavy is, because they have no instructor, nor any to tell them what is to come.

CHRIS. Bowels becometh pilgrims, and thou dost for thy friends as my good Christian did for me when he left me; he mourned for that I would not heed nor regard him, but his Lord and ours did gather up his tears, and put them into his bottle,[12] and now both I and thou, and these my sweet babes, are reaping the fruit and benefit of them. I hope, Mercy, these tears of thine will not be lost; for the truth hath said that "They that sow in tears shall reap in joy," in singing. And that "he that goeth forth and weepeth, bearing precious seed, shall doubtless come again with rejoicing, bringing his sheaves with him."[13]

Then said Mercy,

> Let the Most Blessèd be my guide,
>   If 't be his blessèd will;
> Unto his gate, into his fold,
>   Up to his holy hill.

---

11. Christiana allures her to the Gate which is Christ, and promiseth there to inquire for her. [B]

12. Ps. 56:8.

13. Ps. 126:5, 6.

And let him never suffer me
　To swerve or turn aside
From his free grace, and holy ways,
　Whate'er shall me betide.

And let him gather them of mine,
　That I have left behind;
Lord, make them pray they may be thine,
　With all their heart and mind.

Now my old friend proceeded and said: But when Christiana came up to the Slough of Despond, she began to be at a stand; for, said she, this is the place in which my dear husband had like to a been smothered with mud. She perceived also that notwithstanding the command of the King to make this place for pilgrims good, yet it was rather worse than formerly. So I asked if that was true. Yes, said the old gentleman, too true; for that many there be that pretend to be the King's labourers, and that say they are for mending the King's highway, that bring dirt and dung instead of stones, and so mar instead of mending.[14] Here Christiana therefore, with her boys, did make a stand; but, said Mercy, Come, let us venture, only let us be wary. Then they looked well to the steps, and made a shift to get staggeringly over.

Yet Christiana had like to a been in, and that not once nor twice. Now they had no sooner got over, but they thought they heard words that said unto them, "Blessed is she that believeth, for there shall be a performance of the things that have been told her from the Lord."[15]

Then they went on again; and said Mercy to Christiana, Had I as good ground to hope for a loving reception at the wicket-gate as you, I think no Slough of Despond would discourage me.

Well, said the other, you know your sore, and I know mine; and, good friend, we shall all have enough evil before we come at our journey's end.

For can it be imagined that the people that design to attain such excellent glories as we do, and that are so envied that happiness as we are; but that we shall meet with what fears and scares, with what troubles and afflictions they can possibly assault us with, that hate us?

---

14. Their own carnal conclusions, instead of the Word of life. [B]
15. Luke 1:45.

And now Mr. Sagacity left me to dream out my dreams by myself. Wherefore methought I saw Christiana and Mercy and the boys go all of them up to the gate. To which when they were come, they betook themselves to a short debate about how they must manage their calling at the gate, and what should be said to him that did open to them.[16] So it was concluded, since Christiana was the eldest, that she should knock for entrance, and that she should speak to him that did open, for the rest. So Christiana began to knock; and, as her poor husband did, she knocked and knocked again. But instead of any that answered, they all thought that they heard as if a dog came barking upon them; a dog, and a great one too, and this made the women and children afraid. Nor durst they for a while dare to knock any more, for fear the mastiff should fly upon them.[17] Now therefore they were greatly tumbled up and down in their minds, and knew not what to do. Knock they durst not, for fear of the dog; go back they durst not, for fear the Keeper of that gate should espy them as they so went, and should be offended with them. At last they thought of knocking again, and knocked more vehemently than they did at the first. Then said the Keeper of the gate, Who is there? So the dog left off to bark, and he opened unto them.

Then Christiana made low obeisance, and said, Let not our Lord be offended with his handmaidens, for that we have knocked at his princely gate. Then said the Keeper, Whence come ye, and what is that you would have?

Christiana answered, We are come from whence Christian did come, and upon the same errand as he; to wit, to be, if it shall please you, graciously admitted by this gate into the way that leads to the Celestial City. And I answer, my Lord, in the next place, that I am Christiana, once the wife of Christian, that now is gotten above.

With that the Keeper of the gate did marvel, saying, What, is she become now a pilgrim, that but a while ago abhorred that life? Then she bowed her head and said, Yes, and so are these my sweet babes also.

Then he took her by the hand, and let her in, and said also, "Suffer the little children to come unto me";[18] and with that he shut up

---

16. Prayer should be made with consideration and fear, as well as in faith and hope. [B]

17. The dog, the Devil, an enemy to prayer. [B]

18. Mark 10:14.

the gate. This done, he called to a trumpeter that was above, over the gate, to entertain Christiana with shouting and sound of trumpet for joy. So he obeyed, and sounded, and filled the air with his melodious notes.

Now all this while poor Mercy did stand without, trembling and crying for fear that she was rejected. But when Christiana had gotten admittance for herself and her boys, then she began to make intercession for Mercy.

CHRIS. And she said, My Lord, I have a companion of mine that stands yet without, that is come hither upon the same account as myself; one that is much dejected in her mind, for that she comes, as she thinks, without sending for, whereas I was sent to by my husband's King to come.

Now Mercy began to be very impatient, for each minute was as long to her as an hour;[19] wherefore she prevented Christiana from a fuller interceding for her, by knocking at the gate herself. And she knocked then so loud that she made Christiana to start. Then said the Keeper of the gate, Who is there? And said Christiana, It is my friend.

So he opened the gate, and looked out, but Mercy was fallen down without in a swoon, for she fainted, and was afraid that no gate would be opened to her.

Then he took her by the hand and said, Damsel, I bid thee arise. Oh, Sir, said she, I am faint; there is scarce life left in me. But he answered, That one once said, "When my soul fainted within me, I remembered the Lord, and my prayer came in unto thee, into thy holy temple."[20] Fear not, but stand upon thy feet, and tell me wherefore thou art come.

MERCY. I am come for that unto which I was never invited, as my friend Christiana was. Hers was from the King, and mine was but from her. Wherefore I fear I presume.

KEEP. Did she desire thee to come with her to this place?

MERCY. Yes; and as my Lord sees, I am come. And if there is any grace or forgiveness of sins to spare, I beseech that I, thy poor handmaid, may be partaker thereof.

Then he took her again by the hand, and led her gently in, and said, I pray for all them that believe on me, by what means soever they

---

19. The delays make the hungering soul the ferventer. [B]
20. Jon. 2:7.

come unto me. Then said he to those that stood by, Fetch something, and give it to Mercy to smell on, thereby to stay her fainting. So they fetched her a "bundle of myrrh";[21] and a while after, she was revived.

And now was Christiana and her boys, and Mercy, received of the Lord at the head of the way, and spoke kindly unto by him. Then said they yet further unto him, We are sorry for our sins, and beg of our Lord his pardon, and further information what we must do.

I grant pardon, said he, by word and deed; by word, in the promise of forgiveness; by deed, in the way I obtained it. Take the first from my lips with a kiss, and the other as it shall be revealed.

Now I saw in my dream that he spake many good words unto them, whereby they were greatly gladded. He also had them up to the top of the gate and showed them by what deed they were saved, and told them withal that that sight they would have again as they went along in the way, to their comfort.[22]

So he left them a while in a summer-parlour below, where they entered into a talk by themselves. And thus Christiana began: O Lord! how glad am I that we are got in hither!

MERCY. So you well may; but I of all have cause to leap for joy.

CHRIS. I thought one time, as I stood at the gate (because I had knocked and none did answer) that all our labour had been lost; specially when that ugly cur made such a heavy barking against us.

MERCY. But my worst fear was after I saw that you were taken into his favour, and that I was left behind. Now thought I, 'tis fulfilled which is written, "Two women shall be grinding together; the one shall be taken, and the other left."[23] I had much ado to forbear crying out, Undone! undone!

And afraid I was to knock any more; but when I looked up to what was written over the gate, I took courage. I also thought that I must either knock again or die; so I knocked, but I cannot tell how, for my spirit now struggled betwixt life and death.

CHRIS. Can you not tell how you knocked? I am sure your knocks were so earnest that the very sound of them made me start; I thought I never heard such knocking in all my life. I thought you would a come in by violent hands, or a took the kingdom by storm.[24]

---

21. Song of Sol. 1:13.
22. Christ crucified seen afar off. [B]
23. Matt. 24:41.
24. Matt. 11:12.

MERCY. Alas, to be in my case, who that so was could but a done so? You saw that the door was shut upon me, and that there was a most cruel dog thereabout. Who, I say, that was so fainthearted as I, that would not a knocked with all their might? But pray, what said my Lord to my rudeness? Was he not angry with me?

CHRIS. When he heard your lumbering noise, he gave a wonderful innocent smile. I believe what you did pleased him well enough, for he showed no sign to the contrary. But I marvel in my heart why he keeps such a dog; had I known that before, I fear I should not have had heart enough to have ventured myself in this manner.[25] But now we are in, we are in; and I am glad with all my heart.

MERCY. I will ask, if you please, next time he comes down, why he keeps such a filthy cur in his yard. I hope he will not take it amiss.

Ay, do, said the children, and persuade him to hang him, for we are afraid he will bite us when we go hence.

So at last he came down to them again, and Mercy fell to the ground on her face before him and worshipped, and said, Let my Lord accept the sacrifice of praise which I now offer unto him with the calves of my lips.[26]

So he said to her, Peace be to thee, stand up. But she continued upon her face and said, "Righteous art thou, O Lord, when I plead with thee: yet let me talk with thee of thy judgements."[27] Wherefore dost thou keep so cruel a dog in thy yard, at the sight of which such women and children as we are ready to fly from the gate for fear.

He answered and said, That dog has another owner, he also is kept close in another man's ground; only my pilgrims hear his barking. He belongs to the castle which you see there at a distance, but can come up to the walls of this place. He has frighted many an honest pilgrim from worse to better, by the great voice of his roaring. Indeed he that owneth him doth not keep him of any goodwill to me or mine, but with intent to keep the pilgrims from coming to me, and that they may be afraid to knock at this gate for entrance. Sometimes also he has broken out and has worried some that I loved; but I take all at present patiently. I also give my pilgrims timely help, so they are not delivered up to his power to do to them

---

25. If the soul at first did know all it should meet with in its journey to Heaven it would hardly ever set out. [B]
26. Hos. 14:2 (meaning is doubtful).
27. Jer. 12:1.

what his doggish nature would prompt him to. But what! my pur-
chased one, I trow, hadst thou known never so much beforehand,
thou wouldst not have been afraid of a dog.

The beggars that go from door to door will, rather than they will
lose a supposed alms, run the hazard of the bawling, barking, and
biting too of a dog; and shall a dog, a dog in another man's yard, a
dog whose barking I turn to the profit of pilgrims, keep any from
coming to me? I deliver them from the lions, their "darling from
the power of the dog."[28]

MERCY. Then said Mercy, I confess my ignorance. I spake what I
understood not; I acknowledge that thou dost all things well.[29]

CHRIS. Then Christiana began to talk of their journey, and to
inquire after the way. So he fed them, and washed their feet, and
set them in the way of his steps, according as he had dealt with her
husband before. So I saw in my dream that they walked on in their
way, and had the weather very comfortable to them.

Then Christiana began to sing, saying,

> Blessed be the day that I began
>   A pilgrim for to be;
> And blessèd also be that man
>   That thereto movèd me.
>
> 'Tis true, 'twas long ere I began
>   To seek to live for ever:
> But now I run fast as I can;
>   'Tis better late than never.
>
> Our tears to joy, our fears to faith
>   Are turned, as we see:
> Thus our beginning (as one saith,)
>   Shows what our end will be.

Now there was, on the other side of the wall that fenced in the
way up which Christiana and her companions were to go, a garden, and that garden belonged to him whose was that barking dog
of whom mention was made before. And some of the fruit-trees

---

28. Ps. 22:20, 21.
29. Christians when wise enough acquiesce in the wisdom of their Lord. [B]

that grew in that garden shot their branches over the wall, and being mellow, they that found them did gather them up and oft eat of them to their hurt. So Christiana's boys, as boys are apt to do, being pleased with the trees and with the fruit that did hang thereon, did pluck them, and began to eat. Their mother did also chide them for so doing, but still the boys went on.

Well, said she, my sons, you transgress, for that fruit is none of ours, but she did not know that they did belong to the enemy; I'll warrant you if she had, she would a been ready to die for fear. But that passed, and they went on their way. Now by that they were gone about two bow-shots from the place that let them into the way, they espied two very ill-favoured ones coming down apace to meet them. With that, Christiana and Mercy her friend covered themselves with their veils, and so kept on their journey; the children also went on before, so that at last they met together. Then they that came down to meet them, came just up to the women, as if they would embrace them; but Christiana said, Stand back, or go peaceably by as you should. Yet these two, as men that are deaf, regarded not Christiana's words, but began to lay hands upon them. At that Christiana, waxing very wroth, spurned at them with her feet. Mercy also, as well as she could, did what she could to shift them. Christiana again said to them, Stand back and be gone, for we have no money to lose, being pilgrims, as ye see, and such too as live upon the charity of our friends.

ILL-FAVOURED. Then said one of the two of the men, We make no assault upon you for money, but are come out to tell you that if you will but grant one small request which we shall ask, we will make women of you for ever.

CHRIS. Now Christiana, imagining what they should mean, made answer again, We will neither hear, nor regard, nor yield to what you shall ask. We are in haste, cannot stay; our business is a business of life and death. So again she and her companions made a fresh essay to go past them; but they letted them in their way.

ILL-FAV. And they said, We intend no hurt to your lives; it is another thing we should have.

CHRIS. Ah, quoth Christiana, you would have us body and soul, for I know it is for that you are come; but we will die rather upon the spot, than suffer ourselves to be brought into such snares as shall hazard our well-being hereafter. And with that they both shrieked out and cried, Murder! murder! and so put themselves under those laws that are provided for the protection of women. But the men still made their approach upon them, with design to prevail against them. They therefore cried out again.

Now they being, as I said, not far from the gate in at which they came, their voice was heard from where they were thither; wherefore some of the house came out, and knowing that it was Christiana's tongue, they made haste to her relief. But by that they was got within sight of them, the women were in a very great scuffle; the children also stood crying by. Then did he that came in for their relief call out to the ruffians, saying, What is that thing that you do? Would you make my Lord's people to transgress? He also attempted to take them, but they did make their escape over the wall into the garden of the man to whom the great dog belonged; so the dog became their protector.[30] This Reliever then came up to the women and asked them how they did. So they answered, We thank thy Prince, pretty well; only we have been somewhat affrighted. We thank thee also for that thou camest in to our help, for otherwise we had been overcome.

RELIEVER. So after a few more words, this Reliever said as followeth: I marvelled much when you were entertained at the gate above, being ye knew that ye were but weak women, that you petitioned not the Lord there for a conductor; then might you have avoided these troubles and dangers, for he would have granted you one.

CHRIS. Alas! said Christiana, we were so taken with our present blessing, that dangers to come were forgotten by us; beside, who could have thought that so near the King's palace there should have lurked such naughty[31] ones? Indeed it had been well for us had we asked our Lord for one; but since our Lord knew 'twould be for our profit, I wonder he sent not one along with us.

REL. It is not always necessary to grant things not asked for, lest by so doing they become of little esteem; but when the want of a thing is felt, it then comes under, in the eyes of him that feels it, that estimate that properly is its due, and so consequently will be thereafter used. Had my Lord granted you a conductor, you would not neither so have bewailed that oversight of yours in not asking for one, as now you have occasion to do. So all things work for good, and tend to make you more wary.

---

30. The ill-ones fly to the Devil for relief. [B]
31. Wicked.

CHRIS. Shall we go back again to my Lord, and confess our folly, and ask one?

REL. Your confession of your folly I will present him with. To go back again you will need not, for in all places where you shall come, you will find no want at all; for in every one of my Lord's lodgings which he has prepared for the reception of his pilgrims, there is sufficient to furnish them against all attempts whatsoever. But, as I said, he will be inquired of by them to do it for them; and 'tis a poor thing that is not worth asking for. When he had thus said, he went back to his place, and the pilgrims went on their way.

MERCY. Then said Mercy, What a sudden blank[32] is here! I made account we had now been past all danger, and that we should never see sorrow more.

CHRIS. Thy innocency, my sister, said Christiana to Mercy, may excuse thee much; but as for me, my fault is so much the greater, for that I saw this danger before I came out of the doors, and yet did not provide for it where provision might have been had. I am therefore much to be blamed.

MERCY. Then said Mercy, How knew you this before you came from home? Pray open to me this riddle.

CHRIS. Why, I will tell you. Before I set foot out of doors, one night, as I lay in my bed, I had a dream about this; for methought I saw two men, as like these as ever the world they could look, stand at my bed's feet, plotting how they might prevent my salvation. I will tell you their very words. They said ('twas when I was in my troubles), What shall we do with this woman? for she cries out waking and sleeping for forgiveness. If she be suffered to go on as she begins, we shall lose her as we have lost her husband. This, you know, might a made me take heed, and have provided when provision might a been had.

MERCY. Well, said Mercy, as by this neglect we have an occasion ministered unto us to behold our own imperfections, so our Lord has taken occasion thereby to make manifest the riches of his grace; for he, as we see, has followed us with unasked kindness, and has delivered us from their hands that were stronger than we, of his mere good pleasure.

Thus now when they had talked away a little more time, they drew nigh to a house which stood in the way, which house was

---

32. State of being utterly disconcerted, helpless, nonplussed.

built for the relief of pilgrims; as you will find more fully related in the First Part of these Records of the Pilgrim's Progress. So they drew on towards the house (the House of the Interpreter), and when they came to the door, they heard a great talk in the house. They then gave ear and heard, as they thought, Christiana mentioned by name. For you must know that there went along, even before her, a talk of her and her children's going on pilgrimage. And this thing was the more pleasing to them, because they had heard that she was Christian's wife, that woman who was sometime ago so unwilling to hear of going on pilgrimage. Thus therefore they stood still and heard the good people within commending her, who they little thought stood at the door. At last Christiana knocked as she had done at the gate before. Now when she had knocked, there came to the door a young damsel named Innocent, and opened the door and looked, and behold two women were there.

DAMSEL. Then said the damsel to them, With whom would you speak in this place?

CHRIS. Christiana answered, We understand that this is a privileged place for those that are become pilgrims, and we now at this door are such; wherefore we pray that we may be partakers of that for which we at this time are come, for the day, as thou seest, is very far spent, and we are loath tonight to go any further.

DAMSEL. Pray, what may I call your name, that I may tell it to my Lord within?

CHRIS. My name is Christiana; I was the wife of that pilgrim that some years ago did travel this way, and these be his four children. This maiden also is my companion, and is going on pilgrimage too.

INNOCENT. Then ran Innocent in (for that was her name) and said to those within, Can you think who is at the door? There is Christiana and her children, and her companion, all waiting for entertainment here. Then they leaped for joy, and went and told their master. So he came to the door, and looking upon her he said, Art thou that Christiana whom Christian, the goodman, left behind him, when he betook himself to a pilgrim's life?

CHRIS. I am that woman that was so hard-hearted as to slight my husband's troubles, and that left him to go on in his journey alone, and these are his four children; but now I also am come, for I am convinced that no way is right but this.

INTER. Then is fulfilled that which also is written of the man that said to his son, "Go work today in my vineyard"; and he said to his father, "I will not"; but afterwards repented and went.[33]

CHRIS. Then said Christiana, So be it, Amen. God make it a true saying upon me, and grant that I may be found, at the last, of him in peace without spot and blameless.

INTER. But why standest thou thus at the door? Come in, thou daughter of Abraham. We were talking of thee but now, for tidings have come to us before, how thou art become a pilgrim. Come, children, come in; come, maiden, come in. So he had them all into the house.

So when they were within, they were bidden sit down and rest them; the which when they had done, those that attended upon the pilgrims in the house came into the room to see them. And one smiled, and another smiled, and they all smiled, for joy that Christiana was become a pilgrim. They also looked upon the boys, they stroked them over the faces with the hand, in token of their kind reception of them.[34] They also carried it lovingly to Mercy, and bid all welcome into their Master's house.

After a while, because supper was not ready, the Interpreter took them into his Significant[35] Rooms, and showed them what Christian, Christiana's husband, had seen sometime before. Here therefore they saw the man in the cage, the man and his dream, the man that cut his way through his enemies, and the picture of the biggest of them all, together with the rest of those things that were then so profitable to Christian.

This done, and after these things had been somewhat digested by Christiana and her company, the Interpreter takes them apart again, and has them first into a room where was a man that could look no way but downwards, with a muck-rake in his hand. There stood also one over his head with a celestial crown in his hand, and proffered him that crown for his muck-rake; but the man did neither look up, nor regard, but raked to himself the straws, the small sticks, and dust of the floor.

Then said Christiana, I persuade myself that I know somewhat the meaning of this; for this is a figure of a man of this world, is it not, good Sir?

---

33. Matt. 21:28, 29.
34. Old Saints glad to see the young ones walk in God's ways. [B]
35. Conveying particular meanings; full of meaning.

INTER. Thou hast said the right, said he, and his muck-rake doth show his carnal mind. And whereas thou seest him rather give heed to rake up straws and sticks, and the dust of the floor, than to what he says that calls to him from above with the celestial crown in his hand, it is to show that heaven is but as a fable to some, and that things here are counted the only things substantial. Now whereas it was also showed thee that the man could look no way but downwards, it is to let thee know that earthly things, when they are with power upon men's minds, quite carry their hearts away from God.

CHRIS. Then said Christiana, Oh, deliver me from this muck-rake!

INTER. That prayer, said the Interpreter, has lain by till 'tis almost rusty. "Give me not riches," is scarce the prayer of one of ten thousand.[36] Straws, and sticks, and dust, with most, are the great things now looked after.

With that Mercy and Christiana wept, and said, It is, alas! too true.

When the Interpreter had showed them this, he has them into the very best room in the house (a very brave room it was). So he bid them look round about, and see if they could find anything profitable there. Then they looked round and round; for there was nothing there to be seen but a very great spider on the wall: and that they overlooked.

MERCY. Then said Mercy, Sir, I see nothing; but Christiana held her peace.

INTER. But, said the Interpreter, look again; and she therefore looked again, and said, Here is not anything but an ugly spider, who hangs by her hands upon the wall. Then said he, Is there but one spider in all this spacious room? Then the water stood in Christiana's eyes, for she was a woman quick of apprehension; and she said, Yea, Lord, there is here more than one. Yea, and spiders whose venom is far more destructive than that which is in her. The Interpreter then looked pleasantly upon her, and said, Thou hast said the truth. This made Mercy blush, and the boys to cover their faces. For they all began now to understand the riddle.

Then said the Interpreter again, "The spider taketh hold with her hands (as you see), and is in kings' palaces."[37] And wherefore is this recorded, but to show you that how full of the venom of sin

---

36. Prov. 30:8.
37. Prov. 30:28.

soever you be, yet you may by the hand of faith lay hold of, and dwell in the best room that belongs to the King's house above.

CHRIS. I thought, said Christiana, of something of this; but I could not imagine it all. I thought that we were like spiders, and that we looked like ugly creatures, in what fine room soever we were; but that by this spider, this venomous and ill-favoured creature, we were to learn how to act faith, that came not into my mind. And yet she has taken hold with her hands, as I see, and dwells in the best room in the house. God has made nothing in vain.

Then they seemed all to be glad; but the water stood in their eyes, yet they looked one upon another, and also bowed before the Interpreter.

He had them then into another room, where was a hen and chickens, and bid them observe a while. So one of the chickens went to the trough to drink, and every time she drank she lift up her head and her eyes toward heaven. See, said he, what this little chick doth, and learn of her to acknowledge whence your mercies come, by receiving them with looking up. Yet again, said he, observe and look; so they gave heed and perceived that the hen did walk in a fourfold method toward her chickens. 1. She had a common call, and that she hath all day long. 2. She had a special call, and that she had but sometimes. 3. She had a brooding note. And 4. She had an outcry.

Now, said he, compare this hen to your King, and these chickens to his obedient ones. For, answerable to her, himself has his methods, which he walketh in towards his people; by his common call, he gives nothing; by his special call, he always has something to give; he has also a brooding voice, for them that are under his wing;[38] and he has an outcry to give the alarm when he seeth the enemy come. I chose, my darlings, to lead you into the room where such things are, because you are women, and they are easy for you.

CHRIS. And, Sir, said Christina, pray let us see some more. So he had them into the slaughterhouse, where was a butcher killing of a sheep; and behold the sheep was quiet, and took her death patiently. Then said the Interpreter, You must learn of this sheep to suffer, and to put up wrongs without murmurings and complaints. Behold how quietly she takes her death, and without objecting she suffereth her skin to be pulled over her ears. Your King doth call you his sheep.

---

38. Matt. 23:37.

After this, he led them into his garden, where was great variety of flowers; and he said, Do you see all these? So Christiana said, Yes. Then said he again, Behold the flowers are diverse in stature, in quality, and colour, and smell, and virtue;[39] and some are better than some; also where the gardener hath set them, there they stand, and quarrel not with one another.

Again, he had them into his field, which he had sowed with wheat and corn; but when they beheld, the tops of all were cut off, only the straw remained. He said again, This ground was dunged, and ploughed, and sowed; but what shall we do with the crop? Then said Christiana, Burn some, and make muck of the rest. Then said the Interpreter again, Fruit, you see, is that thing you look for, and for want of that you condemn it to the fire, and to be trodden under foot of men: beware that in this you condemn not yourselves.

Then as they were coming in from abroad, they espied a little robin with a great spider in his mouth. So the Interpreter said, Look here. So they looked, and Mercy wondered, but Christiana said, What a disparagement is it to such a little pretty bird as the robin-redbreast is, he being also a bird above many, that loveth to maintain a kind of sociableness with men; I had thought they had lived upon crumbs of bread, or upon other such harmless matter. I like him worse than I did.

The Interpreter then replied, This robin is an emblem very apt to set forth some professors by; for to sight they are as this robin, pretty of note, colour, and carriages. They seem also to have a very great love for professors that are sincere; and above all other, to desire to sociate with, and to be in their company, as if they could live upon the good man's crumbs. They pretend also that therefore it is that they frequent the house of the godly and the appointments of the Lord; but when they are by themselves, as the robin, they can catch and gobble up spiders, they can change their diet, drink iniquity, and swallow down sin like water.

So when they were come again into the house, because supper as yet was not ready, Christiana again desired that the Interpreter would either show or tell of some other things that are profitable.[40]

Then the Interpreter began and said, The fatter the sow is, the more she desires the mire; the fatter the ox is, the more gamesomely

---

39. Literally, healing or medicinal qualities.
40. Pray, and you will get at that which yet lies unrevealed. [B]

he goes to the slaughter; and the more healthy the lusty man is, the more prone he is unto evil.

There is a desire in women to go neat and fine, and it is a comely thing to be adorned with that that in God's sight is of great price.

'Tis easier watching a night or two, than to sit up a whole year together. So 'tis easier for one to begin to profess well, than to hold out as he should to the end.

Every shipmaster, when in a storm, will willingly cast that overboard that is of the smallest value in the vessel; but who will throw the best out first? None but he that feareth not God.

One leak will sink a ship; and one sin will destroy a sinner.

He that forgets his friend is ungrateful unto him; but he that forgets his Saviour is unmerciful to himself.

He that lives in sin, and looks for happiness hereafter, is like him that soweth cockle, and thinks to fill his barn with wheat or barley.

If a man would live well, let him fetch his last day to him, and make it always his company-keeper.

Whispering and change of thoughts proves that sin is in the world.

If the world, which God sets light by, is counted a thing of that worth with men, what is heaven, that God commendeth?

If the life that is attended with so many troubles is so loth to be let go by us, what is the life above?

Everybody will cry up the goodness of men; but who is there that is, as he should, affected with the goodness of God?

We seldom sit down to meat, but we eat and leave. So there is in Jesus Christ more merit and righteousness than the whole world has need of.

When the Interpreter had done, he takes them out into his garden again, and had them to a tree whose inside was all rotten and gone, and yet it grew and had leaves. Then said Mercy, What means this? This tree, said he, whose outside is fair, and whose inside is rotten, it is to which many may be compared that are in the garden of God; who with their mouths speak high in behalf of God, but indeed will do nothing for him; whose leaves are fair, but their heart good for nothing but to be tinder for the Devil's tinder-box.

Now supper was ready, the table spread, and all things set on the board; so they sat down and did eat, when one had given thanks. And the Interpreter did usually entertain those that lodged with him with music at meals, so the minstrels played. There was also one that did sing, and a very fine voice he had. His song was this:

The Lord is only my support,
And he that doth me feed;
How can I then want anything
Whereof I stand in need?

When the song and music was ended, the Interpreter asked
Christiana what it was that at first did move her to betake herself
to a pilgrim's life. Christiana answered, First, The loss of my husband came into my mind, at which I was heartily grieved; but all
that was but natural affection. Then after that, came the troubles
and pilgrimage of my husband into my mind, and also how like a
churl I had carried it to him as to that. So guilt took hold of my
mind, and would have drawn me into the Pond;[41] but that opportunely I had a dream of the well-being of my husband, and a letter
sent me by the King of that country where my husband dwells, to
come to him. The dream and the letter together so wrought upon
my mind that they forced me to this way.

INTER. But met you with no opposition before you set out of
doors?

CHRIS. Yes, a neighbour of mine, one Mrs. Timorous (she was
akin to him that would have persuaded my husband to go back
for fear of the lions). She all-to-befooled me for, as she called it,
my intended desperate adventure; she also urged what she could
to dishearten me to it: the hardships and troubles that my husband
met with in the way; but all this I got over pretty well. But a
dream that I had of two ill-looked ones, that I thought did plot
how to make me miscarry in my journey, that hath troubled
me much; yea, it still runs in my mind, and makes me afraid of
every one that I meet, lest they should meet me to do me a mischief, and to turn me out of the way. Yea, I may tell my Lord,
though I would not have everybody know it, that between this and
the gate by which we got into the way, we were both so sorely
assaulted that we were made to cry out, Murder! and the two that
made this assault upon us were like the two that I saw in my
dream.

Then said the Interpreter, Thy beginning is good, thy latter end
shall greatly increase. So he addressed himself to Mercy, and said
unto her, And what moved thee to come hither, sweetheart?

---

41. Possibly a variant spelling of "pound," an enclosure, place of confinement, or trap.

Then Mercy blushed and trembled, and for a while continued silent.

INTER. Then said he, Be not afraid, only believe, and speak thy mind.

MERCY. So she began and said, Truly, Sir, my want of experience is that that makes me covet to be in silence, and that also fills me with fears of coming short at last. I cannot tell of visions and dreams as my friend Christiana can; nor know I what it is to mourn for my refusing of the counsel of those that were good relations.

INTER. What was it then, dear heart, that hath prevailed with thee to do as thou hast done?

MERCY. Why, when our friend here was packing up to be gone from our town, I and another went accidentally to see her; so we knocked at the door and went in. When we were within, and seeing what she was doing, we asked what was her meaning. She said, she was sent for to go to her husband; and then she up and told us how she had seen him in a dream, dwelling in a curious[42] place, among immortals, wearing a crown, playing upon a harp, eating and drinking at his Prince's table, and singing praises to him for bringing him thither, &c. Now, methought, while she was telling these things unto us, my heart burned within me; and I said in my heart, If this be true, I will leave my father and my mother, and the land of my nativity, and will, if I may, go along with Christiana.

So I asked her further of the truth of these things, and if she would let me go with her; for I saw now that there was no dwelling, but with the danger of ruin, any longer in our town. But yet I came away with a heavy heart, not for that I was unwilling to come away, but for that so many of my relations were left behind.

And I am come with all the desire of my heart, and will go, if I may, with Christiana unto her husband and his King.

INTER. Thy setting out is good, for thou hast given credit to the truth. Thou art a Ruth, who did, for the love she bare to Naomi, and to the Lord her God, leave father and mother, and the land of her nativity, to come out and go with a people that she knew not heretofore. "The Lord recompense thy work, and full reward be given thee of the Lord God of Israel, under whose wings thou art come to trust."[43]

---

42. Exquisite, excellent.
43. Ruth 2:12.

Now supper was ended, and preparation was made for bed; the women were laid singly alone, and the boys by themselves. Now when Mercy was in bed, she could not sleep for joy, for that now her doubts of missing at last were removed further from her than ever they were before. So she lay blessing and praising God, who had had such favour for her.

In the morning they rose with the sun, and prepared themselves for their departure; but the Interpreter would have them tarry awhile, for, said he, you must orderly go from hence. Then said he to the damsel that first opened unto them. Take them and have them into the garden to the bath,[44] and there wash them and make them clean from the soil which they have gathered by travelling. Then Innocent the damsel took them, and had them into the garden, and brought them to the bath; so she told them that there they must wash and be clean, for so her master would have the women to do that called at his house, as they were going on pilgrimage. They then went in and washed, yea, they and the boys and all; and they came out of that bath, not only sweet and clean, but also much enlivened and strengthened in their joints. So when they came in, they looked fairer a deal than when they went out to the washing.

When they were returned out of the garden from the bath, the Interpreter took them, and looked upon them, and said unto them, "Fair as the moon."[45] Then he called for the seal, wherewith they used to be sealed that were washed in his bath. So the seal was brought, and he set his mark upon them, that they might be known in the places whither they were yet to go. Now the seal was the contents and sum of the passover which the children of Israel did eat when they came out from the land of Egypt, and the mark was set between their eyes.[46] This seal greatly added to their beauty, for it was an ornament to their faces. It also added to their gravity, and made their countenances more like them of angels.

Then said the Interpreter again to the damsel that waited upon these women, Go into the vestry and fetch out garments for these people. So she went and fetched out white raiment, and laid it down before him; so he commanded them to put it on. "It was fine linen, white and clean."[47] When the women were thus adorned,

---

44. The bath Sanctification. [B]
45. Song of Sol. 6:10.

46. Exod. 13:9.
47. Rev. 19:8, 14.

they seemed to be a terror one to the other; for that they could not see that glory each one on herself which they could see in each other. Now therefore they began to esteem each other better than themselves. For you are fairer than I am, said one; and you are more comely than I am, said another. The children also stood amazed to see into what fashion they were brought.

The Interpreter then called for a manservant of his, one Great-heart, and bid him take sword and helmet and shield; and take these my daughters, said he, and conduct them to the house called Beautiful, at which place they will rest next. So he took his weapons and went before them; and the Interpreter said, God speed. Those also that belonged to the family sent them away with many a good wish. So they went on their way and sung:

> This place has been our second stage;
>   Here we have heard and seen
> Those good things that, from age to age,
>   To others hid have been.
> The dung-hill raker, spider, hen,
>   The chicken, too, to me
> Hath taught a lesson; let me then
>   Conformèd to it be.
> The butcher, garden, and the field,
>   The robin and his bait,
> Also the rotten tree doth yield
>   Me argument of weight;
> To move me for to watch and pray,
>   To strive to be sincere;
> To take my cross up day by day,
>   And serve the Lord with fear.

Now I saw in my dream that they went on, and Great-heart went before them; so they went and came to the place where Christian's burden fell off his back, and tumbled into a sepulchre. Here then they made a pause; and here also they blessed God. Now, said Christiana, it comes to my mind what was said to us at the gate, to wit, that we should have pardon by word and deed; by word, that is, by the promise; by deed, to wit, in the way it was obtained. What the promise is, of that I know something; but what it is to have pardon by deed, or in the way that it was obtained, Mr. Great-heart, I suppose you know, wherefore, if you please, let us hear you discourse thereof.

GREAT-HEART. Pardon by the deed done is pardon obtained by some one for another that hath need thereof: not by the person pardoned, but in the way, saith another, in which I have obtained it. So then, to speak to the question more at large, the pardon that you and Mercy and these boys have attained, was obtained by another, to wit, by him that let you in at the gate; and he hath obtained it in this double way. He had performed righteousness to cover you, and spilt blood to wash you in.[48]

CHRIS. But if he parts with his righteousness to us, what will he have for himself?

GREAT-HEART. He has more righteousness than you have need of, or than he needeth himself.

CHRIS. Pray make that appear.

GREAT-HEART. With all my heart; but first I must premise that he of whom we are now about to speak is one that has not his fellow. He has two natures in one person, plain to be distinguished, impossible to be divided. Unto each of these natures a righteousness belongeth, and each righteousness is essential to that nature; so that one may as easily cause the nature to be extinct, as to separate its justice or righteousness from it. Of these righteousnesses, therefore, we are not made partakers so as that they, or any of them, should be put upon us that we might be made just, and live thereby. Besides these, there is a righteousness which this Person has, as these two natures are joined in one. And this is not the righteousness of the Godhead, as distinguished from the manhood; nor the righteousness of the manhood, as distinguished from the Godhead; but a righteousness which standeth in the union of both natures, and may properly be called the righteousness that is essential to his being prepared of God to the capacity of the mediatory office which he was to be intrusted with. If he parts with his first righteousness, he parts with his Godhead; if he parts with his second righteousness, he parts with the purity of his manhood; if he parts with this third, he parts with that perfection that capacitates him to the office of mediation. He has therefore another righteousness, which standeth in performance, or obedience to a revealed will;

---

48. A comment upon what was said at the gate, or a discourse of our being justified by Christ. [B]

and that is it that he puts upon sinners, and that by which their sins are covered. Wherefore he saith, "As by one man's disobedience many were made sinners; so by the obedience of one shall many be made righteous."[49]

CHRIS. But are the other righteousnesses of no use to us?

GREAT-HEART. Yes; for though they are essential to his natures and office, and cannot be communicated unto another, yet it is by virtue of them that the righteousness that justifies is for that purpose efficacious. The righteousness of his Godhead gives virtue to his obedience; the righteousness of his manhood giveth capability to his obedience to justify; and the righteousness that standeth in the union of these two natures to his office, giveth authority to that righteousness to do the work for which it is ordained.

So then, here is a righteousness that Christ, as God, has no need for, for he is God without it; here is a righteousness that Christ, as man, has no need of to make him so, for he is perfect man without it; again, here is a righteousness that Christ, as God-man, has no need of, for he is perfectly so without it. Here then is a righteousness that Christ, as God, as man, as God-man, has no need of, with reference to himself, and therefore he can spare it; a justifying righteousness that he for himself wanteth not, and therefore he giveth it away, hence 'tis called the "gift of righteousness."[50] This righteousness, since Christ Jesus the Lord has made himself under the Law, must be given away; for the Law doth not only bind him that is under it to do justly, but to use charity. Wherefore he must, he ought, by the Law, if he hath two coats, to give one to him that hath none. Now our Lord hath indeed two coats, one for himself and one to spare; wherefore he freely bestows one upon those that have none. And thus, Christiana, and Mercy, and the rest of you that are here, doth your pardon come by deed, or by the work of another man. Your Lord Christ is he that has worked, and has given away what he wrought for to the next poor beggar he meets.

But again, in order to pardon by deed, there must something be paid to God as a price, as well as something prepared to cover us withal. Sin has delivered us up to the just curse of a righteous law; now from this curse we must be justified by way of redemption, a price being paid for the harms we have done, and this is by the

49. Rom. 5:19.
50. Rom. 5:17.

blood of your Lord, who came and stood in your place and stead, and died your death for your transgressions. Thus has he ransomed you from your transgressions by blood, and covered your polluted and deformed souls with righteousness. For the sake of which, God passeth by you, and will not hurt you when he comes to judge the world.

CHRIS. This is brave. Now I see there was something to be learned by our being pardoned by word and deed. Good Mercy, let us labour to keep this in mind; and my children, do you remember it also. But, Sir, was not this it that made my good Christian's burden fall from off his shoulder, and that made him give three leaps for joy?

GREAT-HEART. Yes, it was the belief of this that cut those strings that could not be cut by other means; and it was to give him a proof of the virtue of this, that he was suffered to carry his burden to the Cross.

CHRIS. I thought so; for though my heart was lightful and joyous before, yet it is ten times more lightsome and joyous now. And I am persuaded by what I have felt, though I have felt but little as yet, that if the most burdened man in the world was here, and did see and believe as I now do, 'twould make his heart the more merry and blithe.

GREAT-HEART. There is not only comfort and the ease of a burden brought to us by the sight and consideration of these, but an endeared affection begot in us by it; for who can, if he doth but once think that pardon comes, not only by promise, but thus, but be affected by the way and means of his redemption, and so with the man that hath wrought it for him?

CHRIS. True; methinks it makes my heart bleed to think that he should bleed for me. Oh, thou loving one! Oh, thou Blessed one! Thou deservest to have me, thou hast bought me; thou deservest to have me all, thou hast paid for me ten thousand times more than I am worth! No marvel that this made the water stand in my husband's eyes, and that it made him trudge so nimbly on; I am persuaded he wished me with him, but vile wretch that I was, I let him come all alone. Oh, Mercy, that thy father and mother were here; yea, and Mrs. Timorous also. Nay, I wish now with all my heart that here was Madam Wanton too. Surely, surely, their hearts would be affected; nor could the fear of the one, nor the powerful lusts of the other, prevail with them to go home again, and to refuse to become good pilgrims.

GREAT-HEART. You speak now in the warmth of your affections. Will it, think you, be always thus with you? Besides, this is not communicated to every one, not to every one that did see Jesus bleed. There was that stood by, and that saw the blood run from his heart to the ground, and yet was so far off this that, instead of lamenting, they laughed at him, and instead of becoming his disciples, did harden their hearts against him. So all that you have, my daughters, you have by a peculiar impression made by a divine contemplating upon what I have spoken to you. Remember that 'twas told you that the hen by her common call gives no meat to her chickens. This you have therefore by a special grace.

Now I saw still in my dream that they went on until they were come to the place that Simple, and Sloth, and Presumption, lay and slept in, when Christian went by on pilgrimage; and behold, they were hanged up in irons, a little way off on the other side.

MERCY. Then said Mercy to him that was their guide and conductor, What are those three men? and for what are they hanged there?

GREAT-HEART. These three men were men of very bad qualities. They had no mind to be pilgrims themselves, and whosoever they could, they hindered. They were for sloth and folly themselves, and whoever they could persuade with, they made so too, and withal taught them to presume that they should do well at last. They were asleep when Christian went by; and now you go by, they are hanged.

MERCY. But could they persuade any to be of their opinion?

GREAT-HEART. Yes; they turned several out of the way. There was Slow-pace, that they persuaded to do as they. They also prevailed with one Short-wind, with one No-heart, with one Linger-after-lust, and with one Sleepy-head, and with a young woman her name was Dull, to turn out of the way and become as they. Besides, they brought up an ill report of your Lord, persuading others that he was a taskmaster. They also brought up an evil report of the good land, saying it was not half so good as some pretend it was. They also began to vilify his servants, and to count the very best of them meddlesome, troublesome busybodies. Further, they could call the bread of God, husks; the comforts of his children, fancies; the travel and labour of pilgrims, things to no purpose.

CHRIS. Nay, said Christiana, if they were such, they shall never be bewailed by me. They have but what they deserve; and I think it is well that they hang so near the highway, that others may see and take warning. But had it not been well if their crimes had been engraven on some plate of iron or brass, and left here, even where they did their mischiefs, for a caution to other bad men?

GREAT-HEART. So it is, as you well may perceive, if you will go a little to the wall.

MERCY. No, no, let them hang, and their names rot, and their crimes live for ever against them. I think it a high favour that they were hanged before we came hither; who knows else what they might have done to such poor women as we are? Then she turned it into a song, saying,

> Now then, you three, hang there and be a sign
> To all that shall against the truth combine.
> And let him that comes after fear this end,
> If unto pilgrims he is not a friend.
> And thou, my soul, of all such men beware,
> That unto holiness opposers are.

Thus they went on till they came at the foot of the Hill Difficulty, where again their good friend, Mr. Great-heart, took an occasion to tell them of what happened there when Christian himself went by. So he had them first to the spring. Lo, said he, this is the spring that Christian drank of, before he went up this hill; and then it was clear and good, but now it is dirty with the feet of some that are not desirous that pilgrims here should quench their thirst.[51] Thereat Mercy said, And why so envious, trow? But, said their guide, it will do, if taken up and put into a vessel that is sweet and good; for then the dirt will sink to the bottom, and the water will come out by itself more clear. Thus therefore Christiana and her companions were compelled to do. They took it up and put it into an earthen pot, and so let it stand till the dirt was gone to the bottom, and then they drank thereof.

Next he showed them the two by-ways that were at the foot of the hill, where Formality and Hypocrisy lost themselves. And, said he, these are dangerous paths: two were here cast away when Christian came by. And although, as you see, these ways are since stopped up with chains, posts, and a ditch, yet there are that will choose to adventure here, rather than take the pains to go up this hill.

---

51. Ezek. 34:18, 19. 'Tis difficult getting of good doctrine in erroneous times. [B]

CHRIS. "The way of transgressors is hard."[52] 'Tis a wonder that they can get into those ways without danger of breaking their necks.

GREAT-HEART. They will venture. Yea, if at any time any of the King's servants doth happen to see them, and doth call unto them, and tell them that they are in the wrong ways, and do bid them beware the danger, then they will railingly return them answer and say, "As for the word that thou hast spoken unto us in the name of the King, we will not hearken unto thee; but we will certainly do whatsoever thing goeth out of our own mouths," &c.[53] Nay, if you look a little farther, you shall see that these ways are made cautionary enough, not only by these posts and ditch and chain, but also by being hedged up. Yet they will choose to go there.

CHRIS. They are idle; they love not to take pains; uphill way is unpleasant to them. So it is fulfilled unto them as it is written, "The way of the slothful man is a hedge of thorns."[54] Yea, they will rather choose to walk upon a snare, than to go up this hill, and the rest of this way to the city.

Then they set forward and began to go up the hill, and up the hill they went; but before they got to the top, Christiana began to pant, and said, I daresay this is a breathing hill. No marvel if they that love their ease more than their souls choose to themselves a smoother way. Then said Mercy, I must sit down; also the least of the children began to cry. Come, come, said Great-heart, sit not down here, for a little above is the Prince's arbour. Then took he the little boy by the hand and led him up thereto.

When they were come to the arbour, they were very willing to sit down, for they were all in a pelting heat. Then said Mercy, How sweet is rest to them that labour! And how good is the Prince of pilgrims to provide such resting-places for them! Of this arbour I have heard much; but I never saw it before.[55] But here let us beware of sleeping; for as I have heard, for that it cost poor Christian dear.

Then said Mr. Great-heart to the little ones, Come, my pretty boys, how do you do? What think you now of going on pilgrim-

---

52. Prov. 13:15.
53. Jer. 44:16, 17.
54. Prov. 15:19.
55. Matt. 11:28, 29.

age? Sir, said the least, I was almost beat out of heart; but I thank you for lending me a hand at my need. And I remember now what my mother hath told me, namely, that the way to heaven is as up a ladder, and the way to hell is as down a hill. But I had rather go up the ladder to life, than down the hill to death.

Then said Mercy, But the proverb is, To go down the hill is easy. But James said (for that was his name), The day is coming when, in my opinion, going down the hill will be the hardest of all. 'Tis a good boy, said his master, thou hast given her a right answer. Then Mercy smiled; but the little boy did blush.

CHRIS. Come, said Christiana, will you eat a bit, a little to sweeten your mouths, while you sit here to rest your legs? For I have here a piece of pomegranate, which Mr. Interpreter put in my hand just when I came out of his doors. He gave me also a piece of a honey-comb[56] and a little bottle of spirits. I thought he gave you something, said Mercy, because he called you a to-side. Yes, so he did, said the other, but Mercy, it shall still be as I said it should when at first we came from home: thou shalt be a sharer in all the good that I have because thou so willingly didst become my companion. Then she gave to them, and they did eat, both Mercy and the boys. And said Christiana to Mr. Great-heart, Sir, will you do as we? But he answered, You are going on pilgrimage, and presently I shall return. Much good may what you have do to you. At home I eat the same every day. Now when they had eaten and drank, and had chatted a little longer, their guide said to them, The day wears away, if you think good, let us prepare to be going. So they got up to go, and the little boys went before. But Christiana forgot to take her bottle of spirits with her; so she sent her little boy back to fetch it. Then said Mercy, I think this is a losing place. Here Christian lost his roll; and here Christiana left her bottle behind her. Sir, what is the cause of this? So their guide made answer and said, The cause is sleep or forgetfulness. Some sleep when they should keep awake; and some forget when they should remember; and this is the very cause why often at the resting-places, some pilgrims in some things come off losers. Pilgrims should watch and remember what they had already received under their greatest enjoyments; but for want of doing so, ofttimes their rejoicing ends in tears, and their sunshine in a cloud. Witness the story of Christian at this place.

---

56. Song of Sol. 8:2; 5:1.

When they were come to the place where Mistrust and Timorous met Christian to persuade him to go back for fear of the lions,
they perceived as it were a stage, and before it, towards the road, a
broad plate with a copy of verses written thereon, and underneath,
the reason of the raising up of that stage in that place rendered. The
verses were these:

> Let him who sees this stage take heed
>   Unto his heart and tongue;
> Lest if he do not, here he speed
>   As some have long agone.

The words underneath the verses were, "This stage was built to
punish such upon, who through timorousness or mistrust shall be
afraid to go farther on pilgrimage. Also on this stage both Mistrust
and Timorous were burned through the tongue with a hot iron, for
endeavouring to hinder Christian in his journey."

Then said Mercy, This is much like to the saying of the Beloved,
"What shall be given unto thee? or what shall be done unto thee, thou
false tongue? Sharp arrows of the mighty, with coals of juniper."[57]

So they went on till they came within sight of the lions. Now Mr.
Great-heart was a strong man, so he was not afraid of a lion. But
yet when they were come up to the place where the lions were, the
boys that went before were glad to cringe behind, for they were
afraid of the lions, so they stepped back and went behind. At this
their guide smiled and said, How now, my boys, do you love to go
before when no danger doth approach, and love to come behind so
soon as the lions appear?[58]

Now as they went up, Mr. Great-heart drew his sword with
intent to make a way for the pilgrims in spite of the lions. Then
there appeared one that, it seems, had taken upon him to back the
lions; and he said to the pilgrims' guide, What is the cause of your
coming hither? Now the name of that man was Grim or Bloody-
man, because of his slaying of pilgrims, and he was of the race of
the giants.

GREAT-HEART. Then said the pilgrims' guide, These women and

---

57. Ps. 120:3, 4.
58. An emblem of those that go on bravely when there is no danger, but shrink
when troubles come. [B]

children are going on pilgrimage; and this is the way they must go, and go it they shall, in spite of thee and the lions.

GRIM. This is not their way, neither shall they go therein. I am come forth to withstand them, and to that end will back the lions.

Now to say truth, by reason of the fierceness of the lions, and of the *grim*-carriage of him that did back them, this way had of late lain much unoccupied, and was almost all grown over with grass.

CHRIS. Then said Christiana, Though the highways have been unoccupied heretofore, and though the travellers have been made in time past to walk through by-paths, it must not be so now I am risen, now "I am risen a mother in Israel."[59]

GRIM. Then he swore by the lions, but it should; and therefore bid them turn aside, for they should not have passage there.

GREAT-HEART. But their guide made first his approach unto Grim, and laid so heavily at him with his sword that he forced him to a retreat.

GRIM. Then said he that attempted to back the lions, Will you slay me upon mine own ground?

GREAT-HEART. It is the King's highway that we are in, and in his way it is that thou hast placed thy lions; but these women and these children, though weak, shall hold on their way in spite of thy lions. And with that he gave him again a downright blow and brought him upon his knees. With this blow he also broke his helmet, and with the next he cut off an arm. Then did the giant roar so hideously that his voice frighted the women, and yet they were glad to see him lie sprawling upon the ground. Now the lions were chained, and so of themselves could do nothing. Wherefore when old Grim that intended to back them was dead, Mr. Great-heart said to the pilgrims, Come now and follow me, and no hurt shall happen to you from the lions. They therefore went on, but the women trembled as they passed by them; the boys also looked as if they would die, but they all got by without further hurt.

Now then they were within sight of the porter's lodge, and they soon came up unto it; but they made the more haste after this to go thither, because it is dangerous travelling there in the night. So when they were come to the gate, the guide knocked, and the porter cried, Who is there? But as soon as the guide had said, It is I, he knew his voice, and came down (for the guide had oft before that come

---

59. Judg. 5:6, 7.

thither as a conductor of pilgrims). When he was come down he opened the gate, and seeing the guide standing just before it (for he saw not the women, for they were behind), he said unto him, How now, Mr. Great-heart, what is your business here so late tonight? I have brought, said he, some pilgrims hither, where, by my Lord's commandment, they must lodge; I had been here some time ago, had I not been opposed by the giant that did use to back the lions, but I, after a long and tedious combat with him, have cut him off, and have brought the pilgrims hither in safety.

PORTER. Will you not go in and stay till morning?

GREAT-HEART. No, I will return to my Lord tonight.

CHRIS. O Sir, I know not how to be willing you should leave us in our pilgrimage, you have been so faithful and so loving to us, you have fought so stoutly for us, you have been so hearty in coun-selling of us, that I shall never forget your favour towards us.

MERCY. Then said Mercy, Oh that we might have thy company to our journey's end! How can such poor women as we hold out in a way so full of troubles as this way is, without a friend and defender?

JAMES. Then said James, the youngest of the boys, Pray, Sir, be persuaded to go with us and help us, because we are so weak, and the way so dangerous as it is.

GREAT-HEART. I am at my Lord's commandment. If he shall allot me to be your guide quite through, I will willingly wait upon you. But here you failed at first; for when he bid me come thus far with you, then you should have begged me of him to have gone quite through with you, and he would have granted your request. How-ever, at present, I must withdraw; and so, good Christiana, Mercy, and my brave children, Adieu.

Then the porter, Mr. Watchful, asked Christiana of her country and of her kindred; and she said, I came from the City of Destruc-tion; I am a widow woman, and my husband is dead; his name was Christian, the Pilgrim. How! said the porter, was he your hus-band? Yes, said she, and these are his children; and this, pointing to Mercy, is one of my townswomen. Then the porter rang his bell, as at such times he is wont, and there came to the door one of the damsels, whose name was Humble-mind; and to her the porter said, Go tell it within that Christiana, the wife of Christian, and her children, are come hither on pilgrimage. She went in therefore and told it. But oh, what noise for gladness was there within, when the damsel did but drop that word out of her mouth!

So they came with haste to the porter, for Christiana stood still at the door. Then some of the most grave said unto her, Come in, Christiana, come in, thou wife of that good man; come in, thou blessed woman; come in, with all that are with thee. So she went in, and they followed her that were her children and her companions. Now when they were gone in, they were had into a very large room, where they were bidden to sit down; so they sat down, and the chief of the house was called to see and welcome the guests. Then they came in, and understanding who they were, did salute each other with a kiss, and said Welcome, ye vessels of the grace of God; welcome to us your friends.

Now because it was somewhat late, and because the pilgrims were weary with their journey, and also made faint with the sight of the fight and of the terrible lions, therefore they desired, as soon as might be, to prepare to go to rest. Nay, said those of the family, refresh yourselves first with a morsel of meat; for they had prepared for them a lamb, with the accustomed sauce belonging thereto, for the porter had heard before of their coming, and had told it to them within. So when they had supped, and ended their prayer with a psalm, they desired they might go to rest. But let us, said Christiana, if we may be so bold as to choose, be in that chamber that was my husband's when he was here; so they had them up thither, and they lay all in a room. When they were at rest, Christiana and Mercy entered into discourse about things that were convenient.

CHRIS. Little did I think once, that when my husband went on pilgrimage I should ever have followed.

MERCY. And you as little thought of lying in his bed, and in his chamber to rest, as you do now.

CHRIS. And much less did I ever think of seeing his face with comfort, and of worshipping the Lord the King with him, and yet now I believe I shall.

MERCY. Hark! Don't you hear a noise?

CHRIS. Yes; it is, as I believe, a noise of music, for joy that we are here.

MERCY. Wonderful! music in the house, music in the heart, and music also in heaven, for joy that we are here!

Thus they talked awhile, and then betook themselves to sleep. So in the morning, when these were awake, Christiana said to Mercy:

CHRIS. What was the matter that you did laugh in your sleep tonight? I suppose you were in a dream.

MERCY. So I was, and a sweet dream it was; but are you sure I laughed?

CHRIS. Yes; you laughed heartily; but prithee, Mercy, tell me thy dream.

MERCY. I was a-dreamed that I sat all alone in a solitary place, and was bemoaning of the hardness of my heart. Now I had not sat there long, but methought many were gathered about me to see me, and to hear what it was that I said. So they hearkened, and I went on bemoaning the hardness of my heart. At this, some of them laughed at me, some called me fool, and some began to thrust me about. With that, methought I looked up and saw one coming with wings toward me. So he came directly to me and said, Mercy, what aileth thee? Now when he had heard me make my complaint, he said, Peace be to thee. He also wiped mine eyes with his handkerchief, and clad me in silver and gold. He put a chain about my neck, and earrings in mine ears, and a beautiful crown upon my head.[60] Then he took me by the hand and said, Mercy, come after me. So he went up, and I followed, till we came at a golden gate. Then he knocked; and when they within had opened, the man went in, and I followed him up to a throne, upon which one sat, and he said to me, Welcome, daughter. The place looked bright and twinkling, like the stars, or rather like the sun; and I thought that I saw your husband there. So I awoke from my dream. But did I laugh?

CHRIS. Laugh! ay, and well you might to see yourself so well. For you must give me leave to tell you that I believe it was a good dream; and that, as you have begun to find the first part true, so you shall find the second at last. "God speaks once, yea, twice, yet man perceiveth it not, in a dream, in a vision of the night, when deep sleep falleth upon men, in slumbering upon the bed."[61] We need not, when a-bed, lie awake to talk with God. He can visit us while we sleep, and cause us then to hear his voice. Our heart ofttimes wakes when we sleep, and God can speak to that, either by words, by proverbs, by signs and similitudes, as well as if one was awake.

MERCY. Well, I am glad of my dream; for I hope ere long to see it fulfilled, to the making of me laugh again.

CHRIS. I think it is now high time to rise and to know what we must do.

---

60. Ezek. 16:9–13.
61. Job 33:14, 15.

MERCY. Pray, if they invite us to stay awhile, let us willingly accept of the proffer. I am the willinger to stay awhile here to grow better acquainted with these maids. Methinks Prudence, Piety, and Charity have very comely and sober countenances.

CHRIS. We shall see what they will do. So when they were up and ready, they came down, and they asked one another of their rest, and if it was comfortable or not.

MERCY. Very good, said Mercy; it was one of the best night's lodging that ever I had in my life.

Then said Prudence and Piety, If you will be persuaded to stay here awhile, you shall have what the house will afford.

CHAR. Ay, and that with a very good will, said Charity. So they consented and stayed there about a month or above, and became very profitable one to another. And because Prudence would see how Christiana had brought up her children, she asked leave of her to catechise them. So she gave her free consent. Then she began at the youngest, whose name was James.

PRUDENCE. And she said, Come, James, canst thou tell me who made thee?

JAMES. God the Father, God the Son, and God the Holy Ghost.

PRUD. Good boy. And canst thou tell me who saves thee?

JAMES. God the Father, God the Son, and God the Holy Ghost.

PRUD. Good boy still. But how doth God the Father save thee?

JAMES. By his grace.

PRUD. How doth God the Son save thee?

JAMES. By his righteousness, death, and blood, and life.

PRUD. And how doth God the Holy Ghost save thee?

JAMES. By his illumination, by his renovation, and by his preservation.

Then said Prudence to Christiana, You are to be commended for thus bringing up your children. I suppose I need not ask the rest these questions, since the youngest of them can answer them so well. I will therefore now apply myself to the next youngest.

PRUD. Then she said, Come, Joseph (for his name was Joseph), will you let me catechise you?

JOSEPH. With all my heart.

PRUD. What is man?

JOSEPH. A reasonable creature, so made by God, as my brother said.

PRUD. What is supposed by this word "saved"?

JOSEPH. That man by sin has brought himself into a state of captivity and misery.

PRUD. What is supposed by his being saved by the Trinity?

JOSEPH. That sin is so great and mighty a tyrant, that none can pull us out of its clutches but God; and that God is so good and loving to man, as to pull him indeed out of this miserable state.

PRUD. What is God's design in saving of poor men?

JOSEPH. The glorifying of his name, of his grace and justice, &c., and the everlasting happiness of his creature.

PRUD. Who are they that must be saved?

JOSEPH. Those that accept of his salvation.

PRUD. Good boy, Joseph; thy mother has taught thee well, and thou hast hearkened to what she hath said unto thee.

Then said Prudence to Samuel, who was the eldest but one,

PRUD. Come, Samuel, are you willing that I should catechise you also?

SAMUEL. Yes, forsooth, if you please.

PRUD. What is heaven?

SAM. A place and state most blessed, because God dwelleth there.

PRUD. What is hell?

SAM. A place and state most woeful, because it is the dwelling place of sin, the Devil, and death.

PRUD. Why wouldest thou go to heaven?

SAM. That I may see God, and serve him without weariness; that I may see Christ, and love him everlastingly; that I may have that fulness of the Holy Spirit in me that I can by no means here enjoy.

PRUD. A very good boy also, and one that has learned well.

Then she addressed herself to the eldest, whose name was Matthew; and she said to him, Come, Matthew, shall I also catechise you?

MATT. With a very good will.

PRUD. I ask then, if there was ever anything that had a being antecedent to or before God?

MATT. No, for God is eternal; nor is there anything excepting himself that had a being until the beginning of the first day. "For in six days the Lord made heaven and earth, the sea, and all that in them is."[62]

---

62. Exod. 20:11.

Prud. What do you think of the Bible?

Matt. It is the holy Word of God.

Prud. Is there nothing written therein but what you understand?

Matt. Yes; a great deal.

Prud. What do you do when you meet with such places therein that you do not understand?

Matt. I think God is wiser than I. I pray also that he will please to let me know all therein that he knows will be for my good.

Prud. How believe you as touching the resurrection of the dead?

Matt. I believe they shall rise, the same that was buried: the same in nature, though not in corruption. And I believe this upon a double account: First, because God has promised it; secondly, because he is able to perform it.

Then said Prudence to the boys, You must still hearken to your mother, for she can learn you more. You must also diligently give ear to what good talk you shall hear from others; for, for your sakes do they speak good things. Observe also and that with carefulness, what the heavens and the earth do teach you; but especially be much in the meditation of that Book that was the cause of your father's becoming a pilgrim. I for my part, my children, will teach you what I can while you are here, and shall be glad if you will ask me questions that tend to godly edifying.

Now by that these pilgrims had been at this place a week, Mercy had a visitor that pretended[63] some goodwill unto her, and his name was Mr. Brisk, a man of some breeding, and that pretended to religion; but a man that stuck very close to the world. So he came once or twice or more to Mercy, and offered love unto her. Now Mercy was of a fair countenance, and therefore the more alluring.

Her mind also was, to be always busying of herself in doing; for when she had nothing to do for herself, she would be making of hose and garments for others, and would bestow them upon them that had need. And Mr. Brisk, not knowing where or how she disposed of what she made, seemed to be greatly taken, for that he found her never idle. I will warrant her a good housewife, quoth he to himself.

Mercy then revealed the business to the maidens that were of the house, and inquired of them concerning him, for they did know

---

63. Professed.

him better than she. So they told her that he was a very busy young man, and one that pretended to religion; but was, as they feared, a stranger to the power of that which was good.

Nay then, said Mercy, I will look no more on him, for I purpose never to have a clog to my soul.

Prudence then replied that there needed no great matter of discouragement to be given to him, her continuing so as she had begun to do for the poor would quickly cool his courage.[64]

So the next time he comes he finds her at her old work, a-making of things for the poor. Then said he, What! always at it? Yes, said she, either for myself or for others. And what canst thou earn a day? quoth he. I do these things, saith she, "that I may be rich in good works, laying up in store a good foundation against the time to come, that I may lay hold on eternal life."[65] Why, prithee, what dost thou with them? Clothe the naked, said she. With that his countenance fell. So he forbore to come at her again. And when he was asked the reason why, he said that Mercy was a pretty lass, but troubled with ill conditions.[66]

When he had left her, Prudence said, Did I not tell thee that Mr. Brisk would soon forsake thee? yea, he will raise up an ill report of thee; for notwithstanding his pretence to religion and his seeming love to Mercy, yet Mercy and he are of tempers so different that I believe they will never come together.[67]

MERCY. I might a had husbands afore now, though I spake not of it to any; but they were such as did not like my conditions, though never did any of them find fault with my person. So they and I could not agree.

PRUD. Mercy in our days is little set by, any further than as to its name; the practice, which is set forth by thy conditions, there are but few that can abide.

MERCY. Well, said Mercy, if nobody will have me, I will die a maid, or my conditions shall be to me as a husband. For I cannot change my nature; and to have one that lies cross to me in this, that I purpose never to admit of as long as I live. I had a sister named Bountiful that was married to one of these churls, but he and she could

---

64. Inclination, intention.
65. 1 Tim. 6:18, 19.
66. Personal qualities, morals, behaviour.
67. Mercy in the practice of mercy rejected; while Mercy in the name of mercy is liked. [B]

never agree; but because my sister was resolved to do as she had began, that is, to show kindness to the poor, therefore her husband first cried her down at the cross[68] and then turned her out of his doors.

PRUD. And yet he was a professor, I warrant you.

MERCY. Yes, such a one as he was, and of such as he the world is now full, but I am for none of them all.

Now Matthew, the eldest son of Christiana, fell sick, and his sickness was sore upon him, for he was much pained in his bowels, so that he was with it, at times, pulled as 'twere both ends together. There dwelt also not far from thence one Mr. Skill, an ancient and well-approved physician. So Christiana desired it, and they sent for him, and he came. When he entered the room, and had a little observed the boy, he concluded that he was sick of the gripes.[69] Then he said to his mother, What diet has Matthew of late fed upon? Diet! said Christiana, nothing but that which is wholesome. The physician answered, This boy has been tampering with something that lies in his maw undigested, and that will not away without means. And I tell you, he must be purged, or else he will die.

SAM. Then said Samuel, Mother, mother, what was that which my brother did gather up and eat, so soon as we were come from the gate that is at the head of this way? You know that there was an orchard on the left hand, on the other side of the wall, and some of the trees hung over the wall, and my brother did pluck and did eat.

CHRIS. True, my child, said Christiana, he did take thereof and did eat; naughty boy as he was, I did chide him, and yet he would eat thereof.

SKILL. I knew he had eaten something that was not wholesome food. And that food, to wit, that fruit, is even the must hurtful of all. It is the fruit of Beelzebub's orchard. I do marvel that none did warn you of it; many have died thereof.

CHRIS. Then Christiana began to cry; and she said, O naughty boy! and O careless mother! What shall I do for my son?

SKILL. Come, do not be too much dejected; the boy may do well again, but he must purge and vomit.

CHRIS. Pray, Sir, try the utmost of your skill with him, whatever it costs.

---

68. Publicly condemned her, disclaimed responsibility for her (cross: market-cross; public square).
69. Gripes of conscience. [B]

SKILL. Nay, I hope I shall be reasonable. So he made him a purge, but it was too weak. 'Twas said, it was made of the blood of a goat, the ashes of a heifer, and with some of the juice of hyssop, &c.[70] When Mr. Skill had seen that that purge was too weak, he made him one to the purpose. 'Twas made *ex carne et sanguine Christi.*[71] (You know physicians give strange medicines to their patients.) And it was made up into pills, with a promise or two, and a proportionable quantity of salt.[72] Now he was to take them three at a time fasting, in half a quarter of a pint of the tears of repentance. When this potion was prepared and brought to the boy, he was loath to take it, though torn with the gripes as if he should be pulled in pieces. Come, come, said the physician, you must take it. It goes against my stomach, said the boy. I must have you take it, said his mother. I shall vomit it up again, said the boy. Pray, Sir, said Christiana to Mr. Skill, how does it taste? It has no ill taste, said the doctor; and with that she touched one of the pills with the tip of her tongue. Oh, Matthew, said she, this potion is sweeter than honey. If thou lovest thy mother, if thou lovest thy brothers, if thou lovest Mercy, if thou lovest thy life, take it. So with much ado, after a short prayer for the blessing of God upon it, he took it, and it wrought kindly with him. It caused him to purge, it caused him to sleep and rest quietly; it put him into a fine heat and breathing sweat, and did quite rid him of his gripes. So in little time he got up and walked about with a staff,[73] and would go from room to room, and talk with Prudence, Piety, and Charity, of his distemper, and how he was healed.

So when the boy was healed, Christiana asked Mr. Skill, saying, Sir, what will content you for your pains and care to and of my child? And he said, You must pay the Master of the College of Physicians, according to rules made in that case and provided.[74]

CHRIS. But, Sir, said she, what is this pill good for else?

SKILL. It is an universal pill; 'tis good against all the diseases that pilgrims are incident to, and when it is well prepared, it will keep good, time out of mind.

---

70. Heb. 9.
71. The Latin I borrow. [B] ("Of the flesh and blood of Christ"; see John 6:53–56.)
72. Mark 9:49, 50.
73. A word of God in the hand of his faith. [B]
74. Heb. 13:11–15.

CHRIS. Pray, Sir, make me up twelve boxes of them; for if I can get these, I will never take other physic.

SKILL. These pills are good to prevent diseases, as well as to cure when one is sick. Yea, I dare say it, and stand to it, that if a man will but use this physic as he should, it will make him live for ever. But, good Christiana, thou must give these pills no other way but as I have prescribed;[75] for if you do, they will do no good. So he gave unto Christiana physic for herself, and her boys, and for Mercy; and bid Matthew take heed how he eat any more green plums, and kissed them, and went his way.

It was told you before that Prudence bid the boys that if at any time they would, they should ask her some questions that might be profitable, and she would say something to them.

MATT. Then Matthew, who had been sick, asked her, Why, for the most part, physic should be bitter to our palates?

PRUD. To show how unwelcome the Word of God and the effects thereof are to a carnal heart.

MATT. Why does physic, if it does good, purge, and cause that we vomit?

PRUD. To show that the Word, when it works effectually, cleanseth the heart and mind. For look, what the one doth to the body, the other doth to the soul.

MATT. What should we learn by seeing the flame of our fire go upwards? and by seeing the beams and sweet influences of the sun strike downwards?

PRUD. By the going up of the fire we are taught to ascend to heaven by fervent and hot desires; and by the sun's sending his heat, beams, and sweet influences downwards, we are taught that the Saviour of the world, though high, reacheth down with his grace and love to us below.

MATT. Where have the clouds their water?

PRUD. Out of the sea.

MATT. What may we learn from that?

PRUD. That ministers should fetch their doctrine from God.

MATT. Why do they empty themselves upon the earth?

PRUD. To show that ministers should give out what they know of God to the world.

MATT. Why is the rainbow caused by the sun?

---

75. In a glass of the tears of repentance. [B]

PRUD. To show that the covenant of God's grace is confirmed to us in Christ.

MATT. Why do the springs come from the sea to us through the earth?

PRUD. To show that the grace of God comes to us through the body of Christ.

MATT. Why do some of the springs rise out of the tops of high hills?

PRUD. To show that the spirit of grace shall spring up in some that are great and mighty, as well as in many that are poor and low.

MATT. Why doth the fire fasten upon the candlewick?

PRUD. To show that unless grace doth kindle upon the heart there will be no true light of life in us.

MATT. Why is the wick and tallow, and all, spent to maintain the light of the candle?

PRUD. To show that body and soul, and all, should be at the service of, and spend themselves to maintain in good condition that grace of God that is in us.

MATT. Why doth the pelican pierce her own breast with her bill?

PRUD. To nourish her young ones with her blood, and thereby to show that Christ the blessed so loveth his young, his people, as to save them from death by his blood.

MATT. What may one learn by hearing the cock crow?

PRUD. Learn to remember Peter's sin, and Peter's repentance. The cock's crowing shows also that day is coming on; let then the crowing of the cock put thee in mind of that last and terrible day of judgement.

Now about this time their month was out; wherefore they signified to those of the house that 'twas convenient for them to up and be going. Then said Joseph to his mother, It is convenient that you forget not to send to the house of Mr. Interpreter, to pray him to grant that Mr. Great-heart should be sent unto us, that he may be our conductor the rest of our way. Good boy, said she, I had almost forgot. So she drew up a petition, and prayed Mr. Watchful, the Porter, to send it by some fit man to her good friend Mr. Interpreter; who, when it was come, and he had seen the contents of the petition, said to the messenger, Go tell them that I will send him. When the family where Christiana was saw that they had a purpose to go forward, they called the whole house together to give thanks to their King for sending of them such profitable guests as these. Which done, they said to Christiana, And shall we not show thee something, according as our custom is to do to pilgrims, on which thou mayest meditate when thou art upon the way? So they took Christiana, her children, and Mercy into the closet, and showed them one of the apples that Eve did eat of, and that she also did give to her husband, and that for the eating of which they both were turned out of Paradise, and asked her what she thought that was? Then Christiana said, It is food or poison, I know not which. So they opened the matter to her, and she held up her hands and wondered.

Then they had her to a place and showed her Jacob's ladder.[76] Now at that time there were some angels ascending upon it. So Christiana looked and looked, to see the angels go up; and so did the rest of the company. Then they were going into another place to show them something else; but James said to his mother, Pray bid them stay here a little longer, for this is a curious sight. So they turned again and stood feeding their eyes with this so pleasant a prospect. After this, they had them into a place where did hang up a golden anchor, so they bid Christiana take it down; for, said they, you shall have it with you, for 'tis of absolute necessity that you should, that you may lay hold of that within the veil, and stand steadfast, in case you should meet with turbulent weather, so they were glad thereof.[77] Then they took them and had them to the mount upon which Abraham our father had offered up Isaac his son, and showed them the altar, the wood, the fire, and the knife, for they remain to be seen to this very day.[78] When they had seen it, they held up their hands and blessed themselves, and said, Oh, what a man for love to his Master and for denial to himself was Abraham! After they had showed them all these things, Prudence took them into the dining-room, where stood a pair of excellent virginals; so she played upon them, and turned what she had showed them into this excellent song, saying,

> Eve's apple we have showèd you,
>   Of that be you aware;
> You have seen Jacob's ladder too,

76. Gen. 28:12.
77. Heb. 6:19.
78. Gen. 22.

Upon which angels are.

Upon which angels are.
An anchor you receivèd have,
  But let not these suffice,
Until with Abr'am you have gave
  Your best a sacrifice.

Now about this time one knocked at the door, so the Porter opened, and behold Mr. Great-heart was there; but when he was come in, what joy was there! For it came now fresh again into their minds how but a while ago he had slain old Grim Bloody-man the giant, and had delivered them from the lions.

Then said Mr. Great-heart to Christiana and to Mercy, My Lord hath sent each of you a bottle of wine, and also some parched corn, together with a couple of pomegranates. He has also sent the boys some figs and raisins to refresh you in your way.

Then they addressed themselves to their journey, and Prudence and Piety went along with them. When they came at the gate, Christiana asked the Porter if any of late went by? He said, No, only one some time since, who also told me that of late there had been a great robbery committed on the King's highway, as you go; but, he said, the thieves are taken and will shortly be tried for their lives. Then Christiana and Mercy were afraid; but Matthew said, Mother, fear nothing, as long as Mr. Great-heart is to go with us and be our conductor.

Then said Christiana to the Porter, Sir, I am much obliged to you for all the kindnesses that you have showed me since I came hither; and also for that you have been so loving and kind to my children; I know not how to gratify your kindness. Wherefore, pray, as a token of my respects to you, accept of this small mite; so she put a gold angel[79] in his hand, and he made her a low obeisance and said, Let thy garments be always white, and let thy head want no ointment. Let Mercy live and not die, and let not her works be few. And to the boys he said, Do you fly youthful lusts and follow after godliness with them that are grave and wise; so shall you put gladness into your mother's heart and obtain praise of all that are sober-minded. So they thanked the Porter and departed.

Now I saw in my dream that they went forward until they were

79. A coin.

come to the brow of the hill, where Piety, bethinking herself, cried out, Alas! I have forgot what I intended to bestow upon Christiana and her companions. I will go back and fetch it. So she ran and fetched it. While she was gone, Christiana thought she heard in a grove a little way off, on the right hand, a most curious, melodious note, with words much like these,

> Through all my life thy favour is
>   So frankly showed to me,
> That in thy house for evermore
>   My dwelling-place shall be.

And listening still, she thought she heard another answer it, saying,

> For why? The Lord our God is good,
> His mercy is for ever sure.
> His truth at all times firmly stood,
> And shall from age to age endure.

So Christiana asked Prudence what 'twas that made those curious notes. They are, said she, our country birds; they sing these notes but seldom, except it be at the spring, when the flowers appear, and the sun shines warm, and then you may hear them all day long. I often, said she, go out to hear them; we also ofttimes keep them tame in our house. They are very fine company for us when we are melancholy; also they make the woods, and groves, and solitary places, places desirous to be in.

By this time Piety was come again; so she said to Christiana, Look here, I have brought thee a scheme[80] of all those things that thou hast seen at our house, upon which thou mayest look when thou findest thyself forgetful, and call those things again to remembrance for thy edification and comfort.

Now they began to go down the hill into the Valley of Humiliation. It was a steep hill and the way was slippery; but they were very careful, so they got down pretty well. When they were down in the Valley, Piety said to Christiana, This is the place where Christian

---

80. Diagram, summary, outline.

your husband met with the foul fiend Apollyon, and where they had that dreadful fight that they had; I know you cannot but have heard thereof. But be of good courage; as long as you have here Mr. Great-heart to be your guide and conductor, we hope you will fare the better. So when these two had committed the pilgrims unto the conduct of their guide, he went forward and they went after.

GREAT-HEART. Then said Mr. Great-heart, We need not to be so afraid of this Valley, for here is nothing to hurt us, unless we procure it to ourselves. It is true, Christian did here meet with Apollyon, with whom he also had a sore combat; but that fray was the fruit of those slips that he got in his going down the hill, for they that get slips there must look for combats here. And hence it is that this Valley has got so hard a name; for the common people, when they hear that some frightful thing has befallen such a one in such a place, are of an opinion that that place is haunted with some foul fiend or evil spirit, when, alas! it is for the fruit of their doing that such things do befall them there.

This Valley of Humiliation is of itself as fruitful a place as any the crow flies over; and I am persuaded, if we could hit upon it, we might find somewhere hereabout something that might give us an account why Christian was so hardly beset in this place.

Then James said to his mother, Lo, yonder stands a pillar, and it looks as if something was written thereon; let us go and see what it is. So they went and found there written, "Let Christian's slips before he came hither, and the battles that he met with in this place, be a warning to those that come after." Lo, said their guide, did not I tell you that there was something hereabouts that would give intimation of the reason why Christian was so hard beset in this place? Then turning himself to Christiana, he said, No disparagement to Christian more than to many others whose hap and lot his was. For 'tis easier going up, than down this hill, and that can be said but of few hills in all these parts of the world. But we will leave the good man; he is at rest, he also had a brave victory over his enemy. Let him grant that dwelleth above that we fare no worse, when we come to be tried, than he.

But we will come again to this Valley of Humiliation. It is the best and most useful piece of ground in all those parts. It is fat ground, and, as you see, consisteth much in meadows; and if a man was to come here in the summertime, as we do now, if he knew not anything before thereof, and if he also delighted himself in the sight of his eyes, he might see that that would be delightful to him. Behold how green this Valley is, also how beautiful with lilies. I have also known many labouring men that have got good estates in this Valley of Humiliation. (For God resisteth the proud, but gives more, more grace to the humble.)[81] For indeed it is a very fruitful soil, and doth bring forth by handfuls. Some also have wished that the next way to their Father's house were here, that they might be troubled no more with either hills or mountains to go over; but the way is the way, and there's an end.

Now as they were going along and talking, they espied a boy feeding his father's sheep. The boy was in very mean clothes, but of a very fresh and well-favoured countenance; and as he sat by himself, he sang. Hark, said Mr. Great-heart, to what the shepherd's boy saith. So they hearkened, and he said,

> He that is down needs fear no fall;
>   He that is low, no pride;
> He that is humble ever shall
>   Have God to be his guide.
> I am content with what I have,
>   Little be it, or much:
> And, Lord, contentment still I crave,
>   Because thou savest such.
> Fulness to such a burden is
>   That go on pilgrimage;
> Here little, and hereafter bliss,
>   Is best from age to age.

Then said the guide, Do you hear him? I will dare to say that this boy lives a merrier life, and wears more of that herb called heart's-ease in his bosom, than he that is clad in silk and velvet; but we will proceed in our discourse.

In this Valley our Lord formerly had his country-house; he loved much to be here; he loved also to walk these meadows, for he found the air was pleasant. Besides, here a man shall be free from the noise and from the hurryings of this life. All states are full of

---

81. James 4:6.

noise and confusion, only the Valley of Humiliation is that empty and solitary place. Here a man shall not be so let and hindered in his contemplation, as in other places he is apt to be. This is a Valley that nobody walks in, but those that love a pilgrim's life. And though Christian had the hard hap to meet here with Apollyon, and to enter with him a brisk encounter, yet I must tell you that in former times men have met with angels here, have found pearls here, and have in this place found the words of life.

Did I say, our Lord had here in former days his country-house, and that he loved here to walk? I will add, in this place, and to the people that live and trace[82] these grounds, he has left a yearly revenue to be faithfully paid them at certain seasons, for their maintenance by the way, and for their further encouragement to go on in their pilgrimage.

SAMUEL. Now as they went on, Samuel said to Mr. Great-heart, Sir, I perceive that in this Valley my father and Apollyon had their battle; but whereabout was the fight? for I perceive this Valley is large.

GREAT-HEART. Your father had that battle with Apollyon at a place yonder before us, in a narrow passage just beyond Forgetful Green. And indeed that place is the most dangerous place in all these parts. For if at any time the pilgrims meet with any brunt, it is when they forget what favours they have received, and how unworthy they are of them. This is the place also where others have been hard put to it; but more of the place when we are come to it, for I persuade myself that to this day there remains either some sign of the battle, or some monument to testify that such a battle there was fought.

MERCY. Then said Mercy, I think I am as well in this Valley as I have been anywhere else in all our journey; the place, methinks, suits with my spirit. I love to be in such places where there is no rattling with coaches, nor rumbling with wheels; methinks here one may without much molestation be thinking what he is, whence he came, what he has done, and to what the King has called him; here one may think, and break at heart, and melt in one's spirit, until one's eyes become like the "fishpools of Heshbon."[83] They that go rightly through this Valley of Bacha make it a well; the rain that

---

82. Travel over.
83. Song of Sol. 7:4.

God sends down from heaven upon them that are here also "filleth the pools."[84] This Valley is that from whence also the King will give to his their vineyards;[85] and they that go through it shall sing (as Christian did, for all he met with Apollyon).

GREAT-HEART. It is true, said their guide, I have gone through this Valley many a time, and never was better than when here.

I have also been a conductor to several pilgrims, and they have confessed the same. "To this man will I look (saith the King), even to him that is poor and of a contrite spirit, and that trembles at my Word."[86]

Now they were come to the place where the aforementioned battle was fought. Then said the guide to Christiana, her children, and Mercy, This is the place, on this ground Christian stood, and up there came Apollyon against him. And look, did not I tell you? Here is some of your husband's blood upon these stones to this day; behold also how here and there are yet to be seen upon the place some of the shivers of Apollyon's broken darts; see also how they did beat the ground with their feet as they fought, to make good their places against each other; how also with their by-blows they did split the very stones in pieces. Verily, Christian did here play the man, and showed himself as stout as could, had he been there, even Hercules himself. When Apollyon was beat, he made his retreat to the next Valley, that is called the Valley of the Shadow of Death, unto which we shall come anon.

Lo, yonder also stands a monument, on which is engraven this battle and Christian's victory, to his fame throughout all ages. So because it stood just on the wayside before them, they stepped to it and read the writing, which word for word was this:

> Hard by here was a battle fought,
>   Most strange, and yet most true;
> Christian and Apollyon sought
>   Each other to subdue.
> The man so bravely played the man,
>   He made the fiend to fly;

---

84. Ps. 84:6.
85. Hos. 2:15.
86. Isa. 66:2.

Of which a monument I stand,
The same to testify.

When they had passed by this place, they came upon the borders of the Shadow of Death, and this Valley was longer than the other; a place also most strangely haunted with evil things, as many are able to testify, but these women and children went the better through it because they had daylight, and because Mr. Great-heart was their conductor.

When they were entered upon this Valley, they thought that they heard a groaning as of dead men: a very great groaning. They thought also they did hear words of lamentation spoken, as of some in extreme torment. These things made the boys to quake, the women also looked pale and wan; but their guide bid them be of good comfort.

So they went on a little further, and they thought that they felt the ground begin to shake under them, as if some hollow place was there; they heard also a kind of a hissing, as of serpents, but nothing as yet appeared. Then said the boys, Are we not yet at the end of this doleful place? But the guide also bid them be of good courage, and look well to their feet, lest haply, said he, you be taken in some snare.

Now James began to be sick, but I think the cause thereof was fear; so his mother gave him some of that glass of spirits that she had given her at the Interpreter's house, and three of the pills that Mr. Skill had prepared, and the boy began to revive. Thus they went on till they came to about the middle of the Valley, and then Christiana said, Methinks I see something yonder upon the road before us, a thing of a shape such as I have not seen. Then said Joseph, Mother, what is it? An ugly thing, child; an ugly thing, said she. But mother, what is it like? said he. It is like I cannot tell what, said she. And now it was but a little way off; then said she, It is nigh.

Well, well, said Mr. Great-heart, let them that are most afraid keep close to me. So the fiend came on, and the conductor met it; but when it was just come to him, it vanished to all their sights. Then remembered they what had been said some time ago, "Resist the Devil, and he will fly from you."[87]

They went therefore on, as being a little refreshed; but they had

---

87. James 4:7.

not gone far before Mercy, looking behind her, saw, as she thought, something most like a lion, and it came a great padding pace after, and it had a hollow voice of roaring, and at every roar that it gave it made all the Valley echo, and their hearts to ache, save the heart of him that was their guide. So it came up; and Mr. Great-heart went behind, and put the pilgrims all before him. The lion also came on apace, and Mr. Great-heart addressed himself to give him battle. But when he saw that it was determined that resistance should be made, he also drew back and came no further.

Then they went on again, and their conductor did go before them, till they came at a place where was cast up a pit the whole breadth of the way; and before they could be prepared to go over that, a great mist and darkness fell upon them, so that they could not see. Then said the pilgrims, Alas! now what shall we do? But their guide made answer, Fear not, stand still and see what an end will be put to this also. So they stayed there because their path was marred. They then also thought that they did hear more apparently the noise and rushing of the enemies; the fire also and the smoke of the pit was much easier to be discerned. Then said Christiana to Mercy, Now I see what my poor husband went through; I have heard much of this place, but I never was here afore now. Poor man, he went here all alone in the night; he had night almost quite through the way; also these fiends were busy about him, as if they would have torn him in pieces. Many have spoke of it, but none can tell what the Valley of the Shadow of Death should mean, until they come in it themselves. "The heart knows its own bitterness, and a stranger intermeddleth not with its joy."[88] To be here is a fearful thing.

GREAT-HEART. This is like doing business in great waters, or like going down into the deep; this is like being in the heart of the sea, and like going down to the bottoms of the mountains; now it seems as if the earth with its bars were about us for ever.[89] "But let them that walk in darkness and have no light, trust in the name of the Lord, and stay upon their God."[90] For my part, as I have told you already, I have gone often through this Valley, and have been much harder put to it than now I am, and yet you see I am alive. I would

88. Prov. 14:10.
89. Jon. 2:3–6.
90. Isa. 50:10.

not boast, for that I am not mine own saviour; but I trust we shall have a good deliverance. Come, let us pray for light to him that can lighten our darkness, and that can rebuke not only these, but all the Satans in hell.

So they cried and prayed, and God sent light and deliverance, for there was now no let in their way; no not there, where but now they were stopped with a pit. Yet they were not got through the Valley; so they went on still, and behold great stinks and loathsome smells, to the great annoyance of them. Then said Mercy to Christiana, There is not such pleasant being here as at the gate, or at the Interpreter's, or at the house where we lay last.

Oh, but, said one of the boys, it is not so bad to go through here as it is to abide here always; and for aught I know, one reason why we must go this way to the house prepared for us is, that our home might be made the sweeter to us.

Well said, Samuel, quoth the guide, thou hast now spoke like a man. Why, if ever I get out here again, said the boy, I think I shall prize light and good way better than ever I did in all my life. Then said the guide, We shall be out by and by.

So on they went, and Joseph said, Cannot we see to the end of this Valley as yet? Then said the guide, Look to your feet, for you shall presently be among the snares. So they looked to their feet and went on; but they were troubled much with the snares. Now when they were come among the snares, they espied a man cast into the ditch on the left hand, with his flesh all rent and torn. Then said the guide, That is one Heedless, that was a-going this way; he has lain there a great while. There was one Take-heed with him, when he was taken and slain; but he escaped their hands. You cannot imagine how many are killed hereabout, and yet men are so foolishly venturous as to set out lightly on pilgrimage, and to come without a guide. Poor Christian! it was a wonder that he here escaped; but he was beloved of his God. Also, he had a good heart of his own, or else he could never a done it. Now they drew towards the end of the way; and just there where Christian had seen the cave when he went by, out thence came forth Maul, a giant. This Maul did use to spoil young pilgrims with sophistry; and he called Great-heart by his name, and said unto him, How many times have you been forbidden to do these things? Then said Mr. Great-heart, What things? What things? quoth the giant; you know what things; but I will put an end to your trade. But pray, said Mr. Great-heart, before we fall to it, let us understand wherefore we must fight. (Now the women and children stood trembling, and knew not what to do.) Quoth the giant, You rob the country, and rob it with the worst of thefts. These are but generals, said Mr. Great-heart; come to particulars, man.

Then said the giant, Thou practisest the craft of a kidnapper;[91] thou gatherest up women and children, and carriest them into a strange country, to the weakening of my master's kingdom. But now Great-heart replied, I am a servant of the God of heaven; my business is to persuade sinners to repentance; I am commanded to do my endeavour to turn men, women, and children from darkness to light, and from the power of Satan to God; and if this be indeed the ground of thy quarrel, let us fall to it as soon as thou wilt.

Then the giant came up, and Mr. Great-heart went to meet him; and as he went, he drew his sword, but the giant had a club. So without more ado they fell to it, and at the first blow the giant stroke Mr. Great-heart down upon one of his knees; with that the women and children cried out, so Mr. Great-heart, recovering himself, laid about him in full lusty manner, and gave the giant a wound in his arm. Thus he fought for the space of an hour, to that height of heat that the breath came out of the giant's nostrils as the heat doth out of a boiling cauldron.

Then they sat down to rest them, but Mr. Great-heart betook him to prayer; also the women and children did nothing but sigh and cry all the time that the battle did last.

When they had rested them and taken breath, they both fell to it again, and Mr. Great-heart with a full blow fetched the giant down to the ground. Nay, hold, and let me recover, quoth he; so Mr. Great-heart fairly let him get up. So to it they went again, and the giant missed but little of all-to-breaking Mr. Great-heart's skull with his club.

Mr. Great-heart, seeing that, runs to him in the full heat of his spirit, and pierceth him under the fifth rib; with that the giant began to faint, and could hold up his club no longer. Then Mr. Great-heart seconded his blow, and smote the head of the giant from his shoulders. Then the women and children rejoiced, and Mr. Great-heart also praised God, for the deliverance he had wrought.

---

91. God's ministers counted as kidnappers. [B]

When this was done, they amongst them erected a pillar, and fastened the giant's head thereon, and wrote underneath in letters that passengers might read,

> He that did wear this head was one
>   That pilgrims did misuse;
> He stopped their way, he sparèd none,
>   But did them all abuse;
> Until that I, Great-heart, arose,
>   The pilgrims' guide to be;
> Until that I did him oppose,
>   That was their enemy.

Now I saw that they went to the ascent that was a little way off cast up to be a prospect for pilgrims. (That was the place from whence Christian had the first sight of Faithful his brother.) Wherefore here they sat down and rested; they also here did eat and drink and make merry, for that they had gotten deliverance from this so dangerous an enemy. As they sat thus and did eat, Christiana asked the guide if he had caught no hurt in the battle. Then said Mr. Great-heart, No, save a little on my flesh; yet that also shall be so far from being to my determent, that it is at present a proof of my love to my Master and you, and shall be a means by grace to increase my reward at last.

CHRIS. But were you not afraid, good Sir, when you saw him come with his club?

GREAT-HEART. It is my duty, said he, to distrust my own ability, that I may have reliance on him that is stronger than all.

CHRIS. But what did you think when he fetched you down to the ground at the first blow?

GREAT-HEART. Why, I thought, quoth he, that so my Master himself was served, and yet he it was that conquered at the last.

MATT. When you all have thought what you please, I think God has been wonderful good unto us, both in bringing us out of this Valley, and in delivering us out of the hand of this enemy; for my part, I see no reason why we should distrust our God any more, since he has now, and in such a place as this, given us such testimony of his love as this.

Then they got up and went forward. Now a little before them

stood an oak, and under it, when they came to it, they found an old pilgrim fast asleep; they knew that he was a pilgrim by his clothes, and his staff, and his girdle.

So the guide, Mr. Great-heart, awaked him, and the old gentleman, as he lift up his eyes, cried out, What's the matter? who are you? and what is your business here?

GREAT-HEART. Come, man, be not so hot, here are none but friends; yet the old man gets up and stands upon his guard, and will know of them what they were. Then said the guide, My name is Great-heart; I am the guide of these pilgrims, which are going to the Celestial Country.

HONEST. Then said Mr. Honest, I cry you mercy; I feared that you had been of the company of those that some time ago did rob Little-faith of his money; but now I look better about me, I perceive you are honester people.

GREAT-HEART. Why, what would or could you a done to a helped yourself, if we indeed had been of that company?

HON. Done! Why I would have fought as long as breath had been in me; and had I so done, I am sure you could never have given me the worst on't, for a Christian can never be overcome, unless he shall yield of himself.

GREAT-HEART. Well said, father Honest, quoth the guide; for by this I know thou art a cock of the right kind, for thou hast said the truth.

HON. And by this also I know that thou knowest what true pilgrimage is; for all others do think that we are the soonest overcome of any.

GREAT-HEART. Well, now we are so happily met, pray let me crave your name, and the name of the place you came from.

HON. My name I cannot, but I came from the town of Stupidity; it lieth about four degrees beyond the City of Destruction.

GREAT-HEART. Oh! are you that countryman, then? I deem I have half a guess of you; your name is old Honesty, is it not? So the old gentleman blushed, and said, Not Honesty in the abstract, but Honest is my name; and I wish that my nature shall agree to what I am called.

HON. But Sir, said the old gentleman, how could you guess that I am such a man, since I came from such a place?

GREAT-HEART. I had heard of you before, by my Master, for he knows all things that are done on the earth; but I have often wondered that any should come from your place, for your town is worse than is the City of Destruction itself.[92]

Hon. Yes, we lie more off from the sun, and so are more cold and senseless; but was a man in a mountain of ice, yet if the Sun of Righteousness will arise upon him, his frozen heart shall feel a thaw, and thus it hath been with me.

Great-heart. I believe it, father Honest, I believe it; for I know the thing is true.

Then the old gentleman saluted all the pilgrims with a holy kiss of charity, and asked them of their names, and how they had fared since they set out on their pilgrimage.

Chris. Then said Christiana, My name, I suppose, you have heard of; good Christian was my husband, and these four were his children. But can you think how the old gentleman was taken, when she told him who she was! He skipped, he smiled, and blessed them with a thousand good wishes, saying:

Hon. I have heard much of your husband, and of his travels and wars which he underwent in his days. Be it spoken to your comfort, the name of your husband rings over all these parts of the world: his faith, his courage, his enduring, and his sincerity under all, has made his name famous. Then he turned him to the boys and asked them of their names, which they told him. And then said he unto them: Matthew, be thou like Matthew the publican, not in vice, but virtue. Samuel, said he, be thou like Samuel the prophet, a man of faith and prayer. Joseph, said he, be thou like Joseph in Potiphar's house, chaste, and one that flies from temptation. And James, be thou like James the Just, and like James the brother of our Lord.

Then they told him of Mercy, and how she had left her town and her kindred to come along with Christiana and with her sons. At that the old honest man said, Mercy is thy name? By mercy shalt thou be sustained and carried through all those difficulties that shall assault thee in thy way, till thou shalt come thither where thou shalt look the Fountain of Mercy in the face with comfort.

All this while the guide, Mr. Great-heart, was very much pleased, and smiled upon his companion.

---

92. Stupefied ones are worse than those merely carnal. [B]

Now as they walked along together, the guide asked the old gentleman, if he did not know one Mr. Fearing, that came on pilgrimage out of his parts?

HON. Yes, very well, said he. He was a man that had the root of the matter in him; but he was one of the most troublesome pilgrims that ever I met with in all my days.

GREAT-HEART. I perceive you knew him; for you have given a very right character of him.

HON. Knew him! I was a great companion of his; I was with him most an end;[93] when he first began to think of what would come upon us hereafter, I was with him.

GREAT-HEART. I was his guide from my Master's house to the gates of the Celestial City.

HON. Then you knew him to be a troublesome one.

GREAT-HEART. I did so, but I could very well bear it; for men of my calling are oftentimes entrusted with the conduct of such as he was.

HON. Well then, pray let us hear a little of him, and how he managed himself under your conduct.

GREAT-HEART. Why, he was always afraid that he should come short of whither he had a desire to go. Everything frightened him that he heard anybody speak of, that had but the least appearance of opposition in it. I hear that he lay roaring at the Slough of Despond for about a month together; nor durst he, for all he saw several go over before him, venture, though they, many of them, offered to lend him their hand. He would not go back again neither. The Celestial City, he said, he should die if he came not to it; and yet was dejected at every difficulty, and stumbled at every straw that anybody cast in his way. Well, after he had lain at the Slough of Despond a great while, as I have told you, one sunshine morning, I do not know how, he ventured, and so got over; but when he was over, he would scarce believe it. He had, I think, a Slough of Despond in his mind; a slough that he carried everywhere with him, or else he could never have been as he was. So he came up to the gate— you know what I mean—that stands at the head of this way; and there also he stood a good while before he would adventure to knock. When the gate was opened, he would give back and give place to others, and say that he was not worthy. For, for all he got before

93. Almost always.

some to the gate, yet many of them went in before him. There the poor man would stand shaking and shrinking. I dare say it would have pitied one's heart to have seen him; nor would he go back again. At last he took the hammer that hanged on the gate in his hand, and gave a small rap or two; then one opened to him, but he shrank back as before. He that opened stepped out after him, and said, Thou trembling one, what wantest thou? With that he fell down to the ground. He that spoke to him wondered to see him so faint. So he said to him, Peace be to thee; up, for I have set open the door to thee. Come in, for thou art blessed. With that he gat up and went in trembling; and when he was in, he was ashamed to show his face. Well, after he had been entertained there awhile, as you know how the manner is, he was bid go on his way, and also told the way he should take. So he came till he came to our house. But as he behaved himself at the gate, so did he at my master the Interpreter's door. He lay thereabout in the cold a good while, before he would adventure to call; yet he would not go back. And the nights were long and cold then. Nay, he had a note of necessity in his bosom to my master, to receive him and grant him the comfort of his house, and also to allow him a stout and valiant conductor, because he was himself so chickenhearted a man; and yet for all that he was afraid to call at the door. So he lay up and down thereabouts, till, poor man, he was almost starved. Yea, so great was his dejection that though he saw several others, for knocking, got in, yet he was afraid to venture. At last, I think I looked out of the window, and perceiving a man to be up and down about the door, I went out to him and asked what he was; but, poor man, the water stood in his eyes, so I perceived what he wanted. I went therefore in and told it in the house, and we showed the thing to our Lord. So he sent me out again, to entreat him to come in; but I dare say I had hard work to do it. At last he came in; and I will say that for my Lord, he carried it wonderful lovingly to him. There were but few good bits at the table, but some of it was laid upon his trencher. Then he presented the note, and my Lord looked thereon, and said his desire should be granted. So when he had been there a good while, he seemed to get some heart, and to be a little more comfortable, for my master, you must know, is one of very tender bowels, especially to them that are afraid; wherefore he carried it so towards him as might tend most to his encouragement. Well, when he had had a sight of the things of the place, and was ready to take his journey to go to the city, my Lord, as he did to

Christian before, gave him a bottle of spirits and some comfortable
things to eat. Thus we set forward, and I went before him; but the
man was but of few words, only he would sigh aloud.

When we came to where the three fellows were hanged, he said
that he doubted that that would be his end also. Only he seemed
glad when he saw the Cross and the Sepulchre. There, I confess, he
desired to stay a little to look, and he seemed for a while after to be
a little cheery. When we came at the Hill Difficulty, he made no
stick at that, nor did he much fear the lions. For you must know
that his trouble was not about such things as those; his fear was
about his acceptance at last.

I got him in at the House Beautiful, I think, before he was willing. Also when he was in, I brought him acquainted with the
damsels that were of the place; but he was ashamed to make himself much for company. He desired much to be alone, yet he always
loved good talk, and often would get behind the screen to hear it.
He also loved much to see ancient things, and to be pondering
them in his mind. He told me afterwards that he loved to be in
those two houses from which he came last, to wit, at the gate, and
that of the Interpreter's, but that he durst not be so bold to ask.

When we went also from the House Beautiful down the hill into
the Valley of Humiliation, he went down as well as ever I saw man
in my life; for he cared not how mean he was, so he might be happy
at last. Yea, I think there was a kind of sympathy betwixt that valley and him; for I never saw him better in all his pilgrimage than
when he was in that valley.

Here he would lie down, embrace the ground, and kiss the very
flowers that grew in this valley. He would now be up every morning by break of day, tracing and walking to and fro in this valley.

But when he was come to the entrance of the Valley of the Shadow
of Death, I thought I should have lost my man. Not for that he had
any inclination to go back; that he always abhorred, but he was
ready to die for fear. Oh! the hobgoblins will have me! the hobgoblins will have me! cried he, and I could not beat him out on't. He
made such a noise and such an outcry here, that, had they but heard
him, it was enough to encourage them to come and fall upon us.

But this I took very great notice of, that this valley was as quiet
while he went through it as ever I knew it before or since. I suppose
these enemies here had now a special check from our Lord, and a
command not to meddle until Mr. Fearing was passed over it.

It would be too tedious to tell you of all. We will therefore only mention a passage[94] or two more. When he was come at Vanity Fair, I thought he would have fought with all the men in the fair. I feared there we should both have been knocked o' th' head, so hot was he against their fooleries. Upon the Enchanted Ground he was also very wakeful. But when he was come at the river where was no bridge, there again he was in a heavy case.[95] Now, now, he said, he should be drowned for ever, and so never see that face with comfort that he had come so many miles to behold.

And here also I took notice of what was very remarkable; the water of that river was lower at this time than ever I saw it in all my life. So he went over at last, not much above wet-shod. When he was going up to the gate, Mr. Great-heart began to take his leave of him, and to wish him a good reception above. So he said, I shall, I shall. Then parted we asunder, and I saw him no more.

Hon. Then it seems he was well at last.

Great-heart. Yes, yes. I never had doubt about him; he was a man of a choice spirit, only he was always kept very low, and that made his life so burdensome to himself and so troublesome to others. He was, above many, tender of sin. He was so afraid of doing injuries to others that he often would deny himself of that which was lawful, because he would not offend.

Hon. But what should be the reason that such a good man should be all his days so much in the dark.

Great-heart. There are two sorts of reasons for it: One is, the wise God will have it so. Some must pipe and some must weep. Now Mr. Fearing was one that played upon this bass. He and his fellows sound the sackbut, whose notes are more doleful than the notes of other music are; though indeed some say the bass is the ground of music. And for my part, I care not at all for that profession that begins not in heaviness[96] of mind. The first string that the musician usually touches is the bass, when he intends to put all in tune. God also plays upon this string first, when he sets the soul in tune for himself. Only here was the imperfection of Mr. Fearing, he could play upon no other music but this, till towards his latter end.

---

94. Incident, event.
95. Despondent condition.
96. Sadness, grief.

I make bold to talk thus metaphorically, for the ripening of the wits of young readers; and because, in the book of the Revelations, the saved are compared to a company of musicians that play upon their trumpets and harps, and sing their songs before the throne.

Hon. He was a very zealous man, as one may see by what relation you have given of him. Difficulties, lions, or Vanity Fair, he feared not at all: 'twas only sin, death, and hell that was to him a terror, because he had some doubts about his interest[97] in that celestial country.

Great-heart. You say right. Those were the things that were his troublers, and they, as you have well observed, arose from the weakness of his mind thereabout, not from weakness of spirit as to the practical part of a pilgrim's life. I dare believe that, as the proverb is, he could have bit a firebrand, had it stood in his way; but the things with which he was oppressed no man ever yet could shake off with ease.

Chris. Then said Christiana, This relation of Mr. Fearing has done me good. I thought nobody had been like me, but I see there was some semblance 'twixt this good man and I; only we differed in two things: his troubles were so great, they brake out, but mine I kept within. His also lay so hard upon him, they made him that he could not knock at the houses provided for entertainment; but my trouble was always such as made me knock the louder.

Mercy. If I might also speak my heart, I must say that something of him has also dwelt in me. For I have ever been more afraid of the lake and the loss of a place in Paradise, than I have been of the loss of other things. Oh, thought I, may I have the happiness to have a habitation there, 'tis enough, though I part with all the world to win it.

Matt. Then said Matthew, Fear was one thing that made me think that I was far from having that within me that accompanies salvation; but if it was so with such a good man as he, why may it not go well with me?

James. No fears, no grace, said James. Though there is not always grace where there is the fear of hell, yet to be sure, there is no grace where there is no fear of God.

Great-heart. Well said, James, thou hast hit the mark; for the fear of God is the beginning of wisdom, and to be sure, they that want the beginning have neither middle nor end. But we will here

97. Right to a share in.

conclude our discourse of Mr. Fearing, after we have sent after him this farewell.

> Well, Master Fearing, thou didst fear
>   Thy God, and wast afraid
> Of doing anything, while here,
>   That would have thee betrayed.
> And didst thou fear the lake and pit?
>   Would others did so too.
> For, as for them that want thy wit,
>   They do themselves undo.

Now I saw that they still went on in their talk; for after Mr. Great-heart had made an end with Mr. Fearing, Mr. Honest began to tell them of another, but his name was Mr. Self-will. He pretended himself to be a pilgrim, said Mr. Honest; but I persuade myself he never came in at the gate that stands at the head of the way.

GREAT-HEART. Had you ever any talk with him about it?

HON. Yes, more than once or twice; but he would always be like himself, self-willed. He neither cared for man, nor argument, nor yet example; what his mind prompted him to do, that he would do, and nothing else could he be got to.

GREAT-HEART. Pray, what principles did he hold? for I suppose you can tell.

HON. He held that a man might follow the vices as well as the virtues of the pilgrims; and that if he did both, he should be certainly saved.

GREAT-HEART. How! If he had said, 'tis possible for the best to be guilty of the vices, as well as to partake of the virtues of pilgrims, he could not much have been blamed; for indeed we are exempted from no vice absolutely, but on condition that we watch and strive. But this, I perceive, is not the thing; but if I understand you right, your meaning is that he was of that opinion, that it was allowable so to be.

HON. Ay, ay, so I mean; and so he believed and practised.

GREAT-HEART. But what ground had he for his so saying?

HON. Why, he said he had the Scripture for his warrant.

GREAT-HEART. Prithee, Mr. Honest, present us with a few particulars.

HON. So I will. He said, to have to do with other men's wives had been practised by David, God's beloved; and therefore he could do it. He said, to have more women than one was a thing that Solomon practised; and therefore he could do it. He said, that Sarah and the godly midwives of Egypt lied, and so did save Rahab; and therefore he could do it. He said, that the disciples went at the bidding of their Master, and took away the owner's ass; and therefore he could do so too. He said, that Jacob got the inheritance of his father in the way of guile and dissimulation; and therefore he could do so too.

GREAT-HEART. High base,[98] indeed! And you are sure he was of this opinion?

HON. I have heard him plead for it, bring Scripture for it, bring argument for it, &c.

GREAT-HEART. An opinion that is not fit to be with any allowance in the world.

HON. You must understand me rightly. He did not say that any man might do this; but that those that had the virtues of those that did such things might also do the same.

GREAT-HEART. But what more false than such a conclusion? For this is as much as to say that because good men heretofore have sinned of infirmity, therefore he had allowance to do it of a presumptuous mind; or if because a child, by the blast of the wind or for that it stumbled at a stone, fell down and defiled itself in mire, therefore he might wilfully lie down and wallow like a boar therein. Who could a thought that anyone could so far a been blinded by the power of lust? But what is written must be true: They "stumble at the Word, being disobedient; whereunto also they were appointed."[99]

His supposing that such may have the godly men's virtues, who addict themselves to their vices, is also a delusion as strong as the other. It is just as if the dog should say, I have, or may have, the qualities of the child, because I lick up its stinking excrements. To eat up the sin of God's people is no sign of one that is possessed with their virtues. Nor can I believe that one that is of this opinion can at present have faith or love in him. But I know you have made strong objections against him; prithee, what can he say for himself?

HON. Why, he says, To do this by way of opinion seems abundance more honest than to do it, and yet hold contrary to it in opinion.

GREAT-HEART. A very wicked answer; for though to let loose the

98. Very immoral and degrading.
99. 1 Pet. 2:8.

bridle to lusts, while our opinions are against such things, is bad, yet to sin, and plead a toleration so to do, is worse. The one stumbles beholders accidentally, the other pleads them into the snare.

Hon. There are many of this man's mind, that have not this man's mouth; and *that* makes going on pilgrimage of so little esteem as it is.

Great-heart. You have said the truth, and it is to be lamented; but he that feareth the King of Paradise shall come out of them all.

Chris. There are strange opinions in the world. I know one that said 'twas time enough to repent when they came to die.

Great-heart. Such are not overwise. That man would a been loath, might he have had a week to run twenty miles in for his life, to have deferred that journey to the last hour of that week.

Hon. You say right; and yet the generality of them that count themselves pilgrims do indeed do thus. I am, as you see, an old man, and have been a traveller in this road many a day; and I have taken notice of many things.

I have seen some that have set out as if they would drive all the world afore them, who yet have in few days died as they in the wilderness, and so never got sight of the promised land.

I have seen some that have promised nothing at first setting out to be pilgrims, and that one would a thought could not have lived a day, that have yet proved very good pilgrims.

I have seen some who have run hastily forward, that again have after a little time run as fast just back again.

I have seen some who have spoken very well of a pilgrim's life at first, that after a while have spoken as much against it.

I have heard some, when they first set out for Paradise, say positively there is such a place; who, when they have been almost there, have come back again, and said there is none.

I have heard some vaunt what they would do in case they should be opposed, that have even at a false alarm fled faith, the pilgrim's way, and all.

Now as they were thus in their way, there came one running to meet them, and said, Gentlemen, and you of the weaker sort, if you love life, shift yourselves, for the robbers are before you.

Great-heart. Then said Mr. Great-heart, They be the three that set upon Little-faith heretofore. Well, said he, we are ready for them; so they went on their way. Now they looked at every turning when they should a met with the villains; but whether they heard of Mr. Great-heart, or whether they had some other game, they came not up to the pilgrims.

Christiana then wished for an inn for herself and her children, because they were weary. Then said Mr. Honest, There is one a little before us, where a very honourable disciple, one Gaius, dwells.[100] So they all concluded to turn in thither, and the rather, because the old gentleman gave him so good a report. So when they came to the door, they went in, not knocking, for folks use not to knock at the door of an inn. Then they called for the master of the house, and he came to them. So they asked if they might lie there that night.

GAIUS. Yes, gentlemen, if ye be true men, for my house is for none but pilgrims. Then was Christiana, Mercy, and the boys, the more glad, for that the innkeeper was a lover of pilgrims. So they called for rooms, and he showed them one for Christiana and her children and Mercy, and another for Mr. Great-heart and the old gentleman.

GREAT-HEART. Then said Mr. Great-heart, Good Gaius, what hast thou for supper? for these pilgrims have come far today and are weary.

GAIUS. It is late, said Gaius, so we cannot conveniently go out to seek food; but such as we have you shall be welcome to, if that will content.

GREAT-HEART. We will be content with what thou hast in the house, forasmuch as I have proved thee; thou art never destitute of that which is convenient.

Then he went down and spake to the cook, whose name was Taste-that-which-is-good, to get ready supper for so many pilgrims. This done, he comes up again, saying, Come, my good friends, you are welcome to me, and I am glad that I have a house to entertain you; and while supper is making ready, if you please, let us entertain one another with some good discourse. So they all said, Content.

GAIUS. Then said Gaius, Whose wife is this aged matron? and whose daughter is this young damsel?

GREAT-HEART. The woman is the wife of one Christian, a pilgrim of former times; and these are his four children. The maid is one of her acquaintance; one that she hath persuaded to come with her on pilgrimage. The boys take all after their father, and covet to tread in his steps; yea, if they do but see any place where the old pilgrim

---

100. Rom. 16:23.

hath lain, or any print of his foot, it ministereth joy to their hearts, and they covet to lie or tread in the same.

GAIUS. Then said Gaius, Is this Christian's wife? and are these Christian's children? I knew your husband's father, yea, also his father's father. Many have been good of this stock; their ancestors dwelt first at Antioch.[101] Christian's progenitors (I suppose you have heard your husband talk of them) were very worthy men. They have, above any that I know, showed themselves men of great virtue and courage for the Lord of the pilgrims, his ways, and them that loved him. I have heard of many of your husband's relations that have stood all trials for the sake of the truth. Stephen, that was one of the first of the family from whence your husband sprang, was knocked on the head with stones. James, another of this generation, was slain with the edge of the sword. To say nothing of Paul and Peter, men anciently of the family from whence your husband came, there was Ignatius, who was cast to the lions; Romanus, whose flesh was cut by pieces from his bones; and Polycarp, that played the man in the fire. There was he that was hanged up in a basket in the sun, for the wasps to eat; and he who they put into a sack, and cast him into the sea to be drowned. It would be utterly impossible to count up all of that family that have suffered injuries and death, for the love of a pilgrim's life. Nor can I but be glad to see that thy husband has left behind him four such boys as these. I hope they will bear up their father's name, and tread in their father's steps, and come to their father's end.

GREAT-HEART. Indeed, Sir, they are likely lads; they seem to choose heartily their father's ways.

GAIUS. That is it that I said; wherefore Christian's family is like still to spread abroad upon the face of the ground, and yet to be numerous upon the face of the earth. Wherefore let Christiana look out some damsels for her sons, to whom they may be betrothed, &c., that the name of their father and the house of his progenitors may never be forgotten in the world.

HON. 'Tis pity this family should fall and be extinct.

GAIUS. Fall it cannot, but be diminished it may; but let Christiana take my advice, and that is the way to uphold it.

And Christiana, said this innkeeper, I am glad to see thee and thy friend Mercy together here, a lovely couple. And may I advise, take Mercy into a nearer relation to thee. If she will, let her be given

101. Acts 11:26.

to Matthew, thy eldest son; 'tis the way to preserve you a posterity in the earth. So this match was concluded, and in process of time they were married; but more of that hereafter.

Gaius also proceeded and said, I will now speak on the behalf of women, to take away their reproach. For as death and the curse came into the world by a woman, so also did life and health: "God sent forth his Son, made of a woman."[102] Yea, to show how much those that came after did abhor the act of their mother, this sex, in the Old Testament, coveted children, if happily this or that woman might be the mother of the Saviour of the world.

I will say again that when the Saviour was come, women rejoiced in him before either man or angel. I read not that ever any man did give unto Christ so much as one groat; but the women followed him, and ministered to him of their substance. 'Twas a woman that washed his feet with tears, and a woman that anointed his body to the burial. They were women that wept when he was going to the Cross, and women that followed him from the Cross, and that sat by his Sepulchre when he was buried. They were women that were first with him at his resurrection-morn, and women that brought tidings first to his disciples that he was risen from the dead. Women therefore are highly favoured, and show by these things that they are sharers with us in the grace of life.

Now the cook sent up to signify that supper was almost ready, and sent one to lay the cloth, the trenchers, and to set the salt and bread in order.

Then said Matthew, The sight of this cloth, and of this forerunner of the supper, begetteth in me a greater appetite to my food than I had before.

GAIUS. So let all ministering doctrines to thee in this life, beget in thee a greater desire to sit at the supper of the great King in his kingdom; for all preaching, books, and ordinances here, are but as the laying of the trenchers, and as setting of salt upon the board, when compared with the feast that our Lord will make for us when we come to his house.

So supper came up; and first, a heave-shoulder and a wave-breast[103] was set on the table before them, to show that they must

---

102. Gal. 4:4.

103. The shoulder of an animal lifted up in sacrifice; the breast of an animal lifted up in sacrifice and moved from side to side: see Lev. 7:32–34; 10:14, 15.

begin their meal with prayer and praise to God. The heave-shoulder David lifted his heart up to God with; and with the wave-breast, where his heart lay, with that he used to lean upon his harp when he played. These two dishes were very fresh and good, and they all ate heartily well thereof.

The next they brought up was a bottle of wine, red as blood. So Gaius said to them, Drink freely; this is the juice of the true vine, that makes glad the heart of God and man.[104] So they drank and were merry.

The next was a dish of milk well crumbed; but Gaius said, Let the boys have that, that they may grow thereby.[105]

Then they brought up in course a dish of butter and honey. Then said Gaius, Eat freely of this; for this is good to cheer up and strengthen your judgements and understandings. This was our Lord's dish when he was a child; "Butter and honey shall he eat, that he may know to refuse the evil and choose the good."[106]

Then they brought them up a dish of apples, and they were very good-tasted fruit. Then said Matthew, May we eat apples, since they were such, by and with which the serpent beguiled our first mother?

Then said Gaius,

> Apples were they with which we were beguiled;
> Yet sin, not apples, hath our souls defiled.
> Apples forbid, if eat, corrupt the blood;
> To eat such, when commanded, does us good.
> Drink of his flagons, then, thou church, his dove,
> And eat his apples, who are sick of love.[107]

Then said Matthew, I made the scruple, because I a while since was sick with eating of fruit.

GAIUS. Forbidden fruit will make you sick, but not what our Lord has tolerated.

While they were thus talking, they were presented with another dish, and 'twas a dish of nuts.[108] Then said some at the table, Nuts spoil tender teeth, especially the teeth of children; which when Gaius heard, he said,

---

104. John 15:1–5; Judg. 9:13.
105. 1 Pet. 2:2.
106. Isa. 7:15.

107. Song of Sol. 2:5.
108. Song of Sol. 6:11.

Hard texts are nuts (I will not call them cheaters),
Whose shells do keep their kernels from the eaters.
Ope then the shells, and you shall have the meat;
They here are brought for you to crack and eat.

Then were they very merry, and sat at the table a long time, talking of many things. Then said the old gentleman, My good landlord, while we are cracking your nuts, if you please, do you open this riddle:

A man there was, though some did count him mad,
The more he cast away, the more he had.

Then they all gave good heed, wondering what good Gaius would say; so he sat still awhile, and then thus replied:

He that bestows his goods upon the poor,
Shall have as much again, and ten times more.

Then said Joseph, I dare say, Sir, I did not think you could have found it out.

Oh! said Gaius, I have been trained up in this way a great while; nothing teaches like experience. I have learned of my Lord to be kind, and have found by experience that I have gained thereby: "There is that scattereth, yet increaseth; and there is that withholdeth more than is meet, but it tendeth to poverty. There is that maketh himself rich, yet hath nothing; there is that maketh himself poor, yet hath great riches."[109]

Then Samuel whispered to Christiana his mother, and said, Mother, this is a very good man's house, let us stay here a good while, and let my brother Matthew be married here to Mercy before we go any further.

The which Gaius the host overhearing said, With a very good will, my child.

So they stayed there more than a month, and Mercy was given to Matthew to wife.

While they stayed here, Mercy, as her custom was, would be

---

109. Prov. 11:24; 13:7.

making coats and garments to give to the poor, by which she brought up a very good report upon the pilgrims.

But to return again to our story. After supper the lads desired a bed, for that they were weary with travelling. Then Gaius called to show them their chamber, but said Mercy, I will have them to bed. So she had them to bed, and they slept well, but the rest sat up all night, for Gaius and they were such suitable company that they could not tell how to part. Then after much talk of their Lord, themselves, and their journey, old Mr. Honest, he that put forth the riddle of Gaius, began to nod. Then said Great-heart, What, Sir, you begin to be drowsy; come, rub up. Now here's a riddle for you. Then said Mr. Honest, Let us hear it.

Then said Mr. Great-heart,

> He that will kill, must first be overcome,
> Who live abroad would, first must die at home.

Huh, said Mr. Honest, it is a hard one, hard to expound, and harder to practise. But come, landlord, said he, I will, if you please, leave my part to you; do you expound it, and I will hear what you say.

No, said Gaius, 'twas put to you, and 'tis expected that you should answer it.

Then said the old gentleman,

> He first by grace must conquered be,
>   That sin would mortify;
> And who, that lives, would convince[110] me,
>   Unto himself must die.

It is right, said Gaius; good doctrine and experience teaches this. For first, until grace displays itself and overcomes the soul with its glory, it is altogether without heart to oppose sin; besides, if sin is Satan's cords, by which the soul lies bound, how should it make resistance, before it is loosed from that infirmity?

Secondly, Nor will any, that knows either reason or grace, believe that such a man can be a living monument of grace that is a slave to his own corruptions.

---

110. Overcome.

And now it comes in my mind, I will tell you a story worth the hearing. There were two men that went on pilgrimage: the one began when he was young, the other when he was old. The young man had strong corruptions to grapple with; the old man's were decayed with the decays of nature. The young man trod his steps as even as did the old one, and was every way as light as he. Who now, or which of them, had their graces shining clearest, since both seemed to be alike?

HON. The young man's, doubtless. For that which heads it against the greatest opposition, gives best demonstration that it is strongest; especially when it also holdeth pace with that that meets not with half so much; as, to be sure, old age does not.

Besides, I have observed that old men have blessed themselves with this mistake, namely, taking the decays of nature for a gracious conquest over corruptions, and so have been apt to beguile themselves. Indeed, old men that are gracious are best able to give advice to them that are young, because they have seen most of the emptiness of things. But yet, for an old and a young to set out both together, the young one has the advantage of the fairest discovery of a work of grace within him, though the old man's corruptions are naturally the weakest.

Thus they sat talking till break of day. Now when the family was up, Christiana bid her son James that he should read a chapter; so he read the fifty-third of Isaiah. When he had done, Mr. Honest asked, why it was said that the Saviour is said to come "out of a dry ground"; and also that "he had no form nor comeliness in him"?

GREAT-HEART. Then said Mr. Great-heart, To the first, I answer, Because the church of the Jews, of which Christ came, had then lost almost all the sap and spirit of religion. To the second, I say, The words are spoken in the person of the unbelievers, who, because they want that eye that can see into our Prince's heart, therefore they judge of him by the meanness of his outside. Just like those that know not that precious stones are covered over with a homely crust; who, when they have found one, because they know not what they have found, cast it again away as men do a common stone.

Well, said Gaius, now you are here, and since, as I know, Mr. Great-heart is good at his weapons, if you please, after we have refreshed ourselves, we will walk into the fields, to see if we can do any good. About a mile from hence there is one Slay-good, a giant that does much annoy the King's highway in these parts; and I know whereabout his haunt is. He is master of a number of thieves; 'twould be well if we could clear these parts of him.

So they consented and went, Mr. Great-heart with his sword, helmet, and shield, and the rest with spears and staves.

When they came to the place where he was, they found him with one Feeble-mind in his hands, whom his servants had brought unto him, having taken him in the way. Now the giant was rifling of him, with a purpose after that to pick his bones, for he was of the nature of flesh-eaters.

Well, so soon as he saw Mr. Great-heart and his friends at the mouth of his cave with their weapons, he demanded what they wanted.

GREAT-HEART. We want thee, for we are come to revenge the quarrel of the many that thou hast slain of the pilgrims, when thou hast dragged them out of the King's highway; wherefore come out of thy cave. So he armed himself and came out, and to a battle they went, and fought for above an hour, and then stood still to take wind.

SLAY. Then said the giant, Why are you here on my ground?

GREAT-HEART. To revenge the blood of pilgrims, as I also told thee before. So they went to it again, and the giant made Mr. Great-heart give back, but he came up again, and in the greatness of his mind he let fly with such stoutness at the giant's head and sides, that he made him let his weapon fall out of his hand; so he smote him, and slew him, and cut off his head, and brought it away to the inn. He also took Feeble-mind the pilgrim, and brought him with him to his lodgings. When they were come home, they showed his head to the family, and then set it up, as they had done others before, for a terror to those that shall attempt to do as he hereafter.

Then they asked Mr. Feeble-mind how he fell into his hands?

FEEBLE-MIND. Then said the poor man, I am a sickly man, as you see, and because death did usually once a-day knock at my door, I thought I should never be well at home; so I betook myself to a pilgrim's life, and have travelled hither from the town of Uncertain, where I and my father were born. I am a man of no strength at all of body, nor yet of mind; but would, if I could, though I can but crawl, spend my life in the pilgrim's way. When I came at the gate that is at the head of the way, the Lord of that place did entertain me freely; neither objected he against my weakly looks, nor against my feeble mind, but gave me such things that were necessary for my journey, and bid me hope to the end. When I came to the house of the Interpreter, I received much kindness there; and because the Hill Difficulty was judged too hard for me, I was carried up that by one of his servants. Indeed, I have found much relief from pilgrims, though none was willing to go so softly as I am forced to do; yet still, as they came on, they bid me be of good cheer, and said that it was the will of their Lord that comfort should be given to the feebleminded, and so went on their own pace.[111] When I was come up to Assault Lane, then this giant met with me and bid me prepare for an encounter; but, alas! feeble one that I was, I had more need of a cordial. So he came up and took me. I conceited[112] he should not kill me; also when he had got me into his den, since I went not with him willingly, I believed I should come out alive again. For I have heard that not any pilgrim that is taken captive by violent hands, if he keeps heart-whole towards his Master, is by the laws of Providence to die by the hand of the enemy. Robbed I looked to be, and robbed to be sure I am; but I am, as you see, escaped with life, for the which I thank my King as author, and you as the means. Other brunts I also look for; but this I have resolved on, to wit, to run when I can, to go when I cannot run, and to creep when I cannot go. As to the main, I thank him that loves me, I am fixed; my way is before me, my mind is beyond the river that has no bridge, though I am, as you see, but of a feeble mind.

Hon. Then said old Mr. Honest, Have you not, some time ago, been acquainted with one Mr. Fearing, a pilgrim?

Feeble. Acquainted with him; yes. He came from the town of Stupidity, which lieth four degrees to the northward of the City of Destruction, and as many off of where I was born, yet we were well acquainted, for indeed he was my uncle, my father's brother. He and I have been much of a temper. He was a little shorter than I, but yet we were much of a complexion.

Hon. I perceive you knew him; and I am apt to believe also that you were related one to another, for you have his whitely look, a cast like his with your eye, and your speech is much alike.

Feeble. Most have said so that have known us both; and besides, what I have read in him, I have, for the most part, found in myself.

Gaius. Come, Sir, said good Gaius, be of good cheer, you are welcome to me and to my house, and what thou hast a mind to, call

---

111. 1 Thess. 5:14.
112. Thought.

for freely; and what thou wouldest have my servants do for thee, they will do it with a ready mind.

Then said Mr. Feeble-mind, This is unexpected favour, and as the sun shining out of a very dark cloud. Did Giant Slay-good intend me this favour when he stopped me, and resolved to let me go no further? Did he intend that after he had rifled my pockets, I should go to Gaius, mine host? Yet so it is.

Now just as Mr. Feeble-mind and Gaius were thus in talk, there comes one running, and called at the door, and told that about a mile and a half off there was one Mr. Not-right, a pilgrim, struck dead upon the place where he was with a thunderbolt.

FEEBLE. Alas! said Mr. Feeble-mind, is he slain? He overtook me some days before I came so far as hither, and would be my company-keeper. He also was with me when Slay-good the giant took me; but he was nimble of his heels and escaped. But it seems he escaped to die, and I was took to live.

> What, one would think, doth seek to slay outright,
> Ofttimes delivers from the saddest plight.
> That very Providence, whose face is death,
> Doth ofttimes, to the lowly, life bequeath.
> I taken was, he did escape and flee;
> Hands crossed gives death to him, and life to me.

Now about this time Matthew and Mercy were married. Also Gaius gave his daughter Phebe to James, Matthew's brother, to wife; after which time they yet stayed above ten days at Gaius's house, spending their time and the seasons like as pilgrims use to do.

When they were to depart, Gaius made them a feast, and they did eat and drink and were merry. Now the hour was come that they must be gone; wherefore Mr. Great-heart called for a reckoning: But Gaius told him that at his house it was not the custom for pilgrims to pay for their entertainment. He boarded them by the year, but looked for his pay from the good Samaritan, who had promised him, at his return, whatsoever charge he was at with them, faithfully to repay him.[113] Then said Mr. Great-heart to him,

GREAT-HEART. "Beloved, thou dost faithfully whatsoever thou dost to the brethren and to strangers, which have borne witness of

---

113. Luke 10:35.

thy charity before the church: whom if thou (yet) bring forward on their journey after a godly sort, thou shalt do well."[114]

Then Gaius took his leave of them all, and of his children, and particularly of Mr. Feeble-mind. He also gave them something to drink by the way.

Now Mr. Feeble-mind, when they were going out of the door, made as if he intended to linger; the which when Mr. Great-heart espied, he said, Come, Mr. Feeble-mind, pray do you go along with us. I will be your conductor, and you shall fare as the rest.

FEEBLE. Alas! I want a suitable companion; you are all lusty and strong, but I, as you see, am weak. I choose therefore rather to come behind, lest by reason of my many infirmities I should be both a burden to myself and to you. I am, as I said, a man of a weak and feeble mind, and shall be offended and made weak at that which others can bear. I shall like no laughing; I shall like no gay attire; I shall like no unprofitable questions. Nay, I am so weak a man, as to be offended with that which others have liberty to do. I do not yet know all the truth. I am a very ignorant Christian man; sometimes if I hear some rejoice in the Lord, it troubles me because I cannot do so too. It is with me, as it is with a weak man among the strong, or as with a sick man among the healthy, or as a lamp despised. ("He that is ready to slip with his feet is as a lamp despised, in the thought of him that is at ease.")[115] So that I know not what to do.

GREAT-HEART. But brother, said Mr. Great-heart, I have it in commission to comfort the feebleminded, and to support the weak. You must needs go along with us; we will wait for you; we will lend you our help; we will deny ourselves of some things, both opinionative and practical, for your sake; we will not enter into doubtful disputations before you; we will be made all things to you, rather than you shall be left behind.[116]

Now all this while they were at Gaius's door; and behold, as they were thus in the heat of their discourse, Mr. Ready-to-halt[117] came by, with his crutches[118] in his hand, and he also was going on pilgrimage.

FEEBLE. Then said Mr. Feeble-mind to him, Man, how camest thou hither? I was but just now complaining that I had not a suit-

---

114. 3 John 1–6.
115. Job 12:5.
116. Rom. 14:1; 1 Cor. 9:22.
117. Ps. 38:17. Halt: limp.
118. Promises. [B]

able companion, but thou art according to my wish. Welcome, welcome, good Mr. Ready-to-halt, I hope thee and I may be some help.

READY-TO-HALT. I shall be glad of thy company, said the other; and good Mr. Feeble-mind, rather than we will part, since we are thus happily met, I will lend thee one of my crutches.

FEEBLE. Nay, said he, though I thank thee for thy goodwill, I am not inclined to halt before I am lame. Howbeit, I think, when occasion is, it may help me against a dog.

READY. If either myself or my crutches can do thee a pleasure, we are both at thy command, good Mr. Feeble-mind.

Thus therefore they went on; Mr. Great-heart and Mr. Honest went before, Christiana and her children went next, and Mr. Feeble-mind and Mr. Ready-to-halt came behind with his crutches. Then said Mr. Honest,

HON. Pray, Sir, now we are upon the road, tell us some profitable things of some that have gone on pilgrimage before us.

GREAT-HEART. With a good will. I suppose you have heard how Christian of old did meet with Apollyon in the Valley of Humiliation; and also what hard work he had to go through the Valley of the Shadow of Death. Also I think you cannot but have heard how Faithful was put to it with Madam Wanton, with Adam the First, with one Discontent, and Shame, four as deceitful villains as a man can meet with upon the road.

HON. Yes, I have heard of all this, but indeed good Faithful was hardest put to it with Shame; he was an unwearied one.

GREAT-HEART. Ay; for, as the pilgrim well said, he of all men had the wrong name.

HON. But pray, Sir, where was it that Christian and Faithful met Talkative? That same was also a notable one.

GREAT-HEART. He was a confident fool, yet many follow his ways.

HON. He had like to a beguiled Faithful.

GREAT-HEART. Ay, but Christian put him into a way quickly to find him out. Thus they went on till they came at the place where Evangelist met with Christian and Faithful, and prophesied to them of what should befall them at Vanity Fair.

GREAT-HEART. Then said their guide, Hereabouts did Christian and Faithful meet with Evangelist, who prophesied to them of what troubles they should meet with at Vanity Fair.

HON. Say you so? I dare say it was a hard chapter that then he did read unto them.

GREAT-HEART. It was so; but he gave them encouragement withal. But what do we talk of them? They were a couple of lion-like men; they had set their faces like flint. Don't you remember how undaunted they were when they stood before the judge?

HON. Well, Faithful bravely suffered.

GREAT-HEART. So he did, and as brave things came on't; for Hopeful and some others, as the story relates it, were converted by his death.

HON. Well, but pray go on; for you are well acquainted with things.

GREAT-HEART. Above all that Christian met with after he had passed through Vanity Fair, one By-ends was the arch one.

HON. By-ends! What was he?

GREAT-HEART. A very arch fellow; a downright hypocrite. One that would be religious which way ever the world went; but so cunning that he would be sure neither to lose nor suffer for it. He had his mode of religion for every fresh occasion; and his wife was as good at it as he. He would turn and change from opinion to opinion; yea, and plead for so doing too. But so far as I could learn, he came to an ill end with his by-ends; nor did I ever hear that any of his children were ever of any esteem with any that truly feared God.

Now by this time they were come within sight of the town of Vanity, where Vanity Fair is kept. So when they saw that they were so near the town, they consulted with one another how they should pass through the town; and some said one thing, and some another. At last Mr. Great-heart said, I have, as you may understand, often been a conductor of pilgrims through this town; now I am acquainted with one Mr. Mnason, a Cyprusian by nation, an old disciple, at whose house we may lodge.[119] If you think good, said he, we will turn in there.

Content, said old Honest; Content, said Christiana; Content, said Mr. Feeble-mind; and so they said all. Now you must think it was eventide by that they got to the outside of the town; but Mr. Great-heart knew the way to the old man's house. So thither they came, and he called at the door, and the old man within knew his tongue so soon as ever he heard it; so he opened, and they all came in. Then said Mnason their host, How far have ye come today? So they said, From the house of Gaius our friend. I promise you, said

---

119. Acts 21:16.

he, you have gone a good stitch, you may well be a-weary; sit down. So they sat down.

GREAT-HEART. Then said their guide. Come, what cheer, Sirs? I daresay you are welcome to my friend.

MNASON. I also, said Mr. Mnason, do bid you welcome, and whatever you want, do but say, and we will do what we can to get it for you.

HON. Our great want, a while since, was harbour and good company, and now I hope we have both.

MNASON. For harbour, you see what it is; but for good company, that will appear in the trial.

GREAT-HEART. Well, said Mr. Great-heart, will you have the pilgrims up into their lodging?

MNASON. I will, said Mr. Mnason. So he had them to their respective places; and also showed them a very fair dining-room, where they might be and sup together, until time was come to go to rest.

Now when they were set in their places, and were a little cheery after their journey, Mr. Honest asked his landlord, if there were any store of good people in the town?

MNASON. We have a few, for indeed they are but a few, when compared with them on the other side.

HON. But how shall we do to see some of them? for the sight of good men, to them that are going on pilgrimage, is like to the appearing of the moon and the stars to them that are sailing upon the seas.

Then Mr. Mnason stamped with his foot, and his daughter Grace came up; so he said unto her, Grace, go you, tell my friends, Mr. Contrite, Mr. Holy-man, Mr. Love-saint, Mr. Dare-not-lie, and Mr. Penitent, that I have a friend or two at my house that have a mind this evening to see them.

So Grace went to call them, and they came; and after salutation made, they sat down together at the table.

Then said Mr. Mnason, their landlord, My neighbours, I have, as you see, a company of strangers come to my house; they are pilgrims. They come from afar, and are going to Mount Zion. But who, quoth he, do you think this is? pointing with his finger to Christiana. It is Christiana, the wife of Christian, that famous pilgrim, who with Faithful his brother were so shamefully handled in our town. At that they stood amazed, saying, We little thought to see Christiana, when Grace came to call us; wherefore this is a very comfortable surprise. Then they asked her of her welfare, and if these young men were her husband's sons? And when she had told them they were, they said, The King whom you love and serve make you as your father, and bring you where he is in peace.

HON. Then Mr. Honest (when they were all sat down) asked Mr. Contrite and the rest, in what posture their town was at present?

CONTRITE. You may be sure we are full of hurry in fair-time. It is hard keeping our hearts and spirits in any good order, when we are in a cumbered condition. He that lives in such a place as this is, and that has to do with such as we have, has need of an item[120] to caution him to take heed, every moment of the day.

HON. But how are your neighbours for quietness?

CONTRITE. They are much more moderate now than formerly. You know how Christian and Faithful were used at our town; but of late, I say, they have been far more moderate. I think the blood of Faithful lieth with the load upon them till now; for since they burned him, they have been ashamed to burn any more. In those days we were afraid to walk the streets, but now we can show our heads. Then the name of a professor was odious; now, specially in some parts of our town (for you know our town is large), religion is counted honourable.

Then said Mr. Contrite to them, Pray how fareth it with you in your pilgrimage? How stands the country affected towards you?

HON. It happens to us as it happeneth to wayfaring men; sometimes our way is clean, sometimes foul, sometimes uphill, sometimes downhill; we are seldom at a certainty. The wind is not always on our backs, nor is every one a friend that we meet with in the way. We have met with some notable rubs already, and what are yet behind we know not; but for the most part, we find it true that has been talked of, of old, A good man must suffer trouble.

CONTRITE. You talk of rubs; what rubs have you met withal?

HON. Nay, ask Mr. Great-heart, our guide, for he can give the best account of that.

GREAT-HEART. We have been beset three or four times already. First, Christiana and her children were beset with two ruffians that they feared would a took away their lives. We were beset with Giant Bloody-man, Giant Maul, and Giant Slay-good. Indeed we did rather beset the last, than were beset of him. And thus it was. After we had been some time at the house of "Gaius, mine host,

---

120. Maxim or admonition.

and of the whole church," we were minded upon a time to take our weapons with us, and so go see if we could light upon any of those that were enemies to pilgrims (for we heard that there was a notable one thereabouts). Now Gaius knew his haunt better than I, because he dwelt thereabout, so we looked and looked, till at last we discerned the mouth of his cave; then we were glad and plucked up our spirits. So we approached up to his den, and lo, when we came there, he had dragged by mere force into his net, this poor man, Mr. Feeble-mind, and was about to bring him to his end. But when he saw us, supposing, as we thought, he had had another prey, he left the poor man in his hole and came out. So we fell to it full sore, and he lustily laid about him; but in conclusion he was brought down to the ground, and his head cut off, and set up by the wayside, for a terror to such as should after practise such ungodliness. That I tell you the truth, here is the man himself to affirm it, who was as a lamb taken out of the mouth of the lion.

FEEBLE-MIND. Then said Mr. Feeble-mind, I found this true, to my cost and comfort; to my cost, when he threatened to pick my bones every moment, and to my comfort, when I saw Mr. Great-heart and his friends with their weapons approach so near for my deliverance.

HOLY-MAN. Then said Mr. Holy-man, There are two things that they have need to be possessed with, that go on pilgrimage: courage and an unspotted life. If they have not courage, they can never hold on their way; and if their lives be loose, they will make the very name of a pilgrim stink.

LOVE-SAINT. Then said Mr. Love-saint, I hope this caution is not needful amongst you. But truly, there are many that go upon the road, that rather declare themselves strangers to pilgrimage, than strangers and pilgrims in the earth.[121]

DARE-NOT-LIE. Then said Mr. Dare-not-lie, It is true, they neither have the pilgrim's weed,[122] nor the pilgrim's courage; they go not uprightly, but all awry with their feet; one shoe goes inward, another outward, and their hosen out behind; there a rag, and there a rent, to the disparagement of their Lord.

PENITENT. These things, said Mr. Penitent, they ought to be troubled for; nor are the pilgrims like to have that grace put upon

---

121. Heb. 11:13.
122. Clothing.

them and their pilgrim's progress as they desire, until the way is cleared of such spots and blemishes.

Thus they sat talking and spending the time, until supper was set upon the table, unto which they went and refreshed their weary bodies; so they went to rest. Now they stayed in this fair a great while, at the house of this Mr. Mnason, who in process of time gave his daughter Grace unto Samuel, Christiana's son, to wife, and his daughter Martha to Joseph.

The time, as I said, that they lay here was long (for it was not now as in former times). Wherefore the pilgrims grew acquainted with many of the good people of the town, and did then what service they could. Mercy, as she was wont, laboured much for the poor; wherefore their bellies and backs blessed her, and she was there an ornament to her profession. And to say the truth for Grace, Phebe, and Martha, they were all of a very good nature, and did much good in their place. They were also all of them very fruitful; so that Christian's name, as was said before, was like to live in the world.

While they lay here, there came a monster out of the woods and slew many of the people of the town. It would also carry away their children and teach them to suck its whelps. Now no man in the town durst so much as face this monster; but all men fled when they heard of the noise of his coming.

The monster was like unto no one beast upon the earth; its body was like a dragon, and it had seven heads and ten horns.[123] It made great havoc of children, and yet it was governed by a woman. This monster propounded conditions to men, and such men as loved their lives more than their souls accepted of those conditions. So they came under.

Now this Mr. Great-heart, together with these that came to visit the pilgrims at Mr. Mnason's house, entered into a covenant to go and engage this beast, if perhaps they might deliver the people of this town from the paws and mouth of this so devouring a serpent.

Then did Mr. Great-heart, Mr. Contrite, Mr. Holy-man, Mr. Dare-not-lie, and Mr. Penitent, with their weapons go forth to meet him. Now the monster at first was very rampant, and looked upon these enemies with great disdain, but they so belaboured him, being sturdy men at arms, that they made him make a retreat; so they came home to Mr. Mnason's house again.

123. Rev. 17:3.

The monster, you must know, had his certain seasons to come out in, and to make his attempts upon the children of the people of the town; also these seasons did these valiant worthies watch him in, and did still continually assault him, insomuch that in process of time he became not only wounded, but lame; also he has not made that havoc of the townsmen's children, as formerly he has done. And it is verily believed by some that this beast will die of his wounds.

This therefore made Mr. Great-heart and his fellows of great fame in this town; so that many of the people that wanted their taste of things, yet had a reverend esteem and respect for them. Upon this account therefore it was that these pilgrims got not much hurt here. True, there were some of the baser sort, that could see no more than a mole, nor understand more than a beast; these had no reverence for these men, nor took they notice of their valour or adventures.

Well, the time grew on that the pilgrims must go on their way, wherefore they prepared for their journey. They sent for their friends; they conferred with them; they had some time set apart, therein to commit each other to the protection of their Prince. There was again that brought them of such things as they had, that was fit for the weak and the strong, for the women and the men, and so laded them with such things as was necessary.

Then they set forward on their way; and their friends accompanying them so far as was convenient, they again committed each other to the protection of their King, and parted.

They therefore that were of the pilgrims' company went on, and Mr. Great-heart went before them. Now the women and children being weakly, they were forced to go as they could bear; by this means Mr. Ready-to-halt and Mr. Feeble-mind had more to sympathise with their condition.

When they were gone from the townsmen, and when their friends had bid them farewell, they quickly came to the place where Faithful was put to death; there therefore they made a stand, and thanked him that had enabled him to bear his cross so well, and the rather because they now found that they had a benefit by such a manly suffering as his was.

They went on therefore after this, a good way further, talking of Christian and Faithful, and how Hopeful joined himself to Christian after that Faithful was dead.

Now they were come up with the Hill Lucre, where the silver

mine was which took Demas off from his pilgrimage, and into which, as some think, By-ends fell and perished; wherefore they considered that. But when they were come to the old monument that stood over against the Hill Lucre, to wit, to the pillar of salt that stood also within view of Sodom and its stinking lake, they marvelled, as did Christian before, that men of that knowledge and ripeness of wit, as they were, should be so blinded as to turn aside here. Only they considered again that nature is not affected with the harms that others have met with, specially if that thing upon which they look has an attracting virtue upon the foolish eye.

I saw now that they went on till they came at the river that was on this side of the Delectable Mountains. To the river where the fine trees grow on both sides, and whose leaves, if taken inwardly, are good against surfeits; where the meadows are green all the year long, and where they might lie down safely.

By this riverside in the meadow, there were cotes and folds for sheep, a house built for the nourishing and bringing up of those lambs, the babes of those women that go on pilgrimage. Also there was here one that was intrusted with them, who could have compassion, and that could "gather these lambs with his arm, and carry them in his bosom, and that could gently lead those that were with young."[124] Now to the care of this Man, Christiana admonished her four daughters to commit their little ones, that by these waters they might be housed, harboured, succoured, and nourished, and that none of them might be lacking in time to come. This man, if any of them go astray, or be lost, he will bring them again, he will also "bind up that which was broken, and will strengthen them that are sick."[125] Here they will never want meat, and drink, and clothing; here they will be kept from thieves and robbers, for this man will die before one of those committed to his trust shall be lost. Besides, here they shall be sure to have good nurture and admonition, and shall be taught to walk in right paths, and that you know is a favour of no small account. Also here, as you see, are delicate waters, pleasant meadows, dainty flowers, variety of trees, and such as bear wholesome fruit; fruit not like that that Matthew eat of, that fell over the wall out of Beelzebub's garden, but fruit that procureth health where there is none, and that continueth and increaseth it where it is.

124. Isa. 40:11.
125. Ezek. 34:11–16.

So they were content to commit their little ones to him; and that which was also an encouragement to them so to do, was, for that all this was to be at the charge of the King, and so was as an hospital for young children and orphans.

Now they went on, and when they were come to By-path Meadow, to the stile over which Christian went with his fellow Hopeful, when they were taken by Giant Despair and put into Doubting Castle, they sat down and consulted what was best to be done; to wit, now they were so strong, and had got such a man as Mr. Great-heart for their conductor, whether they had not best to make an attempt upon the giant, demolish his castle, and if there were any pilgrims in it, to set them at liberty before they went any further. So one said one thing, and another said the contrary. One questioned if it was lawful to go upon unconsecrated ground; another said they might, provided their end was good. But Mr. Great-heart said, Though that assertion offered last cannot be universally true, yet I have a commandment to resist sin, to overcome evil, to fight the good fight of faith;[126] and I pray, with whom should I fight this good fight, if not with Giant Despair? I will therefore attempt the taking away of his life and the demolishing of Doubting Castle. Then said he, Who will go with me? Then said old Honest, I will. And so will we too, said Christiana's four sons, Matthew, Samuel, James, and Joseph; for they were young men and strong. So they left the women in the road, and with them Mr. Feeble-mind and Mr. Ready-to-halt with his crutches, to be their guard until they came back; for in that place, though Giant Despair dwelt so near, they keeping in the road, a light child might lead them.[127]

So Mr. Great-heart, old Honest, and the four young men, went to go up to Doubting Castle, to look for Giant Despair. When they came at the castle-gate, they knocked for entrance with an unusual noise. At that the old Giant comes to the gate, and Diffidence his wife follows. Then said he, Who and what is he that is so hardy, as after this manner to molest the Giant Despair? Mr. Great-heart replied, It is I, Great-heart, one of the King of the Celestial Country's conductors of pilgrims to their place; and I demand of thee that thou open thy gates for my entrance. Prepare thyself also to fight, for I am come to take away thy head, and to demolish Doubting Castle.

126. 1 Tim. 6:12.
127. Isa. 11:6.

Now Giant Despair, because he was a giant, thought no man could overcome him; and again, thought he, since heretofore I have made a conquest of angels, shall Great-heart make me afraid? So he harnessed himself and went out. He had a cap of steel upon his head, a breastplate of fire girded to him, and he came out in iron shoes, with a great club in his hand. Then these six men made up to him, and beset him behind and before. Also when Diffidence, the giantess, came up to help him, old Mr. Honest cut her down at one blow. Then they fought for their lives, and Giant Despair was brought down to the ground, but was very loath to die. He struggled hard and had, as they say, as many lives as a cat; but Great-heart was his death, for he left him not till he had severed his head from his shoulders.

Then they fell to demolishing Doubting Castle, that you know might with ease be done, since Giant Despair was dead. They were seven days in destroying of that, and in it of pilgrims they found one Mr. Despondency, almost starved to death, and one Much-afraid, his daughter; these two they saved alive. But it would a made you a-wondered to have seen the dead bodies that lay here and there in the castle-yard, and how full of dead men's bones the dungeon was.

When Mr. Great-heart and his companions had performed this exploit, they took Mr. Despondency and his daughter Much-afraid into their protection; for they were honest people, though they were prisoners in Doubting Castle, to that tyrant Giant Despair. They therefore, I say, took with them the head of the giant (for his body they had buried under a heap of stones) and down to the road and to their companions they came, and showed them what they had done. Now when Feeble-mind and Ready-to-halt saw that it was the head of Giant Despair indeed, they were very jocund and merry. Now Christiana, if need was, could play upon the viol, and her daughter Mercy upon the lute; so since they were so merry disposed, she played them a lesson, and Ready-to-halt would dance. So he took Despondency's daughter, named Much-afraid, by the hand, and to dancing they went in the road. True, he could not dance without one crutch in his hand; but I promise you, he footed it well. Also the girl was to be commended, for she answered the music handsomely.

As for Mr. Despondency, the music was not much to him; he was for feeding rather than dancing, for that he was almost starved. So Christiana gave him some of her bottle of spirits for present relief, and then prepared him something to eat; and in a little time the old gentleman came to himself, and began to be finely revived.

Now I saw in my dream, when all these things were finished, Mr. Great-heart took the head of Giant Despair and set it upon a pole by the highway side, right over against the pillar that Christian erected for a caution to pilgrims that came after, to take heed of entering into his grounds.

Then he writ under it, upon a marble stone, these verses following:

> This is the head of him, whose name only,
> In former times did pilgrims terrify.
> His Castle's down, and Diffidence his wife,
> Brave Master Great-heart has bereft of life.
> Despondency, his daughter Much-afraid,
> Great-heart for them also the man has played;
> Who hereof doubts, if he'll but cast his eye
> Up hither, may his scruples satisfy:
> This head also when doubting cripples dance,
> Doth show from fears they have deliverance.

When these men had thus bravely showed themselves against Doubting Castle, and had slain Giant Despair, they went forward, and went on till they came to the Delectable Mountains, where Christian and Hopeful refreshed themselves with the varieties of the place. They also acquainted themselves with the Shepherds there, who welcomed them, as they had done Christian before, unto the Delectable Mountains.

Now the Shepherds, seeing so great a train follow Mr. Great-heart, for with him they were well acquainted, they said unto him, Good Sir, you have got a goodly company here. Pray, where did you find all these?

Then Mr. Great-heart replied:

> First here's Christiana and her train,
> Her sons, and her sons' wives, who like the Wain[128]
> Keep by the Pole, and do by compass steer,
> From sin to grace, else they had not been here;
> Next here's old Honest come on pilgrimage,

---

128. Charles's Wain (wagon): old name for the Big Dipper.

Ready-to-halt too, who, I dare engage,
True-hearted is, and so is Feeble-mind,
Who willing was not to be left behind;
Despondency, good man, is coming after,
And so also is Much-afraid, his daughter.
May we have entertainment here, or must
We further go? Let's know whereon to trust.

Then said the Shepherds, This is a comfortable company. You are welcome to us, for we have for the feeble as for the strong. Our Prince has an eye to what is done to the least of these; therefore infirmity must not be a block to our entertainment. So they had them to the palace door, and then said unto them, Come in, Mr. Feeble-mind; Come in, Mr. Ready-to-halt; Come in, Mr. Despondency, and Mrs. Much-afraid, his daughter. These, Mr. Great-heart, said the Shepherds to the guide, we call in by name, for that they are most subject to draw back; but as for you, and the rest that are strong, we leave you to your wonted liberty. Then said Mr. Great-heart, This day I see that grace doth shine in your faces, and that you are my Lord's shepherds indeed, for that you have not pushed these diseased,[129] neither with side nor shoulder, but have rather strewed their way into the palace with flowers, as you should.

So the feeble and weak went in, and Mr. Great-heart and the rest did follow. When they were also set down, the Shepherds said to those of the weaker sort, What is it that you would have? For, said they, all things must be managed here to the supporting of the weak, as well as to the warning of the unruly.

So they made them a feast of things easy of digestion, and that were pleasant to the palate, and nourishing; the which when they had received, they went to their rest, each one respectively unto his proper place. When morning was come, because the mountains were high, and the day clear, and because it was the custom of the Shepherds to show to the pilgrims, before their departure, some rarities, therefore after they were ready, and had refreshed themselves, the Shepherds took them out into the fields, and showed them first what they had showed to Christian before.

Then they had them to some new places. The first was to Mount Marvel, where they looked, and behold, a man at a distance that

129. Troubled, distressed (together with modern meaning).

tumbled the hills about with words. Then they asked the Shepherds what that should mean? So they told them that that man was the son of one Great-grace, of whom you read in the First Part of the Records of the Pilgrim's Progress. And he is set there to teach pilgrims how to believe down, or to tumble out of their ways, what difficulties they shall meet with, by faith.[130] Then said Mr. Greatheart, I know him. He is a man above many.

Then they had them to another place, called Mount Innocent; and there they saw a man clothed all in white, and two men, Prejudice and Ill-will, continually casting dirt upon him. Now behold, the dirt, whatsoever they cast at him, would in little time fall off again, and his garments would look as clear as if no dirt had been cast thereat.

Then said the pilgrims, What means this? The Shepherds answered, This man is named Godly-man, and this garment is to show the innocency of his life. Now those that throw dirt at him are such as hate his well-doing; but as you see the dirt will not stick upon his clothes, so it shall be with him that liveth truly innocently in the world. Whoever they be that would make such men dirty, they labour all in vain; for God, by that a little time is spent, will cause that their innocence shall break forth as the light, and their righteousness as the noonday.

Then they took them and had them to Mount Charity, where they showed them a man that had a bundle of cloth lying before him, out of which he cut coats and garments for the poor that stood about him; yet his bundle or roll of cloth was never the less.

Then said they, What should this be? This is, said the Shepherds, to show you that he that has a heart to give of his labour to the poor, shall never want wherewithal. He that watereth shall be watered himself. And the cake that the widow gave to the prophet did not cause that she had ever the less in her barrel.

They had them also to a place where they saw one Fool and one Want-wit, washing of an Ethiopian with intention to make him white; but the more they washed him the blacker he was. They then asked the Shepherds what that should mean. So they told them, saying, Thus shall it be with the vile person. All means used to get such a one a good name shall in conclusion tend but to make him more abominable. Thus it was with the Pharisees, and so shall it be with all hypocrites.

---

130. Mark 11:23, 24.

Then said Mercy, the wife of Matthew, to Christiana, her mother, Mother, I would, if it might be, see the hole in the hill, or that commonly called the by-way to hell. So her mother brake her mind to the Shepherds. Then they went to the door. It was in the side of a hill, and they opened it, and bid Mercy hearken awhile. So she hearkened, and heard one saying, Cursed be my father for holding of my feet back from the way of peace and life; and another said, O that I had been torn in pieces before I had, to save my life, lost my soul; and another said, If I were to live again, how would I deny myself, rather than come to this place. Then there was as if the very earth had groaned and quaked under the feet of this young woman for fear. So she looked white and came trembling away, saying, Blessed be he and she that are delivered from this place.

Now when the Shepherds had shown them all these things, then they had them back to the palace, and entertained them with what the house would afford. But Mercy, being a young and breeding woman, longed for something that she saw there, but was ashamed to ask. Her mother-in-law then asked her what she ailed; for she looked as one not well. Then said Mercy, There is a looking-glass hangs up in the dining-room, off of which I cannot take my mind: if therefore I have it not, I think I shall miscarry. Then said her mother, I will mention thy wants to the Shepherds, and they will not deny it thee. But she said, I am ashamed that these men should know that I longed. Nay, my daughter, said she, it is no shame, but a virtue, to long for such a thing as that. So Mercy said, Then, mother, if you please, ask the Shepherds if they are willing to sell it.

Now the glass was one of a thousand. It would present a man, one way, with his own feature exactly; and turn it but another way, and it would show one the very face and similitude of the Prince of Pilgrims himself. Yea, I have talked with them that can tell, and they have said that they have seen the very crown of thorns upon his head, by looking in that glass; they have therein also seen the holes in his hands, in his feet, and his side. Yea, such an excellency is there in that glass, that it will show him to one where they have a mind to see him; whether living or dead; whether in earth or heaven; whether in a state of humiliation, or in his exaltation; whether coming to suffer, or coming to reign.[131]

---

131. It was the Word of God (James 1:23; 1 Cor. 13:12; 2 Cor. 3:18). [B]

250]   THE PILGRIM'S PROGRESS

Christiana therefore went to the Shepherds apart (now the names of the Shepherds are Knowledge, Experience, Watchful, and Sincere) and said unto them, There is one of my daughters, a breeding woman, that I think doth long for something that she hath seen in this house; and she thinks she shall miscarry, if she shall by you be denied.

EXPERIENCE. Call her, call her; she shall assuredly have what we can help her to. So they called her and said to her, Mercy, what is that thing thou wouldst have? Then she blushed and said, The great glass that hangs up in the dining-room. So Sincere ran and fetched it, and with a joyful consent it was given her. Then she bowed her head, and gave thanks, and said, By this I know that I have obtained favour in your eyes.

They also gave to the other young women such things as they desired, and to their husbands great commendations, for that they had joined with Mr. Great-heart, to the slaying of Giant Despair, and the demolishing of Doubting Castle.

About Christiana's neck the Shepherds put a bracelet, and so they did about the necks of her four daughters; also they put earrings in their ears, and jewels on their foreheads.

When they were minded to go hence, they let them go in peace, but gave not to them those certain cautions which before were given to Christian and his companion. The reason was for that these had Great-heart to be their guide, who was one that was well acquainted with things, and so could give them their cautions more seasonably; to wit, even then when the danger was nigh the approaching.

What cautions Christian and his companion had received of the Shepherds, they had also lost by that the time was come that they had need to put them in practice. Wherefore here was the advantage that this company had over the other.

From hence they went on, singing, and they said,

> Behold, how fitly are the stages set
> For their relief that pilgrims are become!
> And how they us receive without one let,
> That make the other life our mark and home.
> What novelties they have to us they give,
> That we, though pilgrims, joyful lives may live;
> They do upon us, too, such things bestow,
> That show we pilgrims are, where'er we go.

When they were gone from the Shepherds, they quickly came to the place where Christian met with one Turn-away, that dwelt in the town of Apostasy. Wherefore of him Mr. Great-heart, their guide, did now put them in mind, saying, This is the place where Christian met with one Turn-away, who carried with him the character of his rebellion at his back. And this I have to say concerning this man: he would hearken to no counsel, but, once a-falling, persuasion could not stop him. When he came to the place where the Cross and the Sepulchre were, he did meet with one that did bid him look there, but he gnashed with his teeth, and stamped, and said, he was resolved to go back to his own town. Before he came to the gate, he met with Evangelist, who offered to lay hands on him, to turn him into the way again. But this Turn-away resisted him, and having done much despite unto him, he got away over the wall, and so escaped his hand.

Then they went on; and just at the place where Little-faith formerly was robbed, there stood a man with his sword drawn, and his face all bloody. Then said Mr. Great-heart, What art thou? The man made answer, saying, I am one whose name is Valiant-for-truth. I am a pilgrim, and am going to the Celestial City. Now as I was in my way, there were three men did beset me, and propounded unto me these three things: 1. Whether I would become one of them. 2. Or go back from whence I came. 3. Or die upon the place. To the first I answered, I had been a true man a long season, and therefore it could not be expected that I now should cast in my lot with thieves. Then they demanded what I would say to the second. So I told them that the place from whence I came, had I not found incommodity there, I had not forsaken it at all; but finding it altogether unsuitable to me, and very unprofitable for me, I forsook it for this way. Then they asked me what I said to the third. And I told them, My life cost more dear far, than that I should lightly give it away. Besides, you have nothing to do thus to put things to my choice; wherefore at your peril be it if you meddle. Then these three, to wit, Wild-head, Inconsiderate, and Pragmatic,[132] drew upon me, and I also drew upon them.

So we fell to it, one against three, for the space of above three hours. They have left upon me, as you see, some of the marks of their valour, and have also carried away with them some of mine.

---

132. Excessively busy; meddlesome; interfering.

They are but just now gone. I suppose they might, as the saying is, hear your horse dash, and so they betook them to flight.

GREAT-HEART. But here was great odds, three against one.

VALIANT. 'Tis true, but little or more are nothing to him that has the truth on his side. "Though an host should encamp against me," said one, "my heart shall not fear; though war should rise against me, in this will I be confident," etc.[133] Besides, said he, I have read in some records that one man has fought an army. And how many did Sampson slay with the jawbone of an ass!

GREAT-HEART. Then said the guide, Why did you not cry out, that some might have come in for your succour?

VALIANT. So I did, to my King, who I knew could hear and afford invisible help, and that was sufficient for me.

GREAT-HEART. Then said Great-heart to Mr. Valiant-for-truth, Thou hast worthily behaved thyself. Let me see thy sword. So he showed it him. When he had taken it in his hand and looked thereon a while, he said, Ha! it is a right Jerusalem blade.

VALIANT. It is so. Let a man have one of these blades, with a hand to wield it and skill to use it, and he may venture upon an angel with it. He need not fear its holding, if he can but tell how to lay on. Its edges will never blunt. It will cut flesh, and bones, and soul, and spirit, and all.[134]

GREAT-HEART. But you fought a great while; I wonder you were not weary.

VALIANT. I fought till my sword did cleave to my hand; and when they were joined together, as if a sword grew out of my arm, and when the blood ran through my fingers, then I fought with most courage.[135]

GREAT-HEART. Thou hast done well. Thou hast "resisted unto blood, striving against sin."[136] Thou shalt abide by us, come in and go out with us, for we are thy companions.

Then they took him, and washed his wounds, and gave him of what they had to refresh him; and so they went on together. Now as they went on, because Mr. Great-heart was delighted in him (for he loved one greatly that he found to be a man of his hands) and

---

133. Ps. 27:3.
134. Heb. 4:12.
135. The Word; the Faith; Blood. [B]
136. Heb. 12:4.

because there was with his company them that was feeble and weak, therefore he questioned with him about many things; as first, what countryman he was?

VALIANT. I am of Dark-land; for there I was born, and there my father and mother are still.

GREAT-HEART. Dark-land, said the guide; doth not that lie upon the same coast with the City of Destruction?

VALIANT. Yes, it doth. Now that which caused me to come on pilgrimage was this: we had one Mr. Tell-true came into our parts, and he told it about what Christian had done, that went from the City of Destruction; namely, how he had forsaken his wife and children, and had betaken himself to a pilgrim's life. It was also confidently reported how he had killed a Serpent that did come out to resist him in his journey, and how he got through to whither he intended. It was also told what welcome he had at all his Lord's lodgings, specially when he came to the gates of the Celestial City; for there, said the man, he was received with sound of trumpet, by a company of Shining Ones. He told it also how all the bells in the city did ring for joy at his reception, and what golden garments he was clothed with, with many other things that now I shall forbear to relate. In a word, that man so told the story of Christian and his travels, that my heart fell into a burning haste to be gone after him; nor could father or mother stay me. So I got from them, and am come thus far on my way.

GREAT-HEART. You came in at the gate, did you not?

VALIANT. Yes, yes; for the same man also told us that all would be nothing, if we did not begin to enter this way at the gate.

GREAT-HEART. Look you, said the guide to Christiana, the pilgrimage of your husband, and what he has gotten thereby, is spread abroad far and near.

VALIANT. Why, is this Christian's wife?

GREAT-HEART. Yes, that it is; and these are also her four sons.

VALIANT. What! and going on pilgrimage too?

GREAT-HEART. Yes, verily, they are following after.

VALIANT. It glads me at the heart! Good man! How joyful will he be when he shall see them that would not go with him, yet to enter after him in at the gates into the city.

GREAT-HEART. Without doubt it will be a comfort to him; for, next to the joy of seeing himself there, it will be a joy to meet there his wife and his children.

VALIANT. But now you are upon that, pray let me see your opinion about it. Some make a question whether we shall know one another when we are there.

GREAT-HEART. Do they think they shall know themselves then, or that they shall rejoice to see themselves in that bliss? and if they think they shall know and do these, why not know others, and rejoice in their welfare also?

Again, since relations are our second self, though that state will be dissolved there, yet why may it not be rationally concluded that we shall be more glad to see them there, than to see they are wanting?

VALIANT. Well, I perceive whereabouts you are as to this. Have you any more things to ask me about my beginning to come on pilgrimage?

GREAT-HEART. Yes. Was your father and mother willing that you should become a pilgrim?

VALIANT. Oh, no. They used all means imaginable to persuade me to stay at home.

GREAT-HEART. What could they say against it?

VALIANT. They said it was an idle life; and if I myself were not inclined to sloth and laziness, I would never countenance a pilgrim's condition.

GREAT-HEART. And what did they say else?

VALIANT. Why, they told me that it was a dangerous way; yea, the most dangerous way in the world, said they, is that which the pilgrims go.

GREAT-HEART. Did they show wherein this way is so dangerous?

VALIANT. Yes; and that in many particulars.

GREAT-HEART. Name some of them.

VALIANT. They told me of the Slough of Despond, where Christian was well nigh smothered. They told me that there were archers standing ready in Beelzebub's Castle, to shoot them that should knock at the wicket-gate for entrance. They told me also of the wood, and dark mountains, of the Hill Difficulty, of the lions, and also of the three giants, Bloody-man, Maul, and Slay-good. They said, moreover, that there was a foul fiend haunted the Valley of Humiliation, and that Christian was by him almost bereft of life. Besides, said they, you must go over the Valley of the Shadow of Death, where the hobgoblins are, where the light is darkness, where the way is full of snares, pits, traps, and gins. They told me also of Giant Despair, of Doubting Castle, and of the ruins that the pilgrims met with there. Further, they said I must go over the Enchanted Ground, which was dangerous. And that after all this I should find a river, over which I should find no bridge, and that that river did lie betwixt me and the Celestial Country.

GREAT-HEART. And was this all?

VALIANT. No. They also told me that this way was full of deceivers, and of persons that laid await there, to turn good men out of the path.

GREAT-HEART. But how did they make that out?

VALIANT. They told me that Mr. Worldly Wiseman did there lie in wait to deceive. They also said that there was Formality and Hypocrisy continually on the road. They said also that By-ends, Talkative, or Demas would go near to gather me up; that the Flatterer would catch me in his net; or that with green-headed Ignorance I would presume to go on to the gate, from whence he always was sent back to the hole that was in the side of the hill, and made to go the by-way to hell.

GREAT-HEART. I promise you this was enough to discourage; but did they make an end here?

VALIANT. No; stay. They told me also of many that had tried that way of old, and that had gone a great way therein, to see if they could find something of the glory there, that so many had so much talked of from time to time; and how they came back again, and befooled themselves for setting a foot out of doors in that path, to the satisfaction of all the country. And they named several that did so, as Obstinate, and Pliable, Mistrust, and Timorous, Turn-away, and old Atheist, with several more; who, they said, had some of them gone far to see if they could find, but not one of them found so much advantage by going as amounted to the weight of a feather.

GREAT-HEART. Said they anything more to discourage you?

VALIANT. Yes. They told me of one Mr. Fearing, who was a pilgrim; and how he found this way so solitary that he never had a comfortable hour therein. Also that Mr. Despondency had like to been starved therein; yea, and also, which I had almost forgot, that Christian himself, about whom there has been such a noise, after all his ventures for a celestial crown, was certainly drowned in the Black River, and never went foot further, however it was smothered up.

GREAT-HEART. And did none of these things discourage you?

VALIANT. No; they seemed but as so many nothings to me.

GREAT-HEART. How came that about?

VALIANT. Why, I still believed what Mr. Tell-true had said, and that carried me beyond them all.

GREAT-HEART. Then this was your victory, even your faith.

VALIANT. It was so. I believed and therefore came out, got into the way, fought all that set themselves against me, and by believing am come to this place.

> Who would true valour see,
> 　　Let him come hither;
> One here will constant be,
> 　　Come wind, come weather
> There's no discouragement
> Shall make him once relent
> His first avowed intent
> 　　To be a pilgrim.
>
> Who so beset him round
> 　　With dismal stories,
> Do but themselves confound;
> 　　His strength the more is;
> No lion can him fright,
> He'll with a giant fight,
> But he will have a right
> 　　To be a pilgrim.
>
> Hobgoblin nor foul fiend
> 　　Can daunt his spirit;
> He knows he at the end
> 　　Shall life inherit.
> Then fancies fly away,
> He'll fear not what men say;
> He'll labour night and day
> 　　To be a pilgrim.

By this time they were got to the Enchanted Ground, where the air naturally tended to make one drowsy; and that place was all grown over with briars and thorns, excepting here and there, where was an Enchanted Arbour, upon which if a man sits, or in which if a man sleeps, 'tis a question, say some, whether ever he shall rise or wake again in this world. Over this forest therefore they went, both one and the other, and Mr. Great-heart went before, for that he was the guide; and Mr. Valiant-for-truth, he came behind, being there a guard, for fear lest peradventure some fiend, or dragon, or giant, or thief, should fall upon their rear and so do mischief. They went on here, each man with his sword drawn in his hand, for they knew it was a dangerous place. Also they cheered up one another as well as they could; Feeble-mind, Mr. Great-heart commanded, should come up after him, and Mr. Despondency was under the eye of Mr. Valiant.

Now they had not gone far, but a great mist and darkness fell upon them all, so that they could scarce, for a great while, see the one the other; wherefore they were forced, for some time, to feel for one another by words, for they walked not by sight.

But any one must think that here was but sorry going for the best of them all; but how much worse for the women and children, who both of feet and heart were but tender. Yet so it was, that through the encouraging words of he that led in the front, and of him that brought them up behind, they made a pretty good shift to wag along.

The way also was here very wearisome, through dirt and slab-biness.[137] Nor was there on all this ground so much as one inn or victualling-house, therein to refresh the feebler sort. Here there-fore was grunting, and puffing, and sighing. While one tumbleth over a bush, another sticks fast in the dirt; and the children, some of them, lost their shoes in the mire. While one cries out, I am down; and another, Ho! where are you? and a third, The bushes have got such fast hold on me, I think I cannot get away from them.

Then they came at an arbour, warm, and promising much refresh-ing to the pilgrims; for it was finely wrought above head, beautified with greens, furnished with benches and settles. It also had in it a soft couch, whereon the weary might lean. This, you must think, all things considered, was tempting, for the pilgrims already began to be foiled with the badness of the way; but there was not one of them that made so much as a motion to stop there. Yea, for aught I could perceive, they continually gave so good heed to the advice of their guide, and he did so faithfully tell them of dangers, and of the nature of dangers, when they were at them, that usually, when they were nearest to them, they did most pluck up their spirits, and hearten one another to deny the flesh. This arbour was called the

---

137. Muddiness.

Slothful's Friend, on purpose to allure, if it might be, some of the pilgrims there to take up their rest when weary.

I saw then in my dream that they went on in this their solitary ground, till they came to a place at which a man is apt to lose his way. Now though when it was light, their guide could well enough tell how to miss those ways that led wrong, yet in the dark he was put to a stand, but he had in his pocket a map of all ways leading to or from the Celestial City; wherefore he strook a light (for he never goes also without his tinderbox) and takes a view of his book or map, which bids him be careful in that place to turn to the right-hand way. And had he not here been careful to look in his map, they had all, in probability, been smothered in the mud; for just a little before them, and that at the end of the cleanest way too, was a pit, none knows how deep, full of nothing but mud, there made on purpose to destroy the pilgrims in.

Then thought I with myself, who that goeth on pilgrimage, but would have one of these maps about him, that he may look when he is at a stand, which is the way he must take.

They went on then in this Enchanted Ground, till they came to where there was another arbour, and it was built by the highway-side. And in that arbour there lay two men, whose names were Heedless and Too-bold. These two went thus far on pilgrimage; but here, being wearied with their journey, they sat down to rest themselves, and so fell fast asleep. When the pilgrims saw them, they stood still and shook their heads; for they knew that the sleepers were in a pitiful case. Then they consulted what to do, whether to go on and leave them in their sleep, or to step to them and try to awake them. So they concluded to go to them and wake them, that is, if they could; but with this caution, namely, to take heed that themselves did not sit down nor embrace the offered benefit of that arbour.

So they went in and spake to the men, and called each by his name (for the guide, it seems, did know them); but there was no voice nor answer. Then the guide did shake them, and do what he could to disturb them. Then said one of them, I will pay you when I take my money. At which the guide shook his head. I will fight so long as I can hold my sword in my hand, said the other. At that one of the children laughed.

Then said Christiana, What is the meaning of this? The guide said, They talk in their sleep. If you strike them, beat them, or whatever else you do to them, they will answer you after this fashion; or as one of them said in old time, when the waves of the sea did beat upon him, and he slept as one upon the mast of a ship, "When I awake I will seek it again."[138] You know when men talk in their sleep, they say anything, but their words are not governed either by faith or reason. There is an incoherency in their words now, as there was before betwixt their going on pilgrimage and sitting down here. This then is the mischief on't, when heedless ones go on pilgrimage, 'tis twenty to one but they are served thus. For this Enchanted Ground is one of the last refuges that the enemy to pilgrims has. Wherefore it is, as you see, placed almost at the end of the way, and so it standeth against us with the more advantage. For when, thinks the enemy, will these fools be so desirous to sit down, as when they are weary? and when so like to be weary, as when almost at their journey's end? Therefore it is, I say, that the Enchanted Ground is placed so nigh to the Land Beulah, and so near the end of their race. Wherefore let pilgrims look to themselves, lest it happen to them as it has done to these, that, as you see, are fallen asleep, and none can wake them.

Then the pilgrims desired with trembling to go forward; only they prayed their guide to strike a light, that they might go the rest of their way by the help of the light of a lantern. So he struck a light, and they went by the help of that through the rest of this way, though the darkness was very great.[139]

But the children began to be sorely weary; and they cried out unto him that loveth pilgrims, to make their way more comfortable. So by that they had gone a little further, a wind arose that drove away the fog; so the air became more clear.

Yet they were not off (by much) of the Enchanted Ground; only now they could see one another better, and the way wherein they should walk.

Now when they were almost at the end of this ground, they perceived that a little before them was a solemn noise of one that was much concerned. So they went on and looked before them; and behold they saw, as they thought, a man upon his knees, with hands and eyes lift up, and speaking, as they thought, earnestly to one that was above. They drew nigh, but could not tell what he

138. Prov. 23:34, 35.
139. The light of the Word. [B]

said. So they went softly till he had done. When he had done, he got up and began to run towards the Celestial City. Then Mr. Great-heart called after him, saying, Soho! friend, let us have your company, if you go, as I suppose you do, to the Celestial City. So the man stopped, and they came up to him. But so soon as Mr. Honest saw him, he said, I know this man. Then said Mr. Valiant-for-truth, Prithee, who is it? 'Tis one, said he, who comes from where-abouts I dwelt. His name is Stand-fast; he is certainly a right good pilgrim.

So they came up one to another; and presently Stand-fast said to old Honest, Ho! father Honest, are you there? Ay, said he, that I am, as sure as you are there. Right glad am I, said Mr. Stand-fast, that I have found you on this road. And as glad am I, said the other, that I espied you upon your knees. Then Mr. Stand-fast blushed and said, But why, did you see me? Yes, that I did, quoth the other, and with my heart was glad at the sight. Why, what did you think? said Stand-fast. Think! said old Honest, what should I think? I thought we had an honest man upon the road, and therefore should have his company by and by. If you thought not amiss, [said Stand-fast,] how happy am I. But if I be not as I should, I alone must bear it. That is true, said the other; but your fear doth further confirm me that things are right betwixt the Prince of Pilgrims and your soul. For he saith, "Blessed is the man that feareth always."[140]

VALIANT. Well, but brother, I pray thee tell us what was it that was the cause of thy being upon thy knees even now? Was it for that some special mercies laid obligations upon thee, or how?

STAND-FAST. Why, we are, as you see, upon the Enchanted Ground; and as I was coming along, I was musing with myself of what a dangerous road the road in this place was, and how many that had come even thus far on pilgrimage had here been stopped and been destroyed. I thought also of the manner of the death with which this place destroyeth men. Those that die here die of no violent dis-temper. The death which such die is not grievous to them; for he that goeth away in a sleep, begins that journey with desire and pleasure; yea, such acquiesce in the will of that disease.

HON. Then Mr. Honest, interrupting of him, said, Did you see the two men asleep in the arbour?

STAND-FAST. Ay, ay, I saw Heedless and Too-bold there; and for

---

140. Ps. 112:1.

aught I know, there they will lie till they rot. But let me go on in my tale. As I was thus musing, as I said, there was one in very pleasant attire, but old, who presented herself unto me, and offered me three things; to wit, her body, her purse, and her bed. Now the truth is, I was both a-weary and sleepy; I am also as poor as a howlet, and that, perhaps, the witch knew. Well, I repulsed her once and twice, but she put by my repulses, and smiled. Then I began to be angry; but she mattered that nothing at all. Then she made offers again, and said, If I would be ruled by her, she would make me great and happy; for, said she, I am the mistress of the world, and men are made happy by me. Then I asked her name, and she told me it was Madam Bubble. This set me further from her; but she still followed me with enticements. Then I betook me, as you saw, to my knees; and with hands lift up, and cries, I prayed to him that had said he would help. So just as you came up, the gentle-woman went her way. Then I continued to give thanks for this my great deliverance; for I verily believe she intended no good, but rather sought to make stop of me in my journey.

HON. Without doubt her designs were bad. But stay, now you talk of her, methinks I either have seen her, or have read some story of her.

STAND-FAST. Perhaps you have done both.

HON. Madam Bubble! Is she not a tall comely dame, something of a swarthy complexion?

STEAD-FAST. Right, you hit it, she is just such a one.

HON. Doth she not speak very smoothly, and give you a smile at the end of a sentence?

STEAD-FAST. You fall right upon it again, for these are her very actions.

HON. Doth she not wear a great purse by her side; and is not her hand often in it, fingering her money, as if that was her heart's delight?

STAND-FAST. It is just so; had she stood by all this while, you could not more amply have set her forth before me, nor have better described her features.

HON. Then he that drew her picture was a good limner, and he that wrote of her said true.

GREAT-HEART. This woman is a witch, and it is by virtue of her sorceries that this ground is enchanted. Whoever doth lay their head down in her lap had as good lay it down upon that block over which the axe doth hang; and whoever lay their eyes upon her beauty are counted the enemies of God.[141] This is she that maintaineth in their splendour all those that are the enemies of pilgrims. Yea, this is she that hath bought off many a man from a pilgrim's life. She is a great gossiper; she is always, both she and her daughters, at one pilgrim's heels or another, now commending and then preferring the excellencies of this life. She is a bold and impudent slut; she will talk with any man. She always laugheth poor pilgrims to scorn, but highly commends the rich. If there be one cunning to get money in a place, she will speak well of him from house to house. She loveth banqueting and feasting, mainly[142] well; she is always at one full table or another. She has given it out in some places, that she is a goddess, and therefore some do worship her. She has her times and open places of cheating; and she will say and avow it, that none can show a good comparable to hers. She promiseth to dwell with children's children, if they will but love and make much of her. She will cast out of her purse gold like dust, in some places, and to some persons. She loves to be sought after, spoken well of, and to lie in the bosoms of men. She is never weary of commending her commodities, and she loves them most that think best of her. She will promise to some crowns and kingdoms, if they will but take her advice; yet many hath she brought to the halter, and ten thousand times more to hell.

STAND-FAST. Oh, said Stand-fast, what a mercy is it that I did resist her; for whither might she a drawn me?

GREAT-HEART. Whither! Nay, none but God knows whither. But in general, to be sure, she would a drawn thee "into many foolish and hurtful lusts, which drown men in destruction and perdition."[143]

'Twas she that set Absalom against his father, and Jeroboam against his master. 'Twas she that persuaded Judas to sell his Lord, and that prevailed with Demas to forsake the godly pilgrim's life; none can tell of the mischief that she doth. She makes variance betwixt rulers and subjects, betwixt parents and children, 'twixt neighbour and neighbour, 'twixt a man and his wife, 'twixt a man and himself, 'twixt the flesh and the heart.

Wherefore, good Master Stand-fast, be as your name is, and when you have done all, *stand*.[144]

---

141. The World (James 4:4; 1 John 2:15). [B]
142. Very, exceedingly.
143. 1 Tim. 6:9.
144. Eph. 6:13, 14.

At this discourse there was among the pilgrims a mixture of joy and trembling; but at length they brake out and sang:

> What danger is the pilgrim in,
>   How many are his foes!
> How many ways there are to sin
>   No living mortal knows.
>
> Some of the ditch shy are, yet can
>   Lie tumbling in the mire;
> Some, though they shun the frying-pan,
>   Do leap into the fire.

After this, I beheld until they were come unto the Land of Beulah, where the sun shineth night and day. Here, because they were weary, they betook themselves awhile to rest; and because this country was common for pilgrims, and because the orchards and vineyards that were here belonged to the King of the Celestial Country, therefore they were licensed to make bold with any of his things. But a little while soon refreshed them here; for the bells did so ring, and the trumpets continually sound so melodiously, that they could not sleep; and yet they received as much refreshing as if they had slept their sleep ever so soundly. Here also all the noise of them that walked in the streets was, More pilgrims are come to town. And another would answer, saying, And so many went over the water, and were let in at the golden gates today. They would cry again, There is now a legion of Shining Ones just come to town, by which we know that there are more pilgrims upon the road; for here they come to wait for them, and to comfort them after all their sorrow. Then the pilgrims got up and walked to and fro; but how were their ears now filled with heavenly noises, and their eyes delighted with celestial visions! In this land they heard nothing, saw nothing, felt nothing, smelled nothing, tasted nothing, that was offensive to their stomach or mind; only when they tasted of the water of the river over which they were to go, they thought that tasted a little bitterish to the palate, but it proved sweeter when 'twas down.

In this place there was a record kept of the names of them that had been pilgrims of old, and a history of all the famous acts that they had done. It was here also much discoursed, how the river to some had had its flowings, and what ebbings it has had while others have gone over. It has been in a manner dry for some, while it has overflowed its banks for others.

In this place the children of the town would go into the King's gardens and gather nosegays for the pilgrims, and bring them to them with much affection. Here also grew "camphire, with spikenard, and saffron, calamus, and cinnamon, with all its trees of frankincense, myrrh, and aloes, with all chief spices."[145] With these the pilgrims' chambers were perfumed, while they staid here; and with these were their bodies anointed to prepare them to go over the river when the time appointed was come.

Now while they lay here and waited for the good hour, there was a noise in the town that there was a post[146] come from the Celestial City, with matter of great importance to one Christiana, the wife of Christian the pilgrim. So inquiry was made of her, and the house was found out where she was; so the post presented her with a letter, the contents whereof were, "Hail, good woman! I bring thee tidings that the Master calleth for thee, and expecteth that thou shouldst stand in his presence, in clothes of immortality, within these ten days."

When he had read this letter to her, he gave her therewith a sure token that he was a true messenger, and was come to bid her make haste to be gone. The token was an arrow with a point sharpened with love, let easily into her heart, which by degrees wrought so effectually with her, that at the time appointed she must be gone.

When Christiana saw that her time was come, and that she was the first of this company that was to go over, she called for Mr. Great-heart her guide, and told him how matters were. So he told her he was heartily glad of the news, and could have been glad had the post come for him. Then she bid that he should give advice how all things should be prepared for her journey. So he told her, saying, Thus and thus it must be; and we that survive will accompany you to the riverside.

Then she called for her children, and gave them her blessing; and told them that she yet read with comfort the mark that was set in their foreheads, and was glad to see them with her there, and that they had kept their garments so white. Lastly, she

---

145. Song of Sol. 4:13, 14.
146. Messenger.

bequeathed to the poor that little she had, and commanded her sons and her daughters to be ready against the messenger should come for them.

When she had spoken these words to her guide and to her children, she called for Mr. Valiant-for-truth, and said unto him, Sir, you have in all places showed yourself truehearted; be faithful unto death, and my King will give you a crown of life. I would also entreat you to have an eye to my children; and if at any time you see them faint, speak comfortably to them. For my daughters, my sons' wives, they have been faithful, and a fulfilling of the promise upon them will be their end. But she gave Mr. Stand-fast a ring.

Then she called for old Mr. Honest, and said of him, Behold an Israelite indeed, in whom is no guile. Then said he, I wish you a fair day when you set out for Mount Zion, and shall be glad to see that you go over the river dry-shod. But she answered, Come wet, come dry, I long to be gone; for however the weather is in my journey, I shall have time enough when I come there to sit down and rest me and dry me.

Then came in that good man Mr. Ready-to-halt to see her. So she said to him, Thy travel hither has been with difficulty; but that will make thy rest the sweeter. But watch and be ready; for at an hour when you think not, the messenger may come.

After him came in Mr. Despondency and his daughter Much-afraid, to whom she said, You ought with thankfulness for ever to remember your deliverance from the hands of Giant Despair, and out of Doubting Castle. The effect of that mercy is, that you are brought with safety hither. Be ye watchful, and cast away fear; be sober, and hope to the end.

Then she said to Mr. Feeble-mind, Thou wast delivered from the mouth of Giant Slay-good, that thou mightest live in the light of the living for ever, and see thy King with comfort. Only I advise thee to repent thee of thine aptness to fear and doubt of his goodness before he sends for thee, lest thou shouldest, when he comes, be forced to stand before him for that fault with blushing.

Now the day drew on that Christiana must be gone. So the road was full of people to see her take her journey. But behold, all the banks beyond the river were full of horses and chariots, which were come down from above to accompany her to the city-gate. So she came forth and entered the river, with a beckon of farewell to those that followed her to the riverside. The last word she was heard to say here was, I come, Lord, to be with thee and bless thee.

So her children and friends returned to their place, for that those that waited for Christiana had carried her out of their sight. So she went, and called, and entered in at the gate with all the ceremonies of joy that her husband Christian had done before her.

At her departure her children wept; but Mr. Great-heart and Mr. Valiant played upon the well-tuned cymbal and harp for joy. So all departed to their respective places.

In the process of time there came a post to the town again, and his business was with Mr. Ready-to-halt. So he inquired him out, and said to him, I am come to thee in the name of him whom thou hast loved and followed, though upon crutches, and my message is to tell thee that he expects thee at his table to sup with him in his kingdom the next day after Easter; wherefore prepare thyself for this journey.

Then he also gave him a token that he was a true messenger, saying, "I have broken thy golden bowl, and loosed thy silver cord."[147]

After this, Mr. Ready-to-halt called for his fellow-pilgrims and told them, saying, I am sent for, and God shall surely visit you also. So he desired Mr. Valiant to make his will; and because he had nothing to bequeath to them that should survive him but his crutches and his good wishes, therefore thus he said, These crutches I bequeath to my son that shall tread in my steps, with a hundred warm wishes that he may prove better than I have done.

Then he thanked Mr. Great-heart for his conduct and kindness, and so addressed himself to his journey. When he came at the brink of the river, he said, Now I shall have no more need of these crutches, since yonder are chariots and horses for me to ride on. The last words he was heard to say was, Welcome life! So he went his way.

After this, Mr. Feeble-mind had tidings brought him that the post sounded his horn at his chamber-door. Then he came in and told him, saying, I am come to tell thee that thy Master hath need of thee; and that in very little time thou must behold his face in brightness. And take this as a token of the truth of my message: "Those that look out at the windows shall be darkened."

Then Mr. Feeble-mind called for his friends, and told them

---

147. This and the following "tokens" of the messenger are all taken from Eccles. 12:1–7.

what errand had been brought unto him, and what token he had received of the truth of the message. Then he said, Since I have nothing to bequeath to any, to what purpose should I make a will? As for my feeble mind, that I will leave behind me, for that I shall have no need of that in the place whither I go. Nor is it worth bestowing upon the poorest pilgrim; wherefore when I am gone, I desire that you, Mr. Valiant, would bury it in a dunghill. This done, and the day being come in which he was to depart, he entered the river as the rest. His last words were, Hold out faith and patience. So he went over to the other side.

When days had many of them passed away, Mr. Despondency was sent for; for a post was come, and brought this message to him: Trembling man, these are to summon thee to be ready with thy King, by the next Lord's day, to shout for joy for thy deliverance from all thy doubtings.

And said the messenger, that my message is true, take this for a proof; so he gave him "the grasshopper to be a burden unto him." Now Mr. Despondency's daughter, whose name was Much-afraid, said, when she heard what was done, that she would go with her father. Then Mr. Despondency said to his friends, Myself and my daughter, you know what we have been, and how troublesomely we have behaved ourselves in every company. My will and my daughter's is, that our desponds and slavish fears be by no man ever received, from the day of our departure, for ever; for I know that after my death they will offer themselves to others. For, to be plain with you, they are ghosts, the which we entertained when we first began to be pilgrims, and could never shake them off after; and they will walk about and seek entertainment of the pilgrims; but for our sakes, shut ye the doors upon them.

When the time was come for them to depart, they went to the brink of the river. The last words of Mr. Despondency were, Farewell night, welcome day. His daughter went through the river singing, but none could understand what she said.

Then it came to pass, a while after, that there was a post in the town that inquired for Mr. Honest. So he came to his house where he was, and delivered to his hand these lines: Thou art commanded to be ready against this day seven-night, to present thyself before thy Lord, at his Father's house. And for a token that my message is true, "All thy daughters of music shall be brought low." Then Mr. Honest called for his friends, and said unto them, I die, but shall make no will. As for my honesty, it shall go with me; let him that comes after be told of this. When the day that he was to be gone was come, he addressed himself to go over the river. Now the river at that time overflowed the banks in some places; but Mr. Honest in his lifetime had spoken to one Good-conscience to meet him there, the which he also did, and lent him his hand, and so helped him over. The last words of Mr. Honest were, Grace reigns. So he left the world.

After this it was noised abroad that Mr. Valiant-for-truth was taken with a summons by the same post as the other; and had this for a token that the summons was true, "That his pitcher was broken at the fountain." When he understood it, he called for his friends, and told them of it. Then said he, I am going to my Father's; and though with great difficulty I am got hither, yet now I do not repent me of all the trouble I have been at to arrive where I am. My sword I give to him that shall succeed me in my pilgrimage, and my courage and skill to him that can get it. My marks and scars I carry with me, to be a witness for me, that I have fought his battles who now will be my rewarder. When the day that he must go hence was come, many accompanied him to the riverside, into which as he went he said, Death, where is thy sting? And as he went down deeper, he said, Grave, where is thy victory? So he passed over, and all the trumpets sounded for him on the other side.

Then there came forth a summons for Mr. Stand-fast (this Mr. Stand-fast was he that the rest of the pilgrims found upon his knees in the Enchanted Ground), for the post brought it him open in his hands. The contents whereof were, that he must prepare for a change of life, for his Master was not willing that he should be so far from him any longer. At this Mr. Stand-fast was put into a muse. Nay, said the messenger, you need not doubt the truth of my message, for here is a token of the truth thereof: "Thy wheel is broken at the cistern." Then he called unto him Mr. Great-heart, who was their guide, and said unto him, Sir, although it was not my hap to be much in your good company in the days of my pilgrimage, yet since the time I knew you, you have been profitable to me. When I came from home, I left behind me a wife and five small children; let me entreat you, at your return (for I know that you will go and return to your Master's house, in hopes that you may yet be a conductor to more of the holy pilgrims), that you send to my family, and let them be acquainted with all that hath or shall happen unto me. Tell them, moreover, of my happy arrival to this place, and of the present late blessed condition that I am in. Tell them also of Christian, and of Christiana his wife, and how she and her children came after her husband. Tell them also of what a happy end she made, and whither she has gone. I have little or nothing to send to my family, except it be prayers and tears for them; of which it will suffice if thou acquaint them, if peradventure they may prevail. When Mr. Stand-fast had thus set things in order, and the time being come for him to haste him away, he also went down to the river. Now there was a great calm at that time in the river; wherefore Mr. Stand-fast, when he was about halfway in, stood awhile, and talked to his companions that had waited upon him thither, and he said,

This river has been a terror to many; yea, the thoughts of it also have often frightened me. But now, methinks, I stand easy, my foot is fixed upon that, upon which the feet of the priests that bare the ark of the covenant stood, while Israel went over this Jordan. The waters indeed are to the palate bitter, and to the stomach cold; yet the thoughts of what I am going to, and of the conduct that waits for me on the other side, doth lie as a glowing coal at my heart.

I see myself now at the end of my journey, my toilsome days are ended. I am going now to see that head that was crowned with thorns, and that face that was spit upon for me.

I have formerly lived by hearsay and faith; but now I go where I shall live by sight, and shall be with him in whose company I delight myself.

I have loved to hear my Lord spoken of; and wherever I have seen the print of his shoe in the earth, there I have coveted to set my foot too.

His name has been to me as a civet-box; yea, sweeter than all perfumes. His voice to me has been most sweet; and his countenance I have more desired than they that have most desired the light of the sun. His word I did use to gather for my food, and for antidotes against my faintings. He has held me, and I have kept me from mine iniquities; yea, my steps hath he strengthened in his way.

Now while he was thus in discourse, his countenance changed, his strong men bowed under him; and after he had said, Take me, for I come unto thee, he ceased to be seen of them.

But glorious it was to see how the open region was filled with horses and chariots, with trumpeters and pipers, with singers and players on stringed instruments, to welcome the pilgrims as they went up and followed one another in at the beautiful gate of the city.

As for Christian's children, the four boys that Christiana brought with her, with their wives and children, I did not stay where I was till they were gone over. Also since I came away, I heard one say that they were yet alive, and so would be for the increase of the Church in that place where they were for a time.

Shall it be my lot to go that way again, I may give those that desire it an account of what I here am silent about; meantime I bid my reader *Adieu.*

Grace Abounding *to the* Chief *of* Sinners

A PREFACE

Or Brief Account of the Publishing of This Work:
Written by the Author Thereof, and Dedicated to Those Whom God
Hath Counted Him Worthy to Beget to Faith,
by His Ministry in the Word

Children, grace be with you, Amen. I being taken from you in presence, and so tied up, that I cannot perform that duty that from God doth lie upon me, to youward, for your further edifying and building up in faith and holiness, etc., yet that you may see my soul hath fatherly care and desire after your spiritual and everlasting welfare; I now once again, as before from the top of Shenir and Hermon, so now from "the lions' dens, and from the mountains of the leopards,"[1] do look yet after you all, greatly longing to see your safe arrival into the desired haven.

I thank God upon every remembrance of you,[2] and rejoice even while I stick between the teeth of the lions in the wilderness, at the grace, and mercy, and knowledge of Christ our Saviour, which God hath bestowed upon you, with abundance of faith and love. Your hungerings and thirstings also after further acquaintance with the Father, in his Son; your tenderness of heart, your trembling at sin, your sober and holy deportment also, before both God and men, is great refreshment to me: "for you are my glory and joy."[3]

I have sent you here enclosed a drop of that honey, that I have taken out of the carcass of a lion.[4] I have eaten thereof myself also, and am much refreshed thereby. (Temptations when we meet them at first, are as the lion that roared upon Samson; but if we overcome them, the next time we see them, we shall find a nest of honey within them.) The Philistines understand me not.[5] It is a relation of the work

---

1. Song of Sol. 4:8.
2. Phil. 1:3.
3. 1 Thess. 2:20.

4. Judg. 14:5–8.
5. Judg. 14:14.

of God upon my own soul, even from the very first, till now; wherein you may perceive my castings down, and raisings up: for he woundeth, and his hands make whole. It is written in the scripture,[6] "The father to the children shall make known the truth of God." Yea, it was for this reason I lay so long at Sinai,[7] to see the fire, and the cloud, and the darkness, "that I might fear the Lord all the days of my life upon earth, and tell of his wondrous works to my children."[8]

Moses[9] writ of the journeyings of the children of Israel, from Egypt to the land of Canaan; and commanded also, that they did remember their forty years' travel in the wilderness. "Thou shalt remember all the way which the Lord thy God led thee these forty years in the wilderness, to humble thee, and to prove thee, and to know what was in thine heart, whether thou wouldst keep his commandments or no."[10] Wherefore this I have endeavoured to do; and not only so, but to publish it also, that, if God will, others may be put in remembrance of what he hath done for their souls, by reading his work upon me.

It is profitable for Christians to be often calling to mind the very beginnings of grace with their souls. "It is a night to be much observed to the Lord, for bringing them out from the land of Egypt. This is that night of the Lord to be observed of all the children of Israel in their generations."[11] "My God," saith David,[12] "my soul is cast down within me; but I will remember thee from the land of Jordan, and of the Hermonites, from the hill Mizar." He remembered also the lion and the bear, when he went to fight with the giant of Gath.[13]

It was Paul's accustomed manner,[14] and that when tried for his life,[15] even to open before his judges the manner of his conversion: he would think of that day and that hour, in the which he first did meet with grace, for he found it support unto him. When God had brought the children of Israel through the Red Sea, far into the wilderness, yet they must turn quite about thither again, to remember the drowning of their enemies there,[16] for though they sang his praise before, yet "they soon forgot his works."[17]

In this discourse of mine, you may see much; much, I say, of the

---

6. Isa. 38:19.
7. Deut. 4:10, 11.
8. Ps. 78:3–5.
9. Num. 33:1, 2.
10. Deut. 8:2, 3.
11. Exod. 12:42.

12. Ps. 42:6.
13. 1 Sam. 17:36, 37.
14. Acts 22.
15. Acts 24.
16. Num. 14:25.
17. Ps. 106:12, 13.

grace of God towards me: I thank God I can count it much, for it was above my sins, and Satan's temptations too. I can remember my fears, and doubts, and sad months, with comfort; they are as the head of Goliath in my hand. There was nothing to David like Goliath's sword, even that sword that should have been sheathed in his bowels; for the very sight and remembrance of that, did preach forth God's deliverance to him. O the remembrance of my great sins, of my great temptations, and of my great fears of perishing for ever! They bring fresh into my mind the remembrance of my great help, my great support from heaven, and the great grace that God extended to such a wretch as I.

My dear children, call to mind the former days, the years of ancient times; remember also your songs in the night, and commune with your own heart.[18] Yea, look diligently, and leave no corner therein unsearched, for there is treasure hid, even the treasure of your first and second experience of the grace of God toward you. Remember, I say, the Word that first laid hold upon you; remember your terrors of conscience, and fear of death and hell. Remember also your tears and prayers to God; yea, how you sighed under every hedge for mercy. Have you never a hill Mizar[19] to remember? Have you forgot the close, the milk-house, the stable, the barn, and the like, where God did visit your soul? Remember also the Word, the Word, I say, upon which the Lord hath caused you to hope: if you have sinned against light, if you are tempted to blaspheme, if you are down in despair, if you think God fights against you, or if heaven is hid from your eyes, remember 'twas thus with your father, "but out of them all the Lord delivered me."[20]

I could have enlarged much in this my discourse of my temptations and troubles for sin, as also of the merciful kindness and working of God with my soul. I could also have stepped into a style much higher than this in which I have here discoursed, and could have adorned all things more than here I have seemed to do, but I dare not. God did not play in convincing of me; the devil did not play in tempting of me; neither did I play when I sunk as into a bottomless pit, when the pangs of hell caught hold upon me: wherefore I may not play in my relating of them, but be plain and simple,

18. Ps. 77:5–12.
19. Ps. 42:6.
20. 2 Tim. 3:11.

and lay down the thing as it was. He that liketh it, let him receive it; and he that does not, let him produce a better. Farewell.

My dear children,
The milk and honey is beyond this wilderness. God be merciful to you, and grant that you be not slothful to go in to possess the land.

JOHN BUNYAN

GRACE
ABOUNDING TO
THE CHIEF OF SINNERS

———

Or,
A Brief Relation of the Exceeding Mercy of God
in Christ, to His Poor Servant
John Bunyan

———

1. In this my relation of the merciful working of God upon my soul, it will not be amiss if in the first place I do in a few words give you a hint of my pedigree and manner of bringing up, that thereby the goodness and bounty of God towards me may be the more advanced and magnified before the sons of men.

2. For my descent then, it was, as is well known by many, of a low and inconsiderable generation; my father's house being of that rank that is meanest and most despised of all the families in the land. Wherefore I have not here, as others, to boast of noble blood, or of a highborn state according to the flesh; though all things considered, I magnify the heavenly Majesty, for that by this door he brought me into this world, to partake of the grace and life that is in Christ by the gospel.

3. But yet notwithstanding the meanness and inconsiderableness of my parents, it pleased God to put it into their heart to put me to school, to learn both to read and write; the which I also attained, according to the rate of other poor men's children, though to my shame I confess, I did soon lose that little I learned, and that even almost utterly, and that long before the Lord did work his gracious work of conversion upon my soul.

4. As for my own natural life, for the time that I was without God in the world, it was, indeed, "according to the course of this world, and the spirit that now worketh in the children of disobedience."[21]

---

21. Eph. 2:2, 3.

It was my delight to be taken captive by the devil "at his will,"[22] being filled with all unrighteousness; the which did also so strongly work and put forth itself, both in my heart and life, and that from a child, that I had but few equals (especially considering my years, which were tender, being few), both for cursing, swearing, lying, and blaspheming the holy name of God.

5. Yea, so settled and rooted was I in these things that they became as a second nature to me; the which, as I also have with soberness considered since, did so offend the Lord, that even in my childhood he did scare and affright me with fearful dreams, and did terrify me with dreadful visions. For often, after I had spent this and the other day in sin, I have in my bed been greatly afflicted, while asleep, with the apprehensions of devils and wicked spirits, who still, as I then thought, laboured to draw me away with them; of which I could never be rid.

6. Also I should at these years be greatly afflicted and troubled with the thoughts of the day of judgement, and that both night and day, and should tremble at the thoughts of the fearful torments of hell-fire; still fearing that it would be my lot to be found at last amongst those devils and hellish fiends, who are there bound down with the chains and bonds of eternal darkness.

7. These things, I say, when I was but a child, about nine or ten years old, did so distress my soul, that when in the midst of my many sports and childish vanities, amidst my vain companions, I was often much cast down and afflicted in my mind therewith, yet could I not let go my sins. Yea, I was so overcome with despair of life and heaven, that then I should often wish, either that there had been no hell, or that I had been a devil, supposing they were only tormentors; that if it must needs be, that I indeed went thither, I might be rather a tormentor, than tormented myself.

8. A while after, these terrible dreams did leave me, which also I soon forgot; for my pleasures did quickly cut off the remembrance of them, as if they had never been. Wherefore with more greediness, according to the strength of nature, I did still let loose the reins to my lusts and delighted in all transgression against the law of God, so that until I came to the state of marriage, I was the very ringleader of all the youth that kept me company, into all manner of vice and ungodliness.

---

22. 2 Tim. 2:26.

9. Yea, such prevalency had the lusts and fruits of the flesh, in this poor soul of mine, that had not a miracle of precious grace prevented, I had not only perished by the stroke of eternal justice, but had also laid myself open even to the stroke of those laws, which bring some to disgrace and open shame before the face of the world.

10. In these days the thoughts of religion were very grievous to me; I could neither endure it myself, nor that any other should, so that when I have but seen some read in those books that concerned Christian piety, it would be as it were a prison to me. "Then I said unto God, Depart from me, for I desire not the knowledge of thy ways."²³ I was now void of all good consideration; heaven and hell were both out of sight and mind, and as for saving and damning, they were least in my thoughts. "O Lord, thou knowest my life, and my ways were not hid from thee."²⁴

11. Yet this I well remember, that though I could myself sin with the greatest delight and ease, and also take pleasure in the vileness of my companions, yet even then, if I have at any time seen wicked things by those that professed goodness, it would make my spirit tremble. As once above all the rest, when I was in my height of vanity, yet hearing one to swear that was reckoned for a religious man, it had so great a stroke upon my spirit, as it made my heart to ache.

12. But God did not utterly leave me, but followed me still, not now with convictions, but judgements, yet such as were mixed with mercy. For once I fell into a creek of the sea and hardly escaped drowning; another time I fell out of a boat into Bedford river, but mercy yet preserved me alive. Besides, another time being in the field, with one of my companions, it chanced that an adder passed over the highway, so I having a stick in mine hand, struck her over the back, and having stounded her, I forced open her mouth with my stick and plucked her sting out with my fingers, by which act had not God been merciful to me, I might by my desperateness have brought myself to mine end.

13. This also have I taken notice of with thanksgiving: when I was a soldier, I with others were drawn out to go to such a place to besiege it, but when I was just ready to go, one of the company desired to go in my room, to which, when I had consented, he took

---

23. Job 21:14, 15.
24. Ps. 69:5.

my place; and coming to the siege, as he stood sentinel, he was shot into the head with a musket bullet and died.

14. Here, as I said, were judgements and mercy, but neither of them did awaken my soul to righteousness, wherefore I sinned still, and grew more and more rebellious against God, and careless of mine own salvation.

15. Presently after this, I changed my condition into a married state, and my mercy was to light upon a wife whose father was counted godly. This woman and I, though we came together as poor as poor might be (not having so much household-stuff as a dish or spoon betwixt us both), yet this she had for her part, *The Plain Man's Pathway to Heaven,* and *The Practice of Piety,* which her father had left her when he died. In these two books, I should sometimes read with her, wherein I also found some things that were somewhat pleasing to me (but all this while I met with no conviction). She also would be often telling of me what a godly man her father was, and how he would reprove and correct vice, both in his house and amongst his neighbours; what a strict and holy life he lived in his day, both in word and deed.

16. Wherefore these books, with this relation, though they did not reach my heart to awaken it about my sad and sinful state, yet they did beget within me some desires to religion: so that, because I knew no better, I fell in very eagerly with the religion of the times, to wit, to go to church twice a day, and that too with the foremost, and there should very devoutly both say and sing as others did, yet retaining my wicked life. But withal, I was so overrun with the spirit of superstition that I adored, and that with great devotion, even all things (both the high place, priest, clerk, vestments, service, and what else) belonging to the church; counting all things holy that were therein contained, and especially the priest and clerk most happy, and without doubt greatly blessed, because they were the servants, as I then thought, of God, and were principal in the holy temple, to do his work therein.

17. This conceit grew so strong in little time upon my spirit, that had I but seen a priest (though never so sordid and debauched in his life), I should find my spirit fall under him, reverence him, and knit unto him. Yea, I thought for the love I did bear unto them (supposing they were the ministers of God), I could have laid down at their feet and have been trampled upon by them; their name, their garb, and work did so intoxicate and bewitch me.

18. After I had been thus for some considerable time, another thought came into my mind, and that was, whether we were of the Israelites or no, for finding in the scriptures that they were once the peculiar people of God, thought I, if I were one of this race, my soul must needs be happy. Now again I found within me a great longing to be resolved about this question, but could not tell how I should. At last, I asked my father of it, who told me, No, we were not; wherefore then I fell in my spirit, as to the hopes of that, and so remained.

19. But all this while I was not sensible of the danger and evil of sin; I was kept from considering that sin would damn me, what religion soever I followed, unless I was found in Christ. Nay, I never thought of him, nor whether there was one or no. Thus man, while blind, doth wander, but wearieth himself with vanity, for he knoweth not the way to the city of God.[25]

20. But one day (amongst all the sermons our parson made) his subject was to treat of the Sabbath day and of the evil of breaking that, either with labour, sports, or otherwise (now I was, notwithstanding my religion, one that took much delight in all manner of vice, and especially that was the day that I did solace myself therewith). Wherefore I fell in my conscience under his sermon, thinking and believing that he made that sermon on purpose to show me my evil-doing, and at that time I felt what guilt was, though never before, that I can remember; but then I was for the present greatly loaden therewith, and so went home when the sermon was ended, with a great burden on my spirit.

21. This, for that instant, did benumb the sinews of my best delights, and did embitter my former pleasures to me; but behold, it lasted not, for before I had well dined, the trouble began to go off my mind, and my heart returned to its old course. But oh how glad was I, that this trouble was gone from me, and that the fire was put out, that I might sin again without control! Wherefore when I had satisfied nature with my food, I shook the sermon out of my mind, and to my old custom of sports and gaming I returned with great delight.

22. But the same day, as I was in the midst of a game of cat,[26] and having struck it one blow from the hole, just as I was about to

---

25. Eccles. 10:15.
26. A simple game played with a stick striking an oval piece of wood.

strike it the second time, a voice did suddenly dart from heaven into my soul, which said, "Wilt thou leave thy sins, and go to heaven? Or have thy sins, and go to hell?" At this I was put to an exceeding maze;[27] wherefore leaving my cat upon the ground, I looked up to heaven, and was as if I had with the eyes of my understanding, seen the Lord Jesus looking down upon me, as being very hotly displeased with me, and as if he did severely threaten me with some grievous punishment for these, and other my ungodly practices.

23. I had no sooner thus conceived in my mind, but suddenly this conclusion was fastened on my spirit (for the former hint did set my sins again before my face), that I had been a great and grievous sinner, and that it was now too late for me to look after heaven, for Christ would not forgive me, nor pardon my transgressions. Then I fell to musing upon this also, and while I was thinking on it, and fearing lest it should be so, I felt my heart sink in despair, concluding it was too late, and therefore I resolved in my mind, I would go on in sin. For thought I, if the case be thus, my state is surely miserable; miserable, if I leave my sins, and but miserable if I follow them. I can but be damned, and if it must be so, I had as good be damned for many sins, as to be damned for few.

24. Thus I stood in the midst of my play, before all that then were present; but yet I told them nothing. But, I say, I having made this conclusion, I returned desperately to my sport again, and I well remember that presently this kind of despair did so possess my soul, that I was persuaded I could never attain to other comfort than what I should get in sin; for heaven was gone already, so that on that I must not think. Wherefore I found within me a great desire to take my fill of sin, still studying what sin was to be committed, that I might taste the sweetness of it, and I made as much haste as I could to fill my belly with its delicates, lest I should die before I had my desire, for that I feared greatly. In these things, I protest before God, I lie not, neither do I feign this form of speech: these were really, strongly, and with all my heart, my desires; the good Lord, whose mercy is unsearchable, forgive me my transgressions.

25. (And I am very confident that this temptation of the devil is more usual amongst poor creatures than many are aware of, even to overrun their spirits with a scurvy and seared frame of heart and

---

27. Confusion.

benumbing of conscience; which frame, he stilly and slyly supplieth with such despair, that though not much guilt attendeth the soul, yet they continually have a secret conclusion within them, that there is no hopes for them, "for they have loved sins, therefore after them they will go.")[28]

26. Now therefore I went on in sin with great greediness of mind, still grudging that I could not be so satisfied with it as I would. This did continue with me about a month, or more, but one day as I was standing at a neighbour's shop-window, and there cursing and swearing, and playing the madman after my wonted manner, there sat within the woman of the house and heard me, who, though she also was a very loose and ungodly wretch, yet protested that I swore and cursed at that most fearful rate, that she was made to tremble to hear me, and told me further, that I was the ungodliest fellow for swearing that ever she heard in all her life, and that I, by thus doing, was able to spoil all the youth in a whole town, if they came but in my company.

27. At this reproof I was silenced and put to secret shame; and that too, as I thought, before the God of heaven. Wherefore, while I there stood, and hanging down my head, I wished with all my heart that I might be a little child again, that my father might learn me to speak without this wicked way of swearing; for thought I, I am so accustomed to it, that it is but in vain for me to think of a reformation, for I thought it could never be.

28. But how it came to pass I know not, I did from this time forward so leave my swearing, that it was a great wonder to myself to observe it, and whereas before I knew not how to speak unless I put an oath before, and another behind, to make my words have authority, now, I could, without it, speak better and with more pleasantness than ever I could before; all this while I knew not Jesus Christ, neither did I leave my sports and play.

29. But quickly after this, I fell in company with one poor man, that made profession of religion, who, as I then thought, did talk pleasantly of the scriptures and of the matters of religion. Wherefore falling into some love and liking to what he said, I betook me to my Bible and began to take great pleasure in reading, but especially with the historical part thereof; for, as for Paul's epistles, and scriptures of that nature, I could not away with them, being as yet

---

28. Jer. 2:25; 18:12.

but ignorant either of the corruptions of my nature, or of the want and worth of Jesus Christ to save me.

30. Wherefore I fell to some outward reformation, both in my words and life, and did set the commandments before me for my way to heaven; which commandments I also did strive to keep, and, as I thought, did keep them pretty well sometimes, and then I should have comfort; yet now and then should break one, and so afflict my conscience. But then I should repent, and say I was sorry for it, and promise God to do better next time, and there get help again, for then I thought I pleased God as well as any man in England.

31. Thus I continued about a year, all which time our neighbours did take me to be a very godly man, a new and religious man, and did marvel much to see such a great and famous alteration in my life and manners, and indeed so it was, though yet I knew not Christ, nor grace, nor faith, nor hope; and truly as I have well seen since, had I then died, my state had been most fearful. Well, this, I say, continued about a twelvemonth, or more.

32. But, I say, my neighbours were amazed at this my great conversion, from prodigious profaneness, to something like a moral life; and, truly, so they well might, for this my conversion was as great as for Tom of Bethlem[29] to become a sober man. Now, therefore, they began to praise, to commend, and to speak well of me, both to my face, and behind my back. Now, I was, as they said, become godly; now, I was become a right honest man. But O! When I understood that these were their words and opinions of me, it pleased me mighty well; for though, as yet, I was nothing but a poor painted hypocrite, yet I loved to be talked of as one that was truly godly. I was proud of my godliness, and I did all I did either to be seen of, or to be well spoken of, by men. Well, this, I say, continued for about a twelvemonth or more.

33. Now you must know that before that I had taken much delight in ringing,[30] but my conscience beginning to be tender, I thought that such a practice was but vain, and therefore forced myself to leave it; yet my mind hankered, wherefore I should go to the steeple house, and look on, though I durst not ring. But I thought this did not become religion neither, yet I forced myself and would look on still; but quickly after, I began to think, how, if

---

29. A madman.
30. I.e., churchbell ringing.

one of the bells should fall? Then I chose to stand under a main beam that lay overthwart the steeple from side to side, thinking there I might stand sure. But then I should think again, should the bell fall with a swing, it might first hit the wall, and then rebounding upon me, might kill me for all this beam; this made me stand in the steeple door, and now thought I, I am safe enough, for if a bell should then fall, I can slip out behind these thick walls, and so be preserved notwithstanding.

34. So after this, I would yet go to see them ring, but would not go further than the steeple door; but then it came into my head, how if the steeple itself should fall? And this thought (it may fall for ought I know), would when I stood and looked on, continually so shake my mind, that I durst not stand at the steeple door any longer, but was forced to fly, for fear it should fall upon my head.

35. Another thing was my dancing; I was a full year before I could quite leave it. But all this while, when I thought I kept this or that commandment, or did by word or deed anything that I thought were good, I had great peace in my conscience, and should think with myself, God cannot choose but be now pleased with me, yea, to relate it in mine own way, I thought no man in England could please God better than I.

36. But poor wretch as I was, I was all this while ignorant of Jesus Christ, and going about to establish my own righteousness, had perished therein had not God in mercy showed me more of my state by nature.

37. But upon a day, the good providence of God did cast me to Bedford, to work on my calling; and in one of the streets of that town, I came where there were three or four poor women sitting at a door in the sun, and talking about the things of God, and being now willing to hear them discourse, I drew near to hear what they said, for I was now a brisk talker also myself in the matters of religion; but now I may say, "I heard, but I understood not,"[31] for they were far above out of my reach, for their talk was about a new birth, the work of God on their hearts, also how they were convinced of their miserable state by nature. They talked how God had visited their souls with his love in the Lord Jesus, and with what words and promises they had been refreshed, comforted, and supported against the temptations of the devil; moreover, they rea-

---

31. Dan. 12:8.

soned of the suggestions and temptations of Satan in particular,
and told to each other by which they had been afflicted, and how
they were borne up under his assaults. They also discoursed of
their own wretchedness of heart, of their unbelief, and did con-
temn, slight, and abhor their own righteousness, as filthy and
insufficient to do them any good.

38. And methought they spake as if joy did make them speak:
they spake with such pleasantness of scripture language, and with
such appearance of grace in all they said, that they were to me as if
they had found a new world, as if they were people that dwelt
alone, and were not to be reckoned amongst their neighbours.[32]

39. At this I felt my own heart began to shake, as mistrusting
my condition to be naught, for I saw that in all my thoughts about
religion and salvation, the new birth did never enter into my mind,
neither knew I the comfort of the Word and promise, nor the
deceitfulness and treachery of my own wicked heart. As for secret
thoughts, I took no notice of them; neither did I understand what
Satan's temptations were, nor how they were to be withstood and
resisted, etc.

40. Thus therefore when I had heard and considered what they
said, I left them, and went about my employment again, but their
talk and discourse went with me; also my heart would tarry with
them, for I was greatly affected with their words, both because by
them I was convinced that I wanted the true tokens of a truly godly
man, and also because by them I was convinced of the happy and
blessed condition of him that was such a one.

41. Therefore I should often make it my business to be going
again and again into the company of these poor people, for I could
not stay away, and the more I went amongst them, the more I did
question my condition; and, as still I do remember, presently I found
two things within me, at which I did sometimes marvel (especially
considering what a blind, ignorant, sordid, and ungodly wretch
but just before I was): the one was, a very great softness and tenderness of heart, which caused me to fall under the conviction of
what by scripture they asserted, and the other was, a great bending
in my mind to a continual meditating on them, and on all other
good things which at any time I heard or read of.

42. By these things my mind was now so turned, that it lay like a

---

32. Num. 23:9.

horse leech at the vein, still crying out, "Give, give";[33] yea, it was so
fixed on eternity, and on the things about the kingdom of heaven,
that is, so far as I knew, though as yet God knows, I knew but little,
that neither pleasures, nor profits, nor persuasions, nor threats, could
loosen it, or make it let go its hold. And though I may speak it with
shame, yet it is in very deed a certain truth, it would then have been
as difficult for me to have taken my mind from heaven to earth, as I
have found it often since to get it again from earth to heaven.

43. One thing I may not omit, there was a young man in our
town, to whom my heart before was knit more than to any other,
but he being a most wicked creature for cursing and swearing and
whoring, I shook him off and forsook his company, but about a
quarter of a year after I had left him, I met him in a certain lane,
and asked him how he did; he after his old swearing and mad way,
answered, he was well. "But Harry," said I, "why do you swear and
curse thus? What will become of you if you die in this condition?"
He answered me in a great chafe, "What would the devil do for
company if it were not for such as I am?"

44. About this time I met with some Ranters'[34] books that were
put forth by some of our countrymen, which books were also
highly in esteem by several old professors; some of these I read, but
was not able to make a judgement about them. Wherefore, as I
read in them, and thought upon them, feeling myself unable to
judge, I should betake myself to hearty prayer, in this manner: "O
Lord, I am a fool, and not able to know the truth from error; Lord
leave me not to my own blindness, either to approve of, or condemn this doctrine; if it be of God, let me not despise it; if it be of
the devil, let me not embrace it. Lord, I lay my soul, in this matter,
only at thy foot, let me not be deceived, I humbly beseech thee." I
had one religious intimate companion all this while, and that was
the poor man that I spoke of before, but about this time he also
turned a most devilish Ranter, and gave himself up to all manner of
filthiness, especially uncleanness; he would laugh at all exhortations to sobriety. When I laboured to rebuke his wickedness, he
would laugh the more, and pretend that he had gone through all
religions and could never light on the right till now; he told me also
that in little time I should see all professors turn to the ways of the

---

33. Prov. 30:15.
34. Ranters were a radical Christian sect of the mid-seventeenth century.

Ranters. Wherefore abominating those cursed principles, I left his company forthwith, and became to him as great a stranger as I had been before a familiar.

45. Neither was this man only a temptation to me, but my calling lying in the country, I happened to light into several people's company, who though strict in religion formerly, yet were also swept away by these Ranters. These would also talk with me of their ways and condemn me as legal and dark, pretending that they only had attained to perfection that could do what they would and not sin. O these temptations were suitable to my flesh, I being but a young man and my nature in its prime; but God, who had as I hope designed me for better things, kept me in the fear of his name, and did not suffer me to accept of such cursed principles. And blessed be God, who put it into my heart to cry to him to be kept and directed, still distrusting mine own wisdom; for I have since seen even the effect of that prayer in his preserving me, not only from Ranting errors, but from those also that have sprung up since. The Bible was precious to me in those days.

46. And now methought I began to look into the Bible with new eyes, and read as I never did before, and especially the epistles of the apostle Paul were sweet and pleasant to me, and indeed I was then never out of the Bible, either by reading or meditation, still crying out to God, that I might know the truth and way to heaven and glory.

47. And as I went on and read, I lighted on that passage, "To one is given by the Spirit the word of wisdom; to another the word of knowledge by the same Spirit, and to another faith," etc.[35] And though, as I have since seen, that by this scripture the Holy Ghost intends, in special, things extraordinary, yet on me it then did fasten with conviction, that I did want things ordinary, even that understanding and wisdom that other Christians had. On this word I mused, and could not tell what to do, especially this word faith put me to it, for I could not help it, but sometimes must question whether I had any faith or no, for I feared it shut me out of all the blessings that other good people had given them of God; but I was loath to conclude I had no faith in my soul, for if I do so, thought I, then I shall count myself a very castaway indeed.

48. No, said I with myself, though I am convinced that I am an ignorant sot, and that I want those blessed gifts of knowledge and

35. 1 Cor. 12.

understanding that other good people have, yet at a venture I will conclude I am not altogether faithless, though I know not what faith is. For it was showed me, and that too (as I have since seen) by Satan, that those who conclude themselves in a faithless state, have neither rest nor quiet in their souls, and I was loath to fall quite into despair.

49. Wherefore by this suggestion, I was for a while made afraid to see my want of faith, but God would not suffer me thus to undo and destroy my soul, but did continually against this my blind and sad conclusion, create still within me such suppositions that I might in this deceive myself, insomuch that I could not rest content until I did now come to some certain knowledge whether I had faith or no, this always running in my mind: But how if you want faith indeed? But how can you tell you have faith? And besides, I saw for certain, if I had not, I was sure to perish for ever.

50. So that though I endeavoured at the first to look over the business of faith, yet in a little time, I better considering the matter, was willing to put myself upon the trial, whether I had faith or no. But alas, poor wretch, so ignorant and brutish was I, that I knew to this day no more how to do it than I know how to begin and accomplish that rare and curious piece of art, which I never yet saw nor considered.

51. Wherefore while I was thus considering, and being put to my plunge about it (for you must know that as yet I had in this matter broken my mind to no man, only did hear and consider), the tempter came in with this delusion, that there was no way for me to know I had faith, but by trying to work some miracle, urging those scriptures that seem to look that way, for the enforcing and strengthening his temptation. Nay, one day as I was betwixt Elstow and Bedford, the temptation was hot upon me to try if I had faith by doing of some miracle; which miracle at that time was this, I must say to the puddles that were in the horse pads,[36] "Be dry," and to the dry places, "Be you the puddles." And truly one time I was going to say so indeed, but just as I was about to speak, this thought came into my mind, But go under yonder hedge, and pray first, that God would make you able. But when I had concluded to pray, this came hot upon me, that if I prayed and came again and tried to do it and yet did nothing notwithstanding, then besure I

---

36. I.e., paths.

290] JOHN BUNYAN

had no faith, but was a castaway and lost; nay, thought I, if it be so, I will never try yet, but will stay a little longer.

52. So I continued at a great loss, for I thought if they only had faith which could do such wonderful things, then I concluded that for the present I neither had it, nor yet for time to come were ever like to have it. Thus I was tossed betwixt the devil and my own ignorance, and so perplexed, especially at some times, that I could not tell what to do.

53. About this time, the state and happiness of these poor people at Bedford was thus in a kind of vision represented to me: I saw as if they were set on the sunny side of some high mountain, there refreshing themselves with the pleasant beams of the sun, while I was shivering and shrinking in the cold, afflicted with frost, snow, and dark clouds; methought also betwixt me and them I saw a wall that did compass about this mountain. Now, through this wall, my soul did greatly desire to pass, concluding that if I could, I would go even into the very midst of them, and there also comfort myself with the heat of their sun.

54. About this wall I thought myself to go again and again, still prying as I went, to see if I could find some way of passage by which I might enter therein, but none could I find for some time. At the last I saw as it were a narrow gap, like a little doorway in the wall, through which I attempted to pass, but the passage being very strait and narrow, I made many offers to get in, but all in vain, even until I was well-nigh quite beat out by striving to get in. At last, with great striving, methought I at first did get in my head, and after that by a sidelong striving, my shoulders, and my whole body; then was I exceeding glad, and went and sat down in the midst of them, and so was comforted with the light and heat of their sun.

55. Now, this mountain and wall, etc. was thus made out to me: the mountain signified the church of the living God; the sun that shone thereon, the comfortable shining of his merciful face on them that were therein; the wall I thought was the Word that did make separation between the Christians and the world; and the gap which was in this wall, I thought was Jesus Christ, who is the way to God the Father.[37] But for as much as the passage was wonderful narrow, even so narrow that I could not but with great difficulty enter in thereat, it showed me that none could enter into life

---

37. John 14:6; Matt. 7:14.

but those that were in downright earnest, and unless also they left this wicked world behind them; for here was only room for body and soul, but not for body and soul and sin.

56. This resemblance abode upon my spirit many days, all which time I saw myself in a forlorn and sad condition, but yet was provoked to a vehement hunger and desire to be one of that number that did sit in this sunshine. Now also I should pray wherever I was, whether at home or abroad, in house or field, and should also often with lifting up of heart, sing that of the fifty-first Psalm, "O Lord, consider my distress,"[38] for as yet I knew not where I was.

57. Neither as yet could I attain to any comfortable persuasion that I had faith in Christ, but instead of having satisfaction, here I began to find my soul to be assaulted with fresh doubts about my future happiness, especially with such as these, whether I was elected; but how if the day of grace should now be past and gone?

58. By these two temptations I was very much afflicted and disquieted; sometimes by one, and sometimes by the other of them. And first, to speak of that about my questioning my election, I found at this time that though I was in a flame to find the way to heaven and glory, and though nothing could beat me off from this, yet this question did so offend and discourage me that I was, especially at sometimes, as if the very strength of my body also had been taken away by the force and power thereof. This scripture also did seem to me to trample upon all my desires, "it is neither in him that willeth, nor in him that runneth, but in God that sheweth mercy."[39]

59. With this scripture I could not tell what to do, for I evidently saw that unless the great God of his infinite grace and bounty had voluntarily chosen me to be a vessel of mercy, though I should desire and long and labour until my heart did break, no good could come of it. Therefore this would still stick with me, how can you tell you are elected? And what if you should not? How then?

60. O Lord, thought I, what if I should not indeed? It may be you are not, said the tempter: it may be so indeed, thought I. Why then, said Satan, you had as good leave off, and strive no further, for if indeed you should not be elected and chosen of God, there is no talk of your being saved: For it is neither in him that willeth, nor in him that runneth, but in God that sheweth mercy.

---

38. Ps. 51:1.
39. Rom. 9:16.

61. By these things I was driven to my wits' end, not knowing what to say, or how to answer these temptations (indeed I little thought that Satan had thus assaulted me, but that rather it was my own prudence thus to start the question), for that the elect only attained eternal life, that I without scruple did heartily close withal;[40] but that myself was one of them, there lay all the question.

62. Thus therefore for several days I was greatly assaulted and perplexed, and was often, when I have been walking, ready to sink where I went with faintness in my mind. But one day, after I had been so many weeks oppressed and cast down therewith, as I was now quite giving up the ghost of all my hopes of ever attaining life, that sentence fell with weight upon my spirit, "Look at the generations of old, and see, did ever any trust in God and were confounded?"

63. At which I was greatly lightened and encouraged in my soul, for thus at that very instant it was expounded to me: "Begin at the beginning of Genesis, and read to the end of the Revelations, and see if you can find that there was any that ever trusted in the Lord, and was confounded." So coming home, I presently went to my Bible to see if I could find that saying, not doubting but to find it presently, for it was so fresh, and with such strength and comfort on my spirit, that I was as if it talked with me.

64. Well, I looked, but I found it not, only it abode upon me. Then I did ask first this good man, and then another, if they knew where it was, but they knew no such place. At this I wondered that such a sentence should so suddenly and with such comfort and strength seize and abide upon my heart, and yet that none could find it (for I doubted not but it was in holy scripture).

65. Thus I continued above a year and could not find the place, but at last, casting my eye into the Apocrypha books, I found it in Ecclesiasticus 2:10; this at the first did somewhat daunt me, but because by this time I had got more experience of the love and kindness of God, it troubled me the less, especially when I considered that though it was not in those texts that we call holy and canonical, yet for as much as this sentence was the sum and substance of many of the promises, it was my duty to take the comfort of it, and I bless God for that word, for it was of God to me: that word doth still at times shine before my face.

---

40. Accept.

66. After this, that other doubt did come with strength upon me, But how if the day of grace should be past and gone? How if you have overstood the time of mercy? Now I remember that one day as I was walking into the country, I was much in the thoughts of this, but how if the day of grace be past? And to aggravate my trouble, the tempter presented to my mind those good people of Bedford, and suggested thus unto me, that these being converted already, they were all that God would save in those parts, and that I came too late, for these had got the blessing before I came.

67. Now was I in great distress, thinking in very deed that this might well be so. Wherefore I went up and down bemoaning my sad condition, counting myself far worse than a thousand fools, for standing off thus long, and spending so many years in sin as I have done, still crying out, O that I had turned sooner! O that I had turned seven years ago; it made me also angry with myself, to think that I should have no more wit but to trifle away my time till my soul and heaven were lost.

68. But when I had been long vexed with this fear, and was scarce able to take one step more, just about the same place where I received my other encouragement, these words broke in upon my mind, "Compel them to come in, that my house may be filled, and yet there is room."[41] These words, but especially them, "And yet there is room," were sweet words to me; for truly I thought that by them I saw that there was place enough in heaven for me, and moreover, that when the Lord Jesus did speak these words, he then did think of me, and that he knowing the time would come that I should be afflicted with fear, that there was no place left for me in his bosom, did before speak this word and leave it upon record, that I might find help thereby against this vile temptation. This, I then verily believed.

69. In the light and encouragement of this word, I went a pretty while, and the comfort was the more, when I thought that the Lord Jesus should think on me so long ago, and that he should speak them words on purpose for my sake, for I did then think verily that he did on purpose speak them to encourage me withal.

70. But I was not without my temptations to go back again; temptations, I say, both from Satan, mine own heart, and carnal acquaintance. But I thank God, these were outweighed by that

41. Luke 14:22, 23.

sound sense of death and of the day of judgement, which abode, as it were, continually in my view. I should often also think on Nebuchadnezzar, of whom it is said, "He had given him all the kingdoms of the earth."[42] Yet, I thought, if this great man had all his portion in this world, one hour in hell-fire would make him forget all; which consideration was a great help to me.

71. I was also made about this time to see something concerning the beasts that Moses counted clean and unclean. I thought those beasts were types of men; the clean types of them that were the people of God, but the unclean types of such as were the children of the wicked one. Now I read that the clean beasts chewed the cud; that is, thought I, they show us we must feed upon the Word of God. They also parted the hoof; I thought that signified, we must part, if we would be saved, with the ways of ungodly men. And also, in further reading about them, I found that though we did chew the cud as the hare, yet if we walked with claws like a dog, or if we did part the hoof like the swine, yet if we did not chew the cud as the sheep, we were still for all that, but unclean; for I thought the hare to be a type of those that talk of the Word, yet walk in ways of sin, and that the swine was like him that parteth with his outward pollutions, but still wanteth the Word of faith, without which there could be no way of salvation, let a man be never so devout.[43]

After this, I found by reading the Word, that those that must be glorified with Christ in another world, must be called by him here. Called to the partaking of a share in his Word and righteousness, and to the comforts and firstfruits of his Spirit, and to a peculiar interest in all those heavenly things, which do indeed fore-fit the soul for that rest and house of glory which is in heaven above.

72. Here again I was at a very great stand, not knowing what to do, fearing I was not called; for thought I, if I be not called, what then can do me good? None but those who are effectually called inherit the kingdom of heaven. But O how I now loved those words that spake of a Christian's calling! As when the Lord said to one, "Follow me," and to another, "Come after me," and O thought I, that he would say so to me too! How gladly would I run after him.

73. I cannot now express with what longings and breakings in my soul, I cried to Christ to call me. Thus I continued for a time all

---

42. Dan. 5:18, 19.
43. Deut. 14.

on a flame to be converted to Jesus Christ, and did also see at that day such glory in a converted state, that I could not be contented without a share therein. Gold! Could it have been gotten for gold, what could I have given for it! Had I had a whole world, it had all gone ten thousand times over, for this, that my soul might have been in a converted state.

74. How lovely now was every one in my eyes, that I thought to be converted men and women! They shone, they walked like a people that carried the broad seal of heaven about them. O I saw the lot was fallen to them in pleasant places, and they had a goodly heritage.[44] But that which made me sick was that of Christ, in Mark, "He went up into a mountain, and called to him whom he would, and they came unto him."[45]

75. This scripture made me faint and fear, yet it kindled fire in my soul. That which made me fear, was this, lest Christ should have no liking to me, for he called whom he would. But O the glory that I saw in that condition, did still so engage my heart, that I could seldom read of any that Christ did call, but I presently wished, would I had been in their clothes, would I had been born Peter, would I had been born John, or would I had been by, and had heard him when he called them, how would I have cried, O Lord, call me also! But O I feared he would not call me.

76. And truly the Lord let me go thus many months together, and showed me nothing, either that I was already, or should be called hereafter. But at last, after much time spent, and many groans to God, that I might be made partaker of the holy and heavenly calling, that word came in upon me, "I will cleanse their blood that I have not cleansed: for the Lord dwelleth in Zion."[46] These words I thought were sent to encourage me to wait still upon God, and signified unto me, that if I were not already, yet time might come I might be in truth converted unto Christ.

77. About this time I began to break my mind to those poor people in Bedford and to tell them my condition, which when they had heard, they told Mr. Gifford[47] of me, who himself also took occasion to talk with me, and was willing to be well persuaded of

---

44. Ps. 16.
45. Mark 3:13.
46. Joel 3:21.
47. The minister of Bunyan's church in Bedford.

me, though I think but from little grounds; but he invited me to his house, where I should hear him confer with others about the dealings of God with the soul, from all which I still received more conviction, and from that time began to see something of the vanity and inward wretchedness of my wicked heart, for as yet I knew no great matter therein, but now it began to be discovered unto me, and also to work at that rate for wickedness as it never did before. Now I evidently found that lusts and corruptions would strongly put forth themselves within me, in wicked thoughts and desires, which I did not regard before: my desires also for heaven and life began to fail. I found also that whereas before my soul was full of longings after God, now my heart began to hanker after every foolish vanity. Yea, my heart would not be moved to mind that that was good, it began to be careless both of my soul and heaven; it would now continually hang back both to, and in every duty, and was as a clog on the leg of a bird to hinder her from flying.

78. Nay, thought I, now I grow worse and worse, now am I further from conversion than ever I was before; wherefore, I began to sink greatly in my soul, and began to entertain such discouragement in my heart, as laid me as low as hell. If now I should have burned at the stake, I could not believe that Christ had love for me. Alas, I could neither hear him, nor see him, nor feel him, nor savour any of his things: I was driven as with a tempest, my heart would be unclean, the Canaanites would dwell in the land.

79. Sometimes I would tell my condition to the people of God, which when they heard, they would pity me, and would tell me of the promises; but they had as good have told me that I must reach the sun with my finger, as have bidden me receive or rely upon the promise, and as soon as I should have done it, all my sense and feeling was against me, and I saw I had a heart that would sin, and lay under a law that would condemn.

80. (These things have often made me think of that child which the father brought to Christ, "Who while he was yet a coming to him, was thrown down by the devil, and also so rent and torn by him, that he lay and wallowed foaming.")[48]

81. Further, in these days I should find my heart to shut itself up against the Lord, and against his holy Word. I have found my unbelief to set as it were the shoulder to the door to keep him out,

---

48. Luke 9:42; Mark 9:20.

and that too, even then when I have with many a bitter sigh cried, Good Lord, break it open; "Lord, break these gates of brass, and cut these bars of iron asunder."[49] Yet that Word would sometime create in my heart a peaceable pause, "I girded thee, though thou hast not known me."[50]

82. But all this while, as to the act of sinning, I never was more tender than now; my hinder parts was inward: I durst not take a pin or a stick, though but so big as a straw, for my conscience now was sore, and would smart at every touch. I could not now tell how to speak my words for fear I should misplace them: O how gingerly did I then go, in all I did or said! I found myself as on a miry bog, that shook if I did but stir, and as there left both of God, and Christ, and the Spirit, and all good things.

83. But I observe, though I was such a great sinner before conversion, yet God never much charged the guilt of the sins of my ignorance upon me, only he showed me I was lost if I had not Christ because I had been a sinner. I saw that I wanted a perfect righteousness to present me without fault before God and that this righteousness was nowhere to be found but in the person of Jesus Christ.

84. But my original and inward pollution, that, that was my plague and my affliction; that I saw at a dreadful rate always putting forth itself within me, that I had the guilt of to amazement. By reason of that, I was more loathsome in mine own eyes than was a toad, and I thought I was so in God's eyes too: sin and corruption, I said, would as naturally bubble out of my heart, as water would bubble out of a fountain. I thought now that everyone had a better heart than I had; I could have changed heart with anybody, I thought none but the devil himself could equalize me for inward wickedness and pollution of mind. I fell therefore at the sight of mine own vileness, deeply into despair, for I concluded that this condition that I was in could not stand with a state of grace; sure, thought I, I am forsaken of God; sure I am given up, to the devil, and to a reprobate mind, and thus I continued a long while, even for some years together.

85. While I was thus afflicted with the fears of my own damnation, there were two things would make me wonder: the one was, when I saw old people hunting after the things of this life, as if they should live here always; the other was, when I found professors

49. Ps. 107:16.
50. Isa. 45:5.

much distressed and cast down when they met with outward losses, as of husband, wife, child, etc. Lord, thought I, what a do is here about such little things as these? What seeking after carnal things by some, and what grief in others for the loss of them! If they so much labour after, and spend so many tears for the things of this present life, how am I to be bemoaned, pitied, and prayed for! My soul is dying, my soul is damning. Were my soul but in a good condition, and were I but sure of it, ah! how rich should I esteem myself, though blest but with bread and water: I should count those but small afflictions, and should bear them as little burdens. "A wounded spirit who can bear?"[51]

86. And though I was thus troubled and tossed and afflicted with the sight and sense and terror of my own wickedness, yet I was afraid to let this sense and sight go quite off my mind; for I found that unless guilt of conscience was taken off the right way, that is, by the blood of Christ, a man grew rather worse for the loss of his trouble of mind, than better. Wherefore if my guilt lay hard upon me, then I should cry that the blood of Christ might take it off; and if it was going off without it (for the sense of sin would be sometimes as if it would die, and go quite away) then I would also strive to fetch it upon my heart again, by bringing the punishment for sin in hell-fire upon my spirit, and should cry, "Lord, let it not go off my heart but the right way, but by the blood of Christ, and by the application of thy mercy through him to my soul"; for that scripture lay much upon me, "Without shedding of blood there is no remission."[52] And that which made me the more afraid of this was because I had seen some, who though when they were under wounds of conscience, then they would cry and pray, but they seeking rather present ease from their trouble, than pardon for their sin, cared not how they lost their guilt, so they got it out of their mind; and therefore having got it off the wrong way, it was not sanctified unto them, but they grew harder and blinder and more wicked after their trouble. This made me afraid, and made me cry to God the more, that it might not be so with me.

87. And now was I sorry that God had made me a man, for I feared I was a reprobate. I counted man, as unconverted, the most doleful of all the creatures; thus being afflicted and tossed about by

51. Prov. 18:14.
52. Heb. 9:22.

my sad condition, I counted myself alone, and above the most of men unblest.

88. Yea, I thought it impossible that ever I should attain to so much goodness of heart, as to thank God that he had made me a man. Man indeed is the most noble, by creation, of all the creatures in the visible world, but by sin he has made himself the most ignoble. The beasts, birds, fishes, etc., I blessed their condition, for they had not a sinful nature; they were not obnoxious in the sight of God; they were not to go to hell-fire after death. I could therefore have rejoiced had my condition been as any of theirs.

89. In this condition I went a great while, but when comforting time was come, I heard one preach a sermon upon those words in the Song,[53] "Behold thou art fair, my love; behold, thou art fair"; but at that time he made these two words, "My love," his chief and subject matter, from which after he had a little opened the text, he observed these several conclusions: 1. That the church, and so every saved soul, is Christ's love, when loveless; 2. Christ's love without a cause; 3. Christ's love when hated of the world; 4. Christ's love when under temptation and under desertion; 5. Christ's love from first to last.

90. But I got nothing by what he said at present, only when he came to the application of the fourth particular, this was the word he said, "if it be so, that the saved soul is Christ's love when under temptation and desertion; then poor tempted soul, when thou art assaulted and afflicted with temptation, and the hidings of God's face, yet think on these two words, MY LOVE, still."

91. So as I was a going home, these words came again into my thoughts, and I well remember as they came in, I said thus in my heart, what shall I get by thinking on these two words? This thought had no sooner passed through my heart, but the words began thus to kindle in my spirit, "Thou art my love, thou art my love," twenty times together, and still as they ran thus in my mind, they waxed stronger and warmer, and began to make me look up; but being as yet between hope and fear, I still replied in my heart, "But is it true too? But is it true?" at which that sentence fell in upon me, "He wist not that it was true which was done unto him of the angel."[54]

92. Then I began to give place to the Word, which with power did over and over make this joyful sound within my soul, "Thou art

53. Song of Sol. 4:1.
54. Acts 12:9.

my love, thou art my love; and nothing shall separate thee from my love," and with that Rom. 8:39 came into my mind. Now was my heart filled full of comfort and hope, and now I could believe that my sins should be forgiven me; yea, I remember I could not tell how to contain till I got home. I thought I could have spoken of his love, and of his mercy to me, even to the very crows that sat upon the ploughed lands before me, had they been capable to have understood me, wherefore I said in my soul with much gladness, well, I would I had a pen and ink here, I would write this down before I go any further, for surely I will not forget this, forty years hence; but alas! within less than forty days I began to question all again.

93. Yet still at times, I was helped to believe that it was a true manifestation of grace unto my soul, though I had lost much of the life and savour of it. Now about a week or fortnight after this, I was much followed by this scripture, "Simon, Simon, behold, Satan hath desired to have you,"[55] and sometimes it would sound so loud within me, yea, and as it were call so strongly after me, that once above all the rest, I turned my head over my shoulder, thinking verily that some man had behind me called to me, being at a great distance, methought he called so loud, it came as I have thought since to have stirred me up to prayer and to watchfulness. It came to acquaint me that a cloud and a storm was coming down upon me, but I understood it not.

94. Also as I remember, that time as it called to me so loud, it was the last time that it sounded in mine ears, but methinks I hear still with what a loud voice these words, "Simon, Simon," sounded in my ears, I thought verily, as I have told you, that somebody had called after me that was half a mile behind me; and although that was not my name, yet it made me suddenly look behind me, believing that he that called so loud meant me.

95. But so foolish was I, and ignorant, that I knew not the reason of this sound (which as I did both see and feel soon after, was sent from heaven as an alarm to awaken me to provide for what was coming), only it would make me muse and wonder in my mind to think what should be the reason that this scripture, and that at this rate, so often and so loud, should still be sounding and rattling in mine ears. But, as I said before, I soon after perceived the end of God therein.

---

55. Luke 22:31.

96. For about the space of a month after, a very great storm came down upon me, which handled me twenty times worse than all I had met with before. It came stealing upon me, now by one piece, then by another; first all my comfort was taken from me; then darkness seized upon me; after which whole floods of blasphemies, both against God, Christ, and the scriptures, was poured upon my spirit, to my great confusion and astonishment. These blasphemous thoughts were such as also stirred up questions in me against the very being of God, and of his only beloved Son; as whether there were in truth a God or Christ, or no? And whether the holy scriptures were not rather a fable and cunning story, than the holy and pure Word of God?

97. The tempter also would much assault me with this: How can you tell but that the Turks had as good scriptures to prove their Mahomet the Saviour, as we have to prove our Jesus is; and could I think that so many ten thousands in so many countries and kingdoms should be without the knowledge of the right way to heaven (if there were indeed a heaven) and that we only, who live but in a corner of the earth, should alone be blest therewith? Everyone doth think his own religion rightest, both Jews, and Moors, and Pagans; and how if all our faith, and Christ, and scriptures, should be but a think-so too?

98. Sometime I have endeavoured to argue against these suggestions, and to set some of the sentences of blessed Paul against them; but alas! I quickly felt when I thus did such arguings as these would return again upon me; though we made so great a matter of Paul, and of his words, yet how could I tell but that in very deed, he, being a subtle and cunning man, might give himself up to deceive with strong delusions, and also take both that pains and travail to undo and destroy his fellows?

99. These suggestions (with many other which at this time I may not, nor dare not utter, neither by word nor pen) did make such a seizure upon my spirit, and did so overweigh my heart, both with their number, continuance, and fiery force, that I felt as if there were nothing else but these from morning to night within me, and as though indeed there could be room for nothing else; and also concluded that God had in very wrath to my soul given me up unto them, to be carried away with them, as with a mighty whirlwind.

100. Only by the distaste that they gave unto my spirit, I felt there was something in me that refused to embrace them; but this

consideration I then only had, when God gave me leave to swallow my spittle, otherwise the noise, and strength, and force of these temptations would drown and overflow, and as it were bury all such thoughts, or the remembrance of any such thing. While I was in this temptation, I should find often my mind suddenly put upon it, to curse and swear, or to speak some grievous thing of God, or Christ his Son, and of the scriptures.

101. Now I thought surely I am possessed of the devil; at other times again I thought I should be bereft of my wits, for instead of lauding and magnifying of God the Lord with others, if I have but heard him spoken of, presently some most horrible blasphemous thought or other would bolt out of my heart against him. So that whether I did think that God was, or again did think there were no such thing, no love, nor peace, nor gracious disposition could I feel within me.

102. These things did sink me into very deep despair, for I concluded that such things could not possibly be found amongst them that loved God. I often, when these temptations have been with force upon me, did compare myself in the case of such a child whom some gipsy hath by force took up under her apron, and is carrying from friend and country; kick sometimes I did, and also scream and cry, but yet I was as bound in the wings of the temptation, and the wind would carry me away. I thought also of Saul and of the evil spirit that did possess him, and did greatly fear that my condition was the same with that of his.[56]

103. In these days, when I have heard others talk of what was the sin against the Holy Ghost, then would the tempter so provoke me to desire to sin that sin, that I was as if I could not, must not, neither should be quiet until I had committed that; now no sin would serve but that. If it were to be committed by speaking of such a word, then I have been as if my mouth would have spoken that word whether I would or no, and in so strong a measure was this temptation upon me, that often I have been ready to clap my hand under my chin, to hold my mouth from opening; and to that end also I have had thoughts at other times to leap with my head downward into some muck-hill hole or other, to keep my mouth from speaking.

104. Now again I blessed the condition of the dog and toad, and

---

56. 1 Sam. 16:14.

counted the estate of everything that God had made, far better than this dreadful state of mine, and such as my companions was: yea, gladly would I have been in the condition of dog or horse, for I knew they had no soul to perish under the everlasting weights of hell for sin, as mine was like to do. Nay, and though I saw this, felt this, and was broken to pieces with it, yet that which added to my sorrow was that I could not find that with all my soul I did desire deliverance. That scripture also did tear and rend my soul in the midst of these distractions, "The wicked are like the troubled sea which cannot rest, whose waters cast up mire and dirt: There is no peace to the wicked, saith my God."[57]

105. And now my heart was, at times, exceeding hard; if I would have given a thousand pounds for a tear, I could not shed one, no, nor sometimes scarce desire to shed one. I was much dejected to think that this should be my lot. I saw some could mourn and lament their sin; and others, again, could rejoice, and bless God for Christ; and others, again, could quietly talk of, and with gladness remember, the Word of God, while I only was in the storm or tempest. This much sunk me; I thought my condition was alone. I should, therefore, much bewail my hard hap; but get out of, or get rid of, these things, I could not.

106. While this temptation lasted, which was about a year, I could attend upon none of the ordinances of God, but with sore and great affliction; yea, then was I most distressed with blasphemies. If I have been hearing the Word, then uncleanness, blasphemies, and despair would hold me as captive there. If I have been reading, then sometimes I had sudden thoughts to question all I read; sometimes again my mind would be so strangely snatched away and possessed with other things, that I have neither known, nor regarded, nor remembered so much as the sentence that but now I have read.

107. In prayer also, I have been greatly troubled at this time. Sometimes I have thought I should see the devil, nay, thought I have felt him behind me pull my clothes. He would be also continually at me in the time of prayer, to have done, break off, make haste, you have prayed enough, and stay no longer, still drawing my mind away. Sometimes also he would cast in such wicked thoughts as these, that I must pray to him, or for him: I have

---

57. Isa. 57:20, 21.

thought sometimes of that, "Fall down," or, "If thou wilt fall down and worship me."[58]

108. Also when because I have had wandering thoughts in the time of this duty, I have laboured to compose my mind and fix it upon God; then with great force hath the tempter laboured to distract me and confound me, and to turn away my mind by presenting to my heart and fancy the form of a bush, a bull, a besom,[59] or the like, as if I should pray to those. To these also he would at some times (especially) so hold my mind, that I was as if I could think of nothing else, or pray to nothing else but to these, or such as they.

109. Yet at times I should have some strong and heart-affecting apprehensions of God, and the reality of the truth of his gospel: but O how would my heart at such times put forth itself with inexpressible groanings! My whole soul was then in every word, I should cry with pangs after God, that he would be merciful to me; but then I should be daunted again with such conceits as these. I should think that God did mock at these my prayers, saying, and that in the audience of the holy angels, this poor simple wretch doth hanker after me, as if I had nothing to do with my mercy, but to bestow it on such as he: alas poor fool! how art thou deceived, it is not for such as thee to have favour with the Highest.

110. Then hath the tempter come upon me also with such discouragements as these: You are very hot for mercy, but I will cool you; this frame shall not last always; many have been as hot as you for a spirit, but I have quenched their zeal (and with this such and such who were fallen off, would be set before mine eyes) then I should be afraid that I should do so too. But, thought I, I am glad this comes into my mind; well, I will watch and take what heed I can. Though you do, said Satan, I shall be too hard for you; I will cool you insensibly, by degrees, by little and little. What care I, saith he, though I be seven years in chilling your heart, if I can do it at last; continual rocking will lull a crying child asleep. I will ply it close, but I will have my end accomplished: though you be burning hot at present, yet if I can pull you from this fire, I shall have you cold before it be long.

111. These things brought me into great straits, for as I at present could not find myself fit for present death, so I thought to live long would make me yet more unfit; for time would make me for-

58. Matt. 4:9.
59. A broom.

get all and wear even the remembrance of the evil of sin, the worth of heaven, and the need I had of the blood of Christ to wash me, both out of mind and thought. But I thank Christ Jesus, these things did not at present make me slack my crying, but rather did put me more upon it ("like her who met with the Adulterer"),[60] in which days that was a good word to me, after I had suffered these things a while, "I am persuaded that neither height, nor depth, nor death nor life, etc. shall separate us from the love of God, which is in Christ Jesus."[61] And now I hoped long life should not destroy me, nor make me miss of heaven.

112. Yet I had some supports in this temptation, though they were then all questioned by me: that in the third [chapter] of Jeremiah, at the first, was something to me, and so was the consideration of the fifth verse of that chapter, that though we have spoken and done as evil things as we could, yet we should cry unto God, "My Father, thou art the guide of my youth," and should return unto him.

113. I had also once a sweet glance from that in 2 Cor. 5:21: "For he hath made him to be sin for us, who knew no sin, that we might be made the righteousness of God in him." I remember also that one day, as I was sitting in a neighbour's house, and there very sad at the consideration of my many blasphemies, and as I was saying in my mind, what ground have I to think that I, who have been so vile and abominable, should ever inherit eternal life, that word came suddenly upon me, "What shall we say to these things? If God be for us, who can be against us?";[62] that also was an help unto me, "Because I live, you shall live also."[63] But these were but hints, touches, and short visits, though very sweet when present, only they lasted not, but like to Peter's sheet, of a sudden were caught up from me to heaven again.[64]

114. But afterwards the Lord did more fully and graciously discover himself unto me, and indeed did quite not only deliver me from the guilt that by these things was laid upon my conscience, but also from the very filth thereof, for the temptation was removed, and I was put into my right mind again, as other Christians were.

115. I remember that one day as I was travelling into the coun-

---

60. Deut. 22:25.
61. Rom. 8:38.
62. Rom. 8:31.

63. John 14:19.
64. Acts 10:16.

try, and musing on the wickedness and blasphemy of my heart, and considering of the enmity that was in me to God; that scripture came in my mind, "He hath made peace by the blood of his cross,"[65] by which I was made to see both again, and again, and again, that day, that God and my soul were friends by this blood; yea, I saw that the justice of God and my sinful soul could embrace and kiss each other through this blood. This was a good day to me; I hope I shall not forget it.

116. At another time, as I was sitting by the fire in my house, and musing on my wretchedness, the Lord made that also a precious word unto me, "For as much then as the children are partakers of flesh and blood, he also himself likewise took part of the same, that through death he might destroy him that had the power of death, that is the devil: and deliver those who through the fear of death were all their lifetime subject to bondage."[66] I thought that the glory of these words was then so weighty on me, that I was both once and twice ready to swoon as I sat, yet not with grief and trouble, but with solid joy and peace.

117. At this time also I sat under the ministry of holy Mr. Gifford, whose doctrine, by God's grace, was much for my stability. This man made it much his business to deliver the people of God from all those false and unsound rests that by nature we are prone to take and make to our souls. He pressed us to take special heed, that we took not up any truth upon trust, as from this or that or another man or men, but to cry mightily to God, that he would convince us of the reality thereof, and set us down therein by his own Spirit in the holy Word; for, said he, if you do otherwise, when temptations come, if strongly, you not having received them with evidence from heaven, will find you want that help and strength now to resist, as once you thought you had.

118. This was as seasonable to my soul, as the former and latter rain in their season, for I had found, and that by sad experience, the truth of these his words. (For I had felt, "no man can say," especially when tempted of the devil, "that Jesus Christ is Lord, but by the holy Ghost.")[67] Wherefore I found my soul through grace very apt to drink in this doctrine, and to incline to pray to God that in

---

65. Col. 1:20.
66. Heb. 2:14, 15.
67. 1 Cor. 12:3.

nothing that pertained to God's glory and my own eternal happiness, he would suffer me to be without the confirmation thereof
from heaven, for now I saw clearly there was an exceeding difference betwixt the notions of flesh and blood and the revelations of
God in heaven; also a great difference between that faith that is
fained and according to man's wisdom, and of that which comes by
a man being born thereto of God.[68]

119. But, O! now, how was my soul led from truth to truth by
God! even from the birth and cradle of the son of God to his ascen-
sion and second coming from heaven to judge the world.

120. Truly I then found upon this account the great God was
very good unto me, for to my remembrance there was not any
thing that then I cried to God to make known and reveal unto me,
but he was pleased to do it for me, I mean not one part of the gospel
of the Lord Jesus, but I was orderly led into it; methought I saw
with great evidence, from the relation of the four evangelists, the
wonderful work of God in giving Jesus Christ to save us, from his
conception and birth, even to his second coming to judgement;
methought I was as if I had seen him born, as if I had seen him
grow up, as if I had seen him walk through this world, from the
cradle to his cross, to which also when he came, I saw how gently
he gave himself to be hanged and nailed on it for my sins and
wicked doings; also as I was musing on this his progress, that
dropped on my spirit, "He was ordained for the slaughter."[69]

121. When I have considered also the truth of his resurrection,
and have remembered that word, "Touch me not Mary," etc., I
have seen, as if he leaped at the grave's mouth, for joy that he was
risen again, and had got the conquest over our dreadful foes.[70] I
have also in the spirit seen him a man on the right hand of God the
Father for me, and have seen the manner of his coming from
heaven to judge the world with glory, and have been confirmed in
these things by these scriptures following: Acts 1:9, 10; Acts 7:56;
Acts 10:42; Heb. 7:24; Heb. 8:38; Rev. 1:18; 1 Thess. 4:17, 18.

122. Once I was much troubled to know whether the Lord Jesus
was both man as well as God, and God as well as man; and truly in
those days, let men say what they would, unless I had it with evi-

---

68. Matt. 16:15; 1 John 5:1.
69. 1 Pet. 1:19, 20.
70. John 20:17.

dence from Heaven, all was nothing to me, I counted not myself set down in[71] any truth of God. Well, I was much troubled about this point, and could not tell how to be resolved. At last, that in the fifth [chapter] of the Revelations came into my mind, "And I beheld, and lo, in the midst of the throne and of the four beasts, and in the midst of the elders stood a lamb"; in the midst of the throne, thought I, there is his Godhead; in the midst of the elders, there is his manhood. But O methought this did glister, it was a goodly touch and gave me sweet satisfaction; that other scripture also did help me much in this, "To us a child is born, to us a son is given; and the government shall be upon his shoulder: and his name shall be called Wonderful, Counsellor, the mighty God, the everlasting Father, the Prince of Peace," etc.[72]

123. Also besides these teachings of God in his Word, the Lord made use of two things to confirm me in these things: the one was the errors of the Quakers, and the other was the guilt of sin, for as the Quakers did oppose his truth, so God did the more confirm me in it, by leading me into the scriptures that did wonderfully maintain it.

124. The errors that this people then maintained were: 1. That the holy scriptures were not the Word of God. 2. That every man in the world had the Spirit of Christ, grace, faith, etc. 3. That Christ Jesus, as crucified, and dying 1,600 years ago, did not satisfy divine justice for the sins of the people. 4. That Christ's flesh and blood was within the saints. 5. That the bodies of the good and bad that are buried in the churchyard shall not arise again. 6. That the resurrection is past with good men already. 7. That that man Jesus, that was crucified between two thieves on Mount Calvary, in the land of Canaan, by Jerusalem, was not ascended up above the starry heavens. 8. That he should not, even the same Jesus that died by the hands of the Jews, come again at the last day, and as man judge all nations, etc.

125. Many more vile and abominable things were in those days fomented by them, by which I was driven to a more narrow search of the scriptures, and was, through their light and testimony, not only enlightened, but greatly confirmed and comforted in the truth; and as I said, the guilt of sin did help me much, for still as that would come upon me, the blood of Christ did take it off again, and again, and again, and that too, sweetly, according to the scrip-

---

71. Committed to.
72. Isa. 9:6.

tures. O friends, cry to God to reveal Jesus Christ unto you, "there is none teacheth like him."

126. It would be too long for me here to stay, to tell you in particular how God did set me down in all the things of Christ, and how he did, that he might so do, lead me into his words, yea and also how he did open them unto me, make them shine before me, and cause them to dwell with me, talk with me, and comfort me over and over, both of his own being, and the being of his Son, and Spirit, and Word, and Gospel.

127. Only this, as I said before, I will say unto you again, that in general he was pleased to take this course with me, first to suffer me to be afflicted with temptation concerning them, and then reveal them to me; as sometimes I should lie under great guilt for sin, even crushed to the ground therewith, and then the Lord would show me the death of Christ, yea and so sprinkle my conscience with his blood, that I should find, and that before I was aware, that in that conscience, where but just now did reign and rage the law, even there would rest and abide the peace and love of God through Christ.

128. Now had I an evidence, as I thought, of my salvation from Heaven, with many golden seals thereon, all hanging in my sight; now could I remember this manifestation, and the other discovery of grace with comfort, and should often long and desire that the last day were come, that I might for ever be inflamed with the sight, and joy, and communion of him, whose head was crowned with thorns, whose face was spit on, and body broken, and soul made an offering for my sins. For whereas before I lay continually trembling at the mouth of hell, now methought I was got so far therefrom that I could not, when I looked back, scarce discern it; and O thought I, that I were fourscore years old now, that I might die quickly, that my soul might be gone to rest.

129. But before I had got thus far out of these my temptations, I did greatly long to see some ancient godly man's experience, who had writ some hundreds of years before I was born; for, for those who had writ in our days, I thought (but I desire them now to pardon me) that they had writ only that which others felt, or else had, through the strength of their wits and parts, studied to answer such objections as they perceived others were perplexed with, without going down themselves into the deep. Well, after many such longings in my mind, the God in whose hands are all our days and ways,

did cast into my hand, one day, a book of Martin Luther, his commentary on the Galatians, so old that it was ready to fall piece from piece, if I did but turn it over. Now I was pleased much that such an old book had fallen into my hand, the which, when I had but a little way perused, I found my condition in his experience, so largely and profoundly handled, as if his book had been written out of my heart. This made me marvel; for thus, thought I, this man could not know anything of the state of Christians now, but must needs write and speak of the experience of former days.

130. Besides, he doth most gravely also, in that book debate of the rise of these temptations, namely, blasphemy, desperation, and the like, shewing that the law of Moses, as well as the devil, death, and hell, hath a very great hand therein; the which at first was very strange to me, but considering and watching, I found it so indeed. But of particulars here I intend nothing, only this methinks I must let fall before all men, I do prefer this book of Mr. Luther upon the Galatians (excepting the Holy Bible), before all the books that ever I have seen, as most fit for a wounded conscience.

131. And now I found, as I thought, that I loved Christ dearly. O methought my soul cleaved unto him, my affections cleaved unto him. I felt love to him as hot as fire, and now, as Job said, I thought I should die in my nest; but I did quickly find that my great love was but little, and that I, who had, as I thought, such burning love to Jesus Christ, could let him go again for a very trifle. God can tell how to abase us and can hide pride from man. Quickly after this my love was tried to purpose.

132. For after the Lord had in this manner thus graciously delivered me from this great and sore temptation, and had set me down so sweetly in the faith of his holy gospel, and had given me such strong consolation and blessed evidence from heaven touching my interest in his love through Christ, the tempter came upon me again, and that with a more grievous and dreadful temptation than before.

133. And that was to sell and part with this most blessed Christ, to exchange him for the things of this life, for any thing. The temptation lay upon me for the space of a year, and did follow me so continually, that I was not rid of it one day in a month, no not sometimes one hour in many days together, unless I was asleep.

134. And though in my judgement I was persuaded that those who were once effectually in Christ (as I hoped, through his grace, I had seen myself) could never lose him for ever, "for the land shall

not be sold for ever, for the land is mine," saith God,[73] yet it was a continual vexation to me to think that I should have so much as one such thought within me against a Christ, a Jesus, that had done for me as he had done; and yet then I had almost none others, but such blasphemous ones.

135. But it was neither my dislike of the thought, nor yet any desire and endeavour to resist it, that in the least did shake or abate the continuation or force and strength thereof; for it did always in almost whatever I thought, intermix itself therewith, in such sort that I could neither eat my food, stoop for a pin, chop a stick, or cast mine eye to look on this or that, but still the temptation would come, "Sell Christ for this, or sell Christ for that; sell him, sell him."

136. Sometimes it would run in my thoughts not so little as an hundred times together, sell him, sell him, sell him. Against which, I may say, for whole hours together I have been forced to stand as continually leaning and forcing my spirit against it, lest haply before I were aware, some wicked thought might arise in my heart that might consent thereto, and sometimes also the tempter would make me believe I had consented to it; then should I be as tortured on a rack for whole days together.

137. This temptation did put me to such scares lest I should at sometimes, I say, consent thereto, and be overcome therewith, that by the very force of my mind in labouring to gainsay and resist this wickedness, my very body also would be put into action or motion, by way of pushing or thrusting with my hands or elbows, still answering, as fast as the destroyer said, "Sell him," I will not, I will not, I will not, I will not, no not for thousands, thousands, thousands of worlds; thus reckoning lest I should in the midst of these assaults, set too low a value of him, even until I scarce well knew where I was, or how to be composed again.

138. At these seasons he would not let me eat my food at quiet, but forsooth, when I was set at the table at my meat, I must go hence to pray, I must leave my food now, just now, so counterfeit holy would this devil be. When I was thus tempted, I should say in myself, "Now I am at my meat, let me make an end." "No," said he, "you must do it now, or you will displease God, and despise Christ." Wherefore I was much afflicted with these things, and because of the sinfulness of my nature (imagining that these things

---

73. Lev. 25:23.

were impulses from God), I should deny to do it as if I denied God; and then should I be as guilty because I did not obey a temptation of the devil, as if I had broken the law of God indeed.

139. But to be brief, one morning as I did lie in my bed, I was, as at other times, most fiercely assaulted with this temptation, to sell and part with Christ; the wicked suggestion still running in my mind, "sell him, sell him, sell him," as fast as a man could speak, against which also in my mind, as at other times I answered, no, no, not for thousands, thousands, thousands, at least twenty times together. But at last, after much striving, even until I was almost out of breath, I felt this thought pass through my heart, "Let him go if he will!" and I thought also that I felt my heart freely consent thereto. O, the diligence of Satan! O, the desperateness of man's heart!

140. Now was the battle won, and down fell I, as a bird that is shot from the top of a tree, into great guilt and fearful despair; thus getting out of my bed, I went moping into the field, but God knows with as heavy a heart as mortal man, I think, could bear, where for the space of two hours, I was like a man bereft of life, and as now past all recovery, and bound over to eternal punishment.

141. And withal, that scripture did seize upon my soul, "Or profane person, as Esau, who for one morsel of meat sold his birthright; for you know how that afterwards when he would have inherited the blessing, he was rejected, for he found no place of repentance, though he sought it carefully with tears."[74]

142. Now was I as one bound, I felt myself shut up unto the judgement to come; nothing now for two years together would abide with me, but damnation, and an expectation of damnation. I say, nothing now would abide with me but this, save some few moments for relief, as in the sequel you will see.

143. These words were to my soul like fetters of brass to my legs, in the continual sound of which I went for several months together. But about ten or eleven o'clock one day, as I was walking under a hedge, full of sorrow and guilt, God knows, and bemoaning myself for this hard hap, that such a thought should arise within me, suddenly this sentence bolted in upon me, "The blood of Christ remits all guilt." At this I made a stand in my spirit; with that, this word took hold upon me, "The blood of Jesus Christ his Son cleanseth us from all sin."[75]

---

74. Heb. 12:16.   75. 1 John 1:7.

144. Now I began to conceive peace in my soul, and methought I saw as if the tempter did leer and steal away from me, as being ashamed of what he had done. At the same time also I had my sin and the blood of Christ thus represented to me, that my sin when compared to the blood of Christ was no more to it than this little clot or stone before me, is to this vast and wide field that here I see. This gave me good encouragement for the space of two or three hours, in which time also methought I saw by faith the Son of God as suffering for my sins. But because it tarried not, I therefore sunk in my spirit under exceeding guilt again.

145. But chiefly by the aforementioned scripture, concerning Esau's selling of his birthright, for that scripture would lie all day long, all the week long, yea, all the year long in my mind and hold me down, so that I could by no means lift up myself; for when I would strive to turn me to this scripture or that for relief, still that sentence would be sounding in me, "For ye know, how that afterward, when he would have inherited the blessing he found no place of repentance, though he sought it carefully with tears."

146. Sometimes, indeed, I should have a touch from that in Luke 22:31, "I have prayed for thee, that thy faith fail not"; but it would not abide upon me; neither could I indeed, when I considered my state, find ground to conceive in the least that there should be the root of that grace within me, having sinned as I had done. Now was I tore and rent in heavy case, for many days together.

147. Then began I with sad and careful heart to consider of the nature and largeness of my sin, and to search in the Word of God, if I could in any place espy a word of promise, or any encouraging sentence by which I might take relief. Wherefore I began to consider that third [chapter] of Mark, "All manner of sins and blasphemies shall be forgiven unto the sons of men, wherewith soever they shall blaspheme," which place, methought, at a blush, did contain a large and glorious promise for the pardon of high offences; but considering the place more fully, I thought it was rather to be understood as relating more chiefly to those who had, while in a natural estate, committed such things as there are mentioned, but not to me, who had not only received light and mercy, but that had both after and also contrary to that so slighted Christ as I had done.

148. I feared therefore that this wicked sin of mine might be that sin unpardonable, of which he there thus speaketh, "But he that shall blaspheme against the Holy Ghost, hath never forgive-

ness, but is in danger of eternal damnation,"[76] and I did the rather give credit to this, because of that sentence in the Hebrews, "For you know how that afterwards, when he would have inherited the blessing he was rejected; for he found no place of repentance, though he sought it carefully with tears." For this struck always with me.

149. And now was I both a burden and a terror to myself, nor did I ever so know, as now, what it was to be weary of my life and yet afraid to die. O, how gladly now would I have been anybody but myself! Any thing but a man! And in any condition but mine now! For it was impossible for me to be forgiven my transgression, and to be saved from wrath to come.

150. And now began I to labour to call again time that was past, wishing a thousand times twice told that the day was yet to come when I should be tempted to such a sin, concluding with great indignation, both against my heart and all assaults, how I would rather have been torn in pieces than found a consenter thereto: but alas! these thoughts and wishings, and resolvings, were now too late to help me; the thought had passed my heart, God hath let me go, and I am fallen. "O," thought I, "that it was with me as in months past, as in the days when God preserved me!"[77]

151. Then again, being loath and unwilling to perish, I began to compare my sin with others, to see if I could find that any of those that are saved had done as I had done. So I considered David's adultery and murder[78] and found them most heinous crimes, and those too committed after light and grace received. But yet by considering, I perceived that his transgressions were only such as were against the law of Moses, from which the Lord Christ could with the consent of his Word deliver him, but mine was against the gospel, yea, against the Mediator thereof; I had sold my Saviour.

152. Now again should I be as if racked upon the wheel, when I considered, that, besides the guilt that possessed me, I should be so void of grace, so bewitched. What, thought I, must it be no sin but this? Must it needs be the "great transgression"?[79] Must that wicked one touch my soul?[80] O what stings did I find in all these sentences!

153. What? thought I, is there but one sin that is unpardonable?

---

76. Mark 3:29.   79. Ps. 19:13.
77. Job 29:2.   80. 1 John 5:18.
78. 2 Sam. 11.

But one sin that layeth the soul without the reach of God's mercy, and must I be guilty of that? Must it needs be that? Is there but one sin among so many millions of sins, for which there is no forgiveness, and must I commit this? O! unhappy sin! O unhappy man! These things would so break and confound my spirit, that I could not tell what to do; I thought at times they would have broke my wits, and still to aggravate my misery, that would run in my mind, "You know how that afterwards when he would have inherited the blessing, he was rejected." O! none knows the terrors of those days but myself.

154. After this, I came to consider of Peter's sin which he committed in denying his master, and indeed this came nighest to mine of any that I could find, for he had denied his Saviour as I, and that after light and mercy received; yea, and that too, after warning given him. I also considered that he did it both once and twice, and that after time to consider betwixt. But though I put all these circumstances together, that if possible I might find help, yet I considered again, that his was but a denial of his master, but mine was a selling of my Saviour. Wherefore I thought with myself, that I came nearer to Judas, than either to David or Peter.

155. Here again, my torment would flame out, and afflict me; yea, it would grind me as it were to powder, to discern the preservation of God towards others, while I fell into the snare, for in my thus considering of other men's sins, and comparing of them with my own, I could evidently see how God preserved them notwithstanding their wickedness, and would not let them, as he had let me, to become a son of perdition.

156. But O, how did my soul at this time prize the preservation that God did set about his people! Ah, how safely did I see them walk, whom God had hedged in! They were within his care, protection, and special providence: though they were full as bad as I by nature, yet because he loved them, he would not suffer them to fall without the range of mercy. But as for me, I was gone, I had done it, he would not preserve me, nor keep me, but suffered me, because I was a reprobate, to fall as I had done. Now did those blessed places, that spake of God's keeping his people, shine like the sun before me, though not to comfort me, but to show me the blessed state and heritage of those whom the Lord had blessed.

157. Now I saw, that as God had his hand in all providences and dispensations that overtook his elect, so he had his hand in all the

temptations that they had to sin against him, not to animate them
unto wickedness, but to choose their temptations and troubles for
them, and also to leave them, for a time, to such sins only as might
not destroy, but humble them, as might not put them beyond, but
lay them in the way of the renewing of his mercy. But O, what love,
what care, what kindness and mercy did I now see, mixing itself
with the most severe and dreadful of all God's ways to his people!
He would let David, Hezekiah, Solomon, Peter, and others fall,
but he would not let them fall into sin unpardonable, nor into hell
for sin. O! thought I, these be the men that God hath loved; these
be the men that God, though he chastized them, keeps them in
safety by him, and them whom he makes to abide under the
shadow of the Almighty. But all these thoughts added sorrow,
grief, and horror to me, as whatever I now thought on, it was killing to me. If I thought how God kept his own, that was killing to
me; if I thought of how I was falling myself, that was killing to me.
As all things wrought together for the best, and to do good to them
that were the called, according to his purpose, so I thought that all
things wrought for my damage, and for my eternal overthrow.

158. Then again, I began to compare my sin with the sin of
Judas, that if possible I might find that mine differed from that
which in truth is unpardonable; and, O thought I, if it should differ from it, though but the breadth of an hair, what a happy condition is my soul in! And by considering, I found that Judas did his
intentionally, but mine was against my prayer and strivings; besides,
his was committed with much deliberation, but mine in a fearful
hurry, on a sudden. All this while I was tossed to and fro, like the
locusts,[81] and driven from trouble to sorrow, hearing always the
sound of Esau's fall in mine ears, and of the dreadful consequences
thereof.

159. Yet this consideration about Judas's sin was for a while
some little relief unto me, for I saw I had not, as to the circumstances, transgressed so foully as he; but this was quickly gone again,
for I thought with myself there might be more ways than one to
commit the unpardonable sin, and that too, there might be degrees
of that, as well as of other transgressions. Wherefore, for ought I
yet could perceive, this iniquity of mine might be such as might
never be passed by.

---

81. Ps. 109:23.

160. I was often now ashamed that I should be like such an ugly man as Judas. I thought also how loathsome I should be unto all the saints at the day of judgement, insomuch that now I could scarce see a good man, that I believed had a good conscience, but I should feel my heart tremble at him, while I was in his presence. O! now I saw a glory in walking with God, and what a mercy it was to have a good conscience before him.

161. I was much about this time tempted to content myself, by receiving some false opinion, as that there should be no such thing as a day of judgement, that we should not rise again, and that sin was no such grievous thing. The tempter suggesting thus, "For if these things should indeed be true, yet to believe otherwise, would yield you ease for the present. If you must perish, never torment yourself so much beforehand, drive the thoughts of damning out of your mind, by possessing your mind with some such conclusions that Atheists and Ranters use to help themselves withal."

162. But O! when such thoughts have passed through my heart, how as it were within a step hath death and judgement been in my view! Methought the judge stood at the door. I was as if 'twas come already, so that such things could have no entertainment; but methinks I see by this that Satan will use any means to keep the soul from Christ. He loveth not an awakened frame of spirit; security, blindness, darkness, and error is the very kingdom and habitation of the wicked one.

163. I found it hard work now to pray to God, because despair was swallowing me up. I thought I was as with a tempest driven away from God, for always when I cried to God for mercy, this would come in, "'Tis too late; I am lost, God hath let me fall, not to my correction, but condemnation: My sin is unpardonable, and I know, concerning Esau, how that, after he had sold his birthright, he would have received the blessing, but was rejected." About this time, I did light on that dreadful story of that miserable mortal, Francis Spira,[82] a book that was to my troubled spirit as salt, when rubbed into a fresh wound; every sentence in that book, every groan of that man, with all the rest of his actions in his dolours, as his tears, his prayers, his gnashing of teeth, his wringing of hands, his twining and twisting, languishing and pining away under that

---

82. An Italian of the Reformation era who converted from Protestantism to Catholicism and died miserably.

mighty hand of God that was upon him, was as knives and daggers
in my soul, especially that sentence of his was frightful to me, "Man
knows the beginning of sin, but who bounds the issues thereof?"
Then would the former sentence, as the conclusion of all, fall like a
hot thunderbolt again upon my conscience, "for you know how
that afterwards, when he would have inherited the blessing, he was
rejected; for he found no place of repentance, though he sought it
carefully with tears."

164. Then was I struck into a very great trembling, insomuch
that at some times I could for whole days together feel my very
body as well as my mind to shake and totter under the sense of the
dreadful judgement of God, that should fall on those that have
sinned that most fearful and unpardonable sin. I felt also such a
clogging and heat at my stomach by reason of this my terror that I
was, especially at some times, as if my breastbone would have split
in sunder. Then I thought of that concerning Judas, "who by his
falling headlong, burst asunder, and all his bowels gushed out."[83]

165. I feared also that this was the mark that the Lord did set on
Cain, even continued fear and trembling under the heavy load of
guilt that he had charged on him for the blood of his brother Abel.
Thus did I wind, and twine, and shrink under the burden that was
upon me; which burden also did so oppress me, that I could neither
stand nor go, nor lie either at rest or quiet.

166. Yet that saying would sometimes come to my mind, "He
hath received gifts for the rebellious."[84] The rebellious? thought I,
why surely they are such as once were under subjection to their
Prince, even those who after they have sworn subjection to his government, have taken up arms against him; and this, thought I, is
my very condition: once I loved him, feared him, served him, but
now I am a rebel. I have sold him. I have said, let him go if he will,
but yet he has gifts for rebels, and then why not for me?

167. This sometimes I thought on, and should labour to take
hold thereof, that some, though small, refreshment might have
been conceived by me; but in this also I missed of my desire, I was
driven with force beyond it, like a man that is going to the place of
execution, even by that place where he would fain creep in, and
hide himself, but may not.

---

83. Acts 1.
84. Ps. 68:18.

168. Again, after I had thus considered the sins of the saints in particular, and found mine went beyond them, then I began to think thus with myself: set case I should put all theirs together and mine alone against them, might I not then find some encouragement? For if mine, though bigger than any one, yet should but be equal to all, then there is hope: for that blood that hath virtue enough to wash away all theirs, hath also virtue enough to do away mine, though this one be full as big, if no bigger, than all theirs. Here again I should consider the sin of David, of Solomon, of Manasseh, of Peter and the rest of the great offenders, and should also labour what I might, with fairness, to aggravate and heighten their sins by several circumstances: but, alas! 'twas all in vain.

169. I should think with myself that David shed blood to cover his adultery, and that by the sword of the children of Ammon, a work that could not be done but by continuance and deliberate contrivance, which was a great aggravation to his sin. But then this would turn upon me: ah, but these were but sins against the law from which there was a Jesus sent to save them, but yours is a sin against the Saviour, and who shall save you from that?

170. Then I thought on Solomon, and how he sinned, in loving strange women, in falling away to their idols, in building them temples, in doing this after light, in his old age, after great mercy received, but the same conclusion that cut me off in the former consideration, cut me off as to this; namely, that all those were but sins against the law, for which God had provided a remedy, but I had sold my Saviour, and there now remained no more sacrifice for sin.

171. I would then add to those men's sins the sins of Manasseh,[85] how that he built altars for idols in the house of the Lord, he also observed times, used enchantments, had to do with wizards, was a witch, had his familiar spirits, burned his children in the fire in sacrifice to devils, and made the streets of Jerusalem run down with the blood of innocents. These, thought I, are great sins, since of a bloody colour, yea, it would turn again upon me, "they are none of them of the nature of yours, you have parted with Jesus! You have sold your Saviour!"

172. This one consideration would always kill my heart, my sin was point-blank against my Saviour, and that too at that height, that I had in my heart said of him, "Let him go if he will." O!

---

85. 2 Kings 21.

methoughts, this sin was bigger than the sins of a country, of a kingdom, or of the whole world, no one pardonable, nor all of them
together, was able to equal mine, mine outwent them every one.

173. Now I should find my mind to flee from God, as from the
face of a dreadful judge; yet this was my torment, I could not escape
his hand. ("It is a fearful thing to fall into the hands of the living
God.")[86] But blessed be his grace, that scripture in these flying fits
would call, as running after me, "I have blotted out as a thick cloud
thy transgressions, and as a cloud thy sins: return unto me, for I have
redeemed thee."[87] This, I say, would come in upon my mind, when
I was fleeing from the face of God; for I did flee from his face, that
is, my mind and spirit fled before him. By reason of his highness, I
could not endure; then would the text cry, "Return unto me, for I
have redeemed thee." Indeed, this would make me make a little
stop, and, as it were, look over my shoulder behind me, to see if I
could discern that the God of grace did follow me with a pardon in
his hand, but I could no sooner do that, but all would be clouded
and darkened again by that sentence, "For you know how that afterwards, when he would have inherited the blessing, he found no place
of repentance, though he sought it carefully with tears." Wherefore I
could not return, but fled, though at some times it cried "Return,
return," as if it did holler after me; but I feared to close in therewith,
lest it should not come from God, for that other, as I said was still
sounding in my conscience, "For you know how that afterwards,
when he would have inherited the blessing, he was rejected," etc.

174. Once as I was walking to and fro in a good man's shop,
bemoaning to myself in my sad and doleful state, afflicting myself
with self-abhorrence for this wicked and ungodly thought; lamenting also this hard hap of mine, for that I should commit so great a
sin, greatly fearing I should not be pardoned; praying also in my
heart, that if this sin of mine did differ from that against the Holy
Ghost, the Lord would show it me; and being now ready to sink
with fear, suddenly there was as if there had rushed in at the window, the noise of wind upon me, but very pleasant, and as if I heard
a voice speaking, "Didst ever refuse to be justified by the blood of
Christ?" And withal my whole life of profession past was in a
moment opened to me, wherein I was made to see that designedly

---

86. Heb. 10:31.
87. Isa. 44:22.

I had not; so my heart answered groaningly "No." Then fell with power that word of God upon me, "see that ye refuse not him that speaketh."[88] This made a strange seizure upon my spirit; it brought light with it, and commanded a silence in my heart of all those tumultuous thoughts that before did use, like masterless hellhounds, to roar and bellow, and make a hideous noise within me. It showed me, also, that Jesus Christ had yet a work of grace and mercy for me, that he had not, as I had feared, quite forsaken and cast off my soul; yea, this was a kind of chide for my proneness to desperation, a kind of a threatening me if I did not, notwithstanding my sins and the heinousness of them, venture my salvation upon the Son of God. But as to my determining about this strange dispensation, what it was, I knew not; from whence it came, I knew not. I have not yet in twenty years' time been able to make a judgement of it. I thought then what here I should be loath to speak. But verily that sudden rushing wind was as if an angel had come upon me; but both it and the salutation I will leave until the day of judgement, only this I say, it commanded a great calm in my soul, it persuaded me there might be hope. It showed me, as I thought, what the sin unpardonable was, and that my soul had yet the blessed privilege to fly to Jesus Christ for mercy. But, I say, concerning this dispensation, I know not what yet to say unto it, which was also in truth the cause that at first I did not speak of it in the book. I do now, also, leave it to be thought on by men of sound judgement. I lay not the stress of my salvation thereupon, but upon the Lord Jesus, in the promise; yet, seeing I am here unfolding of my secret things I thought it might not be altogether inexpedient to let this also show itself, though I cannot now relate the matter as there I did experience it. This lasted in the savour of it, for about three or four days, and then I began to mistrust and to despair again.

175. Wherefore still my life hung in doubt before me, not knowing which way I should tip; only this I found my soul desire, even to cast itself at the foot of grace by prayer and supplication. But O 'twas hard for me now to bear the face to pray to this Christ for mercy, against whom I had thus most vilely sinned! It was hard work, I say, to offer to look him in the face against whom I had so vilely sinned; and, indeed, I have found it as difficult to come to God by prayer, after backsliding from him, as to do any other thing. O

---

88. Heb. 12:25.

the shame that did now attend me! especially when I thought I am now a-going to pray to him for mercy that I had so lightly esteemed but a while before! I was ashamed; yea, even confounded, because this villainy had been committed by me, but I saw there was but one way with me—I must go to him and humble myself unto him, and beg that he, of his wonderful mercy, would show pity to me, and have mercy upon my wretched sinful soul.

176. Which when the tempter perceived, he strongly suggested to me, that I ought not to pray to God, for prayer was not for any in my case, neither could it do me good, because I had rejected the Mediator, by whom all prayers came with acceptance to God the Father, and without whom no prayer could come into his presence; wherefore now to pray, is but to add sin to sin. Yea, now to pray, seeing God hath cast you off, is the next way to anger and offend him more than ever you did before.

177. For God (said he) hath been weary of you for these several years already, because you are none of his; your bawling in his ears hath been no pleasant voice to him, and therefore he let you sin this sin, that you might be quite cut off, and will you pray still? This the devil urged, and set forth by that in Numbers, which Moses said to the children of Israel, "that because they would not go up to possess the land when God would have them, therefore for ever after he did bar them out from thence, though they prayed they might with tears."[89]

178. As 'tis said in another place, Exod. 21:14: "The man that sins presumptuously, shall be taken from God's altar, that he may die," even as Joab was by King Solomon, when he thought to find shelter there.[90] These places did pinch me very sore, yet my case being desperate, I thought with myself, I can but die, and if it must be so, it shall once be said, that such a one died at the foot of Christ in prayer. This I did, but with great difficulty, God doth know, and that because, together with this, still that saying about Esau would be set at my heart, even like a flaming sword, to keep the way of the tree of life, lest I should take thereof, and live. O who knows how hard a thing I found it to come to God in prayer!

179. I did also desire the prayers of the people of God for me, but I feared that God would give them no heart to do it; yea, I

89. Num. 14:36, 37, etc.
90. 1 Kings 2:28, etc.

trembled in my soul to think that some or other of them shortly would tell me, that God had said those words to them that he once did say to the prophet concerning the children of Israel, "Pray not for this people, for I have rejected them."[91] So, "pray not for him, for I have rejected him." Yea, I thought that he had whispered this to some of them already, only they durst not tell me so, neither durst I ask them of it, for fear if it should be so, it would make me quite beside myself. "Man knows the beginning of sin," (said Spira) "but who bounds the issues thereof?"

180. About this time I took an opportunity to break my mind to an ancient Christian, and told him all my case. I told him also that I was afraid that I had sinned the sin against the Holy Ghost, and he told me, he thought so too. Here therefore I had but cold comfort, but, talking a little more with him, I found him, though a good man, a stranger to much combat with the devil. Wherefore I went to God again as well as I could, for mercy still.

181. Now also did the tempter begin to mock me in my misery, saying, that seeing I had thus parted with the Lord Jesus, and provoked him to displeasure who should have stood between my soul and the flame of devouring fire, there was now but one way, and that was, to pray that God the Father would be the Mediator betwixt his Son and me, that we might be reconciled again, and that I might have that blessed benefit in him that his blessed saints enjoyed.

182. Then did that scripture seize upon my soul, "He is of one mind, and who can turn him?"[92] O I saw 'twas as easy to persuade him to make a new world, a new covenant, or new Bible besides that we have already, as to pray for such a thing. This was to persuade him that what he had done already was mere folly, and persuade with him to alter, yea, to disannul the whole way of salvation; and then would that saying rent my soul asunder, "Neither is there salvation in any other, for there is none other name under heaven, given amongst men, whereby we must be saved."[93]

183. Now the most free, and full, and gracious words of the gospel were the greatest torment to me; yea, nothing so afflicted me as the thoughts of Jesus Christ. For the remembrance of a Saviour, because I had cast him off, brought both the villainy of my sin, and

---

91. Jer. 11:14.
92. Job 23:13.
93. Acts 4:12.

my loss by it, to mind. Nothing did twinge my conscience like this. Every time that I thought of the Lord Jesus, of his grace, love, goodness, kindness, gentleness, meekness, death, blood, promises and blessed exhortations, comforts and consolations, it went to my soul like a sword; for still, unto these my considerations of the Lord Jesus, these thoughts would make place for themselves in my heart: "Ay, this is the Jesus the loving Saviour, the Son of God, whom thou hast parted with, whom you slighted, despised, and abused. This is the only Saviour, the only Redeemer, the only one that could so love sinners as to wash their sins in his own most precious blood: but you have no part nor lot in this Jesus, you have put him away from you, you have said in your heart, 'Let him go if he will.' Now, therefore, you are severed from him; you have severed yourself from him. Behold, then, his goodness, but you yourself be no partaker of it." O thought I, what have I lost! What have I parted with! What have I disinherited my poor soul of! O! 'tis sad to be destroyed by the grace and mercy of God; to have the Lamb, the Saviour, turn lion and destroyer.[94] I also trembled, as I have said, at the sight of the saints of God, especially at those that greatly loved him, and that made it their business to walk continually with him in this world; for they did both in their words, their carriages, and all their expressions of tenderness and fear to sin against their precious Saviour, condemn, lay guilt upon, and also add continual affliction and shame unto my soul. The dread of them was upon me, and I trembled at God's Samuels.[95]

184. Now also the tempter began afresh to mock my soul another way, saying, that Christ indeed did pity my case, and was sorry for my loss. But for as much as I had sinned, and transgressed as I had done, he could by no means help me, nor save me from what I feared, for my sin was not of the nature of theirs, for whom he bled and died, neither was it counted with those that were laid to his charge when he hanged on the tree; therefore unless he should come down from heaven, and die anew for this sin, though indeed he did greatly pity me, yet I could have no benefit of him. These things may seem ridiculous to others, even as ridiculous as they were in themselves, but to me they were most tormenting cogitations. Every of them augmented my misery, that Jesus Christ should have so

---

94. Rev. 6.
95. 1 Sam. 16:4.

much love as to pity me when he could not help me; nor did I think that the reason why he could not help me was because his merits were weak, or his grace and salvation spent on them already, but because his faithfulness to his threatening would not let him extend his mercy to me. Besides, I thought, as I have already hinted, that my sin was not within the bounds of that pardon that was wrapped up in a promise; and if not, then I knew assuredly, that it was more easy for heaven and earth to pass away than for me to have eternal life. So that the ground of all these fears of mine did arise from a steadfast belief that I had of the stability of the holy Word of God, and, also, from my being misinformed of the nature of my sin.

185. But O how this would add to my affliction, to conceit that I should be guilty of such a sin, for which he did not die! These thoughts would so confound me, and imprison me, and tie me up from faith, that I knew not what to do. But O thought I, that he would come down again, O that the work of man's redemption was yet to be done by Christ; how would I pray him, and entreat him to count and reckon this sin amongst the rest for which he died! But this scripture would strike me down, as dead, "Christ being raised from the dead, dieth no more: death hath no more dominion over him."[96]

186. Thus, by the strange and unusual assaults of the tempter, was my soul, like a broken vessel, driven, as with the winds, and tossed sometimes headlong into despair; sometimes upon the covenant of works, and sometimes to wish that the new covenant, and the conditions thereof, might so far forth as I thought myself concerned, be turned another way, and changed. But in all these, I was but as those that jostle against the rocks; more broken, scattered, and rent. O, the unthought of imaginations, frights, fears, and terrors that are affected by a thorough application of guilt, yielding to desperation! This is the man that hath his dwelling among the tombs with the dead, that is always crying out, and cutting himself with stones.[97] But I say, all in vain; desperation will not comfort him, the old covenant will not save him. Nay, heaven and earth shall pass away before one jot or tittle of the word and law of grace shall fall or be removed: this I saw, this I felt, and under this I groaned. Yet this advantage I got thereby, namely, a further confirmation of the certainty of the

---

96. Rom. 6:9.
97. Mark 5:2–5.

way of salvation, and that the scriptures were the Word of God. O!
I cannot now express what then I saw and felt of the steadiness of
Jesus Christ, the rock of man's salvation, what was done could not
be undone, added to, nor altered; I saw, indeed, that sin might drive
the soul beyond Christ, even the sin which is unpardonable, but woe
to him that was so driven, for the Word would shut him out.

187. Thus was I always sinking, whatever I did think or do. So
one day I walked to a neighbouring town, and sat down upon a settle[98] in the street, and fell into a very deep pause about the most
fearful state my sin had brought me to, and after long musing, I
lifted up my head, but methought I saw as if the sun that shineth in
the heavens did grudge to give me light, and as if the very stones in
the street, and tiles upon the houses, did bend themselves against
me. Methought that they all combined together to banish me out of
the world; I was abhorred of them, and unfit to dwell among them,
or be partaker of their benefits, because I had sinned against the
Saviour. O how happy now was every creature over I was, for they
stood fast, and kept their station, but I was gone and lost.

188. Then breaking out in the bitterness of my soul, I said to
myself, with a grievous sigh, "How can God comfort such a wretch
as I?" I had no sooner said it, but this returned upon me, as an echo
doth answer a voice, "This sin is not unto death." At which I was as if
I had been raised out of a grave, and cried out again, "Lord, how
couldst thou find out such a word as this?" For I was filled with
admiration at the fitness, and also at the unexpectedness of the sentence. The fitness of the word, the rightness of the timing of it: the
power, and sweetness, and light, and glory that came with it also, was
marvellous to me to find. I was now, for the time, out of doubt, as
to that about which I so much was in doubt before, my fears before
were, that my sin was not pardonable, and so that I had no right to
pray, to repent, etc., or that if I did, it would be of no advantage or
profit to me, but now, thought I, if this sin is not unto death, then it is
pardonable, therefore from this I have encouragement to come to
God by Christ for mercy, to consider the promise of forgiveness, as
that which stands with open arms to receive me as well as others;
this, therefore, was a great easement to my mind, to wit, that my sin
was pardonable, that it was not the sin unto death.[99] None but those

---

98. A bench.
99. 1 John 5:16, 17.

that know what my trouble (by their own experience) was, can tell what relief came to my soul by this consideration; it was a release to me, from my former bonds, and a shelter from my former storm, I seemed now to stand upon the same ground with other sinners and to have as good right to the Word and prayer as any of they.

189. Now, I say, I was in hopes that my sin was not unpardonable, but that there might be hopes for me to obtain forgiveness. But O how Satan now did lay about him, for to bring me down again! But he could by no means do it, neither this day, nor the most part of the next, for this good sentence stood like a mill-post at my back. Yet towards the evening of the next day, I felt this word begin to leave me, and to withdraw its supportation from me, and so I returned to my old fears again, but with a great deal of grudging and peevishness, for I feared the sorrow of despair; nor could my faith now longer retain this word.

190. But the next day at evening, being under many fears, I went to seek the Lord; and as I prayed, I cried, and my soul cried to him in these words, with strong cries: "O Lord, I beseech thee show me that thou hast loved me with an everlasting love."[100] I had no sooner said it, but with sweetness it returned upon me, as an echo or sounding again, "I have loved thee with an everlasting love." Now I went to bed at quiet, also when I awaked the next morning, it was fresh upon my soul and I believed it.

191. But yet the tempter left me not, for it could not be so little as an hundred times that he that day did labour to break my peace. O the combats and conflicts that I did then meet with! As I strove to hold by this word, that of Esau would fly in my face, like to lightning. I should be sometimes up and down twenty times in an hour. Yet God did bear me up, and keep my heart upon this word, from which I had also for several days together very much sweetness and comfortable hopes of pardon. For thus it was made out to me, "I loved thee whilst thou wast committing this sin, I loved thee before, I love thee still, and I will love thee for ever."

192. Yet I saw my sin most barbarous, and a filthy crime, and could not but conclude, and that with great shame and astonishment, that I had horribly abused the holy Son of God; wherefore I felt my soul greatly to love and pity him, and my bowels to yearn towards him, for I saw he was still my friend, and did reward me

---

100. Jer. 31:3.

good for evil. Yea, the love and affection that then did burn within to my Lord and Saviour Jesus Christ, did work at this time such a strong and hot desire of revengement upon myself for the abuse I had done unto him, that, to speak as then I thought, had I had a thousand gallons of blood within my veins, I could freely then have spilt it all at the command and feet of this my Lord and Saviour.

193. And as I was thus in musing, and in my studies how to love the Lord, and to express my love to him, that saying came in upon me, "If thou, Lord, shouldest mark iniquity, O Lord, who should stand? But there is forgiveness with thee, that thou mayest be feared."[101] These were good words to me, especially the latter part thereof, to wit, that there is forgiveness with the Lord, that he might be feared; that is, as then I understood it, that he might be loved, and had in reverence, for it was thus made out to me, "that the great God did set so high an esteem upon the love of his poor creatures, that rather than he would go without their love he would pardon their transgressions."

194. And now was that word fulfilled on me, and I was also refreshed by it, "Then shall they be ashamed and confounded, and never open their mouth any more because of their shame, when I am pacified towards thee for all that thou hast done, saith the Lord God."[102] Thus was my soul at this time (and as I then did think for ever) set at liberty from being again afflicted with my former guilt and amazement.

195. But before many weeks were over, I began to despond again, fearing lest notwithstanding all that I had enjoyed, that yet I might be deceived and destroyed at the last, for this consideration came strong into my mind, that whatever comfort and peace I thought I might have from the Word of the promise of life, yet unless there could be found in my refreshment a concurrence and agreement in the scriptures, let me think what I will thereof, and hold it never so fast, I should find no such thing at the end: "For the Scriptures cannot be broken."[103]

196. Now began my heart again to ache, and fear I might meet with disappointment at the last. Wherefore I began with all seriousness to examine my former comfort, and to consider whether

---

101. Ps. 130:3, 4.
102. Ezek. 16:36.
103. John 10:35.

one that had sinned as I have done, might with confidence trust upon the faithfulness of God laid down in those words by which I had been comforted, and on which I had leaned myself; but now was brought those sayings to my mind, "For it is impossible for those who were once enlightened and have tasted of the heavenly gift, and were made partakers of the Holy Ghost, and have tasted the good word of God, and the powers of the world to come; if they shall fall away, to renew them again unto repentance."[104] "For if we sin wilfully after we have received the knowledge of the truth, there remains no more sacrifice for sin, but a certain fearful looking for of judgement and fiery indignation, which shall devour the adversaries."[105] "Even as Esau, who for one morsel of meat sold his birthright; for ye know how that afterwards, when he would have inherited the blessing, he was rejected; for he found no place of repentance, though he sought it carefully with tears."[106]

197. Now was the Word of the gospel forced from my soul, so that no promise or encouragement was to be found in the Bible for me, and now would that saying work upon my spirit to afflict me, "Rejoice not, O Israel, for joy, as other people,"[107] for I saw indeed there was cause of rejoicing for those that held Jesus; but as for me, I had cut myself off by my transgressions, and left myself neither foothold, nor handhold amongst all the stays and props in the precious Word of life.

198. And truly I did now feel myself to sink into a gulf, as an house whose foundation is destroyed. I did liken myself in this condition unto the case of some child that was fallen into a mill-pit, who thought it could make some shift to scrabble and sprawl in the water, yet because it could find neither hold for hand nor foot, therefore at last it must die in that condition. So soon as this fresh assault had fastened on my soul, that scripture came into my heart, "This is for many days,"[108] and indeed I found it was so, for I could not be delivered nor brought to peace again until well-nigh two years and an half were completely finished. Wherefore these words, though in themselves they tended to discouragement, yet to me, who feared this condition would be eternal, they were at some times as an help and refreshment to me.

---

104. Heb. 6.
105. Heb. 10.
106. Heb. 12.

107. Hos. 9:1.
108. Dan. 10:14.

199. For, thought I, "many days" are not for ever; "many days" will have an end; therefore seeing I was to be afflicted not a few, but "many days," yet I was glad it was but "for many days." Thus, I say, I could restore myself sometimes, and give myself a help. For as soon as ever the words came in, at first I knew my trouble would be long, yet this would be but sometimes, for I could not always think on this, nor ever be helped by it though I did.

200. Now while these scriptures lay before me, and laid sin anew at my door, that saying in the eighteen[th chapter] of Luke, with others, did encourage me to prayer. Then the tempter again laid at me very sore, suggesting, that neither the mercy of God, nor yet the blood of Christ, did at all concern me, nor could they help me, for my sin; therefore it was but in vain to pray. Yet, thought I, I will pray. But, said the tempter, your sin is unpardonable. Well, said I, I will pray. 'Tis no boot, said he. Yet, said I, I will pray. So I went to prayer to God, and while I was at prayer, I uttered words to this effect: "Lord, Satan tells me, that neither thy mercy, nor Christ's blood is sufficient to save my soul; Lord, shall I honour thee most by believing thou wilt and canst, or him, by believing thou neither wilt nor canst? Lord, I would fain honour thee by believing thou wilt and canst."

201. And as I was thus before the Lord, that scripture fastened on my heart, "O man, great is thy faith,"[109] even as if one had clapped me on the back, as I lay on my knees before God, yet I was not able to believe this, that this was a prayer of faith, till almost six months after, for I could not think that I had faith, or that there should be a word for me to act faith on; therefore I should still be as sticking in the jaws of desperation, and went mourning up and down in a sad condition, crying, "Is his mercy clean gone? Is his mercy clean gone for ever?" And I thought sometimes, even while I was groaning in these expressions, they did seem to make a question whether it was or no; yet I greatly feared it was.

202. There was nothing now that I longed for more than to be put out of doubt as to this thing in question, and as I was vehemently desiring to know if there was hope, these words came rolling into my mind, "Will the Lord cast off for ever? And will he be favourable no more? Is his mercy clean gone for ever? Doth his promise fail for evermore? Hath God forgotten to be gracious? Hath he in

---

109. Matt. 15:28.

anger shut up his tender mercies?"[110] and all the while they run in my mind, methought I had this still as the answer, 'tis a question whether he hath or no; it may be he hath not. Yea, the interrogatory seemed to me to carry in it a sure affirmation that indeed he had not, nor would so cast off, but would be favourable, that his promise doth not fail, and that he had not forgotten to be gracious, nor would in anger shut up tender mercy; something also there was upon my heart at the same time which I now cannot call to mind, which with this text did sweeten my heart, and made me conclude that his mercy might not be quite gone, not clean gone for ever.

203. At another time I remember I was again much under the question, whether the blood of Christ was sufficient to save my soul? In which doubt, I continued from morning till about seven or eight at night; and at last, when I was, as it were, quite worn out with fear lest it should not lay hold on me, those words did sound suddenly within me, "*He is able*": but methought this word *able,* was spoke so loud unto me, it showed such a *great* word, it seemed to be writ in *great* letters, and gave such a jostle to my fear and doubt (I mean for the time it tarried with me, which was about a day), as I never had from that, all my life either before or after that.[111]

204. But one morning when I was again at prayer and trembling under the fear of this, that no word of God could help me, that piece of a sentence darted in upon me, "*My grace is sufficient.*"[112] At this methought I felt some stay, as if there might be hope, but O how good a thing is it for God to send his Word! For about a fortnight before, I was looking on this very place, and then I thought it could not come near my soul with comfort, and threw down my book in a pet; then I thought it was not large enough for me, no, not large enough, but now it was as if it had arms of grace so wide that it could not only enclose me, but many more besides.

205. By these words I was sustained, yet not without exceeding conflicts, for the space of seven or eight weeks. For my peace would be in and out sometimes twenty times a day—comfort now, and trouble presently; peace now, and before I could go a furlong, as full of fear and guilt as ever heart could hold. And this was not only now and then, but my whole seven weeks' experience. For this

---

110. Ps. 77:7–9.
111. Heb. 7:25.
112. 2 Cor. 12:9.

about the sufficiency of grace, and that of Esau's parting with his birthright, would be like a pair of scales within my mind, sometimes one end would be uppermost, and sometimes again the other, according to which would be my peace or trouble.

206. Therefore I still did pray to God, that he would come in with this scripture more fully on my heart, to wit, that he would help me to apply the whole sentence, for as yet I could not. That he gave, I gathered, but farther I could not go, for as yet it only helped me to hope there might be mercy for me, "My grace is sufficient"; and though it came no farther, it answered my former question, to wit, that there was hope. Yet, because "for thee" was left out, I was not contented, but prayed to God for that also. Wherefore, one day as I was in a meeting of God's people, full of sadness and terror, for my fears again were strong upon me, and as I was now thinking, my soul was never the better, but my case most sad and fearful, these words did with great power suddenly break in upon me, "My grace is sufficient for thee, my grace is sufficient for thee, my grace is sufficient for thee"; three times together, and, O methought that every word was a mighty word unto me; as "my," and "grace," and "sufficient," and "for thee." They were then, and sometimes are still, far bigger than others be.

207. At which time, my understanding was so enlightened, that I was as though I had seen the Lord Jesus look down from heaven through the tiles upon me, and direct these words unto me; this sent me mourning home, it broke my heart, and filled me full of joy, and laid me as low as the dust, only it stayed not long with me, I mean in this glory and refreshing comfort, yet it continued with me for several weeks, and did encourage me to hope. But so soon as that powerful operation of it was taken off my heart, that other about Esau returned upon me as before; so my soul did hang as in a pair of scales again, sometimes up, and sometimes down, now in peace, and anon again in terror.

208. Thus I went on for many weeks, sometimes comforted, and sometimes tormented, and, especially at some times my torment would be very sore, for all those scriptures forenamed in the Hebrews would be set before me, as the only sentences that would keep me out of Heaven. Then again I should begin to repent, that ever that thought went through me; I should also think thus with myself, why, how many scriptures are there against me? There are but three or four, and cannot God miss them, and save me for all

them? Sometimes again I should think, O if it were not for these three or four words, now how might I be comforted! And I could hardly forbear at some times, but to wish them out of the book.

209. Then methought I should see as if both Peter, and Paul, and John, and all the writers did look with scorn upon me, and hold me in derision, and as if they said unto me, All our words are truth, one of as much force as another; it is not we that have cut you off, but you have cast away yourself. There is none of our sentences that you must take hold upon but these, and such as these; "It is impossible; there remains no more sacrifice for sin."[113] "And it had been better for them not to have known the will of God, than after they have known it, to turn from the holy commandment delivered unto them."[114] "For the Scriptures cannot be broken."[115]

210. These, as the elders of the city of refuge, I saw were to be the judges both of my case and me, while I stood with the avenger of blood at my heels, trembling at their gate for deliverance; also with a thousand fears and mistrusts, that they would shut me out for ever.[116]

211. Thus was I confounded, not knowing what to do nor how to be satisfied in this question, whether the scriptures could agree in the salvation of my soul? I quaked at the apostles; I knew their words were true, and that they must stand for ever.

212. And I remember one day, as I was in diverse frames of spirit, and considering that these frames were still according to the nature of the several scriptures that came in upon my mind; if this of grace, then I was quiet, but if that of Esau, then tormented. Lord, thought I, if both these scriptures would meet in my heart at once, I wonder which of them would get the better of me. So methought I had a longing mind that they might come both together upon me; yea, I desired of God they might.

213. Well, about two or three days after, so they did indeed; they bolted both upon me at a time, and did work and struggle strangely in me for a while. At last, that about Esau's birthright began to wax weak, and withdraw, and vanish; and this about the sufficiency of grace prevailed, with peace and joy. And as I was in a muse about this thing, that scripture came home upon me, "Mercy rejoiceth against judgement."[117]

---

113. Heb. 10:26.
114. 2 Pet. 2:21.
115. John 10:35.

116. Josh. 20:3, 4.
117. James 2:13.

214. This was a wonderment to me, yet truly I am apt to think it was of God, for the word of the law and wrath must give place to the word of life and grace, because, though the word of condemnation be glorious, yet the word of life and salvation doth far exceed in glory.[118] Also that Moses and Elias must both vanish, and leave Christ and his saints alone.

215. This scripture also did now most sweetly visit my soul, "And him that cometh to me I will in no wise cast out."[119] O the comfort that I have had from this word, "in no wise!" as who should say, by no means, for nothing, whatever he hath done. But Satan would greatly labour to pull this promise from me, telling of me, that Christ did not mean me, and such as I, but sinners of a lower rank, that had not done as I had done. But I should answer him again, Satan, there is in this word no such exception, but "him that comes, him, any him, him that cometh to me, I will in no wise cast out." And this I well remember still, that of all the slights that Satan used to take this scripture from me, yet he never did so much as put this question, but do you come aright? And I have thought the reason was, because he thought I knew full well what coming aright was; for I saw that to come aright, was to come as I was, a vile and ungodly sinner, and to cast myself at the feet of mercy, condemning myself for sin. If ever Satan and I did strive for any word of God in all my life, it was for this good word of Christ; he at one end and I at the other. O, what work did we make! It was for this in John, I say, that we did so tug and strive: he pulled and I pulled but, God be praised, I got the better of him, I got some sweetness from it.

216. But, notwithstanding all these helps and blessed words of grace, yet that of Esau's selling of his birthright would still at times distress my conscience; for though I had been most sweetly comforted, and that but just before, yet when that came into mind, 'twould make me fear again. I could not be quite rid thereof, 'twould every day be with me. Wherefore now I went another way to work, even to consider the nature of this blasphemous thought; I mean if I should take the words at the largest, and give them their own natural force and scope, even every word therein. So when I had thus considered, I found that if they were fairly taken, they would amount to this, that I had freely left the Lord Jesus Christ to his

118. 2 Cor. 3:8–11; Mark 9:5–7; John 6:37.
119. John 6:37.

choice, whether he would be my Saviour or no, for the wicked words were these, "Let him go if he will." Then that scripture gave me hope, "I will never leave thee nor forsake thee."[120] O Lord, said I, but I have left thee; then it answered again, "but I will not leave thee." For this I thank God also.

217. Yet I was grievous afraid he should, and found it exceeding hard to trust him, seeing I had so offended him. I could have been exceeding glad that this thought had never befallen, for then I thought I could with more ease and freedom abundance have leaned upon his grace. I see it was with me as it was with Joseph's brethren, the guilt of their own wickedness did often fill them with fears, that their brother would at last despise them.[121]

218. But above all the scriptures that yet I did meet with, that in the twentieth [chapter] of Joshua was the greatest comfort to me, which speaks of the slayer that was to flee for refuge. "And if the avenger of blood pursue the slayer, then," saith Moses, "they that are the elders of the city of refuge, shall not deliver him into his hand; because he smote his neighbour unwittingly, and hated him not aforetime." O blessed be God for this word! I was convinced that I was the slayer, and that the avenger of blood pursued me, that I felt with great terror; only now it remained that I inquire, whether I have right to enter the city of refuge? So I found, that he must not, "who lay in wait to shed blood." It was not the wilful murderer, but he who "unwittingly" did it, he who did "unawares shed blood," not out of spite, or grudge, or malice, he that shed it unwittingly, even he who did not "hate his neighbour before." Wherefore,

219. I thought verily I was the man that must enter, for because I had smitten my neighbour "unwittingly, and hated him not aforetime." I hated him not aforetime, no I prayed unto him, was tender of sinning against him; yea, and against this wicked temptation, I had strove for a twelvemonth before. Yea, and also when it did pass through my heart, it did it in spite of my teeth; wherefore I thought I had right to enter this city, and the elders, which are the apostles, were not to deliver me up. This therefore was great comfort to me, and did give me much ground of hope.

220. Yet being very critical, for my smart had made me that I knew not what ground was sure enough to bear me, I had one ques-

---

120. Heb. 13:5.
121. Gen. 50:15–18.

tion that my soul did much desire to be resolved about, and that was, "Whether it be possible for any soul that hath indeed sinned the unpardonable sin, yet after that to receive, though but the least true spiritual comfort from God through Christ?" the which, after I had much considered, I found the answer was, No, they could not, and that for these reasons:

221. First, because those that have sinned that sin, they are debarred a share in the blood of Christ, and being shut out of that, they must needs be void of the least ground of hope, and so of spiritual comfort, "for to such there remains no more sacrifice for sins."[122] Secondly, because they are denied a share in the promise of life: they shall never be forgiven, neither in this world nor in that which is to come.[123] Thirdly, the Son of God excludes them also from a share in his blessed intercession, being for ever ashamed to own them both before his holy Father, and the blessed angels in heaven.[124]

222. When I had with much deliberation considered of this matter, and could not but conclude that the Lord had comforted me, and that too after this my wicked sin, then methought I durst venture to come nigh unto those most fearful and terrible scriptures, with which all this while I had been so greatly affrighted, and on which indeed before I durst scarce cast mine eye (yea, had much ado an hundred times to forbear wishing of them out of the Bible, for I thought they would destroy me), but now, I say, I began to take some measure of encouragement, to come close to them, to read them and consider them, and to weigh their scope and tendency.

223. The which when I began to do, I found their visage changed, for they looked not so grimly on me as before I thought they did. And first, I came to the sixth [chapter] of the Hebrews, yet trembling for fear it should strike me, which, when I had considered, I found that the falling there intended was a falling quite away; that is, as I conceived, a falling from, and an absolute denial of, the gospel of remission of sins by Christ, for from them the apostle begins his argument.[125] Secondly, I found that this falling away must be openly, even in the view of the world, even so as to "put Christ to an open shame." Thirdly, I found that those he there intendeth were for ever shut up of God both in blindness, hardness, and

---

122. Heb. 10:26, 27.
123. Matt. 12:32.
124. Mark 8.
125. Heb. 6:1–3.

impenitency: "It is impossible they should be renewed again unto repentance." By all these particulars, I found, to God's everlasting praise, my sin was not the sin in this place intended.

First, I confessed I was fallen, but not fallen away, that is, from the profession of faith in Jesus unto eternal life.

Secondly, I confessed that I had put Jesus Christ to shame by my sin, but not to open shame. I did not deny him before men, nor condemn him as a fruitless one before the world.

Thirdly, nor did I find that God had shut me up, or denied me to come, though I found it hard work indeed to come to him by sorrow and repentance; blessed be God for unsearchable grace.

224. Then I considered that in the tenth [chapter] of the Hebrews, and found that the wilful sin there mentioned, is not every wilful sin, but that which doth throw off Christ, and then his commandments too. Secondly, that must also be done openly, before two or three witnesses, to answer that of the law.[126] Thirdly, this sin cannot be committed but with great despite done to the Spirit of grace, despising both the dissuasions from that sin, and the persuasions to the contrary; but the Lord knows, though this my sin was devilish, yet it did not amount to these.

225. And as touching that in the twelfth [chapter] of the Hebrews, about Esau's selling his birthright, though this was that which killed me, and stood like a spear against me; yet now I did consider, first, that his was not a hasty thought against the continual labour of his mind, but a thought consented to and put in practice likewise, and that too after some deliberation (Gen. 25). Secondly, it was a public and open action, even before his brother, if not before many more; this made his sin of a far more heinous nature than otherwise it would have been. Thirdly, he continued to slight his birthright: "He did eat and drink, and went his way; thus Esau DESPISED his birthright"; yea, twenty years after he was found to despise it still, "And Esau said, 'I have enough, my brother, keep that thou hast to thyself.'"[127]

226. Now as touching this, that "Esau sought a place of repentance"; thus I thought: first, this was not for the birthright, but for the blessing; this is clear from the apostle, and is distinguished by Esau himself, "He hath taken away my birthright" (that is, for-

---

126. Heb. 10:28.
127. Gen. 33:9.

merly) "and now he hath taken away my blessing also."[128] Secondly, now this being thus considered, I came again to the apostle, to see what might be the mind of God in a New Testament style and sense concerning Esau's sin. And so far as I could conceive, this was the mind of God, that the birthright signified regeneration, and the blessing the eternal inheritance, for so the apostle seems to hint, "Lest there be any profane person, as Esau, who for one morsel of meat sold his birthright," as if he should say, Lest there be any person amongst you that shall cast off those blessed beginnings of God that at present are upon him, in order to a new birth, lest they become as Esau, even be rejected afterwards, when they would inherit the blessing.

227. For many there are, who in the day of grace and mercy despise those things which are indeed the birthright to heaven, who yet when the deciding day appears, will cry as loud as Esau, "Lord, Lord open to us"; but then, as Isaac would not repent, no more will God the Father, but will say, "I have blessed these, yea, and they shall be blessed"; but as for you, "Depart you are workers of iniquity."[129]

228. When I had thus considered these scriptures, and found that thus to understand them was not against but according to other scriptures, this still added further to my encouragement and comfort, and also gave a great blow to that objection, to wit, that the scriptures could not agree in the salvation of my soul. And now remained only the hinder part of the tempest, for the thunder was gone beyond me, only some drops did still remain, that now and then would fall upon me. But because my former frights and anguish were very sore and deep, therefore it did oft befall me still as it befalleth those that have been scared with fire, I thought every voice was fire, fire; every little touch would hurt my tender conscience.

229. But one day, as I was passing in the field, and that too with some dashes on my conscience, fearing lest yet all was not right, suddenly this sentence fell upon my soul, "Thy righteousness is in heaven," and methought withal, I saw with the eyes of my soul Jesus Christ at God's right hand, there, I say, as my righteousness; so that wherever I was, or whatever I was doing, God could not say of me, "He wants my righteousness," for that was just before him.

---

128. Gen. 27:36.
129. Gen. 27:32; Luke 13:25–27.

I also saw moreover, that it was not my good frame of heart that made my righteousness better, nor yet my bad frame that made my righteousness worse; for my righteousness was Jesus Christ himself, "the same yesterday, and today, and for ever."[130]

230. Now did my chains fall off my legs indeed, I was loosed from my affliction and irons, my temptations also fled away, so that from that time those dreadful scriptures of God left off to trouble me; now went I also home rejoicing, for the grace and love of God. So when I came home, I looked to see if I could find that sentence, "Thy righteousness is in heaven," but could not find such a saying, wherefore my heart began to sink again, only that was brought to my remembrance, "He of God is made unto us wisdom, righteousness, sanctification, and redemption"; by this word I saw the other sentence true.[131]

231. For by this scripture, I saw that the man Christ Jesus, as he is distinct from us, as touching his bodily presence, so he is our righteousness and sanctification before God. Here therefore I lived, for some time, very sweetly at peace with God through Christ; O methought Christ! Christ! there was nothing but Christ that was before my eyes. I was not now only for looking upon this and the other benefit of Christ apart, as of his blood, burial, or resurrection, but considered him as a whole Christ, as he in whom all these, and all his other virtues, relations, offices, and operations met together, and that as he sat on the right hand of God in heaven.

232. 'Twas glorious to me to see his exaltation, and the worth and prevalency of all his benefits, and that because of this; now I could look from myself to him, and should reckon that all those graces of God that now were green in me, were yet but like those cracked groats and four-pence-halfpennies that rich men carry in their purses, when their gold is in their trunks at home. O I saw my gold was in my trunk at home, in Christ my lord and Saviour! Now Christ was all; all my wisdom, all my righteousness, all my sanctification, and all my redemption.

233. Further, the Lord did also lead me into the mystery of union with this Son of God, that I was joined to him, that I was flesh of his flesh, and bone of his bone; and now was that a sweet word to me in Eph. 5:30. By this also was my faith in him, as my

---

130. Heb. 13:8.
131. 1 Cor. 1:30.

righteousness, the more confirmed to me; for if he and I were one, then his righteousness was mine, his merits mine, his victory also mine. Now could I see myself in heaven and earth at once; in heaven by my Christ, by my head, by my righteousness and life, though on earth by my body or person.

234. Now I saw Christ Jesus was looked on of God, and should also be looked on by us as that common or public person, in whom all the whole body of his elect are always to be considered and reckoned, that we fulfilled the law by him, rose from the dead by him, got the victory over sin, death, the devil, and hell, by him. When he died we died, and so of his resurrection, "Thy dead men shall live, together with my dead body shall they arise," saith he,[132] and again, "After two days he will revive us: and the third day we shall live in his sight,"[133] which is now fulfilled by the sitting down of the Son of Man on the right hand of the Majesty of the heavens, according to that to the Ephesians, "He hath raised us up together, and made us sit together in heavenly places in Christ Jesus."[134]

235. Ah, these blessed considerations and scriptures, with many others of a like nature, were in those days made to spangle in mine eyes, so that I have cause to say, "Praise ye the Lord God in his sanctuary, praise him in the firmament of his power, praise him for his mighty acts, praise him according to his excellent greatness."[135]

236. Having thus in few words given you a taste of the sorrow and affliction that my soul went under by the guilt and terror that this my wicked thought did lay me under, and having given you also a touch of my deliverance therefrom, and of the sweet and blessed comfort that I met with afterwards (which comfort dwelt about a twelvemonth with my heart, to my unspeakable admiration), I will now (God willing) before I proceed any further, give you in a word or two, what, as I conceive, was the cause of this temptation; and also after that, what advantage at the last it became unto my soul.

237. For the causes, I conceived they were principally two, of which two also I was deeply convinced all the time this trouble lay upon me. The first was, for that I did not, when I was delivered from the temptation that went before, still pray to God to keep me

---

132. Isa. 26:19.
133. Hos. 6:2.
134. Eph. 2:6.
135. Ps. 150:1, 2.

from temptations that were to come, for though, as I can say in truth, my soul was much in prayer before this trial seized me, yet then I prayed only, or at the most principally, for the removal of present troubles, and for fresh discoveries of love in Christ, which I saw afterwards was not enough to do; I also should have prayed that the great God would keep me from the evil that was to come.

238. Of this I was made deeply sensible by the prayer of holy David, who when he was under present mercy, yet prayed that God would hold him back from sin and temptation to come: "For then," saith he, "shall I be upright, I shall be innocent from the GREAT transgression."[136] By this very word was I galled and condemned, quite through this long temptation.

239. That also was another word that did much condemn me for my folly, in the neglect of this duty, Heb. 4:16, "Let us therefore come boldly to the throne of grace, that we may obtain mercy, and find grace to help in time of need." This I had not done, and therefore was suffered thus to sin and fall, according to what is written, "Pray, that ye enter not into temptation,"[137] and truly this very thing is to this day of such weight and awe upon me, that I dare not, when I come before the Lord, go off my knees until I entreat him for help and mercy against the temptations that are to come. And I do beseech thee, reader, that thou learn to beware of my negligence by the affliction that for this thing I did for days, and months, and years, with sorrow undergo.

240. Another cause of this temptation was, that I had tempted God; and on this manner did I do it. Upon a time my wife was great with child, and before her full time was come, her pangs, as of a woman in travail, were fierce and strong upon her, even as if she would immediately have fallen in labour, and been delivered of an untimely birth. Now at this very time it was, that I had been so strongly tempted to question the being of God, wherefore as my wife lay crying by me, I said, but with all secrecy imaginable, even thinking in my heart, "Lord, if thou wilt now remove this sad affliction from my wife, and cause that she be troubled no more therewith this night" (and now were her pangs just upon her) "then I shall know that thou canst discern the most secret thoughts of the heart."

241. I had no sooner said it in my heart but her pangs were

---

136. Ps. 19:13.
137. Luke 22:40.

taken from her, and she was cast into a deep sleep, and so she continued till morning; at this I greatly marvelled, not knowing what to think, but after I had been awake a good while, and heard her cry no more, I fell to sleeping also. So when I waked in the morning, it came upon me again, even what I had said in my heart the last night, and how the Lord had showed me that he knew my secret thoughts, which was a great astonishment unto me for several weeks after.

242. Well, about a year and an half afterwards, that wicked sinful thought, of which I have spoken before, went through my wicked heart, even this thought, "Let Christ go if he will"; so when I was fallen under guilt for this, the remembrance of my other thought, and of the effect thereof, would also come upon me with this retort, which carried also rebuke along with it, "Now you may see that God doth know the most secret thoughts of the heart!"

243. And with this, that of the passages that was betwixt the Lord, and his servant Gideon, fell upon my spirit; how because that Gideon tempted God with his fleece both wet and dry, when he should have believed and ventured upon his word, therefore the Lord did afterwards so try him, as to send him against an innumerable company of enemies, and that too, as to outward appearance, without any strength or help.[138] Thus he served me, and that justly, for I should have believed his word, and not have put an "if" upon the all-seeingness of God.

244. And now to show you something of the advantages that I also gained by this temptation. And first, by this I was made continually to possess in my soul a very wonderful sense both of the being and glory of God, and of his beloved Son; in the temptation before, my soul was perplexed with unbelief, blasphemy, hardness of heart, questions about the being of God, Christ, the truth of the Word, and certainty of the world to come. I say, then I was greatly assaulted and tormented with atheism, but now the case was otherwise; now was God and Christ continually before my face, though not in a way of comfort, but in a way of exceeding dread and terror. The glory of the holiness of God did at this time break me to pieces, and the bowels and compassion of Christ did break me as on the wheel, for I could not consider him but as a lost and rejected Christ, the remembrance of which was at the continual breaking of my bones.

138. Judg. 6, 7.

245. The scriptures now also were wonderful things unto me. I saw that the truth and verity of them were the keys of the kingdom of heaven; those the scriptures favour, they must inherit bliss, but those they oppose and condemn must perish forevermore. O this word, "For the Scriptures cannot be broken," would rend the caul of my heart, and so would that other, "Whose sins ye remit, they are remitted, but whose sins ye retain, they are retained."[139] Now I saw the apostles to be the elders of the city of refuge,[140] those they were to receive in, were received to life, but those that they shut out, were to be slain by the avenger of blood.

246. O! One sentence of the scriptures did more afflict and terrify my mind, I mean those sentences that stood against me (as sometimes I thought they every one did), more, I say, than an army of forty thousand men that might have come against me. Woe be to him against whom the scriptures bend themselves.

247. By this temptation I was made to see more into the nature of the promise than ever I was before. For I lying now trembling under the mighty hand of God, continually torn and rent by the thunderings of his justice; this made me, with careful heart and watchful eye, with great seriousness to turn over every leaf, and with much diligence mixed with trembling, to consider every sentence, together with its natural force and latitude.

248. By this temptation also, I was greatly beaten off my former foolish practice, of putting by the word of promise when it came into my mind. For now, though I could not suck that comfort and sweetness from the promise, as I had done at other times, yet, like to a man a-sinking, I should catch at all I saw; formerly I thought I might not meddle with the promise, unless I felt its comfort, but now 'twas no time thus to do, the avenger of blood too hardly did pursue me.

249. Now therefore I was glad to catch at that word, which yet I feared I had no ground nor right to own; and even to leap into the bosom of that promise, that yet I feared did shut its heart against me. Now also I should labour to take the word as God had laid it down, without restraining the natural force of one syllable thereof. O what did I now see in the blessed sixth [chapter] of John, "And him that comes to me, I will in no wise cast out."[141] Now I began to

139. John 20:23.
140. Josh. 20:4.
141. John 6:37.

consider with myself, that God had a bigger mouth to speak with, than I had heart to conceive with; I thought also with myself, that he spake not his words in haste, or in an unadvised heat, but with infinite wisdom and judgement, and in very truth and faithfulness.[142]

250. I should in these days, often in my greatest agonies, even flounce towards the promise (as the horses do towards sound ground, that yet stick in the mire), concluding (though as one almost bereft of his wits through fear), on this I will rest and stay, and leave the fulfilling of it to the God of heaven that made it. O! many a pull hath my heart had with Satan, for the blessed sixth [chapter] of John. I did not now, as at other times, look principally for comfort (though O how welcome would it have been unto me!), but now a word, a word to lean a weary soul upon, that I might not sink for ever! 'twas that I hunted for.

251. Yea, often when I have been making to the promise, I have seen as if the Lord would refuse my soul for ever; I was often as if I had run upon the pikes, and as if the Lord had thrust at me, to keep me from him, as with a flaming sword. Then I should think of Esther, who went to petition the king contrary to the law.[143] I thought also of Benhadad's servants, who went with ropes upon their heads to their enemies for mercy;[144] the woman of Canaan also, that would not be daunted, though called dog by Christ,[145] and the man that went to borrow bread at midnight[146] were great encouragements unto me.

252. I never saw those heights and depths in grace, and love, and mercy, as I saw after this temptation. Great sins do draw out great grace, and where guilt is most terrible and fierce, there the mercy of God in Christ, when showed to the soul, appears most high and mighty; when Job had passed through his captivity, "he had twice as much as he had before."[147] Blessed be God for Jesus Christ our Lord. Many other things I might here make observation of, but I would be brief, and therefore shall at this time omit them; and do pray God that my harms may make others fear to offend, lest they also be made to bear the iron yoke as I did.

I had two or three times, at or about my deliverance from this temptation, such strange apprehensions of the grace of God, that I could hardly bear up under it; it was so out of measure amazing,

---

142. 2 Sam. 7:28.
143. Esther 4:16.
144. 1 Kings 20:31, etc.

145. Matt. 15:22, etc.
146. Luke 11:5–8, etc.
147. Job 42:10.

when I thought it could reach me, that I do think, if that sense of it had abode long upon me, it would have made me incapable for business.

253. Now I shall go forward to give you a relation of other of the Lord's dealings with me, of his dealings with me at sundry other seasons, and of the temptations I then did meet withal. I shall begin with what I met with when I first did join in fellowship with the people of God in Bedford. After I had propounded to the church, that my desire was to walk in the order and ordinances of Christ with them, and was also admitted by them; while I thought of that blessed ordinance of Christ, which was his last supper with his disciples before his death, that scripture, "Do this in remembrance of me,"[148] was made a very precious word unto me; for by it the Lord did come down upon my conscience with the discovery of his death for my sins, and as I then felt, did as if he plunged me in the virtue of the same. But behold, I had not been long a partaker at the ordinance, but such fierce and sad temptations did attend me at all times therein, both to blaspheme the ordinance, and to wish some deadly thing to those that then did eat thereof, that lest I should at any time be guilty of consenting to these wicked and fearful thoughts, I was forced to bend myself all the while to pray to God to keep me from such blasphemies; and also to cry to God to bless the bread and cup to them, as it went from mouth to mouth. The reason of this temptation I have thought since was, because I did not, with that reverence as became me, at first approach to partake thereof.

254. Thus I continued for three-quarters of a year, and could never have rest nor ease; but at last the Lord came in upon my soul with that same scripture by which my soul was visited before, and after that, I have been usually very well and comfortable in the partaking of that blessed ordinance, and have I trust therein discerned the Lord's body as broken for my sins, and that his precious blood had been shed for my transgressions.

255. Upon a time I was somewhat inclining to a consumption, wherefore, about the spring, I was suddenly and violently seized with much weakness in my outward man; insomuch that I thought I could not live. Now began I afresh to give myself up to a serious examination after my state and condition for the future, and of my evidences for that blessed world to come. For it hath, I bless the

---

148. Luke 22:19.

name of God, been my usual course, as always, so especially in the
day of affliction, to endeavour to keep my interest in life to come,
clear before mine eye.

256. But I had no sooner begun to recall to mind my former
experience of the goodness of God to my soul, but there came
flocking into my mind an innumerable company of my sins and
transgressions, amongst which these were at this time most to my
affliction, namely, my deadness, dulness, and coldness in holy duties,
my wanderings of heart, my wearisomeness in all good things, my
want of love to God, his ways and people, with this at the end of
all, "Are these the fruits of Christianity? Are these the tokens of a
blessed man?"

257. At the apprehension of these things, my sickness was dou-
bled upon me, for now was I sick in my inward man, my soul was
clogged with guilt. Now also was my former experience of God's
goodness to me quite taken out of my mind, and hid as if it had
never been, nor seen. Now was my soul greatly pinched between
these two considerations, "Live I must not, Die I dare not." Now I
sunk and fell in my spirit, and was giving up all for lost, but as I
was walking up and down in the house, as a man in a most woeful
state, that word of God took hold of my heart, "Ye are justified
freely by his grace, through the redemption that is in Christ
Jesus."[149] But O what a turn it made upon me!

258. Now was I as one awakened out of some troublesome sleep
and dream, and listening to this heavenly sentence, I was as if I had
heard it thus expounded to me: Sinner, thou thinkest that because
of thy sins and infirmities, I cannot save thy soul, but behold my
Son is by me, and upon him I look, and not on thee, and will deal
with thee according as I am pleased with him. At this I was greatly
lightened in my mind, and made to understand that God could justify a sinner at any time, it was but looking upon Christ, and
imputing of his benefits to us, and the work was forthwith done.

259. And as I was thus in a muse, that scripture also came with
great power upon my spirit, "Not by works of righteousness that
we have done, but according to his mercy he hath saved us," etc.;[150]
now was I got on high, I saw myself within the arms of grace and
mercy, and though I was before afraid to think of a dying hour, yet

149. Rom. 3:24.
150. 2 Tim. 1:9; Titus 3:5.

now I cried, Let me die. Now death was lovely and beautiful in my sight, for I saw we shall never live indeed till we be gone to the other world. O methought this life is but a slumber in comparison of that above. At this time also I saw more in those words, "Heirs of God"[151] than ever I shall be able to express while I live in this world: "Heirs of God"! God himself is the portion of the saints; this I saw and wondered at, but cannot tell you what I saw.

260. Again, as I was at another time very ill and weak, all that time also the tempter did beset me strongly (for I find he is much for assaulting the soul, when it begins to approach towards the grave, then is his opportunity) labouring to hide from me my former experience of God's goodness; also setting before me the terrors of death and the judgement of God, insomuch, that at this time, through my fear of miscarrying for ever (should I now die), I was as one dead before death came, and was as if I had felt myself already descending into the pit. Methought, I said, there was no way but to hell I must; but behold, just as I was in the midst of those fears, these words of the angels carrying Lazarus into Abraham's bosom[152] darted in upon me, as who should say, "So it shall be with thee when thou dost leave this world." This did sweetly revive my spirit, and help me to hope in God, which when I had with comfort mused on awhile, that word fell with great weight upon my mind, "O death, where is thy sting? O grave, where is thy victory?"[153] At this I became both well in body and mind at once, for my sickness did presently vanish, and I walked comfortably in my work for God again.

261. At another time, though just before I was pretty well and savoury in my spirit, yet suddenly there fell upon me a great cloud of darkness, which did so hide from me the things of God and Christ, that I was as if I had never seen or known them in my life; I was also so overrun in my soul with a senseless heartless frame of spirit, that I could not feel my soul to move or stir after grace and life by Christ. I was as if my loins were broken, or as if my hands and feet had been tied or bound with chains. At this time also I felt some weakness to seize my outward man, which made still the other affliction the more heavy and uncomfortable.

---

151. Rom. 8:17.
152. Luke 16:22.
153. 1 Cor. 15:55.

262. After I had been in this condition some three or four days, as I was sitting by the fire, I suddenly felt this word to sound in my heart, "I must go to Jesus"; at this my former darkness and atheism fled away, and the blessed things of heaven were set within my view. While I was on this sudden thus overtaken with surprise, Wife, said I, is there ever such a scripture, "I must go to Jesus"? She said she could not tell; therefore I sat musing still to see if I could remember such a place. I had not sat above two or three minutes, but that came bolting in upon me, "And to an innumerable company of angels," and withal, Hebrews the twelfth [chapter] about the mount Zion was set before mine eyes.[154]

263. Then with joy I told my wife, O now I know, I know! But that night was a good night to me, I never had but few better; I longed for the company of some of God's people, that I might have imparted unto them what God had showed me. Christ was a precious Christ to my soul that night. I could scarce lie in my bed for joy, and peace, and triumph, through Christ; this great glory did not continue upon me until morning, yet that twelfth [chapter] of the author to the Hebrews[155] was a blessed scripture to me for many days together after this.

264. The words are these, "You are come to mount Zion, to the city of the living God, to the heavenly Jerusalem, and to an innumerable company of angels, to the general assembly and church of the first-born, which are written in heaven, and to God the judge of all, and to the spirits of just men made perfect, and to Jesus the mediator of the New Testament, and to the blood of sprinkling, that speaketh better things than that of Abel": through this blessed sentence the Lord led me over and over, first to this word, and then to that, and showed me wonderful glory in every one of them. These words also have oft since this time been great refreshment to my spirit. Blessed be God for having mercy on me.

---

154. Heb. 12:22–24.
155. Heb. 12:21–23.

A Brief Account of the Author's Call to the Work of the Ministry

265. And now I am speaking my experience, I will in this place thrust in a word or two concerning my preaching the Word, and of God's dealing with me in that particular also, for after I had been about five or six years awakened, and helped myself to see both the want and worth of Jesus Christ our Lord, and also enabled to venture my soul upon him, some of the most able among the saints with us, I say the most able for judgement, and holiness of life, as they conceived, did perceive that God had counted me worthy to understand something of his will in his holy and blessed Word, and had given me utterance in some measure to express, what I saw, to others for edification; therefore, they desired me, and that with much earnestness, that I would be willing at some time to take in hand in one of the meetings to speak a word of exhortation unto them.

266. The which, though at the first it did much dash and abash my spirit, yet being still by them desired and entreated, I consented to their request, and did twice at two several assemblies (but in private) though with much weakness and infirmity, discover my gift amongst them; at which they not only seemed to be, but did solemnly protest as in the sight of the great God, they were both affected and comforted, and gave thanks to the Father of Mercies for the grace bestowed on me.

267. After this, sometimes when some of them did go into the country to teach, they would also that I should go with them; where, though as yet I did not, nor durst not make use of my gift in an open way, yet more privately still, as I came amongst the good people in those places, I did sometimes speak a word of admonition unto them also, the which they, as the other, received with rejoicing at the mercy of God to me, professing their souls were edified thereby.

268. Wherefore, to be brief, at last, being still desired by the church, after some solemn prayer to the Lord, with fasting, I was more particularly called forth, and appointed to a more ordinary and public preaching the Word, not only to and amongst them that believed, but also to offer the gospel to those who had not yet received the faith thereof: about which time I did evidently find in my mind a secret pricking forward thereto (though I bless God not for desire of vainglory, for at that time I was most sorely afflicted with the fiery darts of the devil, concerning my eternal state).

269. But yet could not be content unless I was found in the exercise of my gift, unto which also I was greatly animated, not only by the continual desires of the godly, but also by the saying of Paul to the Corinthians, "I beseech you, brethren (ye know the household of Stephanas, that it is the first-fruits of Achaia, and that they have addicted themselves to the ministry of the saints) that you submit yourselves unto such, and to every one that helpeth with us and laboureth."[156]

270. By this text I was made to see that the Holy Ghost never intended that men who have gifts and abilities should bury them in the earth, but rather did command and stir up such to the exercise of their gift, and also did commend those that were apt and ready so to do, "they have addicted themselves to the ministry of the saints." This scripture in these days did continually run in my mind, to encourage me, and strengthen me in this my work for God. I have been also encouraged from several other scriptures and examples of the godly, both specified in the Word and other ancient histories.[157]

271. Wherefore, though of myself, of all the saints the most unworthy, yet I, but with great fear and trembling at the sight of my own weakness, did set upon the work, and did according to my gift, and the proportion of my faith, preach that blessed gospel that God had showed me in the holy Word of truth, which when the Country understood, they came in to hear the Word by hundreds, and that from all parts, though upon sundry and diverse accounts.

272. And I thank God, he gave unto me some measure of bowels and pity for their souls, which also did put me forward to labour with great diligence and earnestness to find out such a word as might, if God would bless it, lay hold of and awaken the conscience; in which also the good Lord had respect to the desire of his servant, for I had not preached long, before some began to be touched by the Word, and to be greatly afflicted in their minds at the apprehension of the greatness of their sin, and of their need of Jesus Christ.

273. But I at first could not believe that God should speak by me to the heart of any man, still counting myself unworthy, yet those who thus were touched, would love me, and have a peculiar respect for me; and though I did put it from me that they should be awakened by

---

156. 1 Cor. 16:15, 16.
157. Acts 8:4; 18:24, 25, etc.; 1 Pet. 4:10; Rom. 12:6; Foxe's *Acts and Monuments* [1563].

me, still they would confess it and affirm it before the saints of God, they would also bless God for me (unworthy wretch that I am!) and count me God's instrument that showed to them the way of salvation.

274. Wherefore seeing them in both their words and deeds to be so constant, and also in their hearts so earnestly pressing after the knowledge of Jesus Christ, rejoicing that ever God did send me where they were, then I began to conclude it might be so, that God had owned in his work such a foolish one as I; and then came that word of God to my heart with much sweet refreshment, "The blessing of them that were ready to perish is come upon me; yea, I caused the widow's heart to sing for joy."[158]

275. At this therefore I rejoiced, yea, the tears of those whom God did awaken by my preaching would be both solace and encouragement to me; for I thought on those sayings, "Who is he that maketh me glad but the same that is made sorry by me?"[159] and again, "Though I be not an apostle to others, yet doubtless I am unto you, for the seal of mine apostleship are ye in the Lord."[160] These things therefore were as another argument unto me that God had called me to and stood by me in this work.

276. In my preaching of the Word, I took special notice of this one thing, namely, that the Lord did lead me to begin where his Word begins with sinners, that is, to condemn all flesh, and to open and allege that the curse of God by the law doth belong to and lay hold on all men as they come into the world, because of sin. Now this part of my work I fulfilled with great sense, for the terrors of the law, and guilt for my transgressions, lay heavy on my conscience. I preached what I felt, what I smartingly did feel, even that under which my poor soul did groan and tremble to astonishment.

277. Indeed I have been as one sent to them from the dead; I went myself in chains to preach to them in chains, and carried that fire in my own conscience that I persuaded them to beware of. I can truly say, and that without dissembling, that when I have been to preach, I have gone full of guilt and terror even to the pulpit door, and there it hath been taken off, and I have been at liberty in my mind until I have done my work, and then immediately, even before I could get down the pulpit stairs, have been as bad as I was

---

158. Job 29:13.
159. 2 Cor. 2:2.
160. 1 Cor. 9:2.

before. Yet God carried me on, but surely with a strong hand: for neither guilt nor hell could take me off my work.

278. Thus I went for the space of two years, crying out against men's sins, and their fearful state because of them. After which, the Lord came in upon my own soul with some staid peace and comfort through Christ, for he did give me many sweet discoveries of his blessed grace through him. Wherefore now I altered in my preaching (for still I preached what I saw and felt); now therefore I did much labour to hold forth Jesus Christ in all his offices, relations, and benefits unto the world, and did strive also to discover, to condemn and remove those false supports and props on which the world doth both lean, and by them fall and perish. On these things also I staid as long as on the other.

279. After this, God led me into something of the mystery of union with Christ; wherefore that I discovered and showed to them also. And when I had travelled through these three chief points of the Word of God, about the space of five years or more, I was caught in my present practice and cast into prison, where I have lain above as long again, to confirm the truth by way of suffering, as I was before in testifying of it according to the scriptures, in a way of preaching.

280. When I have been in preaching, I thank God my heart hath often, all the time of this and the other exercise, with great earnestness cried to God that he would make the Word effectual to the salvation of the soul, still being grieved lest the enemy should take the Word away from the conscience, and so it should become unfruitful. Wherefore I should labour so to speak the Word, as that thereby (if it were possible) the sin and the person guilty might be particularized by it.

281. Also when I have done the exercise, it hath gone to my heart to think the Word should now fall as rain on stony places, still wishing from my heart, O that they who have heard me speak this day, did but see as I do, what sin, death, hell, and the curse of God, is; and also what the grace, love, and mercy of God is, through Christ, to men in such a case as they are, who are yet estranged from him; and indeed I did often say in my heart before the Lord, "That if to be hanged up presently before their eyes, would be a means to awaken them, and confirm them in the truth, I gladly should be contented."

282. For I have been in my preaching, especially when I have been engaged in the doctrine of life by Christ, without works, as if

an angel of God had stood by at my back to encourage me. O it hath been with such power and heavenly evidence upon my own soul, while I have been labouring to unfold it, to demonstrate it, and to fasten it upon the conscience of others, that I could not be contented with saying, I believe and am sure; methought I was more than sure, if it be lawful so to express myself, that those things which then I asserted, were true.

283. When I went first to preach the Word abroad, the doctors and priests of the country did open wide against me; but I was persuaded of this, not to render railing for railing, but to see how many of their carnal professors I could convince of their miserable state by the law, and of the want and worth of Christ, for thought I, "This shall answer for me in time to come, when they shall be for my hire before their face."[161]

284. I never cared to meddle with things that were controverted and in dispute amongst the saints, especially things of the lowest nature, yet it pleased me much to contend with great earnestness for the Word of faith, and the remission of sins by the death and sufferings of Jesus. But I say, as to other things, I should let them alone, because I saw they engendered strife, and because I saw that they neither in doing, nor in leaving undone, did commend us to God to be his. Besides, I saw my work before me did run in another channel, even to carry an awakening word; to that therefore did I stick and adhere.

285. I never endeavoured to, nor durst make use of other men's lines[162] (though I condemn not all that do), for I verily thought, and found by experience, that what was taught me by the Word and Spirit of Christ could be spoken, maintained, and stood to, by the soundest and best established conscience, and though I will not now speak all that I know in this matter, yet my experience hath more interest in that text of scripture, Gal. 1:11, 12 than many amongst men are aware.

286. If any of those who were awakened by my ministry did after that fall back (as sometimes too many did) I can truly say their loss hath been more to me than if one of my own children, begotten of my body, had been going to its grave; I think verily I may speak it without an offence to the Lord, nothing hath gone so near

---

161. Gen. 30:33.
162. Rom. 15:18.

me as that, unless it was the fear of the loss of the salvation of my own soul. I have counted as if I had goodly buildings and lordships in those places where my children were born. My heart hath been so wrapped up in the glory of this excellent work, that I counted myself more blessed and honoured of God by this, than if he had made me the emperor of the Christian world, or the lord of all the glory of earth without it! O that word, "He that converteth a sinner from the error of his way, doth save a soul from death."[163] "The fruit of the righteous, is a tree of life; and he that winneth souls, is wise."[164] "They that be wise, shall shine as the brightness of the firmament; and they that turn many to righteousness, as the stars for ever and ever."[165] "For what is our hope, or joy, or crown of rejoicing? Are not even ye in the presence of our Lord Jesus Christ at his coming? For ye are our glory and joy."[166] These, I say, with many others of a like nature, have been great refreshments to me.

287. I have observed, that where I have had a work to do for God, I have had first as it were the going of God upon my spirit to desire I might preach there. I have also observed, that such and such souls in particular have been strongly set upon my heart, and I stirred up to wish for their salvation; and that these very souls have after this been given in as the fruits of my ministry. I have also observed, that a word cast in by the by hath done more execution in a sermon than all that was spoken besides. Sometimes also when I have thought I did no good, then I did most of all; and at other times when I thought I should catch them, I have fished for nothing.

288. I have also observed this that where there hath been a work to do upon sinners, there the devil hath begun to roar in the hearts, and by the mouths of his servants. Yea, oftentimes when the wicked world hath raged most, there hath been souls awakened by the Word: I could instance particulars, but I forbear.

289. My great desire in fulfilling my ministry was to get into the darkest places in the country, even amongst those people that were furthest off of profession, yet not because I could not endure the light (for I feared not to show my gospel to any) but because I found my spirit did lean most after awakening and converting

---

163. James 5:20.
164. Prov. 11:30.
165. Dan. 12:3.
166. 1 Thess. 2:19, 20.

work, and the Word that I carried did lead itself most that way; "Yea, so have I strived to preach the gospel, not where Christ was named, lest I should build upon another man's foundation."[167]

290. In my preaching, I have really been in pain, and have as it were travailed to bring forth children to God; neither could I be satisfied unless some fruits did appear in my work: if I were fruitless, it mattered not who commended me, but if I were fruitful, I cared not who did condemn. I have thought of that, "He that winneth souls is wise,"[168] and again, "Lo children are an heritage of the Lord; and the fruit of the womb is his reward: as arrows in the hand of a mighty man, so are children of the youth, happy is the man that hath filled his quiver with them, they shall not be ashamed, but they shall speak with the enemies in the gate."[169]

291. It pleased me nothing to see people drink in opinions if they seemed ignorant of Jesus Christ, and the worth of their own salvation. Sound conviction for sin, especially for unbelief, and an heart set on fire to be saved by Christ, with strong breathings after a truly sanctified soul: that was it that delighted me; those were the souls I counted blessed.

292. But in this work, as in all other, I had my temptations attending me, and that of diverse kinds, as sometimes I should be assaulted with great discouragement, therein fearing that I should not be able to speak the Word at all to edification, nay, that I should not be able to speak sense unto the people; at which times I should have such a strange faintness and strengthlessness seize upon my body, that my legs have scarce been able to carry me to the place of exercise.

293. Sometimes again, when I have been preaching, I have been violently assaulted with thoughts of blasphemy, and strongly tempted to speak them with my mouth before the congregation. I have also at some times, even when I have begun to speak the Word with much clearness, evidence, and liberty of speech, yet been before the ending of that opportunity so blinded, and so estranged from the things I have been speaking, and have also been so straitened in my speech, as to utterance before the people, that I have been as if I had not known or remembered what I have been about; or as if my head had been in a bag all the time of the exercise.

---

167. Rom. 15:20.
168. Prov. 11:30.
169. Ps. 127:3–5.

294. Again, when at sometimes I have been about to preach upon some smart and scorching portion of the Word, I have found the tempter suggest, What! Will you preach this? This condemns yourself; of this your own soul is guilty; wherefore preach not of it at all, or if you do, yet so mince it as to make way for your own escape, lest instead of awakening others, you lay that guilt upon your own soul, as you will never get from under.

295. But I thank the Lord I have been kept from consenting to these so horrid suggestions, and have rather, as Samson, bowed myself with all my might, to condemn sin and transgression wherever I found it, yea though therein also I did bring guilt upon my own conscience; "Let me die," thought I, "with the Philistines,"[170] rather than deal corruptly with the blessed Word of God, "Thou that teachest another, teachest thou not thyself?"[171] It is far better that thou do judge thyself, even by preaching plainly to others, than that thou, to save thyself, imprison the truth in unrighteousness: blessed be God for his help also in this.

296. I have also, while found in this blessed work of Christ, been often tempted to pride and liftings up of heart, and though I dare not say, I have not been infected with this, yet truly the Lord of his precious mercy hath so carried it towards me, that for the most part I have had but small joy to give way to such a thing; for it hath been my every-day's portion to be let into the evil of my own heart, and still made to see such a multitude of corruptions and infirmities therein, that it hath caused hanging down of the head under all my gifts and attainments: I have felt this thorn in the flesh[172] the very mercy of God to me.

297. I have had also together with this, some notable place or other of the Word presented before me, which word hath contained in it some sharp and piercing sentence concerning the perishing of the soul, notwithstanding gifts and parts; as for instance, that hath been of great use unto me, "Though I speak with the tongue of men and of angels, and have not charity, I am become as sounding brass, and a tinkling cymbal."[173]

298. A tinkling cymbal is an instrument of music with which a

---

170. Judg. 16:29, 30.
171. Rom. 2:21.
172. 2 Cor. 12:8, 9.
173. 1 Cor. 13:1, 2.

skilful player can make such melodious and heart-inflaming music, that all who hear him play can scarcely hold from dancing; and yet, behold the cymbal hath not life, neither comes the music from it, but because of the art of him that plays therewith. So then the instrument at last may come to nought and perish, though in times past such music hath been made upon it.

299. Just thus I saw it was and will be with them who have gifts, but want saving grace. They are in the hand of Christ, as the cymbal in the hand of David, and as David could with the cymbal make that mirth in the service of God, as to elevate the hearts of the worshippers, so Christ can use these gifted men, as with them to affect the souls of his people in his church, yet when he hath done all hang them by, as lifeless, though sounding cymbals.

300. This consideration therefore, together with some others, were for the most part as a maul on the head of pride and desire of vainglory. What, thought I, shall I be proud because I am a sounding brass? Is it so much to be a fiddle? Hath not the least creature that hath life, more of God in it than these? Besides, I knew 'twas love should never die, but these must cease and vanish; so I concluded a little grace, a little love, a little of the true fear of God, is better than all these gifts. Yea, and I am fully convinced of it, that it is possible for a soul that can scarce give a man an answer but with great confusion as to method, I say it is possible for them to have a thousand times more grace, and so to be more in love and favour of the Lord, than some who by virtue of the gift of knowledge, can deliver themselves like angels.

301. Thus, therefore, I came to perceive, that though gifts in themselves were good to the thing for which they are designed, to wit, the edification of others, yet empty and without power to save the soul of him that hath them, if they be alone; neither are they, as so, any sign of man's state to be happy, being only a dispensation of God to some, of whose improvement, or nonimprovement, they must, when a little life more is over, give an account to him that is ready to judge the quick and the dead.

302. This showed me, too, that gifts being alone, were dangerous, not in themselves, but because of those evils that attend them that have them, to wit, pride, desire of vainglory, self-conceit, etc., all of which were easily blown up at the applause and commendation of every unadvised Christian, to the endangering of a poor creature to fall into the condemnation of the devil.

303. I saw therefore that he that hath gifts had need be let into a sight of the nature of them, to wit, that they come short of making of him to be in a truly saved condition, lest he rest in them, and so fall short of the grace of God.

304. He hath also cause to walk humbly with God, and be little in his own eyes, and to remember withal, that his gifts are not his own, but the church's; and that by them he is made a servant to the church, and that he must give at last an account of his stewardship unto the Lord Jesus; and to give a good account, will be a blessed thing!

305. Let all men therefore prize a little with the fear of the Lord (gifts indeed are desirable), but yet great grace and small gifts are better than great gifts and no grace. It doth not say, the Lord gives gifts and glory, but the Lord gives grace and glory! And blessed is such an one to whom the Lord gives grace, true grace, for that is a certain forerunner of glory.

306. But when Satan perceived that his thus tempting, and assaulting of me, would not answer his design, to wit, to overthrow my ministry, and make it ineffectual as to the ends thereof, then he tried another way, which was to stir up the minds of the ignorant and malicious, to load me with slanders and reproaches; now therefore I may say, that what the devil could devise, and his instruments invent, was whirled up and down the country against me, thinking, as I said, that by that means they should make my ministry to be abandoned.

307. It began therefore to be rumoured up and down among the people, that I was a witch, a Jesuit, a highwayman, and the like.

308. To all which, I shall only say, God knows that I am innocent. But as for mine accusers, let them provide themselves to meet me before the tribunal of the Son of God, there to answer for these things (with all the rest of their iniquities), unless God shall give them repentance for them, for the which I pray with all my heart.

309. But that which was reported with the boldest confidence was that I had my misses, my whores, my bastards, yea, two wives at once, and the like. Now these slanders (with the other) I glory in, because but slanders, foolish, or knavish lies, and falsehoods cast upon me by the devil and his seed; and should I not be dealt with thus wickedly by the world, I should want one sign of a saint, and child of God. "Blessed are ye" (said the Lord Jesus) "when men shall revile you, and persecute you, and shall say all manner of evil

against you falsely for my sake; rejoice, and be exceeding glad, for great is your reward in heaven; for so persecuted they the prophets which were before you."[174]

310. These things therefore upon mine own account trouble me not, no, though they were twenty times more than they are. I have a good conscience, and whereas they speak evil of me, as an evil-doer, they shall be ashamed that falsely accuse my good conversation[175] in Christ.

311. So then, what shall I say to those that have thus bespattered me? Shall I threaten them? Shall I chide them? Shall I flatter them? Shall I entreat them to hold their tongues? No, not I: were it not for that these things make them ripe for damnation that are the authors and abettors, I would say unto them, "report it!" because 'twill increase my glory.

312. Therefore I bind these lies and slanders to me as an ornament; it belongs to my Christian profession, to be vilified, slandered, reproached, and reviled. And since all this is nothing else, as my God and my conscience do bear me witness, I rejoice in reproaches for Christ's sake.

313. I also calling all those fools, or knaves, that have thus made it anything of their business to affirm any of the things aforenamed of me, namely, that I have been naught with other women, or the like, when they have used to the utmost of their endeavours, and made the fullest inquiry that they can, to prove against me truly, that there is any woman in heaven, or earth, or hell, that can say, I have at any time, in any place, by day or night, so much as attempted to be naught with them; and speak I thus, to beg mine enemies into a good esteem of me? No, not I. I will in this beg relief of no man: believe, or disbelieve me in this, all is a case[176] to me.

314. My foes have missed their mark in this their shooting at me. I am not the man, I wish that they themselves be guiltless; if all the fornicators and adulterers in England were hanged by the neck till they be dead, John Bunyan, the object of their envy, would be still alive and well. I know not whether there be such a thing as a woman breathing under the copes of the whole heaven but by their apparel, their children, or by common fame, except my wife.

---

174. Matt. 5:11–12.
175. Manner of behaving.
176. I.e., it is all the same.

315. And in this I admire the wisdom of God, that he made me shy of women from my first conversation until now. Those know, and can also bear me witness, with whom I have been most intimately concerned, that it is a rare thing to see me carry it pleasant towards a woman; the common salutation of a woman I abhor, 'tis odious to me in whosoever I see it. Their company alone, I cannot away with. I seldom so much as touch a woman's hand, for I think these things are not so becoming me. When I have seen good men salute those women that they have visited, or that have visited them, I have at times made my objection against it, and when they have answered, that it was but a piece of civility, I have told them, it is not a comely sight. Some indeed have urged the holy kiss but then I have asked why they made baulks, why they did salute the most handsome, and let the ill-favoured go; thus, how laudable soever such things have been in the eyes of others, they have been unseemly in my sight.

316. And now for a windup in this matter, I call on not only men, but angels, to prove me guilty of having carnally to do with any woman save my wife, nor am I afraid to do it a second time, knowing that I cannot offend the Lord in such a case, to call God for a record upon my soul, that in these things I am innocent. Not that I have been thus kept, because of any goodness in me more than any other, but God has been merciful to me, and has kept me, to whom I pray that he will keep me still, not only from this, but from every evil way and work, and preserve me to his heavenly kingdom. Amen.

317. Now as Satan laboured by reproaches and slanders to make me vile among my countrymen, that, if possible, my preaching might be made of none effect, so there was added hereto a long and tedious imprisonment, that thereby I might be frighted from my service for Christ, and the world terrified, and made afraid to hear me preach, of which I shall in the next place give you a brief account.

A Brief Account of the Author's Imprisonment

318. Having made profession of the glorious gospel of Christ a long time, and preached the same about five years, I was apprehended at a meeting of good people in the country (amongst whom, had they let me alone, I should have preached that day, but they took me away from amongst them), and had me before a justice, who, after I had offered security for my appearing at the next

sessions yet committed me, because my sureties would not consent to be bound that I should preach no more to the people.

319. At the sessions after, I was indicted for an upholder and maintainer of unlawful assemblies and conventicles, and for not conforming to the national worship of the Church of England; and after some conference there with the justices, they taking my plain dealing with them for a confession, as they termed it, of the indictment, did sentence me to perpetual banishment, because I refused to conform. So being again delivered up to the gaoler's hands, I was had home to prison again, and there have lain now complete twelve years, waiting to see what God would suffer these men to do with me.

320. In which condition I have continued with much content through grace, but have met with many turnings and goings upon my heart both from the Lord, Satan, and my own corruptions; by all which (glory be to Jesus Christ) I have also received, among many things, much conviction, instruction, and understanding, of which at large I shall not here discourse, only give you, in a hint or two, a word that may stir up the godly to bless God, and to pray for me, and also to take encouragement, should the case be their own, "Not to fear what men can do unto them."[177]

321. I never had in all my life so great an inlet into the Word of God as now; the scriptures that I saw nothing in before, are made in this place and state to shine upon me. Jesus Christ also was never more real and apparent than now; here I have seen him, and felt him indeed: O that word, "We have not preached unto you cunningly devised fables"[178] and that, "God raised Christ from the dead, and gave him glory, that your faith and hope might be in God"[179] were blessed words unto me in this my imprisoned condition.

322. These three or four scriptures also have been great refreshment, in this condition, to me: John 14:1–4; John 16:33; Col. 3:3, 4; Heb. 12:22–4. So that sometimes, when I have been in the savour of them, I have been able to laugh at destruction, "and to fear neither the horse nor his rider."[180] I have had sweet sights of the forgiveness of my sins in this place, and of my being with Jesus in another world: "O the mount Zion, the heavenly Jerusalem, the innumerable com-

---

177. Heb. 13:6.
178. 2 Pet. 1:16.
179. 1 Pet. 1:21.
180. Job 39:18.

pany of angels, and God the judge of all, and the spirits of just men made perfect, and Jesus,"[181] have been sweet unto me in this place. I have seen that here, that I am persuaded I shall never, while in this world, be able to express; I have seen a truth in that scripture, "Whom having not seen, ye love; in whom, though now ye see him not, yet believing, ye rejoice with joy unspeakable, and full of glory."[182]

323. I never knew what it was for God to stand by me at all turns, and at every offer of Satan to afflict me, etc., as I have found him since I came in hither, for look how fears have presented themselves, so have supports and encouragements; yea, when I have started even as it were at nothing else but my shadow, yet God, as being very tender of me, hath not suffered me to be molested, but would with one scripture and another strengthen me against all, insomuch that I have often said, "Were it lawful, I could pray for greater trouble, for the greater comfort's sake."[183]

324. Before I came to prison, I saw what was coming, and had especially two considerations warm upon my heart; the first was, how to be able to endure, should my imprisonment be long and tedious; the second was, how to be able to encounter death, should that be here my portion. For the first of these, that scripture, Col. 1:11, was great information to me, namely, to pray to God "to be strengthened with all might, according to his glorious power, unto all patience and long-suffering with joyfulness": I could seldom go to prayer before I was imprisoned, but for not so little as a year together, this sentence or sweet petition, would as it were thrust itself into my mind, and persuade me that if ever I would go through long-suffering, I must have all patience, especially if I would endure it joyfully.

325. As to the second consideration, that saying, 2 Cor. 1:9, was of great use unto me, "But we had the sentence of death in ourselves, that we might not trust in ourselves, but in God that raiseth the dead." By this scripture I was made to see that if ever I would suffer rightly, I must first pass a sentence of death upon everything that can properly be called a thing of this life, even to reckon myself, my wife, my children, my health, my enjoyments and all, as dead to me, and myself as dead to them. "He that loveth father or mother, son or daughter, more than me, is not worthy of me."[184]

---

181. Heb. 12:22–24.
182. 1 Pet. 1:8.

183. Eccles. 7:14; 2 Cor. 1:5.
184. Matt. 10:37.

326. The second was, to live upon God that is invisible; as Paul said in another place, the way not to faint, is "to look not at the things that are seen, but at the things that are not seen; for the things that are seen are temporal; but the things that are not seen, they are eternal."[185] And thus I reasoned with myself; if I provide only for a prison, then the whip comes at unawares, and so does also the pillory; again, if I provide only for these, then I am not fit for banishment; further, if I conclude that banishment is the worst, then if death come, I am surprised; so that I see the best way to go through sufferings is to trust in God through Christ, as touching the world to come; and as touching this world, to "count the grave my house, to make my bed in darkness, and to say to corruption, thou art my father, and to the worm, thou art my mother and sister";[186] that is, to familiarize these things to me.

327. But notwithstanding these helps, I found myself a man, and compassed with infirmities; the parting with my wife and poor children hath oft been to me in this place, as the pulling the flesh from my bones, and that not only because I am somewhat too fond of these great mercies, but also because I should have often brought to my mind the many hardships, miseries, and wants that my poor family was like to meet with, should I be taken from them, especially my poor blind child, who lay nearer my heart than all I had besides. O the thoughts of the hardship I thought my blind one might go under, would break my heart to pieces.

328. Poor child! thought I, what sorrow art thou like to have for thy portion in this world? Thou must be beaten, must beg, suffer hunger, cold, nakedness, and a thousand calamities, though I cannot now endure the wind should blow upon thee. But yet recalling myself, thought I, I must venture you all with God, though it goeth to the quick to leave you. O I saw in this condition I was as a man who was pulling down his house upon the head of his wife and children; yet thought I, I must do it, I must do it, and now I thought of those "two milch kine that were to carry the ark of God into another country, and to leave their calves behind them."[187]

329. But that which helped me in this temptation, was diverse considerations, of which three in special here I will name: the first

---

185. 2 Cor. 4:18.
186. Job 17:13–14.
187. 1 Sam. 6:10–12.

was, the consideration of those two scriptures, "Leave thy fatherless children, I will preserve them alive, and let thy widows trust in
me"; and again, "The Lord said, verily it shall be well with thy
remnant, verily I will cause the enemy to entreat thee well in the
time of evil," etc.[188]

330. I had also this consideration, that if I should now venture
all for God, I engaged God to take care of my concernments; but if
I forsook him and his ways, for fear of any trouble that should
come to me or mine, then I should not only falsify my profession,
but should count also that my concernments were not so sure if left
at God's feet, while I stood to and for his name, as they would be if
they were under my own tuition, though with the denial of the way
of God. This was a smarting consideration, and was as spurs unto
my flesh. That scripture also greatly helped it to fasten the more
upon me, where Christ prays against Judas, that God would disap-
point him in all his selfish thoughts, which moved him to sell his
master. Pray read it soberly, Ps. 109:6, 7, 8, etc.

331. I had also another consideration, and that was, the dread of
the torments of hell, which I was sure they must partake of, that for
fear of the cross do shrink from their profession of Christ, his word
and laws, before the sons of men. I thought also of the glory that he
had prepared for those that in faith, and love, and patience stood to
his ways before them. These things, I say, have helped me, when
the thoughts of the misery that both myself and mine might, for the
sake of my profession, be exposed to, hath lain pinching on my mind.

332. When I have indeed conceited that I might be banished for
my profession, then I have thought of that scripture, "They were
stoned, they were sawn asunder, were tempted, were slain with the
sword, they wandered about in sheepskins and goatskins; being
destitute, afflicted, tormented, of whom the world was not worthy,"[189] for all they thought they were too bad to dwell and abide
amongst them. I have also thought of that saying, "The Holy Ghost
witnesseth in every city, that bonds and afflictions abide me."[190] I
have verily thought that my soul and it have sometimes reasoned
about the sore and sad estate of a banished and exiled condition,
how they are exposed to hunger, to cold, to perils, to nakedness, to

---

188. Jer. 2:24.
189. Heb. 11:37, 38.
190. Acts 20:23.

enemies, and a thousand calamities; and at last it may be to die in a ditch like a poor forlorn and desolate sheep. But I thank God hitherto I have not been moved by these most delicate reasonings, but have rather by them more approved my heart to God.

333. I will tell you a pretty business: I was once above all the rest in a very sad and low condition for many weeks, at which time also I being but a young prisoner, and not acquainted with the laws, had this lay much upon my spirit, that my imprisonment might end at the gallows for ought that I could tell. Now therefore Satan laid hard at me to beat me out of heart, by suggesting thus unto me: But how if when you come indeed to die, you should be in this condition; that is, as not to savour the things of God, nor to have any evidence upon your soul for a better state hereafter? (for indeed at that time all the things of God were hid from my soul).

334. Wherefore when I at first began to think of this, it was a great trouble to me, for I thought with myself, that in the condition I now was in, I was not fit to die, neither indeed did think I could if I should be called to it; besides, I thought with myself, if I should make a scrabbling shift to clamber up the ladder, yet I should either with quaking or other symptoms of faintings, give occasion to the enemy to reproach the way of God and his people, for their timorousness. This therefore lay with great trouble upon me, for methought I was ashamed to die with a pale face, and tottering knees, for such a cause as this.

335. Wherefore I prayed to God that he would comfort me, and give me strength to do and suffer what he should call me to; yet no comfort appeared, but all continued hid. I was also at this time so really possessed with the thought of death, that oft I was as if I was on the ladder, with the rope about my neck, only this was some encouragement to me, I thought I might now have an opportunity to speak my last words to a multitude which I thought would come to see me die; and, thought I, if it must be so, if God will but convert one soul by my very last words, I shall not count my life thrown away, nor lost.

336. But yet all the things of God were kept out of my sight, and still the tempter followed me with, "But whither must you go when you die? What will become of you? Where will you be found in another world? What evidence have you for heaven and glory, and 'an inheritance among them that are sanctified?'"[191] Thus was

---

191. Acts 20:32.

I tossed for many weeks, and knew not what to do; at last this consideration fell with weight upon me, that it was for the Word and way of God that I was in this condition, wherefore I was engaged not to flinch a hair's breadth from it.

337. I thought also, that God might choose whether he would give me comfort now, or at the hour of death, but I might not therefore choose whether I would hold my profession or no; I was bound, but he was free. Yea, 'twas my duty to stand to his Word, whether he would ever look upon me or no, or save me at the last; wherefore, thought I, the point being thus, I am for going on, and venturing my eternal state with Christ, whether I have comfort here or no. If God doth not come in, thought I, I will leap off the ladder even blindfold into eternity, sink or swim, come heaven, come hell. Lord Jesus, if thou wilt catch me, do; if not, I will venture for thy name.

338. I was no sooner fixed upon this resolution, but that word dropped upon me, "Doth Job serve God for nought?"[192] as if the accuser had said, Lord, Job is no upright man, he serves thee for by-respects,[193] hast thou not made a hedge about him, etc., but put forth now thy hand, and touch all that he hath, and he will curse thee to thy face. How now, thought I, is this the sign of an upright soul, to desire to serve God when all is taken from him? Is he a godly man that will serve God for nothing rather than give out? Blessed be God, then, I hope I have an upright heart, for I am resolved (God give me strength) never to deny my profession, though I have nothing at all for my pains; and as I was thus considering, that scripture was set before me, Ps. 44:12, etc.

339. Now was my heart full of comfort, for I hoped it was sincere; I would not have been without this trial for much; I am comforted every time I think of it, and I hope shall bless God for ever for the teaching I have had by it. Many more of the dealings of God towards me I might relate, but these out of the spoils won in battle have I dedicated to maintain the house of God.[194]

---

192. Job 1:9.
193. Different reasons.
194. 1 Chron. 26:27.

The Conclusion

1. Of all the temptations that ever I met with in my life, to question the being of God, and the truth of his gospel, is the worst, and worst to be borne; when this temptation comes, it takes away my girdle from me, and removeth the foundation from under me. O I have often thought of that word, "Have your loins girt about with truth";[195] and of that, "When the foundations are destroyed what can the righteous do?"[196]

2. Sometimes, when, after sin committed, I have looked for sore chastisement from the hand of God, the very next that I have had from him hath been the discovery of his grace. Sometimes, when I have been comforted, I have called myself a fool for my so sinking under trouble. And then, again, when I have been cast down, I thought I was not wise to give such way to comfort. With such strength and weight have both these been upon me.

3. I have wondered much at this one thing, that though God doth visit my soul with never so blessed a discovery of himself, yet I have found again, that such hours have attended me afterwards, that I have been in my spirit so filled with darkness, that I could not so much as once conceive what that God and that comfort was with which I have been refreshed.

4. I have sometimes seen more in a line of the Bible than I could well tell how to stand under, and yet at another time the whole Bible hath been to me as dry as a stick, or rather my heart hath been so dead and dry unto it, that I could not conceive the least dram of refreshment, though I have looked it all over.

5. Of all tears, they are the best that are made by the blood of Christ; and of all joy, that is the sweetest that is mixed with mourning over Christ. O 'tis a goodly thing to be on our knees, with Christ in our arms, before God. I hope I know something of these things.

6. I find to this day seven abominations in my heart: 1. inclinings to unbelief; 2. suddenly to forget the love and mercy that Christ manifesteth; 3. a leaning to the works of the law; 4. wanderings and coldness in prayer; 5. to forget to watch for that I pray for; 6. apt to murmur because I have no more, and yet ready to abuse what I

---

195. Eph. 6:14.
196. Ps. 11:3.

have; 7. I can do none of those things which God commands me, but my corruptions will thrust in themselves; "when I would do good, evil is present with me."[197]

7. These things I continually see and feel, and am afflicted and oppressed with; yet the wisdom of God doth order them for my good: 1. they make me abhor myself; 2. they keep me from trusting my heart; 3. they convince me of the insufficiency of all inherent righteousness; 4. they show me the necessity of flying to Jesus; 5. they press me to pray unto God; 6. they show me the need I have to watch and be sober; 7. and provoke me to look to God through Christ to help me, and carry me through this world.

Amen.

FINIS

197. Rom. 7:21.

I am indeed in prison now
In body, but my mind
Is free to study Christ, and how
Unto me He is kind.

For tho' men keep my outward man
Within their locks and bars,
Yet by the faith of Christ I can
Mount higher than the stars.

Their fetters cannot spirits tame,
Nor tie up God from me;
My faith and hope they cannot lame;
Above them I shall be. . . .

This jail to us is as a hill,
From whence we plainly see
Beyond this world, and take our fill
Of things that lasting be.

From hence we see the emptiness
Of all the world contains;
And here we feel the blessedness
That for us yet remains. . . .

And let us count those things the best
That best will prove at last;
And count such men the only blest
That do such things hold fast. . . .

—*from* "Prison Meditations, A Poem"
by John Bunyan (1665)

SUGGESTIONS FOR FURTHER READING

BUNYAN, JOHN. *The Miscellaneous Works of John Bunyan.* 12 vols. Roger Sharrock, gen. ed. Oxford: Oxford University Press, 1976–90. The standard modern edition of Bunyan. See also Web site listings below.

CALDWELL, PATRICIA. *The Puritan Conversion Narrative.* Cambridge: Cambridge University Press, 1983.

FISH, STANLEY E. *Self-Consuming Artifacts: The Experience of Seventeenth-Century Literature.* Berkeley: University of California Press, 1972.

GREAVES, RICHARD L. *Glimpses of Glory: John Bunyan and English Dissent.* Stanford, Calif.: Stanford University Press, 2002. Not only interprets the full corpus of Bunyan's work but also considers the influence that bouts of depression had on Bunyan's religion and writing.

HILL, CHRISTOPHER. *A Tinker and a Poor Man: John Bunyan and His Church, 1628–1688.* New York: Knopf, 1988; pb. ed. W. W. Norton, 1990. Hill (1912–2003) was the dean of historians of the seventeenth-century English Revolution and author of a dozen other valuable books on it and related subjects.

———. *The World Turned Upside Down: Radical Ideas During the English Revolution.* London: Maurice Temple Smith; pb. repr., Penguin, 1975.

KEEBLE, N. H., ed. *John Bunyan: Conventicle and Parnassus, Tercentenary Essays.* Oxford: Clarendon Press, 1988. An exceptionally fine collection of scholarly essays.

———. *The Literary Culture of Nonconformity in Later Seventeenth-Century England.* Athens: University of Georgia Press, 1987. There are many insights into Bunyan's writings in this excellent general study of dissenting religious literature.

LUXON, THOMAS H. *Literal Figures: Puritan Allegory and the Reformation Crisis in Representation.* Chicago: University of Chicago Press, 1995.

MILLER, PERRY. *Errand into the Wilderness.* Cambridge, Mass.: Harvard University Press, 1975. Important essays on American Puritanism.

NUTTALL, GEOFFREY F. *The Holy Spirit in Puritan Faith and Experience.* Chicago: University of Chicago Press, 1992.

SHARROCK, ROGER. *John Bunyan.* London: Macmillan, 1968; Westport, Conn.: Greenwood Press, 1984.

————. *The Pilgrim's Progress: A Casebook.* London: Macmillan, 1976.

TINDALL, WILLIAM YORK. *John Bunyan: Mechanick Preacher.* New York: Columbia University Press, 1934; repr. Russell & Russell, 1964.

WATKINS, OWEN C. *The Puritan Experience.* London: Routledge & Kegan Paul, 1972.

WEB SITES

Both of these Web sites offer many of Bunyan's works in electronic form:

http://www.johnbunyan.org/ ("John Bunyan Online")

http://acacia.pair.com/Acacia.John.Bunyan/ ("Acacia John Bunyan Online Library")

W. CLARK GILPIN is the Margaret E. Burton Professor of the History of Christianity at the Divinity School, the University of Chicago. From 1990 to 2000, he served as dean of the Divinity School and was recently appointed director of the Martin Marty Center, the Divinity School's institute for advanced research in all fields of the academic study of religion. He has written extensively on Puritanism in both England and New England and is currently completing a book about the letter from prison as a genre of religious literature, which will include a chapter on John Bunyan and his contemporaries.

JOHN F. THORNTON is a literary agent, former publishing executive, and the coeditor, with Katharine Washburn, of *Dumbing Down* (1996) and *Tongues of Angels, Tongues of Men: A Book of Sermons* (1999). He lives in New York City.

SUSAN B. VARENNE is a New York City high school teacher with a strong avocational interest in and wide experience of spiritual literature. She holds an M.A. from the University of Chicago Divinity School and a Ph.D. from Columbia University.